Social and Professional Applications of Actor–Network Theory for Technology Development

Arthur Tatnall
Victoria University, Australia

Information Science
REFERENCE

Managing Director:	Lindsay Johnston
Editorial Director:	Joel Gamon
Book Production Manager:	Jennifer Romanchak
Publishing Systems Analyst:	Adrienne Freeland
Assistant Acquisitions Editor:	Kayla Wolfe
Typesetter:	Erin O'Dea
Cover Design:	Nick Newcomer

Published in the United States of America by
Information Science Reference (an imprint of IGI Global)
701 E. Chocolate Avenue
Hershey PA 17033
Tel: 717-533-8845
Fax: 717-533-8661
E-mail: cust@igi-global.com
Web site: http://www.igi-global.com

Library of Congress Cataloging-in-Publication Data

Social and professional applications of actor-network theory for technology development / Arthur Tatnall, editor.
    p. cm.
 Includes bibliographical references and index.
 Summary: "This book presents a platform for the approaches and implementations of actor-network theory and its relationship with technology development, providing understanding of the usefulness of the social and technical connection"--Provided by publisher.
  ISBN 978-1-4666-2166-4 (hardcover) -- ISBN 978-1-4666-2167-1 (ebook) -- ISBN 978-1-4666-2168-8 (print & perpetual access) 1. Technological innovations--Social aspects. 2. Diffusion of innovations--Social aspects. 3. Information technology--Social aspects. 4. Actor-network theory. I. Tatnall, Arthur.
  HM846.S577 2013
  303.01--dc23
                        2012019281

British Cataloguing in Publication Data
A Cataloguing in Publication record for this book is available from the British Library.

The views expressed in this book are those of the authors, but not necessarily of the publisher.

Table of Contents

Detailed Table of Contents

Chapter 1
Dianne Mulcahy, The University of Melbourne, Australia

In the context of neo-liberal education policy reform, professional teaching standards have become one of the main means of managing improvements to school teaching and assuring its quality. Using the methodology of material semiotics in association with video case data of classroom teaching (in this case, school geography teachers) and their students, the author treats a set of standards in action, towards conducting an ontological inquiry. Bringing the performative perspective of actor-network theory to bear not only is sociality taken into account but also materiality. This paper argues that standards are best understood as shifting assemblies of practice whose nature defines and enacts teacher identity and teacher professional knowledge differently in different locations. The conclusion is drawn that while teaching standards 'clot' and can serve to standardise practices of teaching, they are not stable entities. The variable ontology that they manifest challenges the managerialist impulses that tend to drive standards work in education. Altogether, the paper seeks to augment existing accounts of standards within the field of the sociology of science (Bowker & Star, 1999; Star, 2010; Timmermans & Berg, 2003; Timmermans & Epstein, 2010) and contribute to its subfield, the sociology of standards.

Chapter 2
Michael Tscholl, University of Cambridge, UK
Uma Patel, City University London, UK
Patrick Carmichael, Liverpool John Moores University, UK

This paper presents an account of field research into case-based learning in a management course, guided by the questions: 'what is making change in this setting', and 'where is learning located'. Multiple forms of relations between human and nonhuman entities were identified through extensive research, which, analytically does not sit well with more traditional understandings of learning or case-based learning. A critique of those understandings is offered, drawing on concepts from post-modernism and adopting sensibilities from actor-network theory, follow the action in the setting. The authors demonstrate that the case is an assemblage of heterogeneous connections that are made by the teacher and then by the students in the classroom. In working with ANT sensibilities, examination found that tracing the action offers radically different accounts and possibilities for education research and practice. The pragmatic issues in following the action and the challenge of staying coherent and ambivalent are acknowledged.

Chapter 3

Sue De Vincentis, Deakin University, Australia

Rather than conceptualising the curriculum as a mandate which guides a teacher's task of advancing the knowledge of students, or what the author will call the simple story, the curriculum as an object of complexities is explored in this article. The article considers how approaching the curriculum relationally can be a more fruitful quest than simply accepting that curriculum activity is predetermined, predictable, or standard. Drawing on actor-network theory and the fieldwork resulting from a funded, primary school Arts project in Australia, the curriculum is examined as a relational effect of education. In doing so, it is shown how interdependent webs of heterogeneous relations contribute to this entity called 'the curriculum', encouraging activity to be practised in particular ways, yet suggesting activity could be otherwise.

Chapter 4

Sanna Rimpiläinen, University of Stirling, UK

This paper discusses a methodological dilemma proposed by engaging actor-network theory (ANT) in studying collaborative research practices of researchers in a large interdisciplinary project. The paper sets the context of this large publically funded project ('Ensemble: Semantic Technologies for the Enhancement of Case Based learning') between Education and Computer Sciences, currently being undertaken by a consortium of six UK universities and three international partners. While a strand of ANT states that knowledge 'emerges as continuously generated effects of webs of relations within which they are located' (Law 2007), it is very vague in terms of how precisely does that knowledge emerge and how to study that. The methods -question was further complicated by the existence of multiple, potentially conflicting epistemological positions present at the project – how to study these without having to pass a value judgement in terms of their validity and reliability? The specific focus of the discussion is what might be termed the epistemology of actor-network theory, with particular consideration of the Principle of Symmetry. The paper suggests reading ANT through John Dewey's Pragmatism and assesses ideas to take forward from this discussion in order to study interdisciplinary research work.

Chapter 5

Andrea Quinlan, York University, Canada
Elizabeth Quinlan, University of Saskatchewan, Canada
Desiree Nelson, University of Saskatchewan, Canada

Teaching innovative schools of thought call for innovative methods of instruction. This article investigates the challenges associated with teaching Actor-Network Theory (ANT) and proposes a creative pedagogical approach of 'performing' ANT in the classroom. This article presents a small case study of an instance where this theatrical method was employed in an undergraduate classroom to teach Annemarie Mol's The Body Multiple. Based on the qualitative data collected from reflections of students and the professor, it investigates the successes of this creative pedagogical approach to teach ANT. This article argues that it is only through innovative teaching methods that ANT can be effectively explored in the classroom.

Chapter 6

Petri Nets are tools for the modelling and analysis of the behaviour of systems and analysis of the Petri Net can then reveal important information about the structure and dynamic behaviour of the modelled system. In this article, the author argues that Petri Net concepts (when used qualitatively) are not fundamentally different from those of ANT. For example, the 'places' from Petri Nets bear a strong resemblance to the actors in ANT, and the 'triggers' or 'transitions', are somewhat analogous to ANT's translations. In modelling, places represent conditions and transitions represent events. Tokens may model the resources or data items that are associated with a place or places. The original research that this article is based on was undertaken using an actor-network framework to develop a model for e-Learning for students with Learning Difficulties. This article explores the qualitative use of Petri Nets to supplement this ANT treatment.

Chapter 7

The problematisation of the professional standards for teachers in the UK lifelong learning sector tends to focus on the discourses that the standards embody: discourses that are posited as being based on a restricted or technicist model of professionalism, that fail sufficiently to recognise the lived experiences of teachers within the sector both in terms of professional knowledge and competences, and professional development. This paper takes a different approach, drawing on a branch of material semiotics – actor-network theory – in order to shift the locus of problematisation away from what the standards might mean, to how the standards are physically assembled or instantiated. The paper concludes by suggesting that a first point of problematisation rests not in the discourses that the standards embody, but in the inherent fragilities of any material artefact that has the intention of carrying meaning across spatial, institutional or temporal boundaries.

Chapter 8

This article uses data collected for a study undertaken in the mid-2000s using the Technology Acceptance Model (TAM) to investigate knowledge conversion processes in a Thai Government Ministry. The authors re-analyse this study making use of the power of actor-network theory. The original TAM study, based on technological innovation, investigated the relationship between technology support and management of the knowledge conversion process in a government ministry in Thailand to increase knowledge sharing. The original study found that a number of external variables impacted on the knowledge conversion process, including personal details, training, tools of persuasion, national background and culture, management and policies, employee behaviour, management, and policies and computing support. This paper briefly outlines the findings of the original study and discusses how an ANT study would have approached this material. An analysis is then made of how an Innovation Translation approach differs fundamentally from one using the Technology Acceptance Model.

Chapter 9

    Stasys Lukaitis, RMIT University, Australia

In this paper, the author examines phenomenology and hermeneutics as research traditions and proposes a philosophical basis for their use. The author develops an iterative research process model that meets the needs of socio-technical research into technical innovation. This rigorous hybrid methodology is called hermeneutic phenomenology and is shown to be an excellent approach to dealing with the search for understanding.

Chapter 10

    Fabian Muniesa, Mines ParisTech, Centre de Sociologie de l'Innovation, France

The paper examines, through a case study on the Arizona Stock Exchange, how computerization challenged the definition of the stock exchange in the context of North-American financial markets in the 1990's. It analyses exchange automation in terms of trials of explicitness: the computational formulation of what an exchange is calls for a detailed explication of the (variable, often conflicting and unanticipated) processes and properties of price formation. The paper focuses in particular on the argument of the concentration of liquidity in one single point, which was central to the development of the Arizona Stock Exchange (an electronic call auction). It then asks what kind of revolution is the 'explicitness revolution' in the design of allocation mechanisms.

Chapter 11

    Jim Underwood, University of Technology, Sydney, Australia
    Edin Tabak, Curtin University of Technology, Australia

In this paper, a case study of the evolution of an organisational intranet is used to compare the concepts of "materiality" with actor-network theory's black-boxing. The authors argue that information systems need to become material through "due process". Through this paper, questions arise as to what types of material allies are useful in this process, and whether these allies can co-evolve (or "co-materialise") with the system. In this case there seemed to be existing technical actors, but the authors question whether this is always the case.

Chapter 12

    Tiko Iyamu, Tshwane University of Technology, South Africa

Despite impressive technical advances in tools and methodologies and the organizational insights provided by many years of academic and business research, the underperformance of Information Technology (IT) remains. In the past and even today, organizations experience difficulty in managing technology, changing from system to system, implementing new technology, maintaining compatibility with existing technologies, and changing from one business process to another. These challenges impact significantly on business performance and will continue to do so if not addressed. As a result, many organizations have deployed Enterprise Architecture (EA) in an attempt to address these challenges. However, the design and development of EA has proven to be easier than its institutionalization. The study explored the development and implementation of EA to determine the factors, which influences the institutionalization. Two case studies were conducted and Actor-Network Theory (ANT) was employed in the analysis of the data.

Chapter 13

Magdalena Bielenia-Grajewska, University of Gdansk, Poland

In this article, an attempt will be made to discuss how websites create and maintain the online identity of medical care providers. To discuss this issue in greater detail, the author has chosen Actor-Network-Theory since an ANT approach makes it possible to study the role of living and nonliving entities in shaping the online identity of healthcare suppliers and to concentrate on the networks and systems within e-healthcare as well as the flows and interrelations constituting it. The primary aim of this research is to show the communicative aspect of healthcare corporate websites by using the selected notions of ANT methodology and their potential implications for corporate identity creation and maintenance.

Chapter 14

Johanes Eka Priyatma, Sanata Dharma University, Indonesia
Zainal Abidin Mohamed, Universiti Putra, Malaysia

Leadership has been identified as one of the critical factors in the successful development of e-government projects especially so in developing countries. Unfortunately, empirical studies linking the outcome of e-government projects and the role of leadership are very limited. Moreover, these studies did not comprehensively discuss the role of leadership in implementing e-government projects involving social, political, and technological transformation. Using the four moments of Actor Network Theory (ANT) translation framework, this paper presents detailed actions taken by leaders in the development of a local e-government project. The paper argues that ANT translation provides an appropriate framework to trace and monitor how leadership has been practiced effectively in an e-government project in a developing country.

Chapter 15

Antonio Díaz Andrade, Auckland University of Technology, New Zealand, & Universidad ESAN,
* Peru*
Samuel Ekundayo, Auckland University of Technology, New Zealand

Both actor-network theory and activity theory call attention to the coexistence of people and technology. Although both theories provide analytical tools to understand the nature of the reciprocal action-shaping of humans and nonhumans, each puts emphasis on different conceptual elements of human activity. In this paper, the authors examine both activity theory and actor-network theory and present their similarities and differences, limitations, and complementarities. Using the theoretical lenses of both theories, the authors trace the evolution of an ordinary artifact to illustrate how researchers on the sociology of technology and innovations can benefit from these parallel theoretical approaches.

Chapter 16
A Socio-Technical Study of the Adoption of Internet Technology in Banking, Re-Interpreted as an
Innovation Using Innovation Translation 207

Salim Al-Hajri, Higher College of Technology, Oman
Arthur Tatnall, Victoria University, Australia

This article presents a re-interpretation of research done in the mid-2000s on uptake of Internet technologies in the banking industry in Oman, compared with that in Australia. It addresses the question: What are the enablers and the inhibitors of Internet technology adoption in the Omani banking industry compared with those in the Australian banking industry? The research did not attempt a direct comparison of the banking industries in these two very different countries, but rather considered Internet technology adoption in Oman, informed by the more mature Australian experience. The original study considered Internet banking as an innovation and used an approach to theorising this innovation that was based on Diffusion of Innovations and the Technology Acceptance Model (TAM). Given the socio-technical nature of this investigation, however, another approach to adoption of innovations was worth investigating, and this article reports a re-interpretation of the original study using innovation translation from actor-network theory (ANT).

Chapter 17
Emerging Standardization 221

Antonio Cordella, London School of Economics and Political Science, UK

This paper discusses the dynamics associated with the implementation and deployment of an information infrastructure designed to standardize work practices. The analysis is based on a case study conducted in a pharmaceutical R&D organization. The infrastructure in use, comprising a computerized system and surrounding organizational procedures, seems to support work practices not always as originally planned. The paper discusses the role played by local characteristics, contingencies, and practices in shaping a standardization protocol implemented to standardize work practices. Building on actor-network theory, the paper concludes that the standardization of work practices is the result of the dynamic interplay between technology and its users, rather than the consequence of a planned and well-defined design project.

Preface

INTRODUCTION

Actor-network theory (ANT) proffers an account for socio-technical research in which neither social nor technical positions are privileged. This is in marked contrast with many other approaches that treat the social and the technical in entirely different ways. These other approaches are then either:

- Technologically driven with a focus on the technical aspects, so treating 'the social' as the context in which the events take place, or
- Socially driven where relatively stable social categories are used to explain technological change and the emphasis is on an investigation of social interactions, relegating the technology to context.

Actor-Network Theory originated from research in the social studies of science in the 1980s, principally by Bruno Latour, Michel Callon, and John Law. ANT was designed as an approach to socio-technical research that would treat the contributions of both human and non-human actors fairly and in the same way and considers the world to be full of hybrid entities containing both human and non-human elements. In this socio-technical order nothing is purely social and nothing is purely technical. Law and Callon describe this more explicitly in the following way:

Explanations of social and technical change must avoid three traps. Two of these take the form of reductionisms. Social reductionism, the doctrine that relatively stable social categories can explain technical change, and technological reductionism, the converse view, that technological change automatically shapes society, are both one-sided, incomplete, and misleading (MacKenzie and Wajcman 1985). But even if the social and the technical are both taken to be important, there is a third trap to avoid. This is the notion that the technical and the social evolve as a result of separate processes and only subsequently interact. By contrast, our aim has been to suggest that they are jointly created in a single process. (Law and Callon 1988:295,296)

In actor-network theory, an actor is any human or non-human entity that is able to make its presence individually felt (Law 1987) by other actors and is made up only of its interactions with these other actors (Law 1992; de Vries 1995). ANT is thus concerned with studying the mechanics of power as this occurs through construction and maintenance of networks made up of both human and non-human actors. Callon (1986) argues that an actor can also be considered, at times, as a black box, as we do not always need to see the details of the network of interactions that is inside it.

... it turns out that when you look at what technologists actually do, we find out that they pay scant regard to distinctions between technology on the one hand and society, economics, politics, and the rest on the other. (Law and Callon 1988:284)

ACTOR-NETWORK THEORY: A ROSE BY ANY OTHER NAME ...

For some time there has been discussion over the name of what we now call actor-network theory. Some suggest that its name should be changed to something more accurately descriptive such as the sociology of translation or actant-rhyzome ontology, and in a 1999 book Latour remarked that:

I will start by saying that there are four things that do not work with actor-network theory; the word actor, the word network, the word 'theory' and the hyphen. Four nails in the coffin. (Latour 1999:15)

How serious he was about this, however, is open to question as some time later he noted that the name actor-network theory "... is so awkward, so confusing, so meaningless that is deserves to be kept." (Latour 2005: 9). He then went further to say:

I was ready to drop this label for more elaborate ones like 'sociology of translation', 'actant-rhyzome ontology', 'sociology of innovation', and so on, until someone pointed out to me that the acronym A.N.T. was perfectly fit for a blind, myopic, workaholic, trail-sniffing, and collective traveller. An ant writing for other ants, this fits my project very well! (Latour 2005:9)

Using ANT for a Research Framework in Situations Involving Interactions between People and "Things"

Actor-network theory is based on three principles aimed to ensure that both human and non-human actors are treated fairly and in the same way (Callon 1986):

*   Analytical impartiality: Demanded for all actors in the project under consideration, whether they be human or non-human.
*   Generalised symmetry: Offers to explain conflicting viewpoints of the different actors using the same neutral vocabulary that works the same way for human and non-human actors so that neither the social nor the technical elements should then be given any special explanatory status.
*   Elimination of all *a priori* distinctions between the technological and the social as: "ANT was developed to analyse situations in which it is difficult to separate humans and non-humans, and in which the actors have variable forms and competencies." (Callon 1999:183)

In summary, Callon puts it this way:

The rule which we must respect is not to change registers when we move from the technical to the social aspects of the problem studied. (Callon 1986:200)

ANT was designed for use in situations involving people and things – human and non-human actors – and the interactions, influences and associations between them. It was designed, in particular, to give an equal voice to the actions and influences due to the 'things' – the non-human actors.

IJANTTI Research Articles from 2009-2011

The International Journal of Actor-Network Theory and Technological Innovation (IJANTTI) is now (2012) in its fourth year of publication and has generated a substantial amount of research literature on both actor-network theory in its various applications, and also examples and models of technological innovation. What follows is a summary of IJANTTI articles over the first three years, roughly sorted into categories. (Of course, some articles fit into more than one category so this sorting is at best approximate.)

ANT and Educational Research

A large group of ANT articles relates to educational research, covering both school and university levels. An article by Tummons (2009) explores aspects of higher education in further education provision in England. The article focuses on assessment of a teacher-training course for the learning and skills sector and offers ways of conceptualising the responses of the Further Education colleges where the course was actually run to the systems and procedures established by the University which provided the course. The article suggests that the ways in which assessment processes are regulated and ordered are characterised by complexities for which actor-network theory provides an appropriate conceptual framework.

An article by Manning *et al.* (2010) looks at e-learning and blended learning in a university. The article notes that merely defining a policy in relation to the use of e-learning will not necessarily cause the desired result as first the new ideas have to be adopted by all those involved. The authors suggest that educational technology adoption decisions are made at three levels. Firstly, strategic decisions are made by the university to implement a particular package. Secondly individual academics make adoption decisions regarding those aspects of the package they will use in their teaching and how they will use them. The third level consists of a decision on the balance they will make between on-line and face-to-face teaching. This article questions how decisions are made to adopt one e-learning package rather than another. Once the technology is adopted it then questions how individual academics relate to it and make use of it to deliver some or all of their teaching, and to determine the appropriate blend.

Volume 3, Issue 2 of the journal was a special issue based on the use of ANT for educational research. The first article in this issue (Mulcahy 2011) investigates professional teaching standards and notes that in the context of neo-liberal education policy reform, professional teaching standards have become an important means of managing improvements to school teaching and assuring its quality. Bringing the performative perspective of actor-network theory to bear whereby not only sociality but also materiality is taken into account, the author argues that standards are best understood as shifting assemblies of practice whose nature defines and enacts teacher identity and teacher professional knowledge differently in different locations. Tscholl *et al.* (2011) then present an account of field research into case-based learning in a management course, guided by the questions: 'what is making change in this setting', and 'where is learning located'. In working with ANT sensibilities the authors found that tracing the action offers radically different accounts and possibilities for education research and practice. Rather than conceptualising the curriculum as a mandate which guides a teacher's task of advancing the knowledge of students – the simple story – De Vincentis (2011) explores the curriculum as an object of complexities. Drawing on ANT and the fieldwork resulting from a primary school arts project the article examines the curriculum as a relational effect of education and illustrates how interdependent webs of heterogeneous relations contribute to the entity called the curriculum. Rimpiläinen (2011) introduces an interdisciplinary project entitled: "Ensemble: Semantic Technologies to Support the Teaching and Learning of Case Based Learning" set in a Scottish university. The article's specific focus is on the epistemology of actor-network theory and in particular, the principle of symmetry.

Quinlan *et al.* (2011) note that the teaching of innovative schools of thought calls for innovative methods of teaching. They investigate the challenges associated with teaching actor-network theory, and propose and describe the successes of a creative pedagogical approach of 'performing' ANT in the classroom and using this creative pedagogical approach to the teaching of ANT. They argue that it is only through innovative teaching methods that ANT can be effectively explored in the classroom.

In an article on professionalism, Tummons (2011) notes that problematisation of the professional standards for teachers in the UK lifelong learning sector tends to focus on the discourses that the standards embody: discourses that are posited as being based on a restricted or technicist model of professionalism. These fail to recognise the lived experiences of teachers within the sector both in terms of professional knowledge and competence. This article suggests instead an approach drawing on actor-network theory in order to shift the locus of problematisation away from what the standards might mean, to how the standards are physically assembled or instantiated.

In a couple of articles (Tatnall 2009; Tatnall 2010) I investigate the adoption of the programming language: Visual Basic (VB) into the information systems curriculum of an Australian university. VB did this against resistance from two incumbent programming languages, but could not, of course, work alone and so enlisted the assistance of a human ally. The incumbent programming languages, Pick Basic and the Alice machine language simulator, also had their human allies to assist them in resisting the assault of the newcomer. In many ways it is useful to think of all these programming languages as black boxes made up of hybrid entities containing both human and non-human parts along with a conglomeration of networks, interactions and associations. The non-human cannot act alone, but without them the human parts have nothing to contest.

In an article that relates to both education and feminist issues, Rowan and Bigum (2009) note that despite more than 30 years of gender reform in schools, the number of girls enrolled in IT subjects in the post-compulsory years of education has remained persistently low. The article focuses on identifying reasons for this and ways in which the situation could be changed. The authors discuss differences between the researchers' perception of this problem compared with those of the participants, and use ANT to highlight the gaps, tensions and contradictions within the data and to question the extent to which the enrolment of girls in IT is indeed 'a problem'.

Finally, in relation to research in special education, Adam (2011) argues that Petri Net concepts (when used qualitatively) have some similarities to ANT. The original research that this article is based on was undertaken using an actor-network framework to develop a model for e-learning for students with learning difficulties in special schools in Victoria, and this article explores the qualitative use of Petri Nets to supplement this ANT treatment. The article notes that the places from Petri Nets bear a strong resemblance to the actors in ANT, and the triggers or transitions are somewhat analogous to ANT's translations.

ANT and Research into Information and Communications Technologies (ICT)

In the very first issue of IJANTTI, an article by Cecez-Kecmanovic and Nagm (2009) investigates the evaluation of information systems project proposals by using ANT to provide a better understanding of their development and evaluation in practice and ways in which the evaluation process shapes and ensures the selection of the best IS projects. In a later issue, an article by Elbanna (2009) argues that for researchers studying ICT, ANT provides a theoretical inclusion of what used to be considered different poles, in analytically and including a wide array of actors that were formerly considered to be of different nature and from different levels of analysis. Using the analytic perspective of ANT, Linden (2009) relates research examining electronic mailing list discussions by the Linux kernel developers, and found many posts that expressed the developers' dislike for the revised version of the Linux General Public License – but all for different reasons. These opinions provide details of differences between open source software and free software, and illustrate that for a proper understanding there is a need to consider both human and non-human actors. Iyamu (2009) notes that the focus in IT projects has predominantly focused on technologies and less on the non-technical components. His study focused on the connection between the technical and non-technical, including the relationships between actors in the development and implementation of IT strategy.

Cordella (2010) suggests that research into information infrastructures has mainly focused on studying the process that both shapes and stabilises information infrastructures and of studying the role played by information infrastructure in leveraging business performance. Using ANT as an ontological foundation to analyse the relations among actors, this article proposes the concept of information infrastructures in action to highlight their dynamic nature, leading to a consideration of these not as stable entities, but rather as entities performed through relations. In relation to enterprise ICT architecture, Iyamu (2010; 2011) notes that organisations experience difficulty in managing technology, changing from system to system, implementing new technology, maintaining compatibility with existing technologies and changing from one business process to another, and relates two case studies, analysed from an ANT perspective, in order to better understand the related socio-technical influences. Cole (2010) investigates the relationship between the social and the material in ICT and considers this under the banner of socio-materiality.

Another ICT related article (Jonsson and Holmström 2010) focuses on the use of sensors as part of remote diagnostic systems in industrial organisations, noting that context awareness forms a core concern in ubiquitous computing. The study shows that the process of desituating context – capturing context and transferring it to another context – is critical for the successful use of the technology and that by conceptualising the world as heterogeneous socio-technical networks, ANT can help to analyse the intertwined relationship between human agency, technology and contexts to further our knowledge about desituation of context. Evolution of an organisational intranet is the subject of an article by Underwood and Tabak (2011) in which they compare concepts of materiality with actor-network theory's black-boxing. In the article they argue that information systems need to become material through due process and that questions arise as to what types of material allies are useful in this process, and whether these allies can co-evolve with the system.

ANT and Healthcare Research

The information intensive environment of healthcare research has been a topic that has attracted a number of ANT articles. Wickramasinghe and Bali (2009) proffer a network-centric approach to healthcare to allow free and rapid sharing of information and effective knowledge building. They assert that if we are to realise such a vision the application of Social Network Analysis combined with Actor-network Theory (S'ANT), provides useful analytical tools and analyses. In a related article (Wickramasinghe, Bali and Goldberg 2009) the S'ANT approach is advocated as a means to analyse the case for the application of a pervasive technology solution in the form of a wireless-enabled mobile phone to facilitate superior diabetes management.

Investigating the adoption of ICT in medical general practices in a rural area of Victoria, Deering *et al.* (2010) use ANT to analyse the very complex decisions taken in its adoption. These decisions involve many actors, both human and non-human and, rather than characteristics of the technology itself, it is often seemingly unimportant human issues that determine if and how ICT is used in General Practice. In one case, for example, non-adoption was because the father of the present Practice Principal was not comfortable with ICT and as he was not far off retirement no one wanted to make him feel uncomfortable by introducing this technology. An article by Bielenia-Grajewska (2011) uses an ANT approach to discuss how websites create and maintain the online identity of healthcare providers. She indicates that an ANT approach makes it possible to study the role of living and non-living entities in shaping the online identity of healthcare suppliers and to concentrate on the networks and systems within e-healthcare as well as the flows and interrelations constituting it.

Knowledge creation techniques tend to focus on either human or technology aspects of organisational development and less often on process-centric aspects of knowledge generation. In relation to healthcare knowledge exchange, the ability to extract germane knowledge to enable rapid and effective decision making is central. Two more articles (Bali and Wickramasinghe 2010; Wickramasinghe, Tatnall and Bali 2010) suggest that to truly understand knowledge creation and transfer it is important to view knowledge creation and all socio-technical organisational operations that result in knowledge generation through the rich lens of actor-network theory.

Business and Government Research and ANT

Uden and Francis (2009) note that the service sector in now the dominant economy in the industrial world and that services have become the key value driver for companies. The rapid growth of services has implications for academic knowledge creation, education, business practice, and government policy, but there is a lack of understanding of the science underlying the design and operation of service systems requiring new conceptual understandings and theoretical underpinnings. The authors suggest that ANT could be used as a theoretical lens to study the development and adoption of service innovation. Naidoo (2010) writes that despite growth in technology-based service delivery options, implementation of contemporary forms of service channels continues to be for organisations and that current conceptualisations of IS implementation are too narrow and highlight only some aspects of this phenomenon. The article uses the ANT conceptual elements of inscription and translation to describe how the design and use of this self-service technology emerged from co-entanglement between the technological and social.

Another article (Ariani and Yuliar 2009) uses ANT's notion of translation to investigate bio-fuel development in Indonesia. It notes that despite the activities of scientists, business people, policy makers, and farmers, adoption of bio-fuel innovation seems to remain very limited. Kasimin and Ibrahim (2009) point out that in Malaysia, major IT transfer in the public sector is usually due to policy implementation involving central government directives to implementation agencies. Their research has shown that the technology transfer process usually also involved many phases. In the article they described an approach based on actor-network theory and concepts of technology transfer stages and found that ignoring issues emerging from interactions between stakeholders not only delayed the transfer process but also did not fully achieve the original project objectives.

In an article relating a research approach using both Structuration Theory and Actor-Network Theory, Iyamu and Roode (2010) describe IT-business strategy and the way that business uses this either to increase their competitiveness, or often just to survive. The article points out that little is known about non-technical factors, including people, and their impact to the development and implementation of IT strategy and uses these theories to analyse how non-technical factors influence IT strategy.

Based on a case study of the Arizona Stock Exchange, Muniesa (2011) outlines how computerisation challenged the definition of the stock exchange in the context of North American financial markets in the 1990s. The article forms a sociological appraisal of market devices and examines how several kinds of apparatus contribute to the formation and deformation of market realities, in resonance with the viewpoints emphasised throughout ANT

An article by Cordella (2011) discusses the dynamics associated with the implementation and deployment of an information infrastructure designed to standardise work practices, based on a case study conducted in a pharmaceutical research and development organisation. The article discusses the dynamic interplay between technology and its users through the role played by local characteristics, contingencies, and practices in shaping a protocol to standardise work practices. Ekundayo and Diaz Andrade (2011) use ANT and Activity Theory to follow the trajectory of an artefact that makes it possible to go up and, once up there, to go down. We might call it a lift, but the authors avoid this characterisation in order to trace its evolution. From an ANT perspective their analysis of the evolution of this artefact shows the dynamic and provisional characteristics of the network of actors. From an Activity Theory perspective, it reveals how the goal-direction of this artefact mediates our actions. Diaz Andrade (2010) notes that assuming symmetry between human and non-human actors is a fundamental tenet of ANT. The article examines the use of electronic mail systems, especially the automatically generated Out of Office message to emphasise the distinction between agency and intentionality. The notions of intermediaries and mediators are introduced not only to corroborate that the division between the social and the technical is artificial but also to reveal the difference between non-human agency and human intentionality.

Leadership has been identified as one of the critical factor in the successful development of e-government projects in developing countries (Priyatma and Mohamed 2011), but empirical studies linking the outcome of e-government projects and the role of leadership are very limited. This article argues that ANT translation concepts provide an appropriate framework to trace and monitor how leadership has been practiced effectively in an e-government project in a developing country.

Communications, Publishing, and Social Networking

An article by Bielenia-Grajewska (2009) discusses the place of ANT in one type of intercultural communication: translation. The article shows how ANT is useful in this area of cross-cultural communication, raising issues such as translators, translation, languages, texts and units and so involving both human and non-human entities that are treated as an ecosystem.

Zammar (2010) examines the role of the actors in a social network service and considers the triggers and challenges they represent to social networking between today's communities and businesses. The article suggests that a Social Network Service is the product of the evolution of social liaisons and the emergence of online communities of people who are interested in exploring the concerns and activities of others. The author hopes that the article will trigger an exploration of the potential role of ANT in the social network service context.

An article dealing with the spread of open access to scholarly publishing (Kennan, Cecez-Kecmanovic, and Underwood 2010) explores some of the issues associated with giving non-human actors a voice of their own in ANT based research. Does this increase understanding of the issue to hand or does anthropomorphism detract from these? The article discusses these broader issues and presents findings from an ANT field study which investigated the implementation of institutional repositories and their relationship to the spread of open access to scholarly publishing.

Technological Innovation

A new technology will only be adopted if potential users make a decision to do so, and it is useful to consider the adoption of any new technology in terms of innovation theory (Tatnall 2011) for which there are several different approaches, the most significant being: the Theory of Reasoned Action (Fishbein and Ajzen 1975), the Theory of Planned Behaviour (Ajzen 1991), the Technology Acceptance Model (Davis 1986), Diffusion of Innovations (Rogers 1995; Rogers 2003) and Innovation Translation (Latour 1986; Law and Callon 1988; Latour 1996).

In a couple of articles (Tatnall 2009; Tatnall 2009) I examine and compare the Innovation Diffusion and Innovation Translation approaches to theorising technological innovation, giving examples of how each approach is used in different situations. The articles suggest that while there are many advantages to the use of a Translation approach it is too simplistic to suggest that Translation always offers a better approach than Diffusion. It is suggested that a Translation approach typically offers a better understanding of individual adoptions, but that for large scale movements, Diffusion has some value.

Gonçalves and Figueiredo (2010) make use of an ANT approach based on Programs of Action to explore the description of innovation cases to discover internal referents that conveys their meaning. The article revisits examples like the application of ANT to obstetrics and gynaecology and the making and evolution of the computer mouse. It then outlines the case of two firms, one in the semiconductor industry and the other in the plastics mould industry, to illustrate a way to research the building of an ANT view for engineering innovations. In another article (Gonçalves and Figueiredo 2010) they write that as they are deeply involved with ANT applications in engineering domains they often cross through its fundamentals. They point out that envisaging ANT as a paradigm can prove valid in the engineering design field, but that it is sometimes necessary to go back to its roots, and that Obligatory Passage Points and Immutable Mobiles are two of the fundamental concepts that needed to be revisited and unfolded.

The next few articles relate to research making use of innovation theory, but using approaches other than ANT to theorising this.

Making use of a technology-organisation-environment (TOE) framework, Alawneh and Hattab (2009) describe an extended model used to examine technological, organisational and environmental factors that influence e-banking adoption in Jordanian banks. The research described looks at technology readiness, competence, bank size, financial resources commitment, business-IT strategy alignment, adequacy of IT professionals, availability of online revenues, competition intensity or pressure and regulatory support environment. Study of the phenomenon of chasm that often exists in the diffusion of innovation is the topic of the next article (Rayna, Striukova and Landau 2009) that looks at devising a theoretical framework to explain the ability of some firms to cross this chasm, while others cannot. An article by Kripanont *et al.* (2009) describes research which used TAM (and its derivatives) to model adoption of Internet technology by academics in Business Schools in Public Universities in Thailand. In an article examining phenomenology and hermeneutics as research traditions, Lukaitis (2011) proposes a philosophical basis for their use and notes that socio-technical approaches to understanding innovation adoption at core rely upon finding meaning from data that must be interpreted and discusses a way of framing research so that a level of trust can be associated with research outcomes. Data visualisation, using an Innovation Diffusion approach, is the subject of an article by Bingley and Burgess (2009) that describes the development of a visual aid to depict the manner in which Internet applications are being diffused through local sporting associations.

Re-Interpretation of Innovation Research Using ANT

Two articles take innovation research done using the Technology Acceptance Model (TAM) and Innovation Diffusion and re-analyse the data from an ANT perspective. One (Al-Hajri and Tatnall 2011) was based on research done in the mid-2000s on inhibitors to the uptake of Internet technologies in the banking industry in Oman. Given the socio-technical nature of this investigation however, another approach to adoption of innovations was worth investigating, and this article reported a re-interpretation of the original study using innovation translation. The second article (Charnkit and Tatnall 2011) used data collected for a study using TAM to investigate knowledge conversion processes in a Thai Government Ministry. The original TAM study investigated the relationship between technology support and management aimed at increasing knowledge sharing. This paper briefly outlines the findings of the original study and discusses how an ANT study would have approached this material in a quite different manner to that of TAM.

CONCLUSION

From stories of building the French Electric Vehicle (Callon 1986), the TSR2 Military Aircraft (Law 1988), and the Aramis railway system (Latour 1996) to Portuguese Navigation (Law 1986) and Scallops and Fishermen (Callon 1986), research literature on actor-network theory has come a long way. ANT has been around since the mid-1980 but it is only over the last 15 or so years that it has grown to become a fundamental part of the approach of many of us to socio-technical academic research.

Technological innovations are adopted for a variety of reasons, but these are often not the reasons proposed by the instigators and promoters of these technologies, and are often not entirely rational. This paper described the articles, both of ANT and of studies of technological innovation based on other theoretical approaches, from the first three years of the International Journal of Actor-Network Theory and Technological Innovation.

There are those who say that ANT has run its course and needs to change fundamentally and there will always be those who make suggestions like these. For most of us, however, the value of making use of a little or a lot of ANT in our research is clear. We should also be allowed a little freedom to mould and shape ANT to our own needs and taste.

Arthur Tatnall
Victoria University, Australia

REFERENCES

Adam, T. (2011). A Petri Net model for analysing e-learning and learning difficulties. *International Journal of Actor-Network Theory and Technological Innovation, 3*(4), 11–21. doi:10.4018/jantti.2011100102

Ajzen, I. (1991). The theory of planned behavior. *Organizational Behavior and Human Decision Processes, 50*(2), 179–211. doi:10.1016/0749-5978(91)90020-T

Al-Hajri, S., & Tatnall, A. (2011). A Socio-technical study of the adoption of internet technology in banking, re-interpreted as an innovation using innovation translation. *International Journal of Actor-Network Theory and Technological Innovation, 3*(3). doi:10.4018/jantti.2011070103

Alawneh, A., & Hattab, E. (2009). E-banking diffusion in the Jordanian banking services sector: An empirical analysis of key factors. *International Journal of Actor-Network Theory and Technological Innovation, 1*(2), 50–66. doi:10.4018/jantti.2009040104

Ariani, Y., & Yuliar, S. (2009). Opening the Indonesian bio-fuel box: How scientists modulate the social. *International Journal of Actor-Network Theory and Technological Innovation, 1*(2), 12.

Bali, R. K., & Wickramasinghe, N. (2010). RAD and other innovative approaches to facilitate superior project management. *International Journal of Actor-Network Theory and Technological Innovation, 2*(3), 33–39. doi:10.4018/jantti.2010070103

Bielenia-Grajewska, M. (2009). Actor-network theory in intercultural communication – Translation through the prism of innovation, technology, networks and semiotics. *International Journal of Actor-Network Theory and Technological Innovation, 1*(4), 53–69. doi:10.4018/jantti.2009062304

Bielenia-Grajewska, M. (2011). Actor-network-theory in medical e-communication – The role of websites in creating and maintaining healthcare corporate online identity. *International Journal of Actor-Network Theory and Technological Innovation, 3*(1), 39–53. doi:10.4018/jantti.2011010104

Bingley, S., & Burgess, S. (2009). Using data visualisation to represent stages of the innovation-decision process. *International Journal of Actor-Network Theory and Technological Innovation, 1*(2), 13–30. doi:10.4018/jantti.2009040102

Callon, M. (1986). The sociology of an actor-network: The case of the electric vehicle . In Callon, M., Law, J., & Rip, A. (Eds.), *Mapping the dynamics of science and technology* (pp. 19–34). London, UK: Macmillan Press.

Callon, M. (1986). Some elements of a sociology of translation: Domestication of the scallops and the fishermen of St Brieuc Bay . In Law, J. (Ed.), *Power, action & belief. A new sociology of knowledge?* (pp. 196–229). London, UK: Routledge & Kegan Paul.

Callon, M. (1999). Actor-network theory - The market test . In Law, J., & Hassard, J. (Eds.), *Actor network theory and after* (pp. 181–195). Oxford, UK: Blackwell Publishers.

Cecez-Kecmanovic, D., & Nagm, F. (2009). Have you taken your guys on the journey? – An ANT account of IS project evaluation. *International Journal of Actor-Network Theory and Technological Innovation, 1*(1), 1–23. doi:10.4018/jantti.2009010101

Charnkit, P., & Tatnall, A. (2011). Knowledge conversion processes in Thai public organisations seen as an innovation: The re-analysis of a TAM study using innovation translation. *International Journal of Actor-Network Theory and Technological Innovation, 3*(4), 32–45. doi:10.4018/jantti.2011100104

Cole, F. T. H. (2010). Negotiating the socio-material in and about information systems: An approach to native methods. *International Journal of Actor-Network Theory and Technological Innovation, 2*(4), 1–9. doi:10.4018/jantti.2010100101

Cordella, A. (2010). Information infrastructure: An actor-network perspective. *International Journal of Actor-Network Theory and Technological Innovation, 2*(1), 35–52. doi:10.4018/jantti.2010071602

Cordella, A. (2011). Emerging standardization. *International Journal of Actor-Network Theory and Technological Innovation, 3*(3), 49–64. doi:10.4018/jantti.2011070104

Davis, F. (1986). *A technology acceptance model for empirically testing new end-user information systems: Theory and results.* Boston: MIT, Doctor of Philosophy.

De Vincentis, S. (2011). Complexifying the 'visualised' curriculum with actor-network theory. *International Journal of Actor-Network Theory and Technological Innovation, 3*(2). doi:10.4018/jantti.2011040103

de Vries, G. (1995). Should we send Collins and Latour to Dayton, Ohio? *EASST Review, 14*(4).

Deering, P., Tatnall, A., & Burgess, S. (2010). Adoption of ICT in rural medical general practices in Australia - An actor-network study. *International Journal of Actor-Network Theory and Technological Innovation, 2*(1), 54–69. doi:10.4018/jantti.2010071603

Diaz Andrade, A. (2010). From intermediary to mediator and vice versa: On agency and intentionality of a mundane sociotechnical system. *International Journal of Actor-Network Theory and Technological Innovation, 2*(4), 21–29. doi:10.4018/jantti.2010100103

Ekundayo, S., & Diaz Andrade, A. (2011). Mediated action and network of actors: From ladders, stairs and lifts to escalators (and travelators). *International Journal of Actor-Network Theory and Technological Innovation, 3*(3), 21–34. doi:10.4018/jantti.2011070102

Elbanna, A. R. (2009). Actor network theory in ICT research: A wider lens of enquiry. *International Journal of Actor-Network Theory and Technological Innovation, 1*(3), 1–14. doi:10.4018/jantti.2009070101

Fishbein, M., & Ajzen, I. (1975). *Belief, attitude, intention, and behavior: An introduction to theory and research.* Reading, MA: Addison-Wesley.

Gonçalves, F. A., & Figueiredo, J. (2010). How to recognize an immutable mobile when you find one: Translations on innovation and design. *International Journal of Actor-Network Theory and Technological Innovation, 2*(2), 39–53. doi:10.4018/jantti.2010040103

Gonçalves, F. A., & Figueiredo, J. (2010). Negotiating meaning – An ANT approach to the building of innovations. *International Journal of Actor-Network Theory and Technological Innovation, 2*(3), 1–16. doi:10.4018/jantti.2010070101

Iyamu, T. (2010). Theoretical analysis of strategic implementation of enterprise architecture. *International Journal of Actor-Network Theory and Technological Innovation, 2*(3), 17–32. doi:10.4018/jantti.2010070102

Iyamu, T. (2011). Institutionalisation of the enterprise architecture: The actor-network perspective. *International Journal of Actor-Network Theory and Technological Innovation*, *3*(1), 27–38. doi:10.4018/jantti.2011010103

Iyamu, T., & Roode, D. (2010). The use of structuration theory and actor network theory for analysis case study of a financial institution in South Africa. *International Journal of Actor-Network Theory and Technological Innovation*, *2*(1), 1–26. doi:10.4018/jantti.2010071601

Iyamu, T., & Tatnall, A. (2009). An actor-network analysis of a case of development and implementation of IT strategy. *International Journal of Actor-Network Theory and Technological Innovation*, *1*(4), 35–52. doi:10.4018/jantti.2009062303

Jonsson, K., & Holmström, J. (2010). Desituating context in ubiquitous computing: Exploring strategies for the use of remote diagnostic systems for maintenance work. *International Journal of Actor-Network Theory and Technological Innovation*, *2*(3), 40–55. doi:10.4018/jantti.2010070104

Kasimin, H., & Ibrahim, H. (2009). Exploring multi-organizational interaction issues: A case study of information technology transfer in the public sector of Malaysia. *International Journal of Actor-Network Theory and Technological Innovation*, *1*(3), 70–83. doi:10.4018/jantti.2009070105

Kennan, M. A., Cecez-Kecmanovic, D., & Underwood, J. (2010). Having a say: Voices for all the actors in ANT research? *International Journal of Actor-Network Theory and Technological Innovation*, *2*(2), 1–16. doi:10.4018/jantti.2010040101

Kripanont, N., & Tatnall, A. (2009). The role of a modified technology acceptance model in explaining internet usage in higher education in Thailand. *International Journal of Actor-Network Theory and Technological Innovation*, *1*(2), 31–49. doi:10.4018/jantti.2009040103

Latour, B. (1986). The powers of association . In Law, J. (Ed.), *Power, action and belief: A new sociology of knowledge?* (pp. 264–280). London, UK: Routledge & Kegan Paul.

Latour, B. (1996). *Aramis or the love of technology*. Cambridge, MA: Harvard University Press.

Latour, B. (1999). On recalling ANT . In Law, J., & Hassard, J. (Eds.), *Actor network theory and after* (pp. 15–25). Oxford, UK: Blackwell Publishers.

Latour, B. (2005). *Reassembling the social: An introduction to actor-network theory*. Oxford, UK: Oxford University Press.

Law, J. (1986). On the methods of long distance control: Vessels, navigation and the Portuguese route to India . In Law, J. (Ed.), *Power, action and belief: A new sociology of knowledge?* (pp. 234–263). London, UK: Routledge & Kegan Paul.

Law, J. (1987). Technology and heterogeneous engineering: The case of Portuguese expansion . In Bijker, W. E., Hughes, T. P., & Pinch, T. J. (Eds.), *The social construction of technological systems: New directions in the sociology and history of technology* (pp. 111–134). Cambridge, MA: MIT Press.

Law, J. (1988). The anatomy of a socio-technical struggle: The design of the TSR2 . In Elliott, B. (Ed.), *Technology and social process* (pp. 44–69). Edinburgh, UK: Edinburgh University Press.

Law, J. (1992). Notes on the theory of the actor-network: Ordering, strategy and heterogeneity. *Systems Practice, 5*(4), 379–393. doi:10.1007/BF01059830

Law, J., & Callon, M. (1988). Engineering and sociology in a military aircraft project: A network analysis of technological change. *Social Problems, 35*(3), 284–297. doi:10.1525/sp.1988.35.3.03a00060

Linden, L. (2009). Linux kernel developers embracing authors embracing licenses. *International Journal of Actor-Network Theory and Technological Innovation, 1*(3), 15–35. doi:10.4018/jantti.2009070102

Lukaitis, S. (2011). Applying hermeneutic phenomenology to understand innovation adoption. *International Journal of Actor-Network Theory and Technological Innovation, 3*(4), 46–59. doi:10.4018/jantti.2011100105

MacKenzie, D., & Wajcman, J. (Eds.). (1985). *The social shaping of technology: How the refrigerator got its hum*. Milton Keys, UK: Open University Press.

Manning, K., Wong, L., & Tatnall, A. (2010). Aspects of e-learning in a university. *International Journal of Actor-Network Theory and Technological Innovation, 2*(4), 43–52. doi:10.4018/jantti.2010100105

Mulcahy, D. (2011). Performativity in practice: An actor-network account of professional teaching standards. *International Journal of Actor-Network Theory and Technological Innovation, 3*(2), 1–16. doi:10.4018/jantti.2011040101

Muniesa, F. (2011). Is a stock exchange a computer solution? Explicitness, algorithms and the arizona stock exchange. *International Journal of Actor-Network Theory and Technological Innovation, 3*(1), 1–15. doi:10.4018/jantti.2011010101

Naidoo, T. R. (2010). A socio-technical account of an internet-based self-service technology implementation: Why call-centres sometimes 'prevail' in a multi-channel context? *International Journal of Actor-Network Theory and Technological Innovation, 2*(2), 15–34. doi:10.4018/jantti.2010040102

Priyatma, J. E., & Mohamed, Z. A. (2011). Opening the black box of leadership in the successful development of local e-government initiative in a developing country. *International Journal of Actor-Network Theory and Technological Innovation, 3*(3), 1–20. doi:10.4018/jantti.2011070101

Quinlan, A., Quinlan, E., & Nelson, D. (2011). Performing actor-network theory in the post-secondary classroom. *International Journal of Actor-Network Theory and Technological Innovation, 3*(4), 1–10. doi:10.4018/jantti.2011100101

Rayna, T., Striukova, L., & Landau, S. (2009). Crossing the chasm or being crossed out: The case of digital audio players. *International Journal of Actor-Network Theory and Technological Innovation, 1*(3), 36–54. doi:10.4018/jantti.2009070103

Rimpiläinen, S. (2011). Knowledge in networks – Knowing in transactions? *International Journal of Actor-Network Theory and Technological Innovation, 3*(2), 46–56. doi:10.4018/jantti.2011040104

Rogers, E. M. (1995). *Diffusion of innovations*. New York, NY: The Free Press.

Rogers, E. M. (2003). *Diffusion of innovations*. New York, NY: The Free Press.

Rowan, L., & Bigum, C. (2009). What's your problem? ANT reflections on a research project studying girls enrolment in information technology subjects in postcompulsory education. *International Journal of Actor-Network Theory and Technological Innovation, 1*(4), 1–15. doi:10.4018/jantti.2009062301

Tatnall, A. (2009). Information systems, technology adoption and innovation translation. *International Journal of Actor-Network Theory and Technological Innovation, 1*(1), 59–74. doi:10.4018/jantti.2009010104

Tatnall, A. (2009). Innovation translation and innovation diffusion: A comparison of two different approaches to theorising technological innovation. *International Journal of Actor-Network Theory and Technological Innovation, 1*(2), 67–74. doi:10.4018/jantti.2009040105

Tatnall, A. (2010). On actors, networks, hybrids, black boxes and contesting programming languages. *International Journal of Actor-Network Theory and Technological Innovation, 2*(4), 10–20. doi:10.4018/jantti.2010100102

Tatnall, A. (2011). *Information systems research, technological innovation and actor-network theory.* Melbourne, Australia: Heidelberg Press.

Tscholl, M., Patel, U., & Carmichael, P. (2011). (Un)locating learning: Agents of change in case-based learning. *International Journal of Actor-Network Theory and Technological Innovation, 3*(2), 17–31. doi:10.4018/jantti.2011040102

Tummons, J. (2009). Higher education in further education in England: An actor-network ethnography. *International Journal of Actor-Network Theory and Technological Innovation, 1*(3), 55–69. doi:10.4018/jantti.2009070104

Tummons, J. (2011). Deconstructing professionalism: An actor-network critique of professional standards for teachers in the UK lifelong learning sector. *International Journal of Actor-Network Theory and Technological Innovation, 3*(4), 22–31. doi:10.4018/jantti.2011100103

Uden, L., & Francis, J. (2009). Actor-network theory for service innovation. *International Journal of Actor-Network Theory and Technological Innovation, 1*(1), 23–44. doi:10.4018/jantti.2009010102

Underwood, J., & Tabak, E. (2011). Making information systems material through blackboxing: Allies, translation and due process. *International Journal of Actor-Network Theory and Technological Innovation, 3*(1), 16–26. doi:10.4018/jantti.2011010102

Wickramasinghe, N., & Bali, R. (2009). The S'ANT imperative for realizing the vision of healthcare network centric operations. *International Journal of Actor-Network Theory and Technological Innovation, 1*(1), 45–58. doi:10.4018/jantti.2009010103

Wickramasinghe, N., Bali, R., & Goldberg, S. (2009). The S'ANT approach to facilitate a superior chronic disease self-management model. *International Journal of Actor-Network Theory and Technological Innovation, 1*(4), 21–34. doi:10.4018/jantti.2009062302

Wickramasinghe, N., Tatnall, A., & Bali, R. (2010). Using actor-network theory to facilitate a superior understanding of knowledge creation and knowledge transfer. *International Journal of Actor-Network Theory and Technological Innovation, 2*(4), 30–42. doi:10.4018/jantti.2010100104

Zammar, N. (2010). Social network services: The science of building and maintaining online communities, a perspective from actor-network theory. *International Journal of Actor-Network Theory and Technological Innovation, 2*(2), 54–62. doi:10.4018/jantti.2010040104

Chapter 1

Performativity in Practice:
An Actor–Network Account of Professional Teaching Standards

Dianne Mulcahy
The University of Melbourne, Australia

ABSTRACT

In the context of neo-liberal education policy reform, professional teaching standards have become one of the main means of managing improvements to school teaching and assuring its quality. Using the methodology of material semiotics in association with video case data of classroom teaching (in this case, school geography teachers) and their students, the author treats a set of standards in action, towards conducting an ontological inquiry. Bringing the performative perspective of actor-network theory to bear not only is sociality taken into account but also materiality. This paper argues that standards are best understood as shifting assemblies of practice whose nature defines and enacts teacher identity and teacher professional knowledge differently in different locations. The conclusion is drawn that while teaching standards 'clot' and can serve to standardise practices of teaching, they are not stable entities. The variable ontology that they manifest challenges the managerialist impulses that tend to drive standards work in education. Altogether, the paper seeks to augment existing accounts of standards within the field of the sociology of science (Bowker & Star, 1999; Star, 2010; Timmermans & Berg, 2003; Timmermans & Epstein, 2010) and contribute to its subfield, the sociology of standards.

INTRODUCTION

Representationalism separates the world into the ontologically disjoint domains of words and things, leaving itself with the dilemma of their linkage such that knowledge is possible. If words are untethered from the material world, how do representations gain a foothold? (Barad, 2003, p. 811)

DOI: 10.4018/978-1-4666-2166-4.ch001

In the context of neo-liberal education policy reform, professional teaching standards have become one of the main means of managing improvements to teaching and assuring its quality in schools and the wider profession. Providing opportunities for teachers to open up the 'black box' of teaching and learning, and explore these reciprocal processes in an explicit way, they constitute a key element in nations' aspirations to develop world-class standards of teaching. Drawing on video case data of classroom teaching collected as part of a national study of professional teaching standards, and bringing the practice-based, performative perspective of actor-network theory (Law, 2009a; Law & Singleton, 2000) to bear, I argue that standards are best understood as shifting assemblies of practice – a continuing set of practices whose nature defines and enacts teacher identity and teacher professional knowledge differently in different locations. My interest lies largely in what standards are. Taking seriously actor-network theory's idea[1] that objects, like human subjects, can take different forms in different places and practices (Law, 2002; Mol, 2002; Moser, 2008), I trace the development of a set of standards for teaching school geography, towards conducting an ontological inquiry – studying 'what elements, of whichever character, associated in whichever way', make standards be (Mol & Mesman, 1996, p. 429). No longer single entities with essential attributes, objects, like human subjects, not centered and stable. They take their 'point of departure in relations rather than entities' (Sorensen, 2007, p. 24). Thus, 'an object is something people (or … other objects …) act toward and with' (Star, 2010, p. 603).

My article has three substantive sections. In section two, after some preliminary accounts of teaching standards in which the idea of objects taking different forms in different places and practices is introduced, I sketch some research on standards that is set within recent sociology of science.[2] I follow this sketch with a summary of the central tenets of actor-network theory (ANT) accenting its distinctive performative perspective on complex objects such as teaching standards. Next, in section three, a national empirical study of standards for teaching geography in Australian schools is outlined and details describing the methods used to investigate, and simultaneously develop, these standards are given. Data from this study are then worked via the telling of four

stories of these standards that feature the locales or empirical contexts in which this development took place. Accordingly, I trace the life course of these standards, their shifting shape and forms of assembly in classrooms and the wider profession. In section four, I conclude by discussing the distinctiveness of the contribution of ANT to studies of standards within the sociology of science and what this contribution implies for sociology of standards.

PREQUEL: TOWARD AN ONTOLOGICAL INQUIRY – FIRST STEPS

In beginning my ontological inquiry, I start with policy performances of teaching standards. Following Rizvi and Lingard (2010), I take policy to be the 'authoritative allocation of values' and policy around teaching standards to involve the efforts made by governments and regulatory bodies (such as statutory authorities for the regulation and promotion of the teaching profession) to articulate what is valued about teaching and describe the critical features of what teachers know, believe and are able to do. Set firmly within the domain of words (Barad, 2003), 'standards identify what teachers should know and be able to do' (AEEYSOC National Standards Expert Working Group, 2010). This definition carries along with it the idea that what teachers know can be articulated and that teaching is the type of activity that can and should be captured in standards. 'Standards were invented to develop the capacity to have direct knowledge and access to what was previously opaque' (Popkewitz, 2004, p. 245). It assumes that 'what teachers should know and … do' is a somewhat stable object. Separate from practice, it is something that can be captured in a more or less adequate way in teaching standards – a shared and public 'language of practice' (Yinger, 1987). This version of standards is underscored by a 'representationalist belief in the power of words to represent pre-existing things' (Barad, 2003, p. 802).

Let me turn now to academic enactments of standards. Writing in the context of educational reform, Sykes and Plastrik (1993, p. 4) define standards as 'a tool for rendering appropriately precise the making of judgments and decisions in the context of shared meanings and values'. This definition would seem to suggest that standards are technologies (tools) in the service of broader social and cultural agendas. Emphasis is placed on the role that standards play rather than on the nature of standards themselves. In keeping with the definitions above however, standards are constructed as a technology of representation, a language that is able to render the making of judgments and decisions 'appropriately precise'. In my preferred academic definition of standards, a standard is 'any set of agreed-upon rules for the production of (textual or material) objects' (Bowker & Star, 1999, p. 13). In this sociological understanding of standards, stress is placed not only on rules (which, as we know from the later Wittgenstein, do not include their own applications), but also on performativity. Standards do not simply describe pre-existing realities such as the knowledge and skill a teacher should have to teach; they actively produce them. They are 'significant participants in knowledge work' (Ewenstein & Whyte, 2009, p. 9).

Lastly, it is to practice that I turn to provide a less formalistic and detached sense of standards. Standards, I suggest, cannot be detached from their instances. They 'only become significant if we know what they mean in practice by being able to link them to, and see them at work in, different specific circumstances' (Law, 2008, p. 629). Accordingly, I appeal to a data extract taken from a video case study of classroom teaching in which a Year 9 geography teacher is found to be 'standardising' student learning in geography – implicitly using 'agreed upon rules' regarding the teaching of school geography to produce geographers-in-the

making and/or perhaps, learners with a lifelong interest in geography. The teacher begins a lesson sequence in this way:

Looking at the handout please gentlemen, take that in front of you. We're going to work through the different questions quite slowly today so that we're really learning the correct way to do some answers and the first one we are going to look at is the map which is labelled A, alright, so it's showing the location of Melbourne and then Geelong. It's the very first map; could you all look at that please. (It's labelled) A. Now if we look at our handout, the written answer one, it says (reads aloud): 'This data broadsheet introduces us to a range of what we call geographic media'. ... So look through the data A-S, which you've just done, to get a feel for the characteristics of Geelong. Now the first one A is what we call a thematic map. Looking at the map A (reads aloud): 'Name the main land use which is shown on the map'. Now where would a good place be to find that answer if you're looking at a map? (Student response in the background.) The legend. Have a look at the legend, sometimes it's called the key and what is it actually telling us?

In working 'through the different questions quite slowly', the teacher aims to engage this all boys' class in 'really learning the correct way to do some answers'. Here, standards are not so much defined and described, as 'done'. They are an embodied practice: something people and objects (here, handout, data broadsheet) act toward and with (Star, 2010).

A SHORT STORY OF STANDARDS: SOCIOLOGY OF SCIENCE ACCOUNTS

A large proportion of the sociological literature on standards comes from the field of science studies (Timmermans & Epstein, 2010). Drawing on this literature (Bowker & Star, 1999; Lampland & Star, 2009; Star, 2010; Timmermans & Berg, 2003; Timmermans & Epstein, 2010), two 'strategies' for thinking standards can be identified. Following Law and Singleton's (2005) work on complex objects and 'knowing mess', I will call these the epistemological and the ontological. Firstly, and as implied in the prequel above, standards can have different significance for policymakers, academic commentators and practitioners. They can mean different things to different groups; they can be differently interpreted by different groups. Star and Griesemer (1989) in a landmark study within science studies determined that 'boundary objects', which, over time, are inextricably related to standards (Star, 2010, p. 607), act as anchors or bridges between diverse groups. These objects 'are both plastic enough to adapt to local needs and the constraints of the several parties employing them, yet robust enough to maintain a common identity across sites' (Star & Griesemer, 1989, p. 393). Similarly, standards 'have been shown to serve a boundary-bridging function' (Ottinger, 2010, p. 250). In this framing of standards, they reside within representationalism (Barad, 2003). They enable the coming together of multiple and diverse perspectives or views. They are subject to interpretive flexibility or are multi-interpretable. While a generative way to think standards, this framing misses the complexities of standards, the idea that they can simultaneously exist in many different guises.

The second strategy for thinking standards 'moves us from multiple interpretations of objects ... to thinking about multiple objects themselves. This is why we call it ontological' (Law & Singleton, 2005, p. 334). Taken by way of 'the performative turn', this move tends to be made by science studies scholars who draw on the resources of actor-network theory and material-semiotics (Haraway, 1991, 1997; Law, 2002, 2009a; Law & Lien, 2010; Mol, 2002; Moser, 2008). As Barad (2003, p. 802) has it, 'the move towards performative alternatives to representationalism shifts the focus from questions of correspondence between descriptions and reality (e.g., do they mirror nature or culture?) to matters of practices/doings/actions'. She continues: 'performativity is actually a contestation of the unexamined habits of mind that grant language and other forms of representation more power in determining our ontologies than they deserve' (Barad, 2003). Riding on the back of written representations, educational standards may have been accorded more power than they deserve in determining what constitutes quality teaching and the character of the teaching profession? Standards practices are performative. They bring things – teacher knowledge and identities – into being. They don't simply refer to or represent something somewhere else (Sorensen, 2007); they are productive and help to shape and condition the world (Lien & Law, 2010). They create performative effects such as valorising policy agendas that seek to regulate life and learning in schools and policy processes that seek to steer practice at a distance. No longer providing for the coming together of multiple views, they are caught up in and catch others up in multiple worlds. Like other complex entities, entities such as teaching standards are assemblages[3] of other entities and importantly, entities that are other to one another. In this version of the assemblage of heterogeneous entities such as teaching standards, otherness is acknowledged as 'inside' the practices that concern us (e.g. knowledge practices). It has positivity and a non-assimilability that must be recognized, as otherness: that which cannot be assimilated. This makes for ontological tensions which can play out as ontological politics (Mol, 1999).

ACTOR-NETWORK THEORY AND MATERIAL SEMIOTICS: A PERFORMATIVE PERSPECTIVE

A focus on objects brings practice into view and the rich material contexts and dense social relations in which production takes place. An analytical interest in objects also reveals their centrality to the various processes and practices of learning and knowing (Ewenstein & Whyte, 2009, p. 8)

Using insights from a range of theoretical and methodological traditions, including science, technology and society (STS), post-structuralism and material semiotics, actor-network theory is widely known for its 'commitment to practice and the stuff of the world' (Law, 2008, p. 643). As Law tells its development story, 'actor-network theory is what resulted when a non-humanist and post-structuralist sensibility to relationality, materiality, process, enactment and the possibility of alternative epistemic framings bumped into the theoretically informed, materially-grounded, practice-oriented empirical case-study tradition of English language STS' (Law, 2008, p. 632). More pointedly for the purposes of this paper in its concern with shifting assemblies, actor-network theory is 'a disparate family of material-semiotic tools, sensibilities and methods of analysis' that can be used to tell 'stories about "how" relations assemble or don't' (Law, 2009a, p. 141). Instead of asking why things happen, the material semiotics of actor-network theory asks 'how they occur. How they arrange themselves. How the materials of the world (social, technical, documentary, natural, human, animal) get themselves done' (Law, 2008, p. 632, original emphasis).

The assumption is made that nothing has reality, or form, outside its performance in webs of relations with performances being defined as 'material processes, practices, which take place day by day and minute by minute' (Law & Singleton, 2000, p. 775). Law (2009b, p. 1, original emphasis) continues:

If we think performatively, then reality is not assumed to be independent, priori, definite, singular or coherent. Rather the logic is turned upside down. If reality appears (as it usually does) to be independent, prior, definite, singular or coherent then this is because it is being done *that way. ...*

Practices enact realities ... This means that if we want to understand how realities are done or to explore their politics, then we have to attend carefully to practices and ask how they work.

And practices are?

For my purposes, practices are detectable and somewhat ordered sets of material-semiotic relations. To study practices is therefore to undertake the analytical and empirical task of exploring possible patterns of relations, and how it is that these get assembled in particular locations. It is to treat the real as whatever it is that is being assembled, materially and semiotically in a scene of analytical interest (Law, 2009b, p. 1, original emphasis)

The turn to performance has been taken in various disciplinary fields (e.g. human geography, cultural studies, contemporary political theory). ANT's version of this turn affords attention to materiality and multiplicity and, in so doing, promotes investigation of ontological difference.

Since performances are specific, this also leads to multiplicity, so that what appears to be one thing (an "object," "working," "knowledge") may be understood as a set of related performances. More strongly, it suggests that abstraction (including abstract knowledge) is a performance, something enacted in specific locations that has to be reenacted in other locations in further performances if it is to carry. This has all sorts of implications. One is that things don't come to rest in a single form once agreement, or what is called "closure," is achieved. They rumble on and on, as it were, noisy and noisome. (Law & Singleton, 2000, p. 775)

On this reckoning, standards may be understood to assemble, reassemble and disassemble. No longer 'one thing', they are an active practice of standardising or assemblies of this.[4] In holding to the idea that reality does not precede practices but is made through them, ANT attends to the idea that practices have a political life. 'Practices organize and reproduce the distribution of power, knowledge, and the inequalities that go with them' (Nicolini, Gherardi, & Yanow, 2003, p. 24). They have built-in normativities, contributing to 'some worlds-in-progress but not to others' (Moser, 2008, p. 99). The question becomes which worlds we want practices to make.

The Project in Question: Data and Methods

The first empirical phase of the project reported (performed) here was concerned to study what 'accomplished' geography teaching is by documenting what geography teachers, who are deemed accomplished, do. Data were sourced from teachers and students via video recordings of accomplished teaching with identification of accomplished teachers being made by way of purposeful sampling. Thus, members of the Australian Geography Teachers' Association and its affiliates, the peak professional associations for school geography in Australia, were invited to nominate teachers who are widely regarded professionally, using various criteria including reputation for accomplishment within the field of geographic education, years of experience teaching school geography, teaching qualifications, etc. The approach adopted used technically complex methods for video recording classrooms and supplementing the video records with post-lesson video-stimulated interviews with students and the teacher.[5] Eleven case studies (22 lessons altogether) were conducted in eight schools (government and non-government; metropolitan and non-metropolitan) in three major Australian states. Video recordings were made over the course of a sequence of two lessons, each lasting for approximately fifty minutes. The first of the fieldwork tales below concerns one of these case studies.

The second empirical phase of the project sought to study what 'accomplished' geography teaching is by documenting what geography teach-

ers, at different stages of their career, say about accomplished practice, with particular attention to samples of practice from the video-recordings made as part of the first project phase.[6] This phase involved the conduct of teacher panel meetings (focus groups) in five Australian states. Meeting twice over six months, panels of practising geography teachers (64 teachers altogether) were tasked with reviewing video excerpts and related data (e.g. samples of students' work) and responding to a series of semi-structured questions designed to identify elements of accomplished practice. In so doing, these teachers helped develop the standards for teaching school geography. The further fieldwork tales told below − tales two, three and four − are set within the chief 'contexts' of this development, firstly, a panel consultation website comprising various data files; secondly, the teacher panel meetings where data collected from panel members are discussed; and thirdly, the project website on which the 'official standards', 'Professional Standards for Accomplished Teaching of School Geography, can be found (http://www. geogstandards.edu.au/). In tracing the shifting relations of standards through a research project that spans different contexts or locales, I tell a story of multiple enactments of standards and attend to their performative effects (e.g. regulatory effects). Place locations and names of teachers have been altered for reasons of confidentiality.

STANDARDS IN THE MAKING: SHIFTING ASSEMBLIES OF PRACTICE

A Classroom Tale: Standards 'In the Wild'[7] − A Locally Situated Accomplishment

My first empirical context concerns a classroom set within a large government school in a metropolitan area in which a Year 9 geography class is being introduced by its teacher, Simon, to the skill of field sketching (Figure 1) in preparation for a

Figure 1.

Simon executing photo sketch in class   **Students sketching in the field**

fieldwork trip to be made the following week. Here, standards assume the form of mētis – contextualised, situated knowledge and practice (Li, 2005) in which bodies and representations play a leading role.

One of the main skills for this year that we need to develop is field sketching, OK? Now, there are three aspects to field sketching. What we're going to do, I'll tell you what those three aspects are, then I want to give you an example to do, and we're going to simulate doing a field sketch, except it will be a photo sketch, similar sort of idea but we're going to practise it.

What strikes one when researching in geography classrooms is not only the inscription devices (Latour & Woolgar, 1979) used to record and preserve data but also what might be called the manual handling of knowledge through practices of sketching, drawing, illustrating, labelling and annotating. Simon continues:

There are three things to look for. Illustrating: what do you do? You look at the scene that you're looking at and you give it a frame. ... What are the features you want to look at? I can't show everything but I want to look at the main things, the main features. And the technique ... you work from your foreground to your background. From large detail to the smaller detail. Once you've illustrated it, the most important part is to label and annotate because it might not just be you using

that information later on, someone else might too. So, labelling: you need to name those key features that you've drawn. Name them: beach, groyne, sea wall, harbour, cliff ... You're looking at it as a geographer. We're looking at coastal processes and features. So say to yourself: 'What can I see taking place there? What elements can I see? Or what areas? How can I label it?'.

The classroom version of teaching and standards of teaching provides a strong sense of standards as an activity in which people participate as well as of the role and contribution of sensibilities that are not necessarily state-able as standards: 'You're looking at it as a geographer'. Standards are omnipresent: 'There are three things to look for'; 'So say to yourself: "What can I see taking place there? What elements can I see? Or what areas? How can I label it?"'. Teaching and standards of teaching are not read off a lesson plan or a set of standards statements, rather they are enacted. And their enactments are 'material processes, practices, which take place day by day and minute by minute' (Law & Singleton, 2000, p. 775).

Explaining one of the exercises that the students will be asked to take part in when on fieldwork, Simon demonstrates, yet again, the material, 'hands-on' character of classroom teaching:

One of the tasks that we do a couple of times (on fieldwork) is the tunnel vision. Tunnel vision is ... it's actually the opposite. We live in a world, if you

7

think about it, we go around the world walking round like this (head down, Simon's hands are held to his face, narrowing his vision) and you only see what's directly in front of you, where you're heading from A to B and you miss all the detail. In fieldwork, we walk like this (arms outstretched wide, head up) and we see everything. And we see the links between (everything). It's the same thing when we do a tunnel vision; we'll be going down (to the coast) and we'll be doing the tunnel vision in the bus. So for a period of time in the bus, at points, we'll be observing what's taking place on the land either side of us. Right? So that's what a tunnel vision exercise is. ... Your route to school is the tunnel vision you do everyday and never really think about. It's your personal geography; your map of your route to the school.

Along with interested students (or not), teacher explanation and embodied action assemble, bringing standards of teaching and learning into effect: 'In fieldwork, we walk like this'. Teaching standards are part of working professionally – a locally situated accomplishment.

A Tale of a Panel Consultation Website: Standards as Statements-in-the-Making

My second empirical context concerns a consultation website on which samples of accomplished geography teaching drawn from the video case studies, and comments on this teaching by the teachers and students taking part, could be accessed by the teachers participating in panel meetings or focus groups. Like the version of standards above, the consultation website provides a strong sense of standards as an activity in which people participate; this participation however, occurs at a remove from classroom practice. In being asked to review samples of teaching practice, knowledge of standards and the standards themselves are not being produced at the point of performance of situated understandings (Verran,

Christie, Anbins-King, Van Weeren, & Yunupingu, 2007). Rather, this knowledge is a product of the processing of various case data – video, image, text, audio – that teacher participants respond to. It is perceptual, not corporeal. Bodies do not figure in this assembly of practice in quite the way that Simon's body and his students' bodies do: 'Your route to school is the tunnel vision you do everyday and never really think about'. In this assembly of practice, website, empirical materials, viewing diaries and teacher participants come together to create another version of standards for teaching school geography. Here, language and other forms of representation are granted power in determining the character of these standards.

Thus, the participating teachers were asked to complete a viewing diary towards the production of an account of accomplished teaching. Selecting from the 'Samples' menu on the panel consultation website, they reviewed any or all of the following:

Sample 1: Regional centre of Geelong
Sample 2: Concept formation - Relative location
Sample 3: Fieldsketching
Sample 4: Coastal fieldtrip
Sample 5: Cyclone Nargis
Sample 6a: Population growth - Brainstorming
Sample 6b: Predicting the optimum population of Australia
Sample 7: Topographic mapping skills
Sample 8: Computer-based group work - Countries study
Sample 9: Preparing to work in expert groups - The Olympics
Sample 10: After the simulation - Group discussion

A diary entry for each selection was then completed and submitted online. These submissions were 'scaffolded' using a set of questions, the chief of which for present purposes is: 'What counts as accomplished teaching here'? Using 'Sample 3: Fieldsketching' – the case data collected in Simon's classroom and storied above – as an illustrative example, a small number of responses to this question has been selected randomly to give a sense of teachers' submissions:

T1: 'The idea of asking for 3 different ideas – a clearly established framework for an effective lesson. Modelling on the board to show the students exactly "how to". Linking to the students local knowledge – travelling to school and what they observe. An emphasis on personal connections'.

T2: '1. Teacher has a deep knowledge of both content and skill 2. Being able to reduce the elements of a specific geospatial skill to a series of simple steps that students can comprehend'.

T3: 'I'm not sure. The teacher had accomplished skills of geography (fieldwork sketching), but this is not the same as accomplished geography teaching. I guess he was modelling the skill for the students, but as I say, without much explanation of his thinking or reasoning as he was doing it – no 'thinking aloud' was taking place so in a sense what he was doing could have seemed a bit obvious or quite arbitrary, depending on each student's own prior knowledge of, and confidence with, the task he was modelling'.

T4: 'Use of relevant resources. Line drawing as an overlay of actual photo, rather than simply presenting drawing. Guided discovery approach to labelling of diagram and further annotation of processes involved. Link between visual indicators and labelling of processes'.

T5: 'The use of geography terminology. Knowledge of subject matter. Allowing for student interaction (answering questions the teacher asked)'.

T6: 'I feel that the teacher's approach to teaching skills and his overall knowledge of what he is doing comes across extremely well. His approach is focused on teaching a skill in a visual way. His knowledge of the subject area was well developed and specific. He

encouraged students to look at a photo in a very particular geographic way and to annotate it accordingly'.

T7: 'Use of relevant visual to model approach to geographic skill of field sketching. Breaking down the process of completing a sketch into easy steps for students, for example working from foreground to background'.

Standards are depictions that characterise rather than categorise accomplished practice. While well on the way to becoming generalised statements about accomplished geography teaching – 'He encouraged students to look at a photo in a very particular geographic way' – this version of standards is indexed to the specific actions taken by the teacher: 'I guess he was modelling the skill for the students'. A strong sense of the specificity of practices is provided. The teacher participants account for features of accomplished practice, but in a grounded, context-specific way.

A Tale of Teacher Panels: Standards as Statements (Made)

Tracing the movement of standards from the classroom to the profession at large brings me to the third locale in which the standards under study here were produced – that is, teacher panel meetings (16 meetings altogether) in five major Australian states. Small groups of practising geography teachers (64 teachers altogether) met face-to-face twice to engage in discussions about elements of accomplished geography teaching, using video excerpts from the case data collected in classrooms. Held at various sites, the first meeting of each panel ran for approximately five hours with the last hour being given over to identification of elements of accomplished geography teaching. Here, clearly, we are well on the way to standards manifesting as a shared and public 'language of practice' (Yinger, 1987). By way of illustration, a small selection of these elements, as proposed by the participating teachers, are shown in Table 1.

Written in response to the question, 'What is it that the accomplished geography teacher does?', each of these elements is general in nature. The identified elements pertain to the professional practice of geography teaching as a whole. A distillation and 'scaling out' of the contents of accomplished practice occurs – 'Professional practice is improved and maintained through targeted geographical professional development' – with little reference to the 'lived' and contingent conditions of classrooms.

In one seemingly small move, a move made by way of three technologies (Shapin & Schaffer, 1985) – the material technology of post-it notes on which the elements of accomplished geography teaching were recorded;[8] the literary technology of lists which served to specify the elements;[9] and the social technology of gathering together a panel of practising geography teachers who were taken to be able to testify to the character of accomplished geography teaching – standards emerge as representations of teachers' abilities, predispositions, positioning, knowledge and skills. Once organised into categories and sub-categories, these representations comprise standards statements, the currently valued version of standards which can circulate widely and inform the decisions of policymakers and policy advisors who,

in Australia, are engaged currently in creating a national curriculum and establishing the place of subject specialisations such as school geography in this curriculum. A mobile and scaled up practice, it is this version of standards that can produce powerful performative effects (e.g. regulatory and governance effects).

A Tale of Project Products: Standards and Samples

And so we arrive in the final tale of school geography standards in the making at the project website, http://www.geogstandards.edu.au/, where one can find 'the standards' – ideals, not enactments – which now assume the form of a downloadable PDF file (Figure 2) and a set of numbered statements (Figures 3 and 4):

A 'hard' copy, standards brochure is also available for circulation to schools and the professional associations, implying that in this version of standards practice, standards are a stand-alone and stable object that can travel intact across the country if needs be. And, this is what they are in e-publication and print practice as well as more broadly (i.e. processes of education policy reform).

The categories have hardened – 'the nine geography standards' (Figure 5) – and context and con-

Table 1. Sample of the elements of accomplished geography teaching

Predisposition to geographical content knowledge. Connecting with here and now teachable moments	Making connections with other disciplines using a geography lens	Incorporation of spatial concepts (explicit & implicit)	Able to listen, respond, encourage thinking and justification based on data and evidence
Uses classroom episodes that engage students in self directed and peer orientated learning	Uses the language and tools of the subject	Students are encouraged and supported to be active citizens in their world (either locally, nationally, globally)	Fieldwork
Interlinking of human and natural (physical) world	Embraces the use of multi- media, new technologies, spatial technologies	Professional practice is improved and maintained through targeted geographical professional development	Ability to seek to use learning technologies in ways that transform the pedagogy of geographical education
Bringing people/artefacts/ the world into the classroom and taking the students into the world	Teachers see themselves as a Geographer – Studies are always reflecting / using the Geographical Inquiry Approach	Selection of relevant, stimulating and suitable case studies	Incorporation of real world examples and current material/ issues

Figure 2. Project website: home page

tingency have been seemingly stripped away. Yet, I claim, while standards 'clot' in this publication and dissemination practice, heterogeneity remains. On the 'About this site' page of the project website (Figure 5), standards and samples are juxtaposed and introduced thus: 'This site provides access to the nine geography standards and eleven samples of classroom geography teaching. Each of these is designed to offer a basis for professional learning'. While the nine standards are given priority, room is made for another standards reality, standards as samples or situated practice. It is in the space between these standards varieties that discourses and practices of standards other than standardisation and managerialism can present. Challenging the idea of the singularity of standards, I argue that otherness is acknowledged as 'inside' them.

Practising Performativity: The Contribution of Actor-Network Theory

In making my empirical ontology (Law & Lien, 2010), I have traced the trajectory of a specific set of standards in which complex and disparate entities – teachers, students, researchers, classrooms, panel meetings, video recording equipment, websites and so on – have come together variously in a variety of practices (e.g. classroom teaching, diary writing, panel meetings, web-based work)

to create multiplicity. In storying standards as shifting assemblies of practice – a continuing set of practices that manifest differently in different locations – I have attempted to practise performativity, to explore the possibilities presented by a practice-based, material-oriented, methodological approach. Actor-network theory provides for the tracing of these assemblies as well as purchase on the idea that when an assemblage becomes stabilised (as, for example, 'Big S' standards), it 'supplies a complex of knowledge and practice in terms of which certain kinds of problems and solutions become thinkable whereas others are submerged, at least for a time' (Li, 2005, p. 386). In other words, it creates performative effects – here, power-knowledge effects. ANT accents the idea that practices have a political life. This understanding has important implications for objects of research and research itself. Just as the development of a set of teaching standards is a performative practice, contributing to 'some worlds-in-progress but not to others' (Moser, 2008, p. 99), so too is the study of this development. 'All research is performative, in the sense that it helps enact the real' (Markussen, 2005, p. 329). The question becomes which realities we care to make when undertaking it.

Practising performativity 'is meant to underline the political and interventionist possibilities in research' (Markussen, 2005). Grasping these

Figure 3. 'The standards'

Figure 4. 'The standards'

possibilities in the case of the inquiry conducted here involves giving challenge to the currently valued version of standards which privileges representational forms of knowledge over contextualised, situated knowledge; opening up the idea of standards as it is used in the current conjuncture, to 'undo' it and thus also its effects (e.g. standardisation of teaching practice) (Markussen, 2005, p. 332). It also involves directing attention to one's own knowledge practices. Like the object of the inquiry, the inquiry itself should be opened up, 'undone'. Writing in the context of investigating material politics, Law and Mol (2008, p. 142) ask: 'How might writing be done in a way that opens up a space of contestation rather than closing it down?' and add instructively: 'What otherwise appears to be self-evident may be undermined through articulation. … Articulation requires that practices are put into contrast with their others. If other equally possible ways of ordering are presented along with those under study, this helps open up a space of contestation'. In storying my data as shifting assemblies of practice, I attempted to open up just such a space. Representational forms of knowledge and contextualised, situated knowledge are featured in this 'hybrid' knowledge practice; practices are put into contrast with their others. This contrast is of consequence in the context of neo-liberal education policy reform. It brings into view a particular set of practices

(e.g., embodied action, teacher practical judgment and sensibilities) that are often implicit in studies of standards but seldom examined in a focused manner.

Working samples of teaching practice (knowing-in-practice, standards) with and against standards of teaching practice (knowledge representations, Standards), as practitioners are invited to do via the project website storied in the last of the data 'slices' above, presents the possibility of strengthening a specific version of standards (standards) and of calling into question the currently established reality of standards as representational, stable and singular.[10] 'Practising performativity demands such ontological encounters, encounters in which the terms of the real are allowed to shift' (Markussen, 2005, p. 341) and ontological politics (Mol, 1999) to play out.

Towards a Sociology of Standards: Shifting Assemblies of Practice

In attending carefully to practices and asking how they work (Law, 2009b), as actor-network theory is disposed to do, we can account for the prominence of the standards 'movement' in education, without attributing to standards a coherence, unity and formality that they do not have. Practices of data collection and category creation produce the apparent fixity, formality and authority of

Figure 5. Standards and samples

standards. In the case of the standards under study here, the reality of national professional standards is the effect of a vast array of practices such as collecting data in classrooms, 'drilling down' into these data to establish the characteristics of accomplished geography teaching and clustering these characteristics to create key categories of accomplishment. These practices are underscored by the spatial and political processes of 'scaling out' and 'up'. ANT-oriented studies afford an opportunity to 'trace the negotiations and performances through which educational standards achieve and maintain some durable form as a consequence of the socio-material relations in which they are located and performed' (Fenwick, 2010, p. 2, original emphasis) and, in this tracing, identify ontological shifts, such that what appears to be a single, standard reality – The professional standards for x, y, z school subject – becomes 'different realities being enacted in more or less power-saturated practices' (Law, 2008, p. 637).

Why might the making of these ontological shifts matter? As Law has it, 'the question becomes: how to interfere in and diffract realities in particular locations to generate more respectful and less dominatory alternatives. How to trope, to bend versions of the real, to strengthen desirable realities that would otherwise be weak (Law, 2008, p. 637). It can be claimed that representationalism has ruled the field of standards research in education (through for example, the currently well-established education policy interest in, and commitment to, evidenced-based policy). While I do not advocate any romantic return to notions of standards as wisdom of practice (Shulman, 2004),[11] it may be time to revalue practice-based approaches to thinking and doing educational standards whereby teachers' embodied, practical judgments and enacted standards can come into view and come explicitly to count. The performative perspective that I have attempted to practise here does not exclude the idea of representation, but rather 'views it as a specific aspect of performativity' (Jensen, 2005, p. 262). A robust and

responsible sociology of standards will take both into account. Articulating fundamentally different accounts (of standards) and articulating them together – maintaining the tension between the multiple and the seeming singular – provides a good guiding rule for how to go on in sociological research.

REFERENCES

AEEYSOC National Standards Expert Working Group. (2010). *Draft National Professional Standards for Teachers*. Victoria, Australia: Ministerial Council for Education, Early Childhood Development and Youth Affairs.

Barad, K. (2003). Posthumanist performativity: Toward an understanding of how matter comes to matter. *Signs, 28*(3), 801–831. doi:10.1086/345321

Bowker, G., & Star, S. L. (1999). *Sorting things out: Classification and its consequences*. Cambridge, MA: MIT Press.

Ewenstein, B., & Whyte, J. (2009). Knowledge practices in design: The role of visual representations as 'epistemic objects'. *Organization Studies, 30*(1), 7–30. doi:10.1177/0170840608083014

Fenwick, T. (2010). *How standards are performed in education: Fluid fissures and suspended certainty*. Paper presented at the EASST Conference: Practicing Science and Technology, Performing the Social.

Haraway, D. (1991). *Simians, cyborgs, and women: The reinvention of nature*. New York, NY: Routledge.

Haraway, D. (1997). *Modest-witness@second-millennium.FemaleMan-meets-OncoMouse: Feminism and technoscience*. New York, NY: Routledge.

Hutchins, E. (1995). *Cognition in the wild*. Cambridge, MA: MIT Press.

Jensen, C. B. (2005). An experiment in performative history: Electronic patient records as a future-generating device. *Social Studies of Science*, *35*(2), 241–267. doi:10.1177/0306312705047737

Lampland, M., & Star, S. L. (Eds.). (2009). *Standards and their stories: How quantifying, classifying, and formalizing practices shape everyday life*. London, UK: Cornell University Press.

Latour, B., & Woolgar, S. (1979). *Laboratory life: The social construction of scientific facts*. Thousand Oaks, CA: Sage.

Law, J. (2002). *Aircraft stories: Decentering the object in technoscience*. Durham, NC: Duke University Press.

Law, J. (2008). On sociology and STS. *The Sociological Review*, *56*(4), 623–649. doi:10.1111/j.1467-954X.2008.00808.x

Law, J. (2009a). Actor-network theory and material semiotics. In Turner, B. S. (Ed.), *The new Blackwell companion to social theory* (3rd ed., pp. 141–158). Chichester, UK: John Wiley & Sons. doi:10.1002/9781444304992.ch7

Law, J. (2009b). *Collateral realities*. Retrieved from http://www.heterogeneities.net/publications/Law2009CollateralRealities.pdf

Law, J., & Lien, M. (2010). *Slippery: Field notes on empirical ontology*. Retrieved from http://www.sai.uio.no/english/research/projects/newcomers/publications/working-papers-web/Slippery%20revised%2013%20WP%20version.pdf

Law, J., & Mol, A. (2008). Globalisation in practice: On the politics of boiling pigswill. *Geoforum*, *39*(1), 133–143. doi:10.1016/j.geoforum.2006.08.010

Law, J., & Singleton, V. (2000). Performing technology's stories: On social constructivism, performance, and performativity. *Technology and Culture*, *41*(4), 765–775.

Law, J., & Singleton, V. (2005). Object lessons. *Organization*, *12*(3), 331–355. doi:10.1177/1350508405051270

Li, T. M. (2005). Beyond 'the state' and failed schemes. *American Anthropologist*, *107*(3), 383–394. doi:10.1525/aa.2005.107.3.383

Lien, M., & Law, J. (2010). *Emergent aliens: Performing indigeneity and other ways of doing salmon in Norway*. Retrieved from http://www.sai.uio.no/english/research/projects/newcomers/publications/working-papers-web/Emergent%20aliens%20Ethnos%20revised%20WP%20version.pdf

Markussen, T. (2005). Practising performativity: Transformative moments in research. *European Journal of Women's Studies*, *12*(3), 329–344. doi:10.1177/1350506805054273

Mol, A. (1999). Ontological politics: A word and some questions. In Law, J., & Hassard, J. (Eds.), *Actor-network theory and after* (pp. 74–89). London, UK: Blackwell.

Mol, A. (2002). *The body multiple: Ontology in medical practice*. Durham, NC: Duke University Press.

Mol, A., & Law, J. (1994). Regions, networks and fluids: Anaemia and social topology. *Social Studies of Science*, *24*, 641–671. doi:10.1177/030631279402400402

Mol, A., & Mesman, J. (1996). Neonatal food and the politics of theory: Some questions of method. *Social Studies of Science*, *26*(2), 419–444. doi:10.1177/030631296026002009

Moser, I. (2008). Making Alzheimer's disease matter: Enacting, interfering and doing politics of nature. *Geoforum*, *39*(1), 98–110. doi:10.1016/j.geoforum.2006.12.007

Nicolini, D., Gherardi, S., & Yanow, D. (Eds.). (2003). *Knowing in organizations: A practice-based approach*. Armonk, NY: M.E. Sharpe.

Ottinger, G. (2010). Buckets of resistance: Standards and the effectiveness of citizen science. *Science, Technology & Human Values*, *35*(2), 244–270. doi:10.1177/0162243909337121

Popkewitz, T. (2004). Educational standards: Mapping who we are and are to become. *Journal of the Learning Sciences*, *13*(2), 243–256. doi:10.1207/s15327809jls1302_7

Rizvi, F., & Lingard, B. (2010). *Globalizing education policy*. London, UK: Routledge.

Shapin, S., & Schaffer, S. (1985). *Leviathan and the air-pump: Hobbes, Boyle, and the experimental life*. Princeton, NJ: Princeton University Press.

Shulman, L. (2004). *The wisdom of practice: Essays on teaching, learning, and learning to teach*. San Francisco, CA: Jossey-Bass.

Shulman, L. (2007). Practical wisdom in the service of professional practice. *Educational Researcher*, *36*(9), 560–563. doi:10.3102/0013189X07313150

Sorensen, E. (2007). STS goes to school: Spatial imaginaries of technology, knowledge and presence. *Critical Social Studies*, *2*, 15–27.

Star, S. L. (2010). This is not a boundary object: Reflections on the origin of a concept. *Science, Technology & Human Values*, *35*(5), 601–617. doi:10.1177/0162243910377624

Star, S. L., & Griesemer, J. (1989). Institutional ecology, "translations" and boundary objects: Amateurs and professionals in Berkeley's Museum of Vertebrate Zoology, 1907-39. *Social Studies of Science*, *19*, 387–420. doi:10.1177/030631289019003001

Sykes, G., & Plastrik, P. (1993). *Standard setting as educational reform*. Washington, DC: American Association of Colleges for Teachers of Education.

Timmermans, S., & Berg, M. (2003). *The gold standard: The challenge of evidence-based medicine and standardization in health care*. Philadelphia, PA: Temple University Press.

Timmermans, S., & Epstein, S. (2010). A world of standards but not a standard world: Toward a sociology of standards and standardisation. *Annual Review of Sociology*, *36*, 69–89. doi:10.1146/annurev.soc.012809.102629

Verran, H., Christie, M., Anbins-King, B., Van Weeren, T., & Yunupingu, W. (2007). Designing digital knowledge management tools with Aboriginal Australians. *Digital Creativity*, *18*(3), 129–142. doi:10.1080/14626260701531944

Watson, A., & Huntington, O. H. (2008). They're *here* - I can *feel* them: The epistemic spaces of indigenous and western Knowledges. *Social & Cultural Geography*, *9*(3), 257–281. doi:10.1080/14649360801990488

Yinger, R. (1987). Learning the language of practice. *Curriculum Inquiry*, *17*, 293–318. doi:10.2307/1179695

ENDNOTES

1. Explorations of the character of objects have been made in science, technology and society (STS) for at least twenty years (Law & Singleton, 2005). Actor network theory sits under the broad umbrella of STS. It has however, taken a particular interest in complex objects such as alcoholic liver disease (Law & Singleton, 2005), atherosclerosis (Mol, 2002) and anaemia (Mol & Law, 1994) and, in practising 'ontological radicalism' (Law & Singleton, 2005), it goes further than other parts of STS when considering the nature of the objects in the world.

2. Drawing from a wide range of disciplines, the sociology of science runs under a number of names including 'science, technology and society' (STS), 'social studies of science and technology', 'science and technology studies' (STS) and simply, 'science studies'. See Law's (2008) account in 'On sociology and

STS' for a related version of this disciplinary mapping.

3. 'The concept of the assemblage forwarded by Deleuze and Guattari denotes the 'amalgam of places, bodies, voices, skills, practices, technical devices, theories, social strategies and collective work that together constitute ... knowledge/practices' (Watson & Huntington, 2008, p. 272; Wright, 2005, p. 908). As Law (2009a, p. 146) comments, there is little difference between the term agencement – translated as "assemblage" in English – and the term actor-network (heterogeneous network). Thus, I use these terms, or better perhaps, analytical metaphors, largely interchangeably.

4. One cannot presume however, that this practice will automatically result in standardisation.

5. For each of ten classrooms in three major Australian states, two lessons, each lasting around 50 minutes, were videotaped using three cameras. One camera focused on the teacher, a second on individual students as part of a working group, and a third on the whole class as seen from the front of the room. Using as catalyst the video record from the whole class camera, with the teacher camera image inserted as a picture-in-picture image in one corner of the display, teachers were invited to make a reconstructive account of the lesson events deemed critical to student learning. Similarly, students were invited to make an account of lesson events, using as stimulus the video record from the teacher camera, with the individual students' camera image inserted as a picture-in-picture image in one corner of the display.

6. These samples were selected by members of the research team – nine people altogether, including four highly experienced geographic educators and teachers.

7. Here, I invoke the work of Edwin Hutchins (1995) who studied cognition in culturally constituted activities outside the laboratory – 'in the wild'.

8. When identifying elements of accomplished geography teaching, panel participants as a pair, or group of three, were tasked with making their identifications using post-it notes that, once complete, they then placed on A-3 sheets towards constructing a visual 'map' of the emerging standards. The size of the notes (76mm x 128mm) and the flexibility they afforded (should false starts be made regarding any element, a new note could rapidly replace the old) helped produce standards as statements. These seemingly insignificant materials actively enacted standards as succinct statements e.g. 'Selection of relevant, stimulating and suitable case studies'.

9. Once the elements of accomplished geography teaching were identified by panel participants, they were arranged in order of importance. This 'literary' mode of materialising meaning, whereby the emerging standards were written and re-written, arranged and re-arranged, ultimately brought standards as written and numbered statements into effect.

10. The distinction drawn between the terms 'standards' and 'Standards' implies different modes of materialising teaching standards. These standards can assume the form of knowledge representations (Standards) and/or knowledge indexed to action (standards).

11. Having been writing about the wisdom of practice since 1985, Shulman (2007, p. 561) argues that 'the wisdom of practice is a necessary but ultimately insufficient basis for teaching and pedagogical action. Values, visions of the possible and theoretical conceptions of learning, teaching, development, justice, and equity must be drawn upon'.

This work was previously published in the International Journal of Actor-Network Theory and Technological Innovation, Volume 3, Issue 2, edited by Arthur Tatnall, pp. 1-16, copyright 2011 by IGI Publishing (an imprint of IGI Global).

Chapter 2
(Un)Locating Learning:
Agents of Change in Case-Based Learning

Michael Tscholl
University of Cambridge, UK

Uma Patel
City University London, UK

Patrick Carmichael
Liverpool John Moores University, UK

ABSTRACT

This paper presents an account of field research into case-based learning in a management course, guided by the questions: 'what is making change in this setting', and 'where is learning located'. Multiple forms of relations between human and nonhuman entities were identified through extensive research, which, analytically does not sit well with more traditional understandings of learning or case-based learning. A critique of those understandings is offered, drawing on concepts from post-modernism and adopting sensibilities from actor-network theory, follow the action in the setting. The authors demonstrate that the case is an assemblage of heterogeneous connections that are made by the teacher and then by the students in the classroom. In working with ANT sensibilities, examination found that tracing the action offers radically different accounts and possibilities for education research and practice. The pragmatic issues in following the action and the challenge of staying coherent and ambivalent are acknowledged.

INTRODUCTION

The concept of learning and the rallying call to enhance learning are ever present in our culture. If only we could have a comprehensive understanding of human learning (Illeris, 2009). If only learning could be made more fit-for-purpose then society would see a difference. If only the design of learning technology was less technology led and more about how people learn. Those of us who teach and do research into learning recognize the ambivalence of learning in practice. This state of indeterminacy is described by Law (2004) as generalization that can go so far and no further; and by Latour (2005) as uncertainty in the nature of action where in "each course of action a great

DOI: 10.4018/978-1-4666-2166-4.ch002

variety of agents seem to barge in and displace the original goal" (p. 22).

The notion that there are "agent(s) of change" is central in wide ranging discourses around learning and education. Various candidates are proposed as being the prime 'agent (s)' or at least important ones: the learning material, the teacher, the curriculum, the student, and so on. Yet, assigning primacy or even degrees of relevance to particular candidates has also proven to be difficult. The perception of complexity of the educational endeavour, of many elements being inextricably interwoven and interrelated, remains, and much of the history of learning and education research revolves around attempts to disentangle these elements.

In this paper, we adopt sensibilities from actor network-theory (ANT) to tackle the problem in a different way. Rather than trying to isolate elements, we take the position that complexity is the starting point for analysis and description. The question about an agent of change and of there being a locus of learning – adopted traditionally by cognitive and social models of learning – is reframed as showing distribution and dissipation. We support our claims through an empirical examination based on two years of fieldwork on a higher education course on Maritime Operations and Management (MOAM), where teachers and students are engaged in activities that they understand as case-based learning. Drawing on concepts from ANT this paper poses the question 'where is the locus of learning here' and what does this imply for understanding the idea of there being an 'agent of change' in case-based learning.

Case-based learning pedagogy has a long history of research and practice (Stenhouse, 1975) in which the case artifact (usually text or collection of texts) is the focus of attention. The research and practice discourse(s) on case-based learning starts by reifying the case as having an existence at the outset. In this the possibility of bringing about change and learning is firmly located in the case. This is reviewed in the next section called 'The case located'.

In contrast, the next section '(Un)locating the researcher's work' is a retrospective reconstruction of what turned out to be useful, important and also problematic in the doing of research and tracing the things we found in the fieldwork. 'Un(locating) the research setting' connects the account of ANT-ish sensibilities to the field work and orientates the reader to the research setting.

This is followed by two detailed accounts in which the case is notably made as we follow the action. The case is made as we follow the teachers' account of why he chooses it, how he conceives and designs the case. We follow the action again in small-group case exercises, normally thought of being the core of learning with cases. In following the action we find that learners, drawing in material and other sources, transform the task into something that reflects their background, experience and especially the future imagined by them. We conceptualize these as assemblages but find that implications for practice are elusive and this is discussed in the final section of this article.

THE CASE LOCATED

The literature on case-based educational practices offers accounts in which cases have multiple roles and characteristics, and are tightly intertwined with specific pedagogies, in dependence of the domain, institutional aims, learning goals, and other elements. There is, though, a relatively small number of common characteristics and uses of cases. This paper does not require an exhaustive overview of the Case-based learning landscape, but two examples the Business Case Method, and the use of cases to learn/abstract stable knowledge structures – give a sense of the terrain.

In the Business Case Method, cases are practitioner's accounts, narrative reports of real-world situations that give a sense of what the real world of work looks like and how practitioners operate in it (Barnes, Christensen, & Hansen, 1994). The accompanying rubric is that the case here is employed to develop attitudes of mind to address real-world problems and skills, such as information finding and selecting, justifying an analysis, and implementing an action plan to change real problematic situations. The emphasis is on developing persons capable of assuming responsibilities and leadership. Here, cases are codified experiences, stories, fictionalised accounts brought into the classroom.

A second encompassing role for cases is in learning appropriate structures and reasoning with these structures in domains such as law (Baldwin, 1900), medicine (Barrows, 1985), biology (Allen & Tanner, 2003) and other sciences. Here, the acquisition of stable knowledge to be applied in the real world is given prominence, with the case functioning as 'data' from which to abstract. And it is not only the case, but also the pedagogy – variants of Socratic inquiry (Garvin, 2003) – that is at the service of an acquisition-type form of learning. The case is drawn from the world of work but is, within the pedagogy, conceived as a set of information from which to teach generic knowledge.

So in the literature on teaching with cases there is multiplicity in attributes of cases, but it is not their difference that is of concern, but rather what is common to them: a relatively clearly defined idea that cases enveloped within a pedagogy are capable of significantly changing thinking, reasoning, and even personal attitudes or the 'person as a whole'. There is thus considerable faith in the power inscribed on material, with additional emphasis on the ways in which that knowledge is taken up, elaborated, and appropriated. This is particularly evident when interventions for improvements are proposed, which often target different or new content. For example, the adoption of the case method in institutions or new domains is often justified on the grounds of an inclusion of 'representations of real-world situations', with justifications pointing to the need for educational programs to 'become more pragmatic' or 'students demanding to acquire knowledge for immediate applications on the job'. Different knowledge and different associated pedagogy therefore means

different learning, different persons being formed. In this accounting the case construct is taken a prior, but what if this assumption is disrupted in the researcher's work.

UN(LOCATING) THE RESEARCHER'S WORK

A starting point for researchers working with ANT is that things (human or non-human) have no inherent qualities. Everything takes on form and substance as a result of relations/connections, which can be made and unmade, and are also partial and fragmented, shifting and multiple. This relativism is present even when connections stabilize and make categories, such as pedagogy, teaching, learning and assessment. The point is that these categories should not be taken for granted (Bowker & Star, 1999). These starting points help us to construct learning with cases as a space for research. This section covers what we observed as being mobilized in the setting: 'ANT ontological imperatives', 'ANT constructs for following the action', 'ANT-ish sensibilities' and 'Research in action and partial accounting'.

ANT Ontological Imperatives

ANT, from its inception, emphasized the impossibility of identifying one or more factors of interest and linking them in a cause and effect relationship. Latour (1993) called the modern (post-renaissance and -rationalistic) inclination for limiting of the world of interest 'purification'. He argued that we have never been modern and that hybrids of connections proliferate and have always done so. Purification comes about when as researchers we fail to pay attention when we declare *a priori* the limits of what we are prepared to include, irrespective of what we find by following the action.

A number of ANT-influenced studies have shown the fallacies that emerge when researchers begin with a foundational ontology of discovery.

For example, in early accounts on planning in human and machine learning, the primacy of the plan was asserted and reified as a kind of truth. Suchman's (2006) work on plans and situated action claimed, in contrast, that the assertion that human behavior results from a plan, the supposed 'controller' of behavior, is ultimately unsuccessful because actions are locally produced. Another example is the assumption that teaching and learning takes place in specific places and at specific times in educational institutions. In this, pedagogy is confined in a few obvious taken for granted enclosures such as the classroom, the book, the curriculum, or the lesson; and this at the exclusion of what becomes important in practice (Lankshear et al., 1996). Nespor (2003) opens these spaces, and offers an alternative: it is the activities that contextualize rather than the naming of the context that becomes interesting.

ANT-inspired sociological studies pointed out how even the seemingly most discrete action is a conflation of influences that may be distant in time and space (Law, 1986). This raises questions about who or what is acting, implicitly recognizing the under-determination of action: who is, at any moment, having some influence on what is happening should not be answered by reference to some stable entities (which would include cognitive schemas), innate forces or acquired attitudes because it is they that, in the end, need to be explained. Instead, an actor (in an actor-network) is "the moving target of a vast array of entities swarming towards it" (Latour, 2005, p. 46).

However, following the action means grappling with the fieldwork, the reality of collecting data and of analysis. The challenge is that while in 'general nothing is definite' (Law, 2004, p. 65), 'in particular', (in what Law calls the very local), the talk is as if there is singularity. So, cases do exist as well as being made, knowledge is a thing to be acquired, and 'measured' against learning outcomes and through assessments. Therefore, the researcher has to grapple with the assumed singularity while at the same time "allowing for multiple ontologies and the relations among them, rather than explanations relying on multiple perspectives" (Fenwick & Edwards, 2010, p. 146). And if that is not enough there is also the imperative to work with ambivalence "tracing the contradictions and uncertainties at play within and among the networks and the work they do" (Fenwick & Edwards, 2010, p. 146).

ANT Constructs for Following the Action

This section is concerned with those ANT constructs that informed our field research, specifically in terms of what to follow, what counts as data and analysis and how what we found can be written as interfering and changing practice.

ANT offers the term 'assemblage' to describe a gathering of connections between humans, nonhumans and transcendental objects (ideas); and it is assemblages that make things happen. Assemblages are not 'situations' that provide in some way the necessary conditions for something else to be revealed, to be able to act, but are networks of elements where things are achieved. In scientific research, for example, the setup of the instruments, the ordering of the trials, the selection of the participants are an assemblage that make the 'object under study' rather than uncover it (Knorr-Cetina, 1999; Gomart, 2002). For learning, this means that learning isn't simply a cognitive or social achievement, but that it is enacted as a network effect (Fenwick & Edwards, 2010). The framing and reporting of our research in this paper is also an assemblage. We offer an account of our work as researchers but this is not entirely about researcher's choices or rationality influenced by interaction, but "with researchers, objects, humans, and other things, each contributing to forming the research object and the field through their mutual interaction" (Sorensen, 2009, p. 33).

Assemblages are made of human and non-human elements: a technology is as much part of the assemblage as the person using it, the idea that gave rise to it, also the history of the attempts to carry out work before that technology or way of doing things was adopted; there are even other actors that we cannot know about in advance. For example, in our research the groups work around a table in the classroom, even though the task would suggest that the students need to leave the space and go to a space where a computer screen can be shared. This is a traditional classroom dating back two centuries: table and chairs in a room with an obvious front – the teacher's space. In this example objects and the physical space is part of the change and with this 'agency of objects' it becomes even more difficult to identify who or what makes the change (Latour, 2005).

While it is also traditionally acknowledged that objects are in some way important, they are seen as being useful for 'implementing' something envisioned by the human: knifes are tools for cutting, cars for getting somewhere, and textbooks for conveying knowledge. The privileging of the humans' means that the role of objects have a supporting role, certainly necessary and maybe essential, but secondary to the intentions and plans of humans. That is, an array of objects may be used to carry out the same task because what is important is the 'underlying' intention or plan. ANT, instead of studying what objects mean to and in relation with humans (and thus studying the role of objects via the human), analyzes the trace left behind by what objects do. And what they do occurs always in connection with other things, human and non-human.

This object-oriented symmetry, treating all objects (human and non-human) as equally interesting and capable of exerting force, is taken up in this paper as an essential idea alongside the notion of assemblages. In our study, a small-group learning exercise is a network connecting learners, texts, tasks, teachers, even chairs and a blackboard, the institution, the curriculum, and more, all of which in their connectivity produce something. And this something is very different from what is traditionally conceived as 'knowl-edge', intended as the (internal) representation of the world. Maybe the most radical formulation of this stance is Sorensen's "The materiality of learning" where she describes learning as being performed in specific spatial configurations, giving rise to specific forms of knowledge and specific forms of presence (Sorensen, 2009). In a similar vein, texts, diagrams, spreadsheets, and other inscriptions are not to be seen as representations of knowledge, maybe even the same knowledge expressed in different form, but as material objects that change the task by drawing in other material, other people, other things that hitherto were unconnected in that network.

The connecting and un-connecting of things (the formation of assemblages) is an important juncture in tracing associations. The term translation is used to encapsulate that complex dynamic (Latour, 1987), and to describe what happens when heterogeneous elements form links, connect and, in this process, change something. In any particular research we cannot know in advance how the objects will be connected but as a starting point we can say that all objects of interest must be deployed in such a way as to make things happen (Latour, 2004). The action comes from the objects exerting power to change, that which is being translated. The idea of translation reaffirms the commitment to view the production of things as occurring locally, and, more importantly, to describe the gap between what is intentioned and how that becomes 'realized'. So, in the setting we present here, textbooks and slides are written to 'impart knowledge', to change the students' ways of thinking and looking at problems. But the textbook cannot unfold its 'power' without the teacher, the curriculum, the students' intentions and motivations, and their previous knowledge. And, in the process of this unfolding the original intention may or not be realized, but certainly it is not realized in the way and fashion envisioned by the originator.

However the term translation sits uncomfortably with people in our setting when we talk about what we are doing. ANT has a tendency to lyrical discourse and playful language, and some protagonists are adversarial in defence of language experimentation. On the one hand the term translation describes precisely the research activity of tracing the actors, but on the other it is easier to substitute the term with 'transformation' to describe what we observe in the setting. Despite our interests we share the view that one way of understanding learning at this contemporary time (which is another connection to our setting) is by working with people in our research settings and recognising that transformation for them is not only about knowledge or skills but also about worker identities that can perform better (Chappell et al., 2003).

Ant-ish Sensibilities and Paradoxes

There is general recognition that ANT is difficult to write or talk about (Fenwick & Edwards, 2004). We would say it is difficult to do without treating it as a conceptual framework or breaking it up into conceptual insights that are then used as lens to examine data. In this sense it is difficult to work with ANT without destroying or fragmenting it. ANT is also an assemblage that is translated, and there is increasing acknowledgement of these difficulties and also recognition that ANT is work in progress (Law & Hassard, 1999). The multiplicity of ANT is paradoxically both true and also untenable. It is in this spirit that we adopt the phrase ANT-ish sensibilities. In simple terms this means 'doing our best' to follow the action without deciding (too much) in advance what will emerge as important. It also means as far as possible being mindful in the fieldwork of the ANT principles around symmetry, translation and tracing the network assemblages discussed earlier. We opt for the compromise terminology of 'ANT-ish sensibilities' as a way of recognizing the paradoxes of doing ANT research. For example it is impossible in pragmatic terms to follow all the action. There are no answers to juggling the pragmatics of time and space in following the ac-

tion. We also acknowledge that we as researchers have a hinterland which predates our enculturation with ANT and that this identity creeps in as assumptions and interpretation and tendency to privilege humans and words. Finally, while we recognize multiple ontologies and ambivalence at work in the settings, we also find it difficult to act permanently 'multiple' and 'ambivalent'. We become more deliberately definite when we need to explain what we are doing, persuade people to give us access, and write accounts of our research for particular audiences.

(Un)locating the Research Setting

An essential starting point for any funded investigation in our times is defining the scope of the proposed research. This defines what is included and what is not. ANT presents particular difficulties as in principle we want to delay deciding what is important until the fieldwork. Part of the difficulty is that the topics that are part of our research are all assemblies of a myriad other things: cases, learning, learning technologies, learning in groups, and learning and technology design, as well as innovation in these spaces. In practical terms, there is a problem with when and where to follow the action and when to stop. We also recognize the ambivalence of believing in multiplicity and lack of closure; but in talking to teachers and learners, and in writing this paper, we are compelled to make our research concrete and even authoritative. Therefore, this section is recognizably a partial accounting.

The subject of investigation was inscribed in the project proposal document as one of a number of settings. One of the settings is a Masters Program called Maritime Operations and Management offered at an inner City Centre University in London (UK). The course recruits learners with extensive international experience of working in the maritime sector in operational positions, who want to move into leadership and management roles. The setting fits the project goal in that case studies are used to bring complex historical scenarios of national and international failures into the classroom as cases for learning with. The students work on these cases in small teams and are required to develop responses to key questions including resolution strategies. Students are prepared for the case with a series of specialist lectures and have access to resources selected by the teacher, and are also encouraged to do their own research.

The focus of the fieldwork reported in this paper is on an open ended complex problem about how to deal with an old, undocumented, yet at the core well functioning software. The students are required to analyze the problem, and formulate a strategy about how to migrate to newer software, and an organizational structure for carrying out that strategy.

Latour (2005) suggests some strategies for following the action in fieldwork. Drawing on this we concentrated the fieldwork in a number of sites, two of which are relevant here: for one, following the innovation process and for us this was about following the making of the case as a pedagogical artifact. This is the place of the teacher's work, and so a site of fieldwork. The performance of learning with cases takes place in small group setting and this is another site of fieldwork. In these sites, fieldwork included audio and video footage, and rich descriptions, and involved the researcher being part of the field, building trust relationships. Only this could support the kind of ethnomethodological data analysis that enabled us to examine the things in the environment including talk, materials, spaces, and time all of which exerted force.

MAKING THE CASE: THE TEACHER'S PEDAGOGY

In the setting we studied we found very varied accounts of the nature and role of cases, some of them contradictory, some working, as it were, in parallel. In the interviews with the teacher, he describes cases variously as "impressions of the real world", "representations of the many elements in the world", and "a mix of useful and irrelevant information". Cases are thus representations of the real world as well as simulations of the richness and messiness of that world.

In the teacher's view, cases further play a central role to teach problem solving: the learner needs to be trained about how to deal with messy, complex situations, where information may be unavailable; the learner needs to be trained to make decisions and devise actions under conditions of uncertainty. The case here simulates the 'real' in terms of the overload of information and, curiously, also of the absence of information. The teacher's views on problem solving are revealing: "problem solving is the ability to figure out what is relevant and what is not and to make decisions under uncertainty and with little information available". The case as knowledge about a practice recedes into the background, and becomes an element in a view of what problem solving is and how to teach it. The case is designed with irrelevant information and at the same time, to counter student problems with coming to conclusions in the time allotted, the narrative is reduced.

Here the case thus is discursively made the central 'agent of change': the encounter with the 'real' effects change in the students' mind engenders the acquisition of attitudes and skills, and knowledge about the world of work. The stability of knowledge is not questioned; instead, the presumption persists that the engagement with cases – though rich, messy accounts – and the pedagogy – which leaves considerable freedom to the student – at the end leads to the acquisition of stable and durable knowledge including what is commonly called 'skills' such as argumentation, persuasion, etc. The efforts going into designing cases are a testament to these assumptions. They are designed to push students through a trajectory towards becoming independent thinkers and decision-makers.

Yet, we also find the teacher's accounts replete with references to many other elements of education. A central one is the trajectory of the student within a 'career'. There is an emphasis on the students' previous (i.e. undergraduate) form of learning where they "quite passively absorbed knowledge throughout the undergraduate career"; now, they have to be taught how to "think for themselves, find and evaluate rather than being given information" (both quotes are the teacher's). That is, the effectiveness of teaching with cases extends beyond the (imagined) confines of a Master's course or other artificially delimited sites where cases are primarily used. The case derives its effectiveness from the students' trajectory, from them having been undergraduates with a certain attitude and where a certain form of teaching was practiced. The previous mode of absorption of information is as essential for effectiveness as the current activities around the case. And this may be considered only one and the most evident one of the elements on which teaching with cases draws its role as the central 'promoter of change'. The supposedly 'essential' properties of the case, the 'real', the messy', 'the drawn-from-practice' are related to the properties of other learning material ('formal', 'facts') the students have encountered along their trajectory, indeed they are in contrast to them. Previously performed teaching and learning still reverberate in the effect ascribed to teaching with cases; in a sense, the change case-based learning is able to effect is passed on from other elements, rather than flowing from cases as the source. In this way the role of the case cannot be located in the specific 'essence' of the learning material itself.

MAKING THE CASE: THE STUDENTS' WORK

We have argued in the previous section that cases are enmeshed in multiple relations that extend their supposed role as agents of change into other locations and elements, rendering the very conception of a single agent untenable. We continue this argument by presenting our view of

the kind of work that cases do when they are in the classroom, in a space which is presumed to be at the very heart of learning with cases: small-group case-centred discussions. Case-based and group learning are thoroughly intertwined, certainly a legacy of the method's inception a century ago; an often cited justification for their combination is that cases give rise to multiple viewpoints, thus functioning as the 'promoter' of sought conditions of quite specific learning processes.

In much of the literature of group learning, promoting the exchange of ideas, which may lead to reflection and critique, revision of one's own knowledge base (deep learning) and adoption of other's view points, is at the forefront of the discourse. Learning from the more able peer is also cited as a core mechanism of group learning (Dillenbourg et al., 1995). Learning itself is thus cast again in terms of changing conceptions or adoption of other's conceptions. At the outset, thus, when talking about what may effect change, two elements are cited: the group and the case. We found this discourse in the teacher of the management module. Asked about the rationale for group work, he said: "I put them into a group, so they can learn from each other", and "when they work together, they will hear different viewpoints, and this will make them think more deeply about the problem".

The terms 'promoting', 'engendering', and 'giving rise to' delineate again the case as an actor, but a comparably predictable one: these cases do something; they can be used, quite reliably, to carry out the work for which they were designed. The case is conceived as a mediator that can be safely employed to do sought work. A line of argument that is relevant here as well is the lack of structural/essential characteristics of 'the case'; we argued that much in the discussion on how teachers make the case. Here, as there, cases are made, they become something through the assemblage they are part of and indeed do constitute. The case, what it is in the group, does not exist at the outside, but is made.

Figures 1, 3 and 4 are excerpts of talk of a group of Master-level students working on the management case. The figures are transcriptions of group work captured by video and audio, with an observer sitting close to the group, taking notes and pictures. The questions we are interested here is: what is the students' task, what do the students think they have to do? We adapt the insight from ethnomethodology that 'actors are always in the business of mapping out the social context in which they are placed' (Garfinkel, 1967) to a learning situation, and ask the question: 'what do the students' activities tell us about what learning is for them, what 'knowing' means for them'. For the analyst, this mean refraining from usurping the 'actor' (in this case the learner) through some meta-language, to explain through an analytical framework, 'what the actor really means'. Through this lens we will be able to describe how the students make the case, and be able to show the many actants in this situation as well as the problematic and emergent role of the case.

A common assumption of ANT is that assemblages become visible when their 'previous' existence is disturbed (Latour, 2005). And disturbances can come in many forms, among them the simple fact that entities poised for action are unable to go further. Learning situations may be particularly interesting in this respect: "problem" and "tasks" are set in order to move the learner within a space prescribed by a curriculum and/or domain knowledge. The learner thus must go beyond what s/he knows, and enlists, in this situation, a variety of elements. With the assumption of heterogeneity, and the particular lens offered by ANT, what is enlisted and how becomes a worthwhile object of study. When analysing the exercise, we have chosen moments and small segments which appeared to us as instances where the task was transformed, where more or less different assemblages from the ones that proceeded those moments, were made.

An interesting contribution comes at a moment when, after the group (of 5) has split into two groups of 2 (students A and B) and 3 (C, D and E), it returns together. This exchange (Figure 1) tells us also much about what learning becomes, and how activities emerge from the assemblage so far made. The moment is to be seen as much as one where power is performed as a joint working. The 2 students that split early on in the discussion are much more experienced in the field than the others; and further, one of them is the designated presenter (student B), thus he will make the decision of what to present to the plenary. He has temporary power assigned to him through this role. To counter this weight of experience and responsibility, student E mobilizes an authoritative source: a diagram on a lecture slide, i.e. the teacher's voice (line 5). The power struggle is visible when we see, then, that the suggestion is dismissed by student B (line 10), only for it to be taken up again about 10 minutes later (Figure 3). Yet, the mobilization of an artefact (beyond the case text), the role of artefacts as sources of knowledge, is taken up by student B immediately: he mobilizes an alternative resource, his own notes (Figure 1, line 12), performing again decision-making power and responsibility.

By mobilizing the diagram, the teacher-set task is transformed: it becomes one of identifying correspondences between the text and the diagram, with control of the groups' work shifting from diagram to text and back again (Figure 3, line 9). Lines on the diagram are traced with pens, elements pointed to (Figure 2), and then mapped into elements of the text, and vice versa. The narrative order of the text is broken and a new one is imposed, driven by the structure of the diagrammatic representation (Figure 3, lines 3 and 4).

But the mobilization of the slide, first, and then student B's notes, entails further transformations: authority now is given to knowledge inscribed somewhere on an artefact. 'Pointing to' performs authority, and student B's pointing to his own notes performs his expertise and experience, as well as his role in this exercise. And further, the group's discourse includes now mate-

Figure 1. Excerpt of group work: mobilizing material resources

1 (E):	so the management has to …come up…with…ah… the project of, the idea of changing the whole system
2 (B):	yes
3 (E):	this will be, sooo, in the first place I think that we should going to analyze like, ahh, when they told us, yeah (looking at a lecture slide)
4 (E)	browsing through lecture slides
5 (E):	like here (pointing to slide "Typical Large Project Organisation"). If you want to manage a project, there are a number of ways
6 (B):	yes
7 (E):	there is the project manager group, a group of managers that could come up in the company and say "our system is not working well, we need a change.
8 (B):	yeah
9 (E):	think it's not one person, it's…
10 (B):	(interrupting) … it was already decided [13:18] that there is going to be a change. This is about *implementing* that change, i.e. writing a new

Figure 2. Students pointing to elements, following lines on the diagram (for students' talk, see Figure 3)

rial artefacts (beyond the case text): the discourse has become more materialized than it was when it started.

And, indeed, the mobilization of the lecture slides is a turning point in the exercise. The first mobilization arrives at a moment when the group is undecided about what the problem is. An exchange immediately prior to line 1 (in Figure 1) ends with two students trying to clarify the difference between the problem set and the plan they have to develop as part of the solution (Figure 4). The clarification is unsuccessful: the 'problem' is student A's re-statement of the task set by the teacher, and the 'plan' is to carry out that task (Figure 3, line 5: "pull in the document and link it to the new"). Student E's view on what they have to do (see Figure 1, line 1) is similarly only

a re-statement of the task set. When the slide is pointed to, the group suddenly has identified the 'problem': as described above, it becomes one of finding the correspondences between case and diagram elements. In a sense, the moment is one where a sudden encounter or collision causes the assemblage to form, and then take off in a particular direction. There has been a 'machine' set up, which is now ready to work fairly autonomously and with direction. The assemblage so created is an intersection of discourse formation with material practices (Crary, 1992).

A further element that effects the transformation of the task is time. Student B is particularly aware of the need to develop a presentation within temporal limits. He says, "what I've got to say first when I stand up there is how we would address the various problems" (Figure 1, line 10); and, on another occasion, "we have to do all this in 5 minutes". Within this statement time draws boundaries between what should be done and focused upon and what not. It structures the noting down of 'things said' into a few clear points that are more adequate for a presentation to the plenary. It selects those elements of the conversation that are clear, leaving out those that are doubtful, which may be seen merely as interesting reflections. It also re-casts the exercise as one where 'presentation skills' are trained and practiced; the students' future (and the world of work) suddenly has bearing on the task. The outside world comes into the exercise not by the careful representation

Figure 3. Following the mobilization of the diagram (Figure 1) a task (mapping between text and diagram) is carried out

> (A picks up slide 5 'Typical Large...' and points to the lower line 'Senior Team Member') [14:02]
>
> **1 A**: IT staff come here come (underlines the rectangles ('senior team members') with finger) [25:18]
>
> **2 B**: yeah, there (points to the same rectangles) will probably IT staff
>
> **3 A**: there'll have to submit to the project manager (circles lower left rectangle)
>
> **4 B**: yeah, probably. Who would you see as the project sponsor (points to upper left rectangle)
>
> **5 D**: that is basically...the project sponsor would be the organization itself, because...
>
> **6 B**: (interrupting) no, no, this is an individual. Which individual would be the project sponsor, ...the guy who says 'I own this, at the end of the day I am answerable'

of the 'real' – the supposed role of the case – but much more directly and forcefully through the sought performance.

A wide variety of heterogeneous element has taken the students onto different tracks and new tasks, which become one of drawing correspondences, of identifying similarities between elements, developing a presentation, and so on: artefacts (lecture slides, notes), students' professional background, B's role as the presenter, the teacher's advice (to practice doing presentations), and the 20 minutes time for completing the exercise. New assemblages are created, which set off almost autonomously and uncontrollably to carry out the newly specified task, dismissing some and bringing in other elements. The exchanges presented can be discussed in terms of structuring, or better, in how from an assemblage a structure emerges, namely the structure of a list of 'main points' that can be presented to the plenary. And this structure has, importantly, a direction: it tells students what they have to do at a manageable level of detail, and at a level that is within the students' competence. There are plenty of existing structures in the exercise: the narrative flow of the case text, the list of tasks, the diagram, the students' notes, charts depicting events over time, and their development. The structure that emerges is a list, and it may be seen as a simplification of the manifold types of structures used. But it doesn't combine the other structures, it rather is imposed by the kind of presentation to be given, thus also by the audience that expects a short summary of on the "what have you found, what would you do" questions. It is these elements that form the assemblage.

When we trace the development of the exercise, we cannot identify a main influence other than the performance in the presentation. The exercise is hence pulled by that presentation, which is really lying in the future; the most powerful actant is as yet to be made; the case and the group do not exert their influence because and in the way they have been 'designed' at the outset. The students' background and their status within the group, the return of the more experienced senior students to the main group prompts the search for an authoritative source, and it is found in the lecture slide. The lecture slide/diagram then 'takes over' the group effort because it allows for a new task. And further, a more substantial influence of the diagram unfolds much later, when it is taken up after 10 minutes. Initially, the diagram leads to the inclusion of more artefacts into the group, thus transforming the task, but the initial mobilization plants a seed, as it were, whose power emerges only later. We need to look at other elements to see it.

CONCLUSION

We can draw several conclusions from our analysis and argument. We have shown that the 'group work' cannot be understood solely in terms of peer learning or increased reflectivity/

Figure 4. Excerpt of group work preceding Figure 1 and 3: restating the task

```
1 (A): then they have to write the new code

2 (B): yyyes

3 (A): and relate it to the old one

4 (B): [11:33] that's the plan, I mean that is the problem

5 (A): and...well, yeah, actually the problem......how do we
```

deep thinking, something that is found in the practitioner literature, in guidelines of teaching, as well as being embraced by soft-constructivist approaches. Indeed, the group is performed into existence rather than being an a priori 'promoter' of learning processes. Power, sometimes mediated through artifacts (the mobilization of the diagram), plays an essential role. Joint working performs power relationships, something which cannot be subsumed by conceptions drawing on a 'more or less knowledgeable' distinction and modelling the learning within changes in cognitive structures. Material artifacts, background, experiences, institutional demands and structures, assert their presence in the group work and without taking these into account the complexity of the assemblage cannot be expressed.

Turning to case-based learning, what we found runs counter to the current discourse. In the literature there is an expectation that cases act predictably, a belief we found also in the teacher we interviewed. The expectation is that a case does a certain work in achieving learning outcomes, and as such there is no accounting or acknowledgement of the translations involved. For example, the Harvard case method is prescriptive of structure, a way to design cases that has been adopted in other schools. But our analysis of the small-group work has shown that it is a to-be-produced something that pervades the group work. The design of cases, their careful writing, and their evaluation in terms of what things they talk about,

which dimensions it emphasizes, how faithfully does it reflect the actual working practice and/or world, is a poor predictor of learning outcomes.

The 'work' that the case does can only be determined empirically, i.e. after it has been in the classroom; and this 'work' may extend far beyond answering exam questions or the quite immediate return of a student to the world of work. The kind of uncertainty about cases we talk about here is different from the one that sometimes is found in learning discourse. The case construction approach, for example, embraces unpredictability, but remains to some degree welded to the idea that unpredictability does lead to different student thinking, to different attitudes about how to address problems. That is, the relationship between the character of the case and what should be the outcome of an exercise remains.

There are two points here that return us to the introduction of this article. ANT strategies do uncover some patterns, and consistencies that suggest at least the potential for intervention. For example, better understanding of assemblages in case construction could be deployed in the design of cases as teaching assemblages. The point is to recognize that these gains may not be universal and there is no closure. Living with this ambivalence requires a culture change and a slower and more measured approach to changing practices.

The turning to management purposes reminds us that the local assemblages are also part of a network. While we can define success in relation to learning outcomes there are other discourses the students and teachers are part of. In the case method, questions have been posed about whether it is adequate to talk about 'learning' or whether going to one of the normally prestigious schools of management may serve more than anything as a springboard to employment (Argyris, 1980). Our view is that this question is ill posed because the role of the case needs to be determined in relation to the broader assemblage. And we offer an account of this assemblage in this paper.

This brings us to the paradox of working with ANT. ANT at the present time in Higher Education Research is a niche activity. Where academics, and especially sociologists, have heard of ANT, there is a suspicion dating back to the territory wars in sociology in the 1970s when sociology of associations challenged the main stream. In the review section we raised the practical issues around multiplicity and ontological openness while at the same time looking for intervention that does in effect stabilize a particular position. This is almost impossible to explain in simple terms to those taking part in our research. Moreover we cannot explain ourselves without some incoherence and contradictions what multiplicity and ambivalence is.

We began this article with the intention to interfere with the prevailing discourse on learning with cases, but also to acknowledge some of the complications of ANT-ish sensibilities. ANT-ish sensibilities have the potential to trigger a profound shift in education research where the locus of learning is not fixed or predetermined but something else. In our experience working with ANT principles of symmetrical analysis, and acknowledging multiplicity and ambivalence opens up new spaces of possibilities for education research and teaching practice.

REFERENCES

Allen, D. E., & Tanner, K. D. (2003). Approaches to cell biology teaching: Learning in context. *Cell Biology Education, 2,* 73–81. doi:10.1187/cbe.03-04-0019

Argyis, C. (1980). Some limitations of the case method: Experiences in a management development program. *Academy of Management Review, 5,* 291–299. doi:10.2307/257439

Baldwin, S. E. (1900). Teaching law by cases. *Harvard Law Review, 14,* 258. doi:10.2307/1322548

Barnes, L. B., Christensen, C. R., & Hansen, H. (1994). *Teaching and the case method.* Cambridge, MA: Harvard Business School Press.

Barrows, H. (1985). *How to design a problem-based curriculum for pre-clinical years.* New York, NY: Springer.

Bowker, G., & Star, S. L. (1999). *Sorting things out.* Cambridge, MA: MIT Press.

Chappell, C., Rhodes, C., Solomon, N., Tennant, M., & Yates, L. (2003). *Reconstructing the lifelong learner.* London, UK: Routledge. doi:10.4324/9780203464410

Crary, J. (1992). *Techniques of the observer: On vision and modernity in the 19th century.* Cambridge, MA: MIT Press.

Dillenbourg, P., Baker, M., Blaye, A., & O'Malley, C. (1995). The evolution of research on collaborative learning. In Spada, E., & Reiman, P. (Eds.), *Learning in humans and machine: Towards an interdisciplinary learning science* (pp. 189–211). Amsterdam, The Netherlands: Elsevier.

Fenwick, T., & Edwards, R. (2010). *Actor-network theory in education.* London, UK: Routledge.

Garfinkel, H. (1967). *Studies in ethnomethodology.* Upper Saddle River, NJ: Prentice Hall.

Garwin, D. A. (2003). Making the case: Professional education for the world of practice. *Harvard Magazine.*

Gomart, E. (2002). Methadone: Six effects in search for a substance. *Social Studies of Science, 32*(1), 93–135. doi:10.1177/0306312702032001005

Illeris, K. (2009). *Contemporary theories of learning: Learning theorists in their own words.* London, UK: Routledge.

Knorr-Cetina, K. (1999). *Epistemic cultures: How the sciences make knowledge.* Cambridge, MA: Harvard University Press.

Lankshear, C., Peters, M., & Kobel, M. (1996). Critical pedagogy and cyberspace. In Giroux, H., Lankshear, C., McLaren, P., & Peters, M. (Eds.), *Counternarratives: Cultural studies and critical pedagogies in postmodern spaces*. London, UK: Routledge.

Latour, B. (1987). *Science in action*. Cambridge, MA: Harvard University Press.

Latour, B. (2005). *Reassembling the social: An introduction to actor-network theory*. Oxford, UK: Oxford University Press.

Law, J. (1986). On the methods of long-distance control: Vessels, navigation and the Portuguese route to India. In Law, J. (Ed.), *Power, action and belief: A new sociology of knowledge?* (pp. 234–263). Keele, UK: Sociological Review Monograph.

Law, J. (2004). *After method: Mess in social science research*. London, UK: Routledge.

Law, J., & Hassard, J. (Eds.). (1999). *Actor network theory and after*. London, UK: Blackwell.

Nespor, J. (1994). *Knowledge in motion: Space, time and curriculum in undergraduate physics and management*. London, UK: Routledge.

Sorensen, E. (2009). *The materiality of learning: Learning and technology in educational practice*. Cambridge, UK: Cambridge University Press.

Stenhouse, L. S. (1975). *An introduction to curriculum research and development*. London, UK: Heinemann.

Suchman, L. (2006). *Human-machine reconfigurations: Plans and situated actions*. Cambridge, UK: Cambridge University Press.

This work was previously published in the International Journal of Actor-Network Theory and Technological Innovation, Volume 3, Issue 2, edited by Arthur Tatnall, pp. 17-31, copyright 2011 by IGI Publishing (an imprint of IGI Global).

Chapter 3

Complexifying the 'Visualised' Curriculum with Actor–Network Theory

Sue De Vincentis
Deakin University, Australia

ABSTRACT

Rather than conceptualising the curriculum as a mandate which guides a teacher's task of advancing the knowledge of students, or what the author will call the simple story, the curriculum as an object of complexities is explored in this article. The article considers how approaching the curriculum relationally can be a more fruitful quest than simply accepting that curriculum activity is predetermined, predictable, or standard. Drawing on actor-network theory and the fieldwork resulting from a funded, primary school Arts project in Australia, the curriculum is examined as a relational effect of education. In doing so, it is shown how interdependent webs of heterogeneous relations contribute to this entity called 'the curriculum', encouraging activity to be practised in particular ways, yet suggesting activity could be otherwise.

INTRODUCTION

Going back several years, the local primary school attended by my children at the time, advertised in the school newsletter that the school curriculum committee required new members and that interested parents were welcome. Not being particularly excited by canteen duty or volunteering in the uniform shop, I thought a school committee – especially one focused on the curriculum – sounded ideal. As an experienced primary school teacher and post-graduate student this was an area of the

DOI: 10.4018/978-1-4666-2166-4.ch003

school to which I was more than qualified (and interested) to contribute. I signed up immediately. At the first meeting there were a handful of teachers and parents with expertise in a range of professions: even a barrister and a paramedic. As it eventuated the advice of these two parents was more valued than my education knowledge because for this and then subsequent meetings we reviewed school policy – the number of EpiPens to take on school excursions, for instance, and the legality of failing to do so[1]. I was not so much offended by the (lack of) uptake of my 'education expertise' as puzzled by why a curriculum committee was named as such when it was a policy review committee in practice. "Excuse me," I ventured in a later meeting, "We have had three meetings and not discussed the curriculum." The reply was something like this: "Well, as a school we need to have 'a curriculum committee' but we also have a lot of school based policy requiring regular review and updating which must receive input from parents."

How to think about this conundrum? One response could be that in schools the boxes must be ticked in the name of accountability, not to mention liability, and the maximisation of time is often dealt with creatively. This wraps up the dilemma neatly, complete with a bow on top. Is it useful, however, to think about activity in this simplistic way?

One of the misleading consequences of thinking of the curriculum as an object or a thing is that there is an illusion of boundaries (Apple, 2000): that in naming objects they are set in place, are tangible and travel not only readily but in predictable ways (Law, 1999). And this was certainly the assumption undermined with the naming of the above curriculum committee. But the effects of the curriculum are most obvious in the hurly burly activity of the classroom. A number of the educators in the PhD study I conducted referred to the activity of picturing curriculum outcomes as 'visualising the curriculum'. I take this practice of visualising to be the smooth road in a classroom journey and, in this article, question the parameters and potentiality of a rough track. To do this I consider the relations which bring curriculum activity into being and the effects that are produced. Considering 'the curriculum' as a process which only exists through the interdependent activity which generates its existence is how I will approach this discussion. My focus is on how the human and non-human entities which produce this curriculum activity shape each other. I argue that thinking about the curriculum in relational terms is more useful for imagining how taken for granted labels such as 'learning', 'teachers' and 'outcomes' can be distributed more widely.

My aim is to interfere in curriculum realities and this in turn suggests that realities could have been otherwise: alternatives are possible.

'THE CURRICULUM'

The curriculum as an object of educational enquiry has created thought provoking debate in the last decade (Apple, 2000; Moore & Young, 2001; Weiss et al., 2006; Young, 2008). One of the outstanding questions is: What is 'the curriculum'? Conversations surrounding the curriculum imply school activity involving teachers and students: subjects or topics to be taught at an educational institution (Encarta Dictionary, 2010). Centred within a broader framework, the curriculum here in the state of Victoria is framed as the Victorian Essential Learning Standards. According to the Victorian education organisation responsible for curriculum development:

The Victorian Essential Learning Standards (VELS) outline what is important for all Victorian students to learn and develop during their time at school from Prep to Year 10. They provide a clear set of common state-wide standards which schools use to plan student learning programs, assess student progress and report to parents. (Victorian Curriculum and Assessment Authority, 2009)

In line with the standardised, national curriculum being progressively introduced across states and territories in Australia, much of schooling is focused on school based 'standardised' curriculum activities which encourage students to remain in their classrooms in primary school or move from one classroom to another in secondary schools. Curriculum standards pursue a measure of quality based on what is worth knowing and supposedly acts as a mechanism to avoid gaps in student knowledge. Education standardisation is an ideal which suggests that somehow individual performances can be compared in the same terms. Standing on the shoulders of giants (Newton, 1992), I borrow from Di Mulcahy (2010, p. 3) who has done her research on the defining of standards as a measure of teacher quality and provided two definitions. Mulcahy's first, normative definition states that a standard is: "a tool for rendering appropriately precise the making of judgements and decisions in the context of shared meanings and values" (Sykes & Plastik, 1993, p. 4). And in line with her interest in relationality, Mulcahy's preference is to define a standard as "any set of agreed-upon rules for the production of (textual or material) objects" (Bowker & Starr, 1999, p. 13). As Mulcahy (2010, p. 3) explains:

Across the terrain of these two definitions, attention shifts from social and cultural processes (the making of judgements… in the context of shared meanings') to objects (here 'rules') and their agency and effects.

Mulcahy (2010) is reaching for an understanding of standards that are actively produced and constituted in their making: for the shaping of standards as they are brought into being by their enactment – as a conceptual device to demonstrate that standards become real only when they are practised. Standards are typically assumed to possess no such movement. Educators are assumed to attach curriculum standards to classroom activity like the joining of press studs: align the two pieces – curriculum and students – apply some pressure and… snap, the two wayward flaps are secured precisely, effectively, and not least, accountably. Like Mulcahy, I too wish to move beyond such simplistic conceptions of standards and their assumed attachments. My reason for this, I argue, is due to the blinkering effect that standards have on potential ways of doing and knowing: conceptualising other types of activity, considering different ways of conducting activity and textured ways of knowing activity are not encouraged when 'the standard' is the goal. Standards are indifferent to

diversity because their agenda is to homogenise: to purify and singularise activity. However, curriculum standards direct classroom activity.

Metaphorically the curriculum is like a road map linking how teachers can conceptually and practically move from A to B without getting too lost. The preference for relatively safe pretend school experiences rather than the riskier experiences valuing students' efforts which take place in the wider community is in part attributed to the conventional enactment of the curriculum (Bigum, 2004). For many Australian school students this is how education is 'done'. The reasons for schooling being enacted in this way are entwined historically, socially and politically: school building design and the activity which takes place within can be directly attributed to the educational objectives of the Industrial era (Senge et al., 2000). It is a sad but remarkable achievement that schooling has remained largely unchanged for 150 years. And it is not that educators, theorists, academics and policy makers do not embark on valiant attempts at education reform, but that their efforts are akin to incremental inertia (Fullan, 2001). As quite aptly depicted by the haphazard efforts to include computers usefully in school contexts, we are stuck in a rut (Bigum, 2007).

As education is the common denominator linking most people in the developed world, the lack of movement with school reform is partly to do with what people think education should entail: everyone has their individual experiences of school and these are embedded in assumptions and particular ways of thinking about the purpose of schooling (Robinson, 2006; Senge et al., 2000). However, 'the curriculum' and its sidekick 'assessment' are bound up in a wider political education discourse which sees the complexity of educational processes reduced: a reductionist discourse to which we must be attuned or risk being seduced into its web of compliance (Gough, 2009). As Gough (2009, p. 13) explains, "Complexity theorising invites us to understand our physical and social worlds as open, recursive, organic, nonlinear and emergent, and to be suspicious of mechanistic models that assume linear thinking, control and predictability." And here is the crux of the argument. It could be of more benefit to students for school activity to be visualised along these lines. It is perhaps time to question a mode of education focused on an "acritical acceptance of a now internationally rampant vision of schooling, teaching and learning..." based on perfecting standardised testing and, instead, advocate working towards a more ethical conception of education, one which grapples with how to more effectively educate to cater for difference and diversity (Luke, 2002, p. 49): to catalyse concepts of complexity to improve education and society in generative ways (Gough, 2009).

COMPLEXITIES

How to think about complexity? "How to talk about something, how to name it, without reducing it to the homogeneity and fixity of singularity?" (Law, 1997, p. 6). How to appreciate and perform complexity? Theoretically? And politically, Law continues? And I will add, practically? This is a matter of thinking differently: of overcoming embedded ways of seeing and doing. Law and Mol (2002, p. 1) extrapolate:

There is complexity if things relate but don't add up, if events occur but not within the processes of linear time, and if phenomena share a space but cannot be mapped in terms of a single set of three-dimensional coordinates.

Law (1997, p. 7), borrowing from Strathern (1991), has a conceptual tool for assisting with this quandary: the metaphor fractal.

A fractal is a line which occupies more than one dimension but less than two. So a fractional object? Well, this is something that is indeed more than one and less than many. Somewhere inbetween.

Which is difficult to think because it defies the simplicities of singularity - but also the corresponding simplicities of pluralism. That defies a singular universe, visible from a single place, that is inhabited by separate objects. So the thinking is difficult - no, it is not transparent - precisely because it cannot be summed up and reduced to a point. Rendered conformable. Docile. Because it insists on the situated character of knowing. Because it strives to perform something that is difficult.

Strathern (1991, p. xx) uses the image of a coastline to explain fractal: "Whether one looks at a large-scale map or investigates every inlet and rock on the beach, the scale changes make no difference to the amount of irregularity." Both Law and Strathern are alluding to conceptual thinking and forms of textual representation which do not provide answers: concepts which defy definition. This is thinking which places objects as known only as they are situated, as they are performed. The relativising effects of multiple perspectives makes everything seem partial, as does the nature of the partial description of these realities (Strathern, 1991). Such conceptualisation alludes to the rhizomatic: like a pack of rats swarming over each other, where is the beginning and where is the end (Deleuze & Guttari, 1988)? Or Gough's (2004), understanding, drawing on Braidotti (2000) and Scholes (1976), of 'fabulations' to actualise possibilities: an apparatus for undoing power relations through specific, discontinuous yet circulating fictions which rupture cognitive flows thereby enabling an elevation of silences. Complexity then is a way of knowing partial connections (Strathern, 1991) of objects as they are enacted into reality. And in regards to gathering data, complexity is caught up in methods for following the wild and willful ways of entities as they deploy the full range of controversies in which they are immersed (Latour, 2005).

Why is it important to focus on complexities? Because, as depicted in my opening story about the curriculum committee, or rather the lack of one, the simple story – the story which provides 'the answers' – washes away the complexities of the realities in which this curriculum committee is embedded: the practices which enact curriculum realities are ambivalent in the non-fractal account. The simple story assumes that a singular curriculum reality is visualised before the meeting even begins. The more complex story is interested in how entities relate – the curriculum policy documents, school based policy, teachers and parents also in this case: how these relations produce the multiple realities which unfold (Mol, 2002). Thinking in terms of relationality points to the sensibilities of actor-network theory: ANT.

Thinking Like an ANTer: Relationally

Actor-network theory's intellectual origins reside in the empirical work of Michel Callon, Bruno Latour, and John Law who sought to challenge what they saw as ontological flaws underpinning typical approaches to social science inquiry. The trio reported how the social, technical and material are not discrete entities to which separate research methods could be applied and then analysed, but are actors in their own right which shape each other as they too are shaped (Callon, 1986, 1997; Latour, 1987, 1996; Latour & Woolgar, 1979; Law, 1986, 1996). ANT informed texts describe the effects of enacted practices, highlighting how assemblages are gathered and stabilised or not. Objects and humans are translated in their own terms as differences between them are relational and not predetermined: a process called generalised symmetry (Callon, 1986). In line with other material semiotic approaches – that is approaches which describe relational webs of movement – the more contemporary ANT stories acknowledge they are helping to create the realities that they describe (Law, 2007, 2008, 2009).

Recognising that social and material relations perform complex realities, the curriculum has been subject to school based actor-network theory

accounts (Edwards, 2009; Nespor, 1997; Perillo & Mulcahy, 2009) which assists the conceptualisation in this paper and to which I hopefully contribute in some small way. In highlighting complexities a material semiotic approach to analysis recognises that there are multiple enactments of curriculum research or a given story: my enactment of the school curriculum committee is certainly different to the other teachers and parents – there are multiple realities (Mol, 2002). But how to hold the complexities of these multiple realities without losing them: without simplifying? Law (2004, pp. 4-5) argues for a broader and more generous acceptance of alternative research methods, ones which can capture textured realities. In moving away from a singular, cause-effect, metaphysical representation of reality, one in which generalisations about methodological rules and reasoning are unquestionably practised and naturalised, alternative ways of knowing, feeling or understanding various realities need to be considered (Law, 2004): realities which encourage observation and questioning about what it is that entities do – how they relate. When methods and methods' practices support a relational view of reality, what is apparent is that activity produces effects: these are evidence of the social being reworked in continuous and layered processes (Nespor, 2004). Significantly, these relational effects are the results of sociomaterial practices and not causes (Latour, 2005, p. 215). And consequently, what is made clear is that events which happen in our world often exceed our capacity to know them: relational effects cannot be smoothly explained away (Law, 2004).

Conceptualising the curriculum through an actor-network lens highlights complexities in a number of ways. First, thinking relationally makes space for the activity of non-humans. Through an 'association of actants' (Latour, 1994) curriculum activity is shaped by people and technologies or things, suggesting the same generative capacities as extended to education generally by Gough (2009). Conceptualising curriculum activity in this way draws attention to movement, to the ongoing negotiations to gather alliances and the assembling of curriculum relations, how some assemblages become relatively stable, like the policy review committee at our local school, yet others die and wither away such as 'the curriculum committee'. With a focus on relations, assumptions surrounding activity are more obvious: learning that the curriculum committee was by name only, certainly put a spotlight on assumptions (for me at least) but also raised some other interesting questions, such as: How did this incongruence between naming and practices eventuate? Like a chameleon, how did the curriculum act to disguise its true intentions? By thinking about activity as more likely to be enacted in certain ways in particular situations than others, is a possible explanation. Law's (2004, p. 160) notion of hinterland captures this nicely. He states a hinterland is:

... a bundle of indefinitely extending and more or less routinised and costly literary and material relations that include statements about reality and the realities themselves; a hinterland includes inscription devices, and enacts a topography of reality possibilities, impossibilities, and probabilities. A concrete metaphor for absence and presence.

So, through a relational lens, the curriculum is a dynamic and distributed set of more or less routinised practices which shape realities in ways which might be dominant but not conclusive. Now the activity which took place with the curriculum committee at the local school is not so blurry. In this instance the relations which hold curriculum activity in place when parents are involved, are not as durable as those relations requiring school policy to be reviewed. The texts which make stable the respective yet overlapping sets of relations (curriculum and school policy) they represent, enroll parents to relate more positively to one set of relations (school based policy) than the other (the curriculum): unlike the curriculum, with school

based policy there is a temporal urgency ordered through review-by dates and a necessity for parents' input. The curriculum practices are made absent although the curriculum name remains: it is too costly – time and resource wise – to have two committees operating. Visualising curriculum realities relationally highlights ambivalence.

The curriculum also shapes realities in all sorts of interesting ways as I discuss next. Moving away now from the curriculum committee quandary at the centre of the discussion to date, to the more conventional enactment of the curriculum in schools, I discuss a school project organised by a professional artist to illustrate how hinterlands and curriculum realities shape each other in this instance. I also examine the process of visualising the curriculum and consider the realities this process makes present and absent.

TRIBES OF THE MIND

The data underpinning my PhD focused on a City of Melbourne funded Arts project involving four primary schools and ArtPlay, a specialised children's art space at Birrarung Marr on the Yarra River near Federation Square in central Melbourne. The four schools involved in Tribes were all inner city, resource challenged schools whose students were mainly refugees or recently arrived immigrants. This Arts project, called Tribes of the Mind (Tribes), was conceived and implemented by professional artist and art educator, Tim Denton[2]. With the objective of accepting difference and diversity, this project required students to fabricate a culture authenticated by myths and artefacts. Groups of students from the four schools worked independently on the project at their respective schools and ArtPlay for one school term (approximately 12 weeks) and came together at ArtPlay, only once at the end of this time, to share their respective 'cultures'. My research focused on negotiated knowledge practices and the role of experts in school activity. I was based in Jack's

Year 5/6 classroom at Fitzroy Primary School for the duration of this project. Both Year 5/6 classes were involved with Tribes and produced clay masks, totem poles, bamboo shields, and written myths to support their 'culture'.

Although Tribes involved students and educators for only one school term, its preparation began more than a year before as Denton (2007) submitted a proposal for an Arts grant from the City of Melbourne. The Arts grant, if successful provides funds for the artist's time, any extra assistants required and the resources to be used by the schools for the specific project.

1.0 Project details

Tribes of the Mind is a multi-disciplinary project that engages children in the arts through the creation of a tribe. Through a series of workshops facilitated by professional artist and art educator Tim Denton at ArtPlay, the children determine the environment in which their tribe is based and from that discover the culture, traditions, language, and social rules of their group.

Finally the different tribes meet at a Congress where they learn to see and accept one another's differences while staying true to their own identity. (Denton, 2007)

This section of Arts funding proposal text suggests the types of educational activities which will take place in the schools involved with this project, as it must be noted that the Tribes concept has been adapted from its previous New Zealand context where it was conducted with tertiary Arts students. The proposal text implies that there will be activities and discussion surrounding art, culture and social rules. This text positions the Tribes' practices within an acceptable education context, yet is not so prescriptive that there is no room for individual expression – or so it appears. However, like all texts, this section of the proposal is not value neutral or apolitical: amongst however many

other hopeful candidates, without the proposal being accepted by the judging panel – which includes children – Tribes will not be funded and consequently will be an idea committed to paper only. As it eventuates Tribes is funded and four schools choose to participate in the project.

To suggest that Tribes secures the involvement of four schools and the project is enacted as conceived is the simple story. It purifies the social and material negotiations required to enact this project (Latour & Woolgar, 1979): the instances where pivotal resources such as the clay slicer went missing or the resources themselves were in short supply. It is perhaps more valuable to conceptualise the enactment of Tribes as a gathering of human and non-humans entangled in activity: multiple assemblages enacting Tribes in different ways. With this thinking there is no escaping that the Arts funding process shapes how Tribes will be presented to schools; that acceptable school practices shape how Tribes is presented to schools and the Arts funding body; that available resources shape Tribes as do the temporal and spatial idiosyncrasies of the 'typical' school day. Basically, Tribes shapes the schools as the schools shape Tribes, as will be discussed. However, at Fitzroy Primary 'the curriculum' shapes both.

VISUALISING 'THE CURRICULUM'

As the Victorian Curriculum and Assessment Authority (2005) state earlier in this paper, schools use the curriculum learning standards as a planning device to direct and provide accountability for classroom activity. Typically, educators plan school activity in accordance with their respective state (and national) curriculum directives which tend to take the form of standardised curriculum indicators and outcomes: the subjects to be taught and evidence that these have been learnt. Planning curriculum outcomes generally involves anticipating or visualising how various subjects will be approached, scaffolded, accommodate special school themes (such as The Olympic Games) and fit in with pre-existing timetable arrangements: a type of cognitive scenario planning exercise. It is assumed that this process of visualising not only maximises time and resources, but achieves quality, standardised outcomes so that students smoothly progress along the road of education. This type of activity is in keeping with the dominant practices of the education hinterland. Unsurprisingly, the educators at Fitzroy Primary approach Tribes in this way: as a pre-planned, integrated curriculum unit composed of various dovetailed subjects. Once these curriculum objectives are worked into the scope, planning and projection of the project the focus of the teachers is arguably set, enclosed, and determined. Or so it seems.

Is the curriculum an object which somehow dictates what classroom activity should take place or be prioritised? Law (2004, p. 145) argues this is the dominant Euro-American version of method assemblage: the gathering and stabilising of a collective through constancy, passivity and universality to contribute to a singular view of a determinate world. There is a more complex relational way of conceptualising curriculum enactment, however: as a multiple object brought into being by multiple enactments – as an intertwined and fluid politics of curriculum which takes on agency and is made to act by many, from government ministers stipulating the content of key learning areas, by curriculum writers in the Victorian Curriculum and Assessment Authority, to teachers' enactment of curriculum in the classroom. The curriculum is not simply acted out by teachers and students but shaped by many entities and enacted into multiple realities, which makes the visualising of outcomes somewhat problematic, as will be discussed. The alternative on the other hand, unplanned outcomes, draws attention to assumptions about school activity generally and the purpose of the curriculum specifically, especially a curriculum which is supposedly standardised. How can standardised outcomes possibly capture

the multiple enactments of the curriculum? Or of partial curriculum connections? Of curriculum complexities? Questions are raised and 'answers' are scarce. As I will illustrate, the enactment of the curriculum is not simple but complex. From the beginning of the Tribes project the visualised curriculum causes concern for our teachers. The curriculum is a recalcitrant object.

The problem with getting the two classes together is the full curriculum, he adds... (Interview with Jack, 13ᵗʰ August 2008)

Even if Tim were available to attend the school more frequently, Jack and Claire concur, it takes time to coordinate the curriculum to get Tim and both classes together... (Research notes, 11ᵗʰ August 2008)[3]

The project has just begun and Jack and Claire are already caught up in the pursuit of a singular reality: space (the full curriculum) and time (to coordinate it) (Nespor, 2004). Cajoling the curriculum into its rightful place is a fruitless quest because it is not a 'thing' but a dynamic system shaped by webs of relations. Through the multitude of interdependent assemblages responsible for this object entitled the curriculum, the social, like Latour and Woolgar's (1979) summation of laboratory practices, is condensed with other forms of materiality which dissolve, or purify the complexity of relations: the social evaporates and the curriculum becomes an effect of material relations. Statements about reality are stabilised and the cost of challenging these statements is impossibly high (Latour & Woolgar, 1979): such as curriculum standardisation achieving quality and accountability. And this translates into curriculum practices which enact a singular version of reality, or what Law (2006) would refer to as a zone of tension not comfort, of ambivalence.

Complexifying the curriculum means acknowledging the multiple realities which evolve through curriculum activity: practices and their effects cannot be predetermined, pinned down or domesticated. Attempting to explore spaces which are indefinite, displaced and indistinct points more towards "the world as an unformed but generative flux of forces and relations that work to produce particular realities" – fractal spaces which elude categorisation and predictability (Law, 2004, p. 7). What might be some of the elusive (Law, 2004) Tribes' realities? The various curriculum practices (and their effects) mingle, jostle and contingently cohere in the course of Tribes to enact multiple realities.

We also talk about the busyness of school life. This term they are working on Tribes and the Olympics. There is much to do with literacy and numeracy outcomes... the kids' progression points. Jack states that within his class he has a wide range of abilities. Some kids are working at Year 7 level while others come fresh from the English Language School. Balancing the kids' needs is demanding. There is a Maths tutor who comes in once a week to help as part of the Maths improvement program, and it makes a big difference having an extra helper. The tests administered by the tutor provide evidence that all of the kids have improved their number facts over the term. "What happened to the other guy from the Ardoch Foundation who was volunteering with Maths?" I ask. "He hasn't been around this term," Jack states. "You know what it is like getting and keeping volunteers," he says. (Interview with Jack, 25th August 2008)

For Jack the curriculum is standardised, and he is expected to at least aim for standardisation despite a classroom environment consisting of English language challenges, transient students, a government funded weekly Maths tutor, 'balancing the kids' needs', and ephemeral volunteers: despite standardisation being idealistic. Politically and practically, curriculum fluidity is less viscous in some schools than others, it seems.

And the enactment of school curriculum does not begin and end so neatly: its impact travels more widely. According to Fitzroy Primary teachers, the curriculum is also responsible for the limited amount of time available to work on Tribes during school hours, and for not notifying me of times when classroom project work is happening: timetables are masterfully manipulated to not only accommodate special projects such as Tribes, but also to take advantage of spontaneous education offers (a game against another class, or extra time in the computer room); planned education experiences involving others (such as volunteer literacy and numeracy coaches); last minute changes to specialist subjects (where the specialist teacher is required to supervise a group of students when their ill teacher cannot be replaced); and student labour (when chairs need to be relocated for an education cluster meeting based at the school), for example.

Tribes, although designed to coincide (Mol, 2002) with and enhance curriculum outcomes, only coexists (Mol, 2002) with classroom practices in particular ways. Practices tend to be enacted in specific places only if they are compatible with the corresponding hinterland. If the cost (financially, emotionally, habitually, temporally, spatially, physically, for instance) of changing these practices is too high, they are likely to remain, perhaps in some sort of modified form (Latour & Woolgar, 1979). For cash-strapped inner city schools, and resource and time challenged educators dealing with the brunt of postcode inequity (Black, 2007; Vinson, 2007) visualising curriculum outcomes is cheap. This cost effectiveness is reinforced by governments providing maths tutors and philanthropic organisations providing volunteers, thereby contributing to the stabilising and routinised practices of the education hinterland. But there are other relations amplifying the complexities of curriculum enactment.

The curriculum and supporting documentation are not only effects of mainly invisible, dispersed and distributed actors, through dissemination time and space is collapsed via the use of technology: through making curriculum texts available online, alterations and additions appear seamless, as if they were never a mere afterthought[4]. Curriculum content and standardised outcomes can be added to, adjusted or removed with ease through technology. Via durability, mobility and capability, "documents, devices and drilled people" as Law (1986) argues, if placed in the right structure, have the potential to act upon that structure (p. 12). And so it can be seen how labyrinthical, fluid documents shape as they in turn are being shaped through not only material relations responsible for their production, (education ministers, the curriculum writers, project officers, computers, for example) but also by the material relations responsible for their delivery: teacher practices and the material others – worksheets, chalk, tables, parents, students, for example. But, like the school curriculum committee from the beginning of this paper, some relations are more stable than others.

One of the unstable relational effects, for some of the teachers at least, results from the perceived lack of structure/planning of events due to Tribes co-existing with a hinterland external to the school: the Arts funding hinterland. The curriculum, as discussed, regulates and structures time and activity so diligently that negotiating the acceptable ways of another hinterland can be a challenge for teachers. For the Tribes assemblage, the angst of entanglement, relationality and overlapping of various assemblages influenced by the routinised practices of different hinterlands, appears to obstruct the teachers' ability to visualise (Law, 2004, p. 55).

Myth writing time concludes and the students must attend computer skills with another teacher. They pack up quickly and move next door. This gives me an opportunity to clarify a few observations with Jack. He is finding the Tribes project a bit difficult to visualise, and thinks that to date the concepts have been a bit outside the students' experience. And some kids he concedes just like the company of

having an adult beside them or some reassurance. It's a bit like another project that the kids worked on a couple of years previous where the outcome was not apparent from the beginning. In fact it was a bit of a mess to start with... interconnecting communities, with kids and adults making pieces of weaving to represent their cultures, and then all the bits of material were sewn together. In the end it was great, but to begin with it was all over the place. (Interview with Jack, 15th July 2008)

Reflecting on the project now that it is finished, Claire thought that the end product was fantastic. As a concept she couldn't understand how Tribes was going to end up. Claire now understands why the project was organised the way it was. The kids maybe had difficulty understanding the concept in the beginning too, but at the end it was clearer. The project itself was quite open-ended, so Claire couldn't visualise the end display. Tim would have had an idea though, Claire thinks...

In regards to working on Tribes during the term, Claire feels that one doesn't want to be too prescriptive in approaching what has to be done, and that this made the journey a little bit difficult. This kind of thinking is probably a teacher 'thing': eg "Where are we going? The need to be able to visualise how everything will pull together," states Claire. At the time Claire was a bit unclear about the reasons behind the painting of the paper wall, for instance. Claire adds, "Maybe not visualising the whole journey is part of the creative process. The person with the creative vision has it in their head though..." (Interview with Claire, 19th September 2008)

Such sentiments are confirmed by others. Commonly, 'Where are we going?' is broadly planned by educators at the beginning of a school term, fine-tuned on a weekly basis at a year level and then by class teachers for individual classes. For educators, visualising, or the lack of it, traditionally takes place within temporal and structural units of the school day, which are then further segregated into the teaching of disciplinary, key learning areas. The working day in schools is typically highly stratified, repetitive and routine: school begins at 9am; whole school assemblies on Mondays; staff meetings Tuesdays after school, for example. So temporal rigidity in mainstream school settings mediate the effects of the curriculum in regards to teacher control, highlighted in this instance by a project external to the school recruiting resource challenged schools. There are other more invisible relations guiding curriculum practices, however.

In addition to the formal, state and national government organisations attending to curriculum matters, there are profiteers visualising the curriculum in terms of profit margins: international computer vendor companies and text book publishing warehouses, for example, who maintain an active interest in the commodification of education (Apple, 2000; Cuban, 2004; Kenway et al., 1994). Even not-for-profit organisations aligned with legitimate 'educational purposes' visualise opportunities to generate revenue from the curriculum: the Australian Council for Educational Research (ACER), and the varying universities (most notably the University of New South Wales) who provide standardised curriculum focused assessment materials (and a coordinated team of assessors) for schools and families, for example. When it concerns the direction of education and particularly the curriculum, there is money, power and influence at play (Apple, 2000). There are vested interests in the curriculum being done in particular ways.

LEAVING THE COMPASS (OR GPS) AT HOME

The mapping of Tribes is a partial unraveling of multiple, and connected realities that evolve during the course of the project. And the extensive network of relations is more apparent in a school project which travels beyond the school gate. Through relations action is foreground. Latour (2005) suggests that, "Action is not done under the full control of consciousness; action should rather be felt as a node, a knot, and a conglomerate of many surprising sets of agencies that have to be slowly disentangled" (p.44). And so it is for Tribes. However, in reassembling curriculum realities it can be seen that enactment according to the dominant ways of the education hinterland condones a particular course of action. As Claire notes: 'It's probably a teacher thing e.g. "Where are we going?"' The need to visualise the journey. Not being prescriptive makes the journey bumpy, Claire suggests, yet enacting a prescriptive curriculum supposedly enables clearer visualisation – a smoother journey. Similar to Law's (1986, p. 7) Portuguese mariners navigating the route to India, the teachers, when faced with straying from the well known curriculum waters, could sense the jeopardy to "the durability, the mobility, the strength and the capacity of [their] vessel to return." However, the temptation of smooth journeys should be questioned thinks John Law (2006, p. 21):

Beware of techniques for learning that hold out the promise of effortless travel. If they travel at all it is because they propose a metaphysics that is seamless and singular, but the world is not like that. In practice it is bumpy and heterogeneous. (Law, 2006, p. 21)

Although 'the curriculum' is typically referred to as a 'thing', something to be manipulated and cajoled – a deity to be served – like Brown's (2000) concept of knowledge as an ecology, curriculum may be better viewed as a continually reconstructed design process (Apple, 2000) or cosmogram (Hecht, 2007) – a relational map representing interconnected and interdependent sets of practices. Maybe it is time to think of the curriculum more in terms of "knowledge that is in part located in the social networks, institutions and codes of practice built up by knowledge producers over time" (Moore & Young, 2001, p. 456). In such scenarios education is a personal yet distributed concept: it means different things to different people. This could translate to education activities which take into consideration ways to include students in the direction of school projects rather than teachers planning predetermined outcomes attached to disciplinary subjects. Or perhaps, by involving multiple communities – teachers, students, parents (Mulcahy, 2010) and others from outside the community – students could map out what they would individually and collectively hope to gain from school projects which traverse beyond the school gate, using these projects as a mechanism to guide students along their education trajectories. And it is through this concept of education that curriculum visualisation can produce complex, generative activity. Complexifying the curriculum enables consideration of different modes of ordering: of dynamic learning environments which visualise a space for the shaping of curriculum realities which include the students themselves.

ACKNOWLEDGMENT

This article is the culmination of ideas informed by conversations and the sharing of time. Thanks are extended to the generous entities with whom I am entangled.

REFERENCES

Apple, M. (2000). *Official knowledge: Democratic education in a conservative age* (2nd ed.). New York, NY: Routledge.

Bigum, C. (2004). Rethinking schools and community: The knowledge producing school. In Marshall, S., Taylor, W., & Yu, X. H. (Eds.), *Using community informatics to transform regions* (pp. 52–66). Hershey, PA: IGI Global. doi:10.4018/9781591401322.ch004

Bigum, C. (2007, July 3-6). Heads up versus heads in: Approaches to quality in teacher education and computing and communication technologies. In *Proceedings of the Australian Teacher Education Association National Conference*, Wollongong, Australia.

Black, R. (2007). *Crossing the bridge: Overcoming entrenched disadvantage through student-centred learning.* Retrieved from http://www.eric.ed.gov/ERICWebPortal/search/detailmini.jsp?_nfpb=true&_&ERICExtSearch_SearchValue_0=ED501899&ERICExtSearch_SearchType_0=no&accno=ED501899

Brown, J. S., & Conner, M. (2000). *Linking, lurking, listening and learning.* Retrieved from http://linezine.com/2.1/features/jsbmcl4.htm

Callon, M. (1986). Some elements of a sociology of translation: Domestication of the scallops and the fishermen of St Brieuc Bay. In Law, J. (Ed.), *Power, action and belief: A new sociology of knowledge.* London, UK: Routledge.

Callon, M. (1997). *Actor-network theory: The market test.* Retrieved from http://www.lancs.ac.uk/fass/sociology/papers/callon-market-test.pdf

Cuban, L. (2004). *The blackboard and the bottom line.* Cambridge, MA: Harvard University Press.

Deleuze, G., & Guttari, F. (1988). *A thousand plateaus: Capitalism and schizophrenia.* London, UK: Athlone.

Denton, T. (2007). *Tribes of the mind.* Melbourne, Australia: Arts Grant Application.

Edwards, R. (2009). Translating the prescribed into the enacted curriculum in college and school. *Educational Philosophy and Theory.*

Encarta Dictionary. (2010). *Definition: Curriculum.* Retrieved from http://encarta.msn.com/dictionary_1861602023/curriculum.html

Fullan, M. (2001). *The new meaning of educational change* (3rd ed.). New York, NY: Teachers College Press.

Gough, N. (2004). RhizomANTically becoming-cyborg: Performing posthuman pedagogies. *Educational Philosophy and Theory, 36*(3), 253–265. doi:10.1111/j.1469-5812.2004.00066.x

Gough, N. (2009). AARE President's Address 2008: No country for young people? Anxieties in Australian society and education. *Australian Educational Researcher, 36*(2), 1–19.

Hecht, G. (2007). A cosmogram for nuclear things. *Isis, 98*(1), 100–108. doi:10.1086/512834

Kenway, J., Bigum, C., Fitzclarence, L., Collier, J., & Tregenza, K. (1994). *New education in new times*. Geelong, Australia: Deakin University.

Latour, B. (1987). *Science in action: How to follow scientists and engineers through society*. Milton Keynes, UK: Open University Press.

Latour, B. (1994). On technical mediation - philosophy, sociology, genealogy. *Common Knowledge, 3*(2), 29–65.

Latour, B. (1996). *Aramis or the love of technology*. Cambridge, MA: Harvard University Press.

Latour, B. (2005). *Reassembling the social: An introduction to actor-network-theory*. Oxford, UK: Oxford University Press.

Latour, B., & Woolgar, S. (1979). *Laboratory life: The social construction of scientific facts*. Thousand Oaks, CA: Sage.

Law, J. (1986). *On the methods of long distance control: Vessels, navigation, and the Portuguese route to India*. Retrieved from http://www.lancs.ac.uk/fass/sociology/papers/law-methods-of-long-distance-control.pdf

Law, J. (1997). *Topology and the naming of complexity*. Retrieved from http://www.comp.lancs.ac.uk/sociology/papers/Law-Topology-and-Complexity.pdf

Law, J. (1999). After ANT: Complexity, naming and topology. In Law, J. (Ed.), *Actor network theory and after*. London, UK: Blackwell.

Law, J. (2004). *After method: Mess in social science research*. New York, NY: Routledge.

Law, J. (2006). Pinboards and books: Juxtaposing, learning and materiality. In Krit, D., & Winegar, L. T. (Eds.), *Education and technology: Critical perspectives, possible futures*. Lanham, MD: Lexington Books.

Law, J. (2007). *Actor-network theory and material semiotics*. Retrieved from http://www.heterogeneities.net/publications/Law-ANTandMaterial-Semiotics.pdf

Law, J. (2008). On sociology and STS. *The Sociological Review, 56*(4), 623–649. doi:10.1111/j.1467-954X.2008.00808.x

Law, J. (2009). Seeing like a survey. *Cultural Sociology, 3*(2), 239–256. doi:10.1177/1749975509105533

Law, J., & Mol, A. (Eds.). (2002). *Complexities*. Durham, NC: Duke University Press.

Luke, A. (2002). Curriculum, ethics, metanarratives: Teaching and learning beyond the nation. *Curriculum Perspectives, 22*(1), 49–55.

Mol, A. (2002). *The body multiple: Ontology in medical practice*. Durham, NC: Duke University Press.

Moore, R., & Young, M. (2001). Knowledge and the curriculum in the sociology of education: Towards a reconceptualisation. *British Journal of Sociology of Education, 22*(4), 445–461. doi:10.1080/01425690120094421

Mulcahy, D. (2010). Assembling the 'accomplished' teacher: The performativity and politics of professional teaching standards. *Educational Philosophy and Theory*.

Nespor, J. (1997). *Tangled up in school: Politics, space, bodies and signs in the educational process*. Mahwah, NJ: Lawrence Erlbaum.

Nespor, J. (2004). Educational scale-making. *Pedagogy, Culture & Society, 12*(3), 309–326. doi:10.1080/14681360400200205

Newton, I. (1992). Letter to Robert Hooke. In Maury, J. P., & Paris, I. M. (Eds.), *Newton: Understanding the cosmos (New horizons)*. London, UK: Thames & Hudson.

Perillo, S., & Mulcahy, D. (2009). Performing curriculum change in school and teacher education: A practice-based, actor-network theory perspective. *Curriculum Perspectives, 29*(1), 41–52.

Robinson, K. (2006). *Take a chance...let them dance*. Retrieved from http://www.edutopia.org/magazine/ed1article.php?id=Art_1651&issue=oct_06#

Senge, P., Cambron-McCabe, N., Lucas, T., Smith, B., Dutton, J., & Kleiner, A. (2000). *Schools that learn: A fifth discipline fieldbook for educators, parents, and everyone who cares about education*. New York, NY: Doubleday/Currency.

Strathern, M. (1991). *Partial connections*. Savage, MD: Rowman & Littlefield.

Victorian Curriculum and Assessment Authority. (2005). *Victorian essential learning standards: Principles of teaching and learning unpacked*. Retrieved from http://www.education.vic.gov.au/studentlearning/teachingprinciples/principles/unpacked.htm

Victorian Curriculum and Assessment Authority. (2009). *Victorian curriculum and assessment authority homepage*. Retrieved from http://www.vcaa.vic.edu.au/

Vinson, T. (2007). *Dropping off the edge: The distribution of disadvantage in Australia: A report for the Jesuit Social Services and Catholic Social Services Australia*. Retrieved http://www.australiandisadvantage.org.au/pdf/summary.pdf

Weiss, L., McCarthy, C., & Dimitriadis, G. (Eds.). (2006). *Ideology, curriculum, and the new sociology of education: Revisiting the work of Michael Apple*. New York, NY: Routledge.

Young, M. (2008). From constructivism to realism in the sociology of the curriculum. *Review of Research in Education, 32*(1), 1–28. doi:10.3102/0091732X07308969

ENDNOTES

1. With increasing instances of nut allergies causing anaphylactic shock in Australian school students, schools are very mindful of the precautions required to equip teachers with the procedures for dealing with such cases in the eventuality of a student inadvertently coming in contact with nut products. An EpiPen is an auto-injector which administers a dose of epinephrine to combat an allergic reaction to food or stings. Travelling outside the school poses a different set of risks for students where allergies are known or indeed unknown.

2. Tim Denton and Fitzroy Primary School are correct names but all others are pseudonyms to suppress identity.

3. The data included in this paper was not transcribed from a voice recording but derived from research notes and interviews. All notes and interviews were checked by research participants for accuracy of intention.

4. A marvel of technology occurred during my research into the national curriculum board. On one day I was accessing a URL with the address: www.ncb.org.au, and then when I clicked on the same link the following day I was greeted with an entirely new webpage and a new URL in the window: http://www.acara.edu.au/default.asp.

This work was previously published in the International Journal of Actor-Network Theory and Technological Innovation, Volume 3, Issue 2, edited by Arthur Tatnall, pp. 32-45, copyright 2011 by IGI Publishing (an imprint of IGI Global).

Chapter 4
Knowledge in Networks:
Knowing in Transactions?

Sanna Rimpiläinen
University of Stirling, UK

ABSTRACT

This paper discusses a methodological dilemma proposed by engaging actor-network theory (ANT) in studying collaborative research practices of researchers in a large interdisciplinary project. The paper sets the context of this large publically funded project ('Ensemble: Semantic Technologies for the Enhancement of Case Based learning') between Education and Computer Sciences, currently being undertaken by a consortium of six UK universities and three international partners. While a strand of ANT states that knowledge 'emerges as continuously generated effects of webs of relations within which they are located' (Law 2007), it is very vague in terms of how precisely does that knowledge emerge and how to study that. The methods -question was further complicated by the existence of multiple, potentially conflicting epistemological positions present at the project – how to study these without having to pass a value judgement in terms of their validity and reliability? The specific focus of the discussion is what might be termed the epistemology of actor-network theory, with particular consideration of the Principle of Symmetry. The paper suggests reading ANT through John Dewey's Pragmatism and assesses ideas to take forward from this discussion in order to study interdisciplinary research work.

INTRODUCTION

What is called 'knowledge' cannot be understood without understanding what gaining knowledge means. (Latour, 1987, p. 220)

A strand of Actor Network Theory (ANT) states that knowledge, as well as reality, objects etc, 'emerge as continuously generated effects of webs of relations within which they are located'

DOI: 10.4018/978-1-4666-2166-4.ch004

(Law, 2007). This characterization amounts to knowledge being emergent, fluid, contextualized and constructed, produced within heterogeneous material-semiotic-human networks. Being characterised as a sensibility (Law 2007) rather than a theory or a methodology, ANT is notoriously vague in terms of methods. While it offers ways of tracing the networks out of which knowledge is seen as emerging, it offers very little in terms of helping to answer the question of how precisely does that knowledge emerge, and how to study that.

This question became pertinent in trying to find a way of studying the practices of researchers in a large, interdisciplinary research and development project between education and computer sciences. The methods-question was further complicated by the existence of multiple, potentially conflicting epistemological positions present at the project – how to study these without having to pass a value judgment in terms of their validity and reliability? As a potential solution to these questions, this paper proposes examining the ANT take on the emergence of knowledge (reality, objects) through John Dewey's Philosophical Pragmatism and his transactional theory of knowing (Biesta & Burbules, 2003; Biesta, 2009).

There are two layers of research being discussed in this paper: firstly, there is the interdisciplinary project, Ensemble. (In this volume of IJANTTI, there is a paper written by the researchers from the Ensemble-team '(Un)Locating Learning: Agents of Change in Case-Based Learning', pp. 17-31). Secondly, there is a post-graduate research project studying the work of Ensemble, the focus of this paper. The paper starts out by setting the context for Ensemble, followed by a short outline of the study researching the Ensemble-project, and a rationale for writing this paper. This is followed by treating the two theoretical approaches and their takes on 'knowledge'. The paper finishes by assessing the outcomes of reading ANT through Pragmatism and suggests ideas to take forward from this discussion in order to study interdisciplinary research work. The paper is linked to an on-going PhD study.

BACKGROUND

The PhD study discussed here is linked to a large interdisciplinary research and development project Ensemble: Semantic Technologies for the Enhancement of Case Based learning(www.ensemble.ac.uk), carried out by a consortium of six UK universities and three international partners. It brings together researchers broadly from educational studies and computer sciences backgrounds. Ensemble studies a range of Higher Education disciplines, where 'knowledge is complex, changing or contested' (Carmichael & Garcia Marinez, 2009, p. 1) and where case based learning is employed as their chosen pedagogy. The project aims to develop semantic web-applications for enhancing and supporting teaching and learning in those settings. The disciplines, based across three UK universities, include Archaeology, Dance, Educational Studies, International Journalism, Law, Marine Operations and Management, and Plant Sciences. Semantic web refers to a vision of the world-wide-web in a machine readable format enabling machine reasoning and encoding meaning across heterogeneous data sources (Berners-Lee, Hendler, & Lassila, 2001). Semantic technologies are smaller scale applications that make use of the tenets or technologies from this vision, including integration of diverse data types and sources (e.g. text, images, user generated content, legacy databases), advanced search tools, visualisations of data or collaborative functions (Carmichael & Garcia Martinez, 2009; Jordan & Rimpilainen, 2010). While the idea of making the whole World Wide Web semantic is still only a vision, the project takes as its starting point that technologies developed based on this vision offer potential for supporting and enhancing existing teaching and learning practices through opening up possibilities for e.g. reasoning and searching across vast and diverse datasets, through representing and visualising these in different ways or for collaboratively reviewing, tagging and marking data sets (Carmichael & Garcia Martinez, 2009).

The aim of my research is to study - using ethnographic methods and by drawing on sensibilities from Actor-Network Theory - how this type of project between social sciences and sciences is carried out in practice: how are questions on case based learning being investigated within one particular setting, the discipline of Archaeology, and how the outcomes of these investigations subsequently become translated into a more or less tangible object, a piece semantic web technology tailored to the needs of the discipline? Ultimately, this research follows the emergence of an object which at this stage is only being envisaged, through the interplay of heterogeneous human and non-human participants, of interdisciplinary research practices, technology development and design as well as the pedagogical needs and affordances of the discipline.

The formulation of the aims of my research contains a number of implicit assumptions and proposes a number of problems. The first issue has to do with inter-, multi-, or cross-disciplinarity: The Ensemble project has been jointly funded by the Economic and Social Research Council (ESRC), and Engineering and Physical Sciences Research Council (EPSRC) to deliberately create a project team, and a whole research programme Technology Enhanced Learning (TEL), consisting of members from both sides of the traditional divide between the natural and the social sciences. Within the Ensemble team disciplinary mix does not stop at the seemingly tidy groups of Educational Researchers and Computer Scientists. Both fields are in themselves multi-disciplinary. For instance the researchers on Education side of the team have backgrounds e.g. in Sociology, Psychology and Biology. The number of computer scientists in the team is lower, but even in their field the situation is similar – programmers, designers, HCI people are all classed as Computer Scientists. Furthermore, most members' disciplinary backgrounds are varied, some having switched between the natural and social science research, others just crossing disciplines within one or the other 'camp'.

Secondly, the Ensemble project is designed to be collaborative; a number of people working on the same issue with a common goal in mind, within the same framework and a similar set of constraints (these may of course vary depending on the person). This is where the real challenges in studying this set up emerge: people inhabiting a range of epistemological positions having to work together. This situation in practice means the existence of multiple research approaches,

(including e.g. ethnographic research, action and participatory research, and more structured cognitive sciences research) as well as a mixture of epistemological assumptions leading to expectations of the nature and format of the research findings, as well as the way the team should carry out the work it is doing. An added layer in this has to do with my researcher positionality in relation to the project. How is my research approach going to affect what I am able to say about the project?

WHY 'KNOWLEDGE', AND IS IT A NECESSARY CONCEPT?

In line with the unfolding nature of the Ensemble project, my research questions have evolved over time. Starting out from a more traditionally expressed questions, which included assumptions of actors (researchers and software developers), and a pre-defined concept of knowledge as the assumed outcome of a research process, the question has moved away from assuming humans as the only actors, while becoming more specific in terms of focus. Doing this has also freed space for non-human actors and heterogeneous assemblages, as well as multiple outcomes to participate in and emerge out of these processes. The final iterations have become more focused as a result of more engagement with data:

- How is 'case based learning' being investigated in the discipline of Archaeology?
- How does the concept of 'case' become settled in the process?
- How does a piece of 'semantic technology' emerge out of this research and development process?
- What other outcomes does this process yield?

Given that the concept of knowledge has all but vanished from the formulation of the research questions, why is the title of this paper so entwined with the concept of 'knowledge'? The original problem 'how precisely does knowledge emerge from heterogeneous networks', lead gradually to wondering about my researcher positionality and whether it was possible to study diverse inter-disciplinary research practices without having to evaluate their validity and reliability, and without assuming in advance what their outcome might be.

While 'knowledge' is not by any means the only outcome of any research process, and while there is no universally agreed upon definition of what 'knowledge' even is, every single research approach is based on some epistemological and ontological assumptions. These may be explicitly expressed or implicit, but the claims made at the end of these processes are necessarily based on the assumptions held by the given researchers. Therefore it is necessary to talk about 'knowledge' as a place holder for the purposes of argument in this paper, in order to get to a position whence it is possible to approach the interdisciplinary research practices without assumptions about their nature or the outcomes.

Shared Theoretical Aspirations

From the start I have tried to make sense of the research topic with concepts and ideas from Actor-Network Theory (ANT), also known by the name 'material-semiotics' (Law, 2007). There are various stories of the origins of ANT, but most commonly its roots are traced back to late 1970s and early 1980s Paris to the work of Michel Callon and Bruno Latour in the field of Science and Technology Studies (Latour 2005; Law 2007; Fenwick & Edwards 2010). ANT is by no means a unified approach, but has gone through various incarnations over the years depending on disci-pline, research topic or thinker. It is commonly divided in two main strands, the Classic-ANT and After-ANT (Law, 2007). The ANT studies commonly focus on materiality, objects and the emergence of objects. These studies tend to avoid the 'rational human agency', which is common in the humanist tradition.

Philosophical pragmatism has its roots in American and German philosophers, and it is argued that it could be called the first 'truly American philosophical movement' (Biesta & Burbules, 2003, p. 4). However, as with Actor Network Theory, it is not a unified approach, which is why I have to qualify from the start that I will be working with one particular strand of pragmatism: Biesta's (2009b) 'pragmatic read-ing of Dewey's Pragmatism'. Biesta (2009b) takes Dewey's approach to be not only the most influential strand of pragmatism in the 20th century philosophy of science, but also the 'most detailed and developed form of pragmatism where it con-cerns questions about knowledge, reality and the conduct of inquiry' (Biesta, 2009b, p. 3; Biesta & Burbules, 2003).

Before embarking on working with these two approaches it was necessary to establish that they are not in direct contradiction with one another. While there are differences between the two, there are also some interesting synergies. Although the two approaches have emerged at different times and locations, within different philosophical traditions and as a response to different types of problems, it is possible to conclude that they nevertheless share similar theoretical aspirations. Both are critical of the dualistic world view typical of modern western philosophy and epistemology, a divide that has led to the questioning of the capacity of human mind (in-here) ever to know anything reliably of the reality (out-there). This in turn has led to paradigm wars, tug of war between subjectivism and objectivism, mind and matter, and so on. This is generally speaking at the heart of the issue in trying to study interdisciplinary research practices, which often hold different understandings of what 'reliable knowledge' is and how to go about getting it. Both ANT and pragmatism strive to overcome this divide: Dewey's pragmatism starts from the position that there ultimately is no divide between us and the world out there, and that we are always already in touch with reality through transacting with our environments. In the case of ANT, which is a more dispersed approach, this varies. However, e.g. Annemarie Mol's way of treating us as part of the world is to attend to 'events in practice' taking place in heterogeneous networks of everyday life (Biesta & Burbules, 2003; Biesta, 2009b; Mol, 2003; Law, 2004).

Both approaches also emphasize that it is not that there are no divisions between subjects and objects, mind and matter etc. in the world, but that these should not be understood as primordially given entities, but rather as outcomes of our transactions/enactments within the world and thus the networks in which we exist (Law, 1999; Biesta & Burbules, 2003). Furthermore, the two approaches share an understanding of knowledge as not residing in the human mind, or as being about facts-out-there, but as continuously generated in relation to the networked environment, as contextualised, and as warranted, subject to change.

In the following I will first treat Dewey's Pragmatism and its take on the emergence of knowledge, discussing this later in relation to ANT.

PRAGMATISM AND KNOWING

According to Dewey knowing is an activity, something we do (Dewey, 1916; Biesta, 2009b). Acquisition of knowledge is not something that happens in the depths of the human mind; it arises from the combination of transaction of the organism and its environment, and the reflection upon the consequences of that action. In other words, it emerges from action and feeds back into action (Biesta & Burbules, 2003; Biesta, 2009b). Dewey preferred to talk about transactions instead of interactions, as the latter implies two independent interacting entities, while the former 'puts the process first and treats distinctions such as those between subject and object or between organism and environment as functional distinctions emerging from this process – not as

starting points of metaphysical givens" (Biesta & Burbules, 2003, p. 27).

This is the basis of Dewey's Transactional theory of knowing, which offers an understanding of emergence of knowledge that is not based on the dualistic worldview. For Dewey, as living beings we are always already in transaction, and thus in touch, with the world; we engage with it through intervening, manipulating or interacting with it. This implies that no fundamental gap exists between us and the world, and thus our experiences and our knowledge are directly 'of' the world (Biesta, 2009a; Edwards, 2009).

Experience is the most important concept in Dewey's philosophy, referring to the transaction of organisms and their environments (Biesta, 2009a; Mol, 2003). It is through experience that living organisms transacting with their environment are connected with reality (rather than veiled off it as earlier philosophers had believed) (Biesta & Burbules, 2003; Biesta, 2009b).

The organism acts in accordance with its own structure, simple or complex, upon its surroundings. As a consequence the changes produced in the environment react upon the organism and its activities. The living creature undergoes, suffers, the consequence of its own behaviour. This close connection between doing and suffering or undergoing forms what we call experience. (Dewey, 1920, p. 129 as cited in Biesta, 2009b, p. 12)

The difference between experiences of humans and those of other living organisms is that humans' experiences are always mediated by culture – everything that is a product of human action and interaction, the most important one of these being language (Biesta & Burbules, 2003). While experience concerns transaction 'as it is', knowledge has to do with discovering, through reflection, intelligent thought, the conditions and consequences of experience, the possible relationships between our actions and their consequences, thus being able to control, to plan and to direct our actions (as opposed to blind trial and error (Biesta, 2009a, 2009b). This signifies a shift in understanding knowledge as a representation of things 'as they are' (spectator concept of knowledge) to being concerned with the temporal, historical context in which a given thing is situated (Biesta, 2009a, 2009b). This has a further implication: rather than taking the world as something that we make knowledge about, it is in fact something that we create to be able to account for the perceived link between our actions and their consequences. To put it in other words, the world emerges from the connection between our actions and their consequences, rather than existing objectively, independently of our interests and activities (Biesta, 2009a). Thus, for Dewey, knowledge is simultaneously a construction, but also based on reality (Biesta & Burbules, 2003).

KNOWLEDGE ENACTED IN SOCIO-MATERIAL PRACTICES

The concept of knowledge is slightly more problematic to discuss in ANT-terms, for that has altered over the years, or is articulated slightly differently by different thinkers (Law, 2004, 2007; Law & Hassard, 1999, Mol, 2003). As mentioned before, it is often seen as arising as an effect of the webs of relations (Law, 2007), or for instance out series of 'mundane translations with things' (Roth 1996 as cited in Fenwick & Edwards, 2010; Latour, 1999). Therefore, I will discuss the concept of knowledge in ANT primarily through the work of Annemarie Mol, for to me there are clear synergies (albeit differences as well) between Biesta's reading of Dewey and Mol's take on ANT.

Annemarie Mol's (2003) book 'Body Multiple' is an ethnographic study of a disease, atheroclerosis, the hardening of arteries, and the practices of its diagnosis and treatment at a Dutch hospital. For Mol, knowledge (and objects) came into being through enactments that required co-operation both of the patient and the doctor – two humans – and their networked and heterogeneous practices.

Mol (2003) attends to the physicalities of the practice, as well as stories people tell about their lived experiences of their illness. Her focus is not on perspectives of the doctor and the patient on the illness, but their lived experiences of it, and the practice of diagnosing it, which make the illness material and active. In this way, knowledge emerges as enactments in practices, but also, in Classic ANT terms, as an effect of the webs of relations (Law & Hassard, 1999; Law 2007). Mol (2003) further claims that by foregrounding practices (rather than focusing on the object, or subject) in which objects – as well as knowledge and reality - are enacted, these multiply, becoming 'more than one, less than many', hanging together by association (p. 55).

Both Dewey and Mol attend to the lived experience as the way in which we are in touch with the world. For Dewey there are several different modes of experience (Burbules & Biesta, 2003), and they are all equally real: 'things – anything, everything, in the ordinary or non-technical use of the term 'thing' – are what they are experienced as' (Dewey, 1905, p. 158; Biesta, 2009b, p. 13). He relates as an example a horse as experienced by a jockey, a zoologist, a horse-trader and a palaeontologist, whose accounts of the horse might be different, 'however, there is no reason for assuming that the content of only one of them can be real, and that the experiences of the others must necessarily be any less accurate or real' (Biesta, 2009b, p. 13). This is simply due to the zoologist and the horse-trader, for instance, entering the transaction with the horse from a different standpoint, because their personal backgrounds and histories, and their purposes and intentions with the horse are different (Biesta, 2009b). This resonates closely with the above idea of objects and reality multiplying, becoming 'more than one, less than many' through being enacted a-new in different practices, which are constituted by different heterogeneous networks of human and non-human actors. As well as being experienced differently due to the different standpoint for the transaction, it could be also argued that the horse is being 'enacted' differently by the different people engaging with it; a horse enacted by the jockey will be different from that of a zoologist, yet it is the 'same' horse.

While Dewey sees objects (of knowledge) coming into being through transactions, as a result of knowing, Mol and Dewey differ in their understanding of the temporal nature of objects. Mol states that these objects have no shape or form outside the practices in which they come into being. To me this makes objects appear as discontinuing and a-historical, appearing and then disappearing from one practice to the next. The disease may be diagnosed and enacted into being for the first time there and then, but it has arisen out of something, in co-operation between all the heterogeneous participants of the diagnosis. I agree with Mol's argument that the disease will be enacted anew at different parts of the hospital, thus becoming 'more than one, less than many' (Mol, 2003, p. 55), but at the same time, it is not like the doctor and the patient will forget about the disease once the consultation is over. Dewey's idea of (knowledge) objects (something which for instance Mol's diagnosed disease could be seen as) is that they are situated both in time and space, and arise out of the conjunction of the human being and their environment, their personal histories, attitudes, aspirations etc and the way they approach the environment. To him, the objects are both situated and temporal (Biesta & Burbules, 2003). It needs to be added that most ANT studies agree with the latter notion.

Knowing as Human Enterprise? What about the Principle of Symmetry?

Both Dewey and Mol take types of action (transactions, enactments) taking place between an organism and its environment, or between actors (human, non-human) in networks, as a way of leaving the philosophical dualism of subjectivism and objectivism behind. In this way the world can be approached as 'one', as something where

we are already in touch with reality. While the 'mechanism' seems similar, there are things to reflect on further in this conclusion. Let's consider the terminology used to discuss these actions.

Albeit both Dewey and Mol wish to treat the world without assuming a fundamental divide between subjects and objects, the language does not lend itself to talk about these things without making separations. Thus Dewey talks about living organisms and their environment while ANT terminology is divided into humans and non-humans, subjects and objects, the material and the social. Partly these separations coincide: (networks of) humans and non-humans match closely with organism and environment. However, organism encompasses all that is living, from humans to scallops and pine trees. Furthermore, among these pragmatism prioritises organisms with intelligence and language – capacity to reflect upon their actions and their consequences, and to learn in the process; humans, in other words. The 'environment', on the other hand, seems to be treated as a more generic mass of stuff, implying 'everything else' in the context of the transaction, all the living and non-living things that constitute the environment with which the organisms transact. Dewey does not give these any active role in the act of transaction itself; it is something that the organism responds to according to its structure.

Here I would like to argue two things. Firstly, that it would be useful to conceptualise the 'organism-environment' in networked terms, and secondly, taking this conceptualisation, it would be beneficial to think about the transactions in the light of the Principle of generalised symmetry (Callon, 1986). According to that, apart from human subjects, also the non-humans and objects are seen as having agency, or a capacity to 'act', to cause an effect in states of affairs. That organism is seen not only as causing changes in its environment, but also as reacting to the changes in that environment, to me implies that the 'environment', or rather its elements (the network consisting both of living and non-living, human and non-human matter) participating in the transaction have the capacity to cause an effect on states of affairs. This would enable thinking about the transactions and their contexts in more detailed and practical terms.

With regard to knowledge, both approaches agree that it does not live in the heads of human subjects, and that it is emergent and situated. However, in pragmatist terms it is an essentially a human enterprise, with its emphasis on the human capacity to reflect upon action and for intelligent thought. This is the point that could go against the general ANT-take on the world.

ANT works to de-centre the human agency, distributing that, as well as knowledge, out in the heterogeneous networks. This goes back to the Principle of generalised symmetry mentioned above. Callon's aim was to describe the different entities, seen as pertaining either to the 'nature' or the 'social', in similar terms, without privileging humans over non-humans in our understanding of the working of the world (Callon, 1986; Latour, 2005). Often this is mistaken to mean that humans and non-humans, objects and subjects should be treated equally all the time. However, the principle says:

ANT is not, I repeat is not, the establishment of some absurd 'symmetry between humans and non-humans.' To be symmetric, for us, simply means not to impose a priori some spurious asymmetry among human intentional action and a material world of causal relations. (Latour, 2005, p. 76)

Indeed, it does not say there would not be any asymmetries, just that these should not be assumed in advance. Human capacity for reflection, intelligently thinking about ones actions and their consequences, as well as our capacity for language, are something that have been forgotten, or deliberately ignored, in ANT debates (Law, 2007; Sørensen, 2009). This may be due to the desire to treat objects and subjects symmetrically, without privileging the human capacity for intelligent thought (Law, 1999; Latour, 2005; Sørensen, 2009). However, the human actors

are not mindless beings (unlike e.g. scalpels, textbooks or plants). We can communicate and remember things. Like Mol's doctor and patient, we are hybrids (Fenwick & Edwards, 2010), culminations of various networks or socio-material assemblages that exist in time and place; we have memories of previous incidences, case records to refer to and means of recording the present case to compare it with others – in other words, experience. A note book may help in reminding the doctor of the previous diagnosis, but this piece of 'knowledge' would not go anywhere without the thinking, communicating human.

In the context of Actor-Network Theory, where the role of the rational human is often faded out, it is useful to be reminded of the human capacity for intelligent thought and reflection, and the capacity to plan and think ahead. Here I would like to argue then that we go back to the origins of the principle of generalised symmetry and, while not making a priori assumption of asymmetry between the human intentional action and causal relations of the material world, we remain open to the possible asymmetries, which may or may not occur in the networks. These asymmetries may gather around the 'human' as well as the 'non-human' participants. This is an essential clarification to make when studying interdisciplinary research practices, where multiple epistemological assumptions are at play, and where a lot of immaterial, human-related things (theories, methodologies, ideas etc) are communicated and created through and as part of these practices.

What to Take Away from this Discussion?

While John Dewey's transactional theory of knowing and Annemarie Mol's take on ANT may not be fully mutually compatible, approaching the ANT take on knowledge through Dewey's Transactional theory of knowing has worked like a Litmus-test in helping to highlight aspects of ANT that I had found problematic.

In the beginning I posed a question about the precise way in which knowledge actually emerges out of networks. While ANT remains rather hazy on the 'how', Dewey's transactional theory of knowing helped to direct attention to the (trans) actions taking place between an organism and its environment. I have argued that the organism-environment could be conceptualised in networked terms and that the principle of generalised symmetry should be applied to that (trans)action, a move that would help align Dewey's thinking more with that of ANT. Further, Dewey's theory of knowing focussed on the human capacity to reflect upon (trans)actions, and to discover the conditions and the consequences of that action, in order to control, to plan and to direct future ones (Biesta, 2009a, 2009b). In research activity repeated cycles of reflection upon action, and decisions of next steps are evident. Dewey's emphasis on human intelligence lead me back to the origins of the principle of generalised symmetry, to be reminded that it is not that humans and non-humans should be treated equally in all circumstances, but that an asymmetry between these should not be assumed as a given state of affairs. This should remind us to remain open to possible asymmetries, without trying to artificially flatten them out, allowing humans our capacity for intelligent thought and use of language, which makes us 'human' in the first place.

On the basis of this reading, I would like to concentrate on 'action', to doing as the basis for studying the team's research practices. I will approach my data by asking 'who and what participate in the doing and how? What happens next and why?' (Sørensen, 2009), e.g. a data-meeting, in an interview, in writing a paper, in making a presentation, in developing a Semantic Web application. This, I hope, will also point to the 'gatherings' (Latour, 2005) of things, to how things come to be - like the project itself, the research settings, the technology. These are only preliminary thoughts, which need to be further developed through engagement with data.

Furthermore, focusing on action, on doing will have implications to how 'knowledge' is understood. Seeing knowing as arising from the transactions between a human and her environment 'does away with alleged hierarchies between the different approaches and rather helps make the case that different [research] approaches generate different outcomes, different connections between doing and undergoing, between actions and consequences- - '(Biesta, 2009b, p. 19). Approaching data by focussing on action taking place among/ between participants would allow examining what is happening in the project without having to express any particular epistemological values with regard to the validity or reliability of the work being carried out. This does not wipe out epistemological differences between the different research approaches but provides a way of exploring how the differences emerge and manifest themselves. Furthermore, this would also enable the project itself to emerge as multiple, rather than being forced into a singular, unified view (Mol, 2003). 'Knowledge' – as well as other research enactments, the products of transactions - becomes emergent, an outcome of the research process, rather than existing objectively 'out-there', waiting to be picked up by a skilled researcher. This take would allow for multiple types of knowledge and outcomes to co-exist. Thus, 'knowledge' no longer is about representing things 'as they are', but is concerned with the temporal, historical context in which a given thing is situated and created. Knowledge is simultaneously a construct and of the 'real' world (Biesta, 2009b; Edwards, 2009; Fenwick & Edwards, 2010).

CONCLUSION

In this paper I have discussed two theoretical approaches, a strand of Actor Network Theory and Dewey's Pragmatism, and their takes on reality and knowledge in relation to one another. The paper is linked to my postgraduate research project, which studies research practices in an interdisciplinary research and development project. ANT is useful for thinking about relationality and in helping to trace the heterogeneous networks that 'knowledge' is seen as emerging out of, but it does little to answer the question as to how that 'knowledge' emerges. Apart from this methodological puzzle, the paper asked how to study diverse interdisciplinary research practices without having to evaluate their validity and reliability, and without assuming in advance what their outcome might be.

Engaging the two approaches with one another enabled me to focus on action, to doing, taking in place in networks. The ANT rhetoric emphasizing actors and actants, humans and non-humans had shifted my attention away from the action and happenings taking place between the human and non-human participants in the networks, the very thing that makes these networks dynamic.

Dewey's transactional theory of knowing offers a more detailed explanation for how we come to 'know' and learn - through transacting with our environments, and by reflecting on the experience of that transaction, its conditions and consequences, in order to direct and plan our future actions. That Dewey's Pragmatism sees 'knowing' as fundamentally a human enterprise, something that appeared to be in contradiction with ANT principles, made me revisit the origins of the principle of generalised symmetry. This suggested that it is not that there would not be asymmetries between intentional human action and the causal relations of the material world – only that this asymmetry should not be assumed in advance, as an original state of being. Treating humans and non-humans equally at all times is a misunderstanding of this principle.

Further, taking the different research approaches as different ways of transacting with one's environment, thus resulting in different types of 'knowledge', makes it possible to study the interdisciplinary research activity without making epistemological value judgments about the reliability or validity of those approaches, or without assuming in advance what the nature of the outcomes of these processes might be.

Engaging these two theories with one another has been an illuminating experience. While knowledge indeed emerges as an effect of heterogeneous networks, knowing on the other hand is a result of continual transactions we engage in as part of these networks. Through these moves, by concentrating on action and on the heterogeneous participants in that action, it becomes possible to study the emergence of knowledge and other outcomes of interdisciplinary research and development practices, these including the envisaged semantic web application, still under way at the time of the writing, for supporting case based learning and teaching in the discipline of Archaeology.

REFERENCES

Berners-Lee, T., Hendler, J., & Lassila, O. (2001). The Semantic Web. *Scientific American*.

Biesta, G. (2009a). Disciplinarity and interdisciplinarity in the academic study of education: Comparing traditions of educational theorising. In *Proceedings of the Annual Conference of the British Educational Research Association* (pp. 1-15).

Biesta, G. (2009b). How to use pragmatism pragmatically? Suggestions for the 21st century. In *Proceedings of the Annual Meeting of the American Educational Research Association*, San Diego, CA (pp. 1-10).

Biesta, G. (2010). Pragmatism and the philosophical foundations of mixed methods research. In Teddlie, C., & Tashakkori, A. (Eds.), *Handbook of mixed methods research*. London, UK: Sage.

Biesta, G., & Burbules, N. C. (2003). *Pragmatism and educational research*. London, UK: Rowman & Littlefield.

Callon, M. (1986). Some elements of a sociology of translation: Domestication of the scallops and the fishermen of St Brieuc Bay. In Law, J. (Ed.), *Power, action and belief: A new sociology of knowledge?* (pp. 196–223). London, UK: Routledge.

Carmichael, P., & Garcia Martinez, A. (2009, September 30). Semantic technologies to support teaching and learning with cases: Challenges and opportunities. In *Proceedings of the 1st International Workshop on Semantic Web Applications for Learning and Teaching Support in Higher Education*, Nice, France.

Edwards, R. (2009). Materialising theory: Does theory matter? In *Proceedings of the Keynote Symposium on tThe Theory Question in Education*, Manchester, UK.

Fewick, T., & Edwards, R. (2010). *Actor-network theory in education*. London, UK: Routledge.

Latour, B. (1987). *Science in action: How to follow scientists and engineers through society*. Cambridge, MA: Harvard University Press.

Latour, B. (2005). *Reassembling the social: An introduction to actor-network-theory*. Oxford, UK: Oxford University Press.

Law, J. (1999). After ANT: Complexity, naming and topology. In Law, J., & Hassard, J. (Eds.), *Actor network theory and after*. London, UK: Blackwell.

Law, J. (2004). *After method* (1st ed.). London, UK: Routledge.

Law, J. (2007). *Actor network theory and material semiotics*. Retrieved from http://www.heterogeneities.net/publications/Law-ANTandMaterial-Semiotics.pdf

Law, J., & Hassard, J. (Eds.). (1999). *Actor network theory and after*. Chichester, UK: John Wiley & Sons.

Mol, A. (2003). *The body multiple: Ontology in medical practice*. Durham, NC: Duke University Press.

Sørensen, E. (2009). *The materiality of learning: Technology, knowledge in educational practice* (1st ed.). Cambridge, UK: Cambridge University Press.

This work was previously published in the International Journal of Actor-Network Theory and Technological Innovation, Volume 3, Issue 2, edited by Arthur Tatnall, pp. 46-56, copyright 2011 by IGI Publishing (an imprint of IGI Global).

Chapter 5
Performing Actor–Network Theory in the Post-Secondary Classroom

Andrea Quinlan
York University, Canada

Elizabeth Quinlan
University of Saskatchewan, Canada

Desiree Nelson
University of Saskatchewan, Canada

ABSTRACT

Teaching innovative schools of thought call for innovative methods of instruction. This article investigates the challenges associated with teaching Actor-Network Theory (ANT) and proposes a creative pedagogical approach of 'performing' ANT in the classroom. This article presents a small case study of an instance where this theatrical method was employed in an undergraduate classroom to teach Annemarie Mol's The Body Multiple. Based on the qualitative data collected from reflections of students and the professor, it investigates the successes of this creative pedagogical approach to teach ANT. This article argues that it is only through innovative teaching methods that ANT can be effectively explored in the classroom.

INTRODUCTION

There has been a growing recognition within the education literature that traditional, lecture-based models are ineffective for rendering sociological theory meaning and relevant to undergraduate students (Holtzman, 2005; Pedersen, 2010). In response to these changing notions of effective teaching methods, several alternative techniques have been proposed to address these recognized deficiencies in current practices. Some scholars have described alternative pedagogical techniques that draw on the arts and students' creative capacities in the classroom (Phillips, 2000; Lowney, 1998; Gotsch-Thomson, 1990 as cited in Pedersen, 2010). Others have explored how technology can be made to work in the classroom to transform theory into something accessible and engaging for students (Fails, 1988; Sturgis, 1983). And still

DOI: 10.4018/978-1-4666-2166-4.ch005

others have examined techniques of field-based teaching methods, which introduce experiential learning to the instruction of sociological theory (Pedersen, 2010; Hall, 2000).

Despite these moves towards imagining creative and alternative pedagogical approaches, much of this literature has focused on teaching conventional sociological theories, which often appear in undergraduate sociology curricula, such as functionalism, conflict theory, and symbolic interactionism. To our knowledge, there has been no published literature on new techniques for teaching non-conventional, innovative approaches to sociological inquiry. In an effort to expand this existing pedagogical literature, this article begins with the contention that innovative schools of thought call for innovative methods of instruction. New theory calls for new pedagogy.

This article addresses the challenges associated with teaching Actor-Network Theory (ANT), a relatively new approach to sociological inquiry, by proposing an innovative teaching strategy that bridges the divide between the field and the classroom. ANT is by no means limited to the discipline of Sociology and has both roots and applications in many disciplines such as philosophy, history, anthropology, and science and technology studies. However, given that this article focuses on teaching ANT in the context of a sociology course, ANT will be discussed as an innovative approach to sociological inquiry.

There has been a considerable body of ANT literature: the theoretical and methodological (Latour, 2005; Law, 2004; Law & Hassard, 2005), and the empirical (Epstein, 1996; Latour & Woolgar, 1986; Mol, 2002). Yet very little thought has been devoted to how ANT can be effectively taught in the undergraduate classroom. Given the increasing popularity of ANT as a branch of sociological investigation, it seems imperative that methods for the instruction of ANT are offered and critically considered. This article proposes and examines the effectiveness of an inventive method for teaching ANT to undergraduate sociology students. The following turns to a brief description of Actor-Network Theory before moving to an analysis of our approach for teaching ANT.

ACTOR-NETWORK THEORY

Actor-Network Theory stems from the broader branch of inquiry, Science and Technology Studies (STS). ANT shares the central interest of STS in the rapidly changing world of science and technology. ANT has been taken up in a multitude of ways within the discipline of sociology and beyond. However, there are a few commonalities, which tie most ANT studies together. They are as follows.

Most work that draws on ANT reflects an interest in moving beyond what ANT scholars have taken to be the limiting, restrictive practices of social science inquiry (Law, 2005). These authors strive to describe action in local settings in ways that do not confine, obscure, or abstract action. ANT studies trace "actors", which are defined as human and non-human entities that mediate change, as they work to create "networks" of action (Latour, 2005). Work in the field of ANT often tells stories of "complexities", "translations", and "multiplicities" found in science (Law & Mol, 2002).

ANT has its roots in anthropology (Latour & Woolgar, 1987). This history is obvious in the vast number of ethnographic ANT studies (Latour & Woolgar, 1987; Dugdale, 1999; Mol, 2005). Other works in ANT have diverged from this path and have instead conducted socio-historical research (Latour, 1988; Epstein, 1996). What ties all of these works together is a shared interest in developing and changing practices in contemporary or historical science and technology.

Law (2006), a well-known Actor-Network Theorist, asserts that one of the most challenging questions that he is often asked is; what is ANT? He suggests that to define a sociology which speaks about representations as types of translations or "betrayals" is exceedingly difficult (Law, 2000). He concludes by suggesting that perhaps "one might represent Actor-Network Theory by performing it rather than summarizing it" (2006, p. 48). While Law was referring to a textual 'performance' of Actor-Network Theory, this article will explore a theatrical performance of Actor-Network Theory in the classroom. This article will take seriously Law's contention that ANT is best understood through performance, and examine a theatrical method of teaching ANT to undergraduate students.

Neither (Yet Both) Theory or Method

ANT does not sit comfortably on either side of the conventional dichotomy between sociological theory and sociological method, as it is not easily considered either a theory or a method. Speaking for ANT, Law (2007) asserts that despite being named a theory the "actor-network approach is not a theory. Theories usually try to explain why something happens, but actor-network theory is descriptive" (p. 1). Similarly, ANT does not claim to be a sociological method, in the sense of what the term often implies as being a list of method-ological rules to follow to generate a successful research project. Rather, as Latour (2005) stresses, ANT is a "guide…[that] offers suggestions rather than imposing itself" (p. 17). Or as Law (2007) suggests, states that ANT is a "toolkit for telling interesting stories" (p. 1).

Despite this divergence from common concep-tions of theory and method, ANT does include theoretical and methodological insights. However, the way in which these insights are included within ANT differs greatly from those of mainstream sociological approaches. The theoretical, within ANT, is not shaped in the form of explanatory constructs nor is the methodological shaped in steps to follow. Instead, ANT blurs the boundaries between theory and method to form a guide of a possible way to explore.

Because ANT transcends boundaries between theory and method that are deeply embedded within most undergraduate sociology curricula, it introduces significant challenges for teaching ANT to undergraduate sociology students.

This article thus takes up the problem of how ANT can be effectively taught by exploring the value of a theatrical method of teaching ANT. It will investigate the successes of a particular instance where this method was employed in an undergraduate sociology course. This article will argue that it is only through innovative teaching methods, that new schools of thought can be ef-fectively explored in the classroom.

The following will begin with a brief descrip-tion of the ANT text that was used in our example of the theatrical method of teaching ANT. It will then turn to the reflections of students and a professor on their experience with the theatrical method of teaching ANT was used. This article will conclude with a discussion of the necessity of inventive methods of instruction for areas of sociological thought that sit outside of conventional bounds.

This article will draw upon the voices of four students and a professor. Immediately following the exercise, the students involved were asked to write about their reflections on the process of learning ANT through theatrics. Similarly, the professor recorded her reflections on the effec-tiveness of the method of instruction. It is upon these combined qualitative data that this article is built. They are presented in dialogue form, inter-spersed with some narration. While the voice of the students appears in this article to be singular, it is in actual fact the amalgamation of the voices of four students who participated in the particular exercise that will be described. Pseudonyms are used for both the composite student and professor: Sally and Patricia, respectively.

Given the specificity of limited data explored, we make no claims to the universality of the results gleaned from this particular use of the theatrical method. Instead, this work is intended to be a case study of a single instructor and a particular group of students enrolled in a single course, in which an innovative teaching method is introduced.

THE COURSE AND 'THE BODY MULTIPLE'

The example of the theatrical method of teaching ANT explored in this article was used in a Medical Sociology course. The fourth year course was delivered as part of a sociology degree program in a mid-sized Canadian university. The focus of this course was on classical, current and emerging perspectives of the sociological study of medicine. The two sections of the course correspond to two main themes and each of these themes is presented within the context of specific methodological approaches. In the first section of the course, the experience of illness is studied by reading two narratives: first-person representations of the experience of illness/disability (Frank, 1994; Lindbergh, 2001). In the second section, the structures and institutions associated with health and illness are covered by reading an Institutional Ethnography of nursing practice by Campbell and Rankin (2006) and 'The Body Multiple' by Annemarie Mol (2005) outlined next.

The enrolment for this particular course was quite small with 3 undergraduate students and 1 graduate student. Describing the course, the professor, Patricia, remarked:

At the very beginning of the Medical Sociology course, I told the students that this might be a different kind of course than others they had experienced. The class was going to involve many different kinds of activities because people have different learning styles and we want to include something for everyone. Over the term, we invited a couple of guest speakers, conducted several embodied learning activities, and poster presentations by the students.

The exercise described in this article was thus conducted in the context of a very particular course with few students and an objective to experiment with alternative teaching methods.

Annemarie Mol's (2005) text The Body Multiple: Ontology in Medical Practice was selected as one of the several readings assigned in this course. This work served as an example of study that is heavily informed by Actor-Network Theory. In this text, Mol describes her ethnographic work in a Dutch university hospital where she examined the medical and scientific practices involved in the diagnosis and treatment of atherosclerosis. She illustrates how the disease is 'enacted' differently within different locations of the hospital. In the pathology lab, atherosclerosis is defined as that which is under the microscope, whereas in the clinical examination room, atherosclerosis is the pain that a patient feels in their legs. Mol suggests that despite this multiplicity, the different enactments of atherosclerosis "hang together" in ways that make the disease appear singular (p. 5).

Mol's usage of the notions of multiplicity, enactments, and diseases and bodies as objects are challenging to convey in the classroom. Unlike most theoretical concepts in sociology, such as social structure, agency, inequality etc., Mol's terminology is not intended to provide an explanatory framework for understanding empirical data. The language in Mol's study is not intended to explain why particular phenomena are occurring. Rather, it is employed purely for the purposes of aiding description. Unlike most conventional sociological concepts, Mol's terms do not refer to social phenomena that are fixed and stabilized. Instead, Mol's language seeks to illustrate fluidity and instability. Mol's subtle, yet significant, departures from the traditional language of sociology challenges students to shift their understandings of sociological language.

Compounding these difficulties around language is the structural organization of Mol's text. Unlike most other scholarly texts, Mol divides the pages of her book in two: the top half loosely devoted to an exploration of her empirical findings and the bottom half for her theoretical reflections. This introduces significant challenges in teaching Mol's text to undergraduate students, as it is a form that is both complex and uncommon.

Because some students found the format difficult, the class spent a significant amount of time discussing how to navigate through a text that departed from conventional modes of presentation. The format of the book signaled that the course content was entering a new terrain. Without even beginning to read the text, students recognized Mol's work as something different than what they had seen before in the way of required course readings.

To begin the engagement with Mol's work, ANT was introduced with an overview lecture. The subsequent three or four classes were spent on Mol's text, where each chapter was examined through informal discussions involving all the students. We now turn to a discussion of the details and consequences of the theatrical method of teaching ANT that followed the discussions.

USING THEATRICS TO TEACH ANT

Sally: *The professor introduced us to Actor-Network Theory through a lecture using PowerPoint slides. From the ensuing class discussion we began to understand the fundamentals of the theory. We were excited to learn that we would be 'experiencing' the theory, as it was expressed in The Body Multiple, by way of an interactive presentation. A hospital lab technician was invited to come to a subsequent class.*

Patricia: *By bringing a lab technician into the classroom, my hope was that the students could apply ANT to this particular context. In doing so, they would see that the lab is a small node of the hospital network, but that node could be 'exploded' to become a network in and of itself. In turn, the machines and associated processes and practices in the lab are each nodes in themselves.*

Gail was a lab technician with many years of work experience working in a number of hospital laboratories. She had agreed to come to the class to talk with the students about her work. In preparation for her visit, as a group the students constructed

several questions on what they deemed relevant or piqued their curiosity (Appendix). Applying some of the concepts from the Mol book to the context of a hospital lab, students brainstormed the questions motivated by their desire to know about what happens in a hospital laboratory. For instance, Mol's concepts of 'enactment' generated questions such as "how do the various enactments of disease get coordinated in the lab?". After the students had exhausted all their questions, we then grouped them into five main themes/clusters (Appendix).

Sally: *It was difficult to develop questions because we didn't have a starting place. We didn't know whether we should begin with questions about specimens – their collection and analysis – or maybe the work environment.*

As Sally's words suggest, the students had difficulty identifying a starting point for the questions. This particular struggle was used to further the discussion of the methodological embedded within ANT. As many ANT scholars have suggested, networks do not come with predefined maps that contain "you are here" arrows. Like the students in this course, ANT researchers often struggle with the question of where to start an empirical investigation as ANT does not provide a linear, formulaic research technique. Rather, scholars employing ANT often have to use intuition and creativity to locate their point of empirical departure. By struggling through the process of identifying an entry point into their empirical exploration, the students were given the opportunity to experience first-hand an important aspect of ANT studies.

Once the questions were developed by the students, they were then consolidated, thematised, and left on the board when the lab technician arrived so students could refer to them as the class progressed. Students were told that these questions were only a guide and that they were free to pose any other questions that came to them during the discussion. This semi/un-structured format was discussed as an essential aspect of most empirical data collection in ANT studies. It was described as another example of how ANT departs from the traditional, formulaic model of social scientific investigation.

Gail's entrance into the classroom was dramatic. In her lab garb, complete with face mask and gloves, she held up several needles and asked "who's first to give a blood sample?" The stir in the room was palpable. As many students humorously described later, in the moment that Gail entered the classroom, they did not know whether she was there for a class presentation or for a blood collection. By beginning the presentation/interview with these theatrics, Gail helped to bring to lab to the classroom. While they were still firmly seated in their classroom chairs, in the moment of Gail's entrance, the students' experience came closer to what an ethnographic experience in the field may have been like. Given the close ties that many ANT studies have to the ethnographic approach, this brief connection to the ethnographic was an important one. In addition to the illustrative, these theatrics captured the students' attention and interest in the empirical.

Sally: Gail walked into the classroom dressed as she would have if she were actually on the job as a lab tech, complete with gloves, and a mask, holding a needle. We instantly felt what patients feel when approached by a tech to take their blood. It felt like we were in a suspense film, no one wanting to move for fear it could be them. Everyone in the class felt uneasy! Gail said, "so who is ready to give blood?" We all looked at one another wondering if this could be legitimate. We wondered what kind of class we signed up for. None of us were ready to be the guinea pig. My friend offered me as the sacrificial lamb probably for fear that she might be chosen herself. From the moment Gail walked through that door she had us captivated. Her grand entrance in her garb grasped our attention, which transferred to

the PowerPoint that she presented. We were intrigued by the photographs and discussion, some of which came out of our previously brainstormed questions.

In the first suspended moments of the session with Gail, the descriptive aspect of ANT transcended to a performative level. Central concepts of bodies, disease, and medical work in Mol's study were set within the context of the students' own experience of being a patient required to give blood for analysis.

Sally: After what felt like a long time, Gail informed us that we were not going to be giving blood today, which quickly eased our thoughts of bolting from the classroom. This experience of a guest speaker was unlike any I had ever had throughout my entire university career, and one I will not soon forget.

Patricia comments on the effect of unusual approach on the students: "The students' reserve was mixed with curiosity, perhaps because they had experienced, in earlier classes, a number of wildly different teaching methods. But, the use of costume and props, as minimal as these were, brought science into the classroom in a way they had not experienced. It was far from the usual protocols associated with bringing guest speakers to classes."

The session proceeded with Gail shedding her lab coat, mask, and gloves. A slide show ensued of photos that Gail had taken inside the lab. Gail used these photos to articulate a detailed illustration of all the aspects of the lab. In doing this, Gail once again brought the lab to life in the classroom. She illustrated the field the students might have seen through ethnographic observation. The access restrictions on most labs often prevent the possibility of undergraduate students engaging in ethnographies of laboratory work, which precludes the possibility of experiencing this common method of data collection in

ANT studies. However, Gail's vivid, colourful illustration brought the field to the students and introduced the possibility of ethnography within the classroom.

Sally: The lab pictures were very revealing. Most people never get to see what happens in a lab. The "Authorized Personnel Only" sign limits the public's access. So, to have a glimpse of the equipment, the room, and the setup was quite surprising.

After the slide show, the students began to ask their previously developed questions. However, as the interview continued, the students deviated from their questions based on what they had learned about the lab in Gail's presentation. They used the theoretical terms from Mol, such as 'enactment', while adeptly created new questions and reformulated existing questions in response to the slides and their new insights gleaned from the presentation. The students were learning in the moment, adjusting their assumptions about the workings of the lab. The way they had expected the lab to work and how they came to understand to work was very different.

Sally: We were not limited to the questions we created beforehand and this helped us delve into our new understandings. Some of our questions were answered right away. For instance, in the instant viewing of the slide on specimen processors, our questions on how the processing of different specimens became irrelevant. Others spontaneously came to us while Gail was talking.

Just as the students were given the space to formulate their own questions, they were also given the opportunity to deviate from the pre-existing set of questions during the session with the lab technician. In this way, the session replicated what interviews often look like in an ANT studies as aspects of the network emerge; new questions

are formulated and posed. Through this process students not only learned about the intricacies of laboratory work, but the complexities of Mol's work and of ANT more generally.

Sally: The descriptions in the Mol book came to life. I had an 'ahaa' moment when I realized that what Mol was saying in her book was true and applicable to the real world.

The moment the student is describing is what every teacher hopes for: when students connect the theory they are learning to the real world. These 'ahaa' moments are seldom predictable and often times students themselves are not entirely clear what brings about the clarity.

Sally: My curiosity was piqued by the sample analyzing machine. I was intrigued by the way it is cleaned to avoid contamination and how the small percentage of contamination happens, but does not directly affect the sample. All samples are treated as biohazardous, and they are all viewed as contaminated with HIV, etc. to ensure the utmost safest environment. One of the pictures was the rack of blood samples lined up like little soldiers with their identification badges (the barcodes). Right away, I realized that diseases are enacted as blood samples in the lab. I tried not to jump ahead in our questions, but it was hard. When Gail said 'we don't deal with human beings we deal with specimens', I asked 'but when does it become the patient?' She didn't answer the question directly, perhaps because she didn't quite understand it. But, when she told us about the biohazard procedures my question was answered.

In recognizing the enactment of diseases in the lab as blood samples opened up an understanding of the multiplicity of disease, described admirably by Mol. As the Gail described, the procedures designed to standardize the treatment all of the samples during their entire stay in the lab, it became evident to the students that the samples' individual identity was stripped the minute they came through the lab door, but re-assembled with their distinctive features when the test results are evaluated. While as an abstract concept the 'multiplicity of diseases' had little meaning to the students, Gail's photos and vivid description of laboratory work allowed for an understanding of this concept in the empirical context from which it originally emerged.

As Gail described, test done in the lab sometimes result in measures outside of the normal range of values. When this happens the patient characteristics (age, sex, racial profile) come into view. Patient records are retrieved and reviewed, co-workers might be consulted, and often times a phone call is made to the nurse on the patient's ward for additional particularities on the patient and discussions with co-workers.

Patricia: Gail peppered her description of the procedures and practices of evaluating test results with illustrative calculations in the blackboard. We were witness to an interactive dance of numeric values produced by the blood test and the textual representations of the patient, a dance of disease enactment.

The mock calculations put on the blackboard by Gail illustrated the discrepancies between the normal, or expected, numerical values of test results and the particular values acquired from a test of a specific individual are resolved. It made obvious the need for other patient-specific information, such as demographics, medical history and current treatment regimes. The coordination of these two very different types of data was revealed to be part of the way the work of a lab technician is organized to incorporate 'abnormal' measures into how the disease is understood.

A further complicating revelation was how the same numerical value from the same test can be understood in very different ways. Gail offered the illustrative example of a blood sample coming to the lab for a hemoglobin test because it is there is a tentative cancer diagnosis. If the hemoglobin is low, a cancer diagnosis is not an immediate consequence because the technician might identify this patient as being recently been dehydrated.

Patricia: The students were so engaged in the ensuring discussion, we extended the class by at least ½ hour over the allotted time. In our follow-up discussion of what was learned from Gail's visit, the students' spoke of how it altered our understanding of ANT. The discussion closed the loop. The theory was followed by the concrete, a 'visit' into the lab. Then, from the lab, we came back to the theory.

The session with the lab technician illustrated how disease is enacted in the laboratory. While students had an understanding of how disease might be enacted in the lab from Mol's text, they did not have any direct experience. From the session with Gail,, they saw first-hand how those that work in the lab see diseases not as that which is experienced by people, but as abnormal cells and vessel walls. Through this performative exercise, Mol's text, the concepts of enactment and multiplicity, and Actor-Network Theory more generally were all brought to life.

CONCLUSION

This article has explored a method for using theatrics to teach Actor-Network Theory in an undergraduate sociology course. Costumes, props, and visual aids were assembled for the purpose of opening up the students to a greater understanding and appreciation for the complexities of ANT. As a student remarked following the exercise, "for me ANT is like a photomosaic. One of those puzzles with little pictures that together make a big picture. That's what I appreciated about it, with other theories, you are so limited". By 'performing' ANT in the classroom, students were challenged to think beyond simplistic theoretical concepts to a more abstract and nuanced understanding of Mol's The Body Multiple and Actor-Network Theory more generally.

The performative approach to teaching innovative approaches to inquiry proposed in this article seeks to bring the field into the classroom. This move attempts to dissolve the binary that has been constructed in much of the pedagogical literature between the field and the classroom. The assumption associated with this divide is that the experiences that students have in the classroom are distinct and apart from those they have in the field. By bringing the field into the classroom, the performative technique makes it possible to combine the pedagogical potential of the field and the classroom.

As this article has argued the complexity of ANT as an approach to sociological inquiry calls for an innovative method of instruction. The article asserts, by way of example, scholarly and creative pedagogical approaches can be harmonize effectively. The use of performative techniques in teaching sociology, however, is by no means limited to the field of ANT. There are many other branches of sociological thought that could be explored in the classroom using a similar theatrical method, such as the approach of Institutional Ethnography, which similarly transcends the boundaries between sociological theory and method (Smith, 2005). Further thought on how the classroom can be used as a stage to perform innovative sociological approaches is needed. This work offers an entry into these imaginings and raises a call for more critical reflection on creative methods for teaching innovative sociological thought.

REFERENCES

Dugdale, A. (1999). Materiality: Juggling sameness and difference. In Law, J., & Hassard, J. (Eds.), *Actor network theory and after* (pp. 113–133). Oxford, UK: Blackwell.

Epstein, S. (1996). *Impure science*. Berkeley, CA: University of California Press.

Fails, E. (1988). Teaching sociological theory: The development of an experimental strategy. *Teaching Sociology, 16*(3), 256–262. doi:10.2307/1317527

Frank, A. (1994). *At the will of the body*. New York, NY: Mariner Books.

Hall, M. (2000). Clinical sociology in service learning. *Sociological Practice: A Journal of Clinical and Applied Sociology, 2*(1), 33-39.

Holtzman, M. (2005). Teaching sociological theory through active learning: The irrigation exercise. *Teaching Sociology, 33*(2), 206–212. doi:10.1177/0092055X0503300207

Latour, B. (1988). *The pasteurization of France*. Cambridge, MA: Harvard University Press.

Latour, B. (2005). *Reassembling the social: An introduction to actor-network-theory*. Oxford, UK: Oxford University Press.

Latour, B., & Woolgar, S. (1986). *Laboratory life*. Princeton, NJ: Princeton University.

Law, J. (2000). *Networks, relations, cyborgs: On the social study of technology*. Retrieved from http://www.lancs.ac.uk/fass/sociology/papers/law-networks-relations -cyborgs.pdf

Law, J. (2004). *After method: Mess in social science research*. London, UK: Routledge.

Law, J. (2006). Traduction/Trahision: Notes on ANT. *Convergencia, 42*, 47–72.

Law, J. (2007). *Actor network theory and material semiotics*. Retrieved from http://heterogeneities. net/publications/Law2007ANT andMaterialSemiotics.pdf

Law, J., & Hassard, J. (1999). *Actor network theory and after*. Oxford, UK: Blackwell.

Lindbergh, R. (2001). *No more words*. New York, NY: Simon & Schuster.

Mol, A. (2002). *The body multiple: Ontology in medical practice*. Durham, NC: Duke University Press.

Pedersen, D. (2010). Active and collaborative leaning in an undergraduate sociological theory course. *Teaching Sociology, 38*(3), 197–206. doi:10.1177/0092055X10370119

Rankin, J., & Campbell, M. (2006). *Managing to nurse*. Toronto, ON, Canada: University of Toronto Press.

Sturgis, R. (1983). Conversations with theorists: An innovative approach to teaching social theory. *Teaching Sociology, 10*(2), 275–280. doi:10.2307/1317118

APPENDIX

Questions the class developed in preparation for Gail's visit:

1. How does the blood come into the lab? Do you collect it from the patient or does it arrive? What substances, other than blood, are analysed in the lab? Urine? How do they come into the lab?
2. Is it just diseases that are enacted in the lab? Or are patients, too? If so, when and how? How does that get coordinated with the enactment of disease? If you know that the sample you're working on is a kid, does that make a difference? If they have HIV, alcoholism, or are from a marginalized group, does that make a difference in how the patient is enacted? Or if the patient that corresponds to that particular sample you are working on is found to have some disease that you, yourself, have a personal connection to (e.g., you have a family member with cancer) – does that make a difference?
3. What are the actual practices in the lab? How does the work get done? Are you making diagnoses, or, are you simply recording the numbers that you get from the tests you perform? Is there room for error in the test results you generate? If so, what are these? Is there a division of labour such that only certain techs do certain tests? What do you do if a lab request comes in and it seems clear that not all the boxes (each indicating a test) are ticked off as they should be? Is there much variation from lab to lab in these practices?
4. Clashes: Is it possible to get discrepancies in test results using different tests? For instance, what do you do if you are running 3 tests, all for the same disease, and one points in one direction and the other two point in the other direction? Is it possible to get discrepant results using different machines? How do you resolve those?

How Does the Authority of the Physician Come into Play in Resolving Any of these Clashes?

Elizabeth Quinlan was one of the first graduates of the Interdisciplinary studies doctoral program at the University of Saskatchewan, Canada, where she now teaches and researches in the department of sociology. Her interests lie in the intersection of sociology of health, work, and gender. In her CIHR-funded post-doctoral fellowship, she investigated how members of multi-disciplinary health care teams exchange, create, and apply their knowledge in the context of their collective clinical decision-making. Her recent interests include using arts-based participatory research methods to co-create improved working conditions and quality of life. Recently, Quinlan was awarded a New Investigator grant from Saskatchewan Health Research Foundation to Award to use participatory theatre with health care aides to address workplace bullying.

This work was previously published in the International Journal of Actor-Network Theory and Technological Innovation, Volume 3, Issue 4, edited by Arthur Tatnall, pp. 1-10, copyright 2011 by IGI Publishing (an imprint of IGI Global).

Chapter 6

A Petri Net Model for Analysing E-Learning and Learning Difficulties

Tas Adam
Victoria University, Australia

ABSTRACT

Petri Nets are tools for the modelling and analysis of the behaviour of systems and analysis of the Petri Net can then reveal important information about the structure and dynamic behaviour of the modelled system. In this article, the author argues that Petri Net concepts (when used qualitatively) are not fundamentally different from those of ANT. For example, the 'places' from Petri Nets bear a strong resemblance to the actors in ANT, and the 'triggers' or 'transitions', are somewhat analogous to ANT's translations. In modelling, places represent conditions and transitions represent events. Tokens may model the resources or data items that are associated with a place or places. The original research that this article is based on was undertaken using an actor-network framework to develop a model for e-Learning for students with Learning Difficulties. This article explores the qualitative use of Petri Nets to supplement this ANT treatment.

SOCIO-TECHNICAL RESEARCH ON STUDENTS WITH LEARNING DIFFICULTIES (LD)

Students with Learning Difficulties (LD) are catered for in Australia in both 'main stream' schools and in Special Schools. There are over 100 'Special Needs' Schools in Victoria and over 1,200 in Australia to provide education for students with various learning difficulties (learning difficulties/disabilities of general nature, intellectual or physical) that fall into several categories ranging from mild to physical and severe learning difficulties. Table 1 shows the various categories of LD that can be found in the directory of special needs schools.

A useful definition of LD comes from the Learning Disabilities Association of Canada (LDAC) who defines LD as:

A number of disorders which may affect the acquisition, organization, retention, understanding or use of verbal or nonverbal information. These

DOI: 10.4018/978-1-4666-2166-4.ch006

disorders affect learning in individuals who otherwise demonstrate at least average abilities essential for thinking and/or reasoning. As such, learning disabilities are distinct from global intellectual deficiency. (Learning Disabilities Association of Canada, 2002)

ANT AND STUDENTS WITH LD

Special Schools are complex socio-technical entities and research into their curriculum needs to take account of this complexity. The actors involved in the adoption of this technology to assist students with special needs include: students, parents, teachers, school principals, school ICT specialist teachers, the School Council, the Web, computers, Education Department policies, learning technology policy, the school environment, classroom environments, learning approaches and paradigms, delivery methods of instruction, engagement methods, thinking processes, technology infrastructure-bandwidth, curriculum, Internet resources, digital libraries and other schools. In an ANT framework, actors are seen to contest and negotiate with each other in an attempt to influence the final outcome in a direction to their own liking. The Education Department, for example, might want ensure that all schools offer a similar level of service to students and to ensure their accountability. The parents of a student with LD, on the other hand, would want the best for their own child regardless of what was going on in other schools.

A BRIEF INTRODUCTION TO PETRI NETS

Petri Nets were invented in the late 1930s by Carl Adam Petri (1962), and in simple terms these are graphical objects with arcs and transitions. He and Lee (2007) applied Petri Nets to model e-learning platforms or environments. Other studies concentrate on the semantic aspects of e-learning

(Ghaleb et al., 2006) and Park and Kim (2008) have analysed the different layers for e-learning and recommended the modelling with a suitable Petri Net. A full mathematical treatment of Petri Nets is beyond the scope of this article but here is provided a discussion of the basic concepts that are fundamental to the model design. In the article I will argue that although Petri Nets are often used as a tool in quantitative research, they also have a place in qualitative research and especially socio-technical research. The chief attraction of this approach is the way in which the basic aspects of distributed systems are identified conceptually and mathematically, and hence, it is most appropriate to build a model for e-learning on this basis.

According to Petersen (1981), the guiding principles of Petri Net theory in formulating the basic notions of states and change of states (called transitions) are:

1. States and transitions are two intertwined but distinct notions that describe an even handed treatment.
2. Both states and transitions are distributed entities.

Table 1. Summary of special needs categories (adapated from Australian Schools Directory, 2011)

Special Need Category	
General Disabilities	Intellectual Disabilities/ Autism
Hearing Impaired	Learning Difficulties
English Learning	Moderate to High Needs
Distance Education	Multiple Disabilities
Autistic	Physical Disabilities
Emotional Behaviour	Speech / Language Disorders
High Needs	Vision Impaired
Intellectual Disabilities	Young Mothers

3. The extent of change caused by a transition is fixed; it does not depend on the state at which it occurs.

4. A transition is enabled to occur at a state if and only if the fixed extent of change associated with the transition is possible at that state.

Formally, Petri Nets are a mathematical modelling technique with graphical structure representation and applicable to many systems. As a graphical tool Petri Nets can be used as a visual-communication aid similar to flow charts and networks. In addition, tokens (non-negative integers) are assigned to places to simulate the dynamic nature of the system. Thus if we include all attributes then, a Petri Net is a particular kind of directed graph, together with an initial state called the initial marking M_0.

The underlying graph of a Petri Net is a directed, weighted, bipartite graph consisting of two kinds of nodes, called places and transitions, where arcs are either from a place to a transition or from a transition to a place. An example of a Petri Net is shown in Figure 1, where places are represented by circles and transitions are represented by rectangular boxes. One of the early systems modelled by Petri Nets was the Simple Protocol in data communications. Figure 1 shows the places and transitions for the initial marking. By firing transitions, the system can alter its marking and thus reach a new state.

I will argue that Petri Net concepts are not fundamentally different from those of ANT. For example, the 'places' from Petri Nets bear a strong resemblance to the actors in ANT, and the triggers or transitions, are analogous to the translations. In modelling, places represent conditions and transitions represent events. A transition (Murata, 1989) has a certain number of input and output places representing the pre-conditions and post-conditions of the event, respectively. Tokens may model the resources or data items that are associated with a place or places.

As mentioned, Petri Nets are tools for the modelling and analysis of the behaviour of systems. Petri Net theory allows a system to be modelled by a Petri Net (PN), or a mathematical representation of the system. Analysis of the PN can then, hopefully, reveal important information about the structure and dynamic behaviour of the modelled system.

A Petri Net is composed of four parts (Murata, 1989): a set of places P, a set of transitions T, an input function I, and an output function O. The input and output functions relate to transitions and places. The structure of a Petri Net is defined by its places, transitions, Input functions, and Output functions. The formal definition of a Petri Net (Murata, 1989) is a 5-tuple PN = (P, T, F, W, M_0) where:

- $P = \{p_1, p_2, \ldots, p_m\}$ is a finite set of places
- $T = \{t_1, t_2, \ldots, t_n\}$ is a finite set of transitions
- $F \subseteq \{(P \times T) \cup (T \times P)\}$ is a set of arcs
- $W : F \rightarrow \{1, 2, 3, \ldots\}$ is a weight function
- $M_0 : P \rightarrow \{0, 1, 2, 3, \ldots\}$ is the initial marking
- $P \cap T = \varnothing \text{ and } P \cup T \neq \varnothing$

In general, this definition applies to simple nets known in the literature as Place Transition Nets (PTN). In order to handle complex systems, another class of nets has been defined by various researchers; the high-level Petri Nets. To allow for data manipulation (Jensen, 1991) and describe type concepts as in high-level languages, coloured Petri Nets have been defined. These allow places to contain tokens that represent different data values (colour).

Figure 1. Petri net model of simple flow control protocol

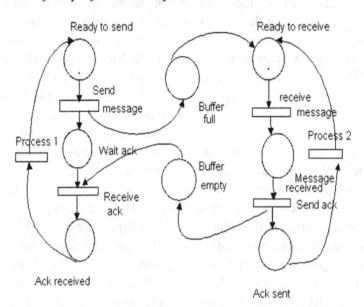

A PETRI NET FOR E-LEARNING

As mentioned, a Petri Net is a graphical tool to model systems. The systems can move from one state to another via triggers or actions (called preconditions). This approach has been used in ICT to model the operation of a computer which consists of several well-known components, like memory, CPU, input/output devices and hard drive(s). Petri Nets have also been used in areas such as data communications protocol modelling (Adam, 1993) and manufacturing.

This article explores whether Petri Nets could be applied to adding value to modelling an approach to e-learning and students with learning difficulties that was based on the use of actor-network theory. The idea was that since the education of people with learning difficulties relies on policy, leadership, staff attitudes, parental beliefs, expectations and support personnel, it may be possibly to define an overall model that captures all actors and their attributes (networks). The basis for this discussion is the e-learning model shown in Figure 2.

Analysis of this e-learning model produced the Petri Net shown in Figure 4 (see later in this article), allows a reader to examine and look for various operations. For example, access to resources (tools and learning objects) and so on is based on certain criteria (preconditions). Similarly, assessment, teaching models and so on, can be argued to fit logically, into a Petri Net description. The benefit of such a modelling approach is that we can treat the educational environment (Special Schools, Principal, Department, Staff) as the resources/places (with tokens) for our Petri Net. Furthermore, we can also incorporate an opportunity cost for LD as was proposed by Petty (2005), in a New Zealand study for the visually impaired. Thus the learning outcomes may be analysed and we can determine the overall impact of ICT in the curriculum where all students have the same opportunity to learn regardless of their individual characteristics.

RATIONALE FOR AN E-LEARNING PETRI NET MODEL

Petri Net models were recently proposed for e-learning by He and Le (2007) and Park and Kim (2008) and a similar model was also proposed by

Figure 2. Learning interface model (Adam et al., 2006)

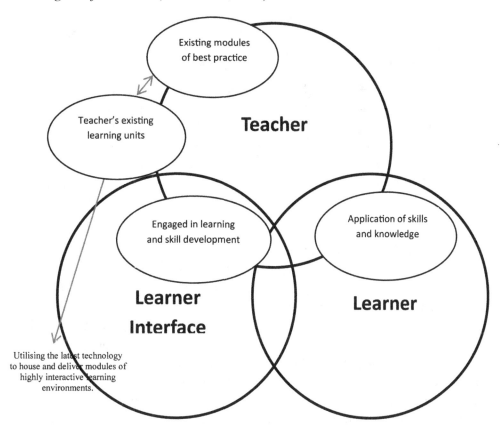

Ghaleb et al. (2006). The study by Ghaleb et al. analysed an e-learning model based on Semantic Web technology and the model includes various services and tools in the context of a semantic portal, such as: course registration, uploading course documents and student assignments, interactive tutorial, announcements, useful links, assessment, and simple semantic search. A metadata-based ontology is introduced for this purpose and added to the model. Although these elements may be a little too complex for LD students, I would argue that the concept of a portal with some modification with adaptive technology (and possibly Widgits) may serve the LD students' community via the forthcoming Ultranet (Tatnall & Dakich, in press) in the State of Victoria, Australia.

The literature provides studies of modelling e-learning with Simple Hierarchical Petri Nets, which were developed in the late 70s by Valette

(1979) and were refined to High-Level Coloured Petri Nets by Jensen (1991). Given the richness of the workflow processes, a Petri Net may also be used to provide the theoretical framework for workflow management, since we can analyse the firing sequences by examining the places (pre-conditions and post-conditions), the transitions (actions), the tokens (process states) and the arcs in the graph (process actions or flows). In fact, He and Le (2007) have proposed a division of two layers: the Learning Process Layer and the Web Service Layer.

LEARNING PROCESS NET

The Learning Process Net is defined by the relationship: Learning process Net = (P,T,T^R,W,Pi,PO), where the following applies: $P = \{P1,$

Figure 3. Cooperative learning as a Petri net

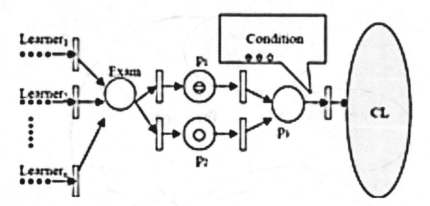

P2,...,Pm} is a finite set of places representing the pre-condition and post-condition in a learning process. *T= {T1, T2,...,Tn}* is a finite set of transitions representing explicit and implicit. The Learning Process Net is Learning Objects Structured Petri Net which describes the structure and mutual dependence of a set of learning objects (LO). It allows us to model the context of each learning object in terms of preconditions (prerequisites) and post-conditions (learning objectives) (Risse & Vatterrott 2004). In this model, one may assume that the Learning Process Net correctly models the mutual dependence of LOs, then, an LO can be completed successfully only if all preconditions are fulfilled (and generate the necessary post-conditions or results in other places). These relations can adequately be described by Petri Nets (Peterson, 1981) where the LOs are modelled by transitions, and preconditions and post-conditions are modelled by places. The context between LOs is modelled by a set of places with token(s). It should be noted that the content of a message is not important as it is not known until run time.

WEB SERVICES NET

Web service behaviour is basically a partially ordered set of activities. Therefore, the transformation from the primitive activities to Petri Net is relatively straightforward (Chi et al., 2005). Activity is modelled by transition and the state of the service is modelled by places. The arrows between places and transitions are used to specify causal relations. We assume that a Petri Net to model a Web service contains one input place (i.e., a place with no incoming arcs) and one output place (i.e. a place with no outgoing arcs). When a token is in its corresponding input place, this means that a Web service meets its precondition(s), whereas a token in the corresponding output place means that the Web service completes its activity. Structured activities are nested activities, for example: sequence, for defining an execution order, switch, for conditional routing, flow, for parallel routing, and while, for looping.

An e-learning environment requires the learning process specifications and deployment of these to the Web Services layer. The model must allow for the individual variation of learners and their self-independence, and in addition, the cooperative attitude of each learner. The individualised customised learning or constructionist learning approach for LD students must optimise the environment by adjusting the weights for the various needs and abilities of the learners. Furthermore, the modelling must allow for the following areas:

- Cooperative learning and team organization,

Figure 4. Petri net model for e-learning and LD

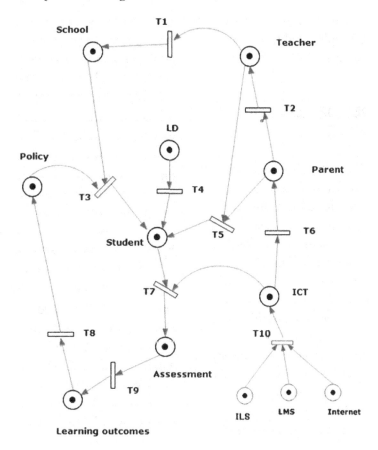

- Investigation of cooperative learning and planning,
- Self-centred, individualised education,
- Co-operation co-work at the team level,
- Sharing of resources,
- Evaluation and self-examination of cooperative learning between teams.

A study by Park and Kim (2008) examine the layers and relationships between layers for e-learning. The study focuses on customised co-operative learning as an approach to e-learning and then applies a Petri Net model to this form of learning. The e-learning environment is separated into three levels: processes, selected processes and sub-processes.

The processes displays basic processes to achieve cooperation learning under e-learning environment and selected processes displays that it can be missed, selected or utilised, depends on status of instructor. And sub- processes displays into sections for detail behaviours of processes or selected processes. Model of cooperative learning at e-learning is divided into 6 steps, education preparation and checking objective, cooperative learning and team organisation, investigation of cooperative learning and planning, self-centered individual education, cooperation co-work at the team, sharing product, evaluation and self-examination of cooperative learning between teams. (Park & Kim 2008)

The above characteristic elements of the e-learning platform can be represented by the Petri Net model for e-learning and Cooperative Learning shown in Figure 3.

PETRI NET MODEL DESIGN FOR E-LEARNING AND LD

When modelling with Petri Nets, it is important to consider the conditions that must be satisfied by the Petri Net. These are referred to as the reachability, dead-marking and boundedness which are defined as follows: Reachability: identifies whether it is possible for a learning process to achieve the desired results or not; Dead marking: used as a number to check for errors in the learning process design; Boundedness: this refers to the number of tokens in a place, either 0 or 1; otherwise this indicates an error. A study by Petty (2005) investigated the opportunity to learn parameters or metrics for the visually impaired. This article has adopted the arguments provided in that study an e-learning framework model for LD students. The main parameters are defined below and an overall formula or expression is given from Petty (2005). The following variables of this model for the proposed Petri Net model for LD are as follows:

- S_i = Vector of student characteristics for student i, including individual and family attributes.
- P_i = Vector of provision for learner i, both mainstream (provided by the school) and specialised (provided by the resource teachers, teacher aides and DEET).
- O_i = Vector of opportunity-to-learn for learner i.
- ε_i = The error term or random variation.

Petty (2005) also defines the following relationship for the opportunity-to-learn for learner

i: $O_i = \beta_0 + \beta_1 S_i + \beta_2 P_i + \varepsilon_i$. This expression shows the opportunity-to-learn is a function of the student characteristics and the educational provision that the student receives. If the independent variables are standardised to a mean of zero, β_0 is the mean opportunity to learn, β_1 is the factor by which the student characteristics are transformed, reflecting how they affect the opportunity-to-learn, and β_2 is the factor by which the provision is transformed to affect opportunity-to-learn. However, as the provision is responsive to the student characteristics, and we can express P_i (the provision vector) as a function of S_i (the vector of student characteristics): $P_i = \alpha_0 + \alpha_1 S_i + \varsigma$ where α_0 is the mean amount of provision and α_1 can be interpreted as the amount of provision added for each 'unit' of disability or special need. Greater level of disability, expressed in S_i (student characteristics), implies a higher value of P_i (provision). The last term ς is an error term associated with the provision vector. It can be argued that the student characteristics are affected by actors and their networks. Thus the provision may be affected by policy, school actors and networks, and therefore, the error term may be considered as a balanced indicator for the provision on LD.

Combining these from above yields the following result:

$$O_i = \beta_0 + \beta_1 S_i + \beta_2(\alpha_0 + \alpha_1 S_i + \varsigma) + \varepsilon_i$$

which can be simplified into the following form: $O_i = k_0 + k_1 S_i$ where k_0 and k_1 are constants or weights that relate to the mean opportunity-to-learn and the adjusted weight or factor for the provision of the resource allocated to LD student i, respectively. Clearly, in proposing an e-learning model for LD students it would be beneficial to consider and explore the nature of the student characteristics (S_i), the provision (P_i) and the opportunity to learn (O_i). For example, a 121-ICT project at a

Special School provided an opportunity for all students in the classroom to use a laptop in their day-to-day work. However, some of the students were also supported by specialist staff or teacher aides, and hence, the provision vector P_i would be different for each LD student as the student characteristics are different. In the Petty (2005) research study, the aim was to determine what P_i (provision) is needed in order to get the desired O_i (opportunity-to-learn), assuming that, S_i the student characteristics were given. Accordingly, the aim is to make good use of resources and thus it is desirable to resolve the question "what is the best way to provide P_i in order to optimise O_i?" Or given limited resources, determine how they should best be used in order to provide the highest amount of opportunity-to-learn, with given student characteristics. A Petri Net e-learning model (based on the Learning Interface Model shown in Figure 4) is shown. This model exhibits triggers (transitions) and places (resources) that are needed to enable the respective triggers (the firing rule).

PETRI NETS VERSUS ANT NETWORKS

The Petri Net uses triggers (transitions) by using resources (places), and consequently, generates new resources (tokens in places). In order for the transition to be activated, the preconditions need to be satisfied. For example, if a computer CPU is to execute a process certain threads and other resources must be available including memory, input devices and output devices for storage. In ANT for a translation to take place, we need actors and their networks to be present and aligned in order for the innovation (proposal) to be accepted, and hence adopted. In this comparison is proposed a logical correspondence between places (resources) and actors, and between transitions and translations.

ANT AND AN ANALYSIS OF THE PETRI NET FOR E-LEARNING MODEL DESCRIBED IN THIS STUDY

The model consists of ten transitions (actions or triggers) T_1-T_{10} and twelve places (resources) which are represented by School, Teacher, Parent, Student, LD, Policy, ICT, Assessment, Learning outcomes, ILS, LMS and Internet. The Petri Net model for LD e-Learning is designed to enable the firing of transitions provided the preconditions from the resources are satisfied. For example, T_7 can only fire if the two places, Student and ICT have a token (resource). The result is the firing of transition T_7, which generates tokens in a place called Assessment. This is equivalent to the actors and their networks in problematising the students' environment and trying to diagnose the skills and knowledge of a student with LD. It follows from the model, that the Learning outcomes (place) is affected by transition T_9, which has a precondition Assessment. The transition T_8 is triggered by the precondition, Learning Outcomes, which would impact Policy. Transition T_3 requires input from places School and Policy to enable its firing and its post conditions are shown by placing resources in the place called Student. The opportunity-to-learn metric may be resourced from the place called Policy.

The model shows the firing of three transitions T_3, T_4 and T_5 must be satisfied (triggered) in order for resources (tokens) to be deposited in the place Student. This operation demonstrates the impact of policy, teachers, parents and LD on students. Transition T_7 is fired when students work with ICT and the post-condition for the place Assessment is affected by the addition of tokens. This models the positive impact of ICT on the learning outcomes that are reached via the firing of transition T_9.

The Petri Net further shows the firing of transition T_{10} is enabled via a combination of e-Learning approaches that require preconditions (resources) from the places ILS, LMS and Internet. These three places may be replaced and enabled by an equivalent single place, Web 2.0 technologies, whose result (output) from the firing of T_{10} is indicated by the post-condition in the place ICT. The operation for the remainder of the transitions can be analysed in a similar manner and these are summarised in Table 2.

Students form their own networks, and so do teachers, parents, and Education Authorities. Consequently it is contended that the Petri Net model presented in Figure 4 can be viewed as a conceptual or logical representation of the interactions and associations of actors, shown in the above summary. The model displays the strong associations and influences or alignments that exist in the learning environment for LD students. If the impact of ICT is to be examined, then we may apply the Petty (2005) model as discussed earlier, and if this is adopted the result will be a model that can be used a standard for evaluating the learning outcomes of LD students with the adoption of ICT. The model shows that if transactions T_3, T_4 and T_5 all fire, then these generate tokens or resources for the place student. Therefore, these can be used as a way of measuring or assessing the opportunity-to-learn, as these directly can generate the student characteristics vector, S_i.

Table 2. Summary of model operation

Transition	Preconditions	Post conditions
T_1	Teacher	School
T_2	Parent	Teacher
T_3	School, Policy	Student
T_4	LD	Student
T_5	Teacher, Parent	Student
T_6	ICT	Parent
T_7	Student, ICT	Assessment
T_8	Learning outcomes	Policy
T_9	Assessment	Learning outcomes
T_{10}	ILS, LMS, Internet	ICT

This model has the potential to determine the opportunity-to-learn cost for each LD student, to analyse the use of ICT as an integral component in the curriculum and its impact on the learning outcomes or achievement for these students. It should be pointed out that there is anecdotal evidence on how computers were introduced in the curriculum. The evidence showed that leadership of prime actors, such as principals, played a significant part in the adoption of computers in the 80s, and hence, they affected the provision vector Pi for each student. As was mentioned earlier in the thesis, the provision vector was influenced by the DSP program in Australian schools in the 80s.

CONCLUSION

The article presented a Petri Net model for e-Learning which is specific to LD students. The model contains the main elements of the teaching and learning environment and this can be applied to Special Schools which are ready to adopt the full potential of ICT. The article also compared an approach using Petri Nets to that using actor-network theory, and contended that they have something in common.

One of the objectives of this study was to propose a model that would determine the risk factors for learning of LD students. The e-Learning model presented here has the capacity to facilitate this objective. The Petri Net model in Figure 4 makes provision for this diagnosis as it can be considered as the opportunity vector in the Petty (2005) model. The learning outcomes and the pathways from school-to-work or further study is an area or field in the LD students' networks that must be accounted for by the proposed model. A careful examination of the model shows that transitions T_4, T_3 and T_7 provide the triggers to analyse the risk factors for e-Learning and LD. In this way, it would be possible to diagnose LD and the provision for effective learning strategies and technologies, relevant to the individual characteristics vector S_i of each LD student.

REFERENCES

Adam, T. (1993). *Modelling and implementing protocols using high level Petri Nets.*

Adam, T., Rigoni, A., & Tatnall, A. (2006). Designing and implementing curriculum for students with special needs: A case study of a thinking curriculum. *Journal of Business Systems. Governance and Ethics, 1*(1), 49–63.

Australian Schools Directory. (2011). *The only guide to all Australian primary and secondary schools.* Retrieved from http://www.australian-schoolsdirectory. com.au/

Chi, Y.-L., Tsai, M.-H., & Lee, C.-W. (2005). A Petri-net based validator in reliability of a composite service. In *Proceedings of the IEEE International Conference on e-Technology, e-Commerce and e-Service* (pp. 450-453).

Ghaleb, F., Daoud, S., & Hasna, A., ALJa'am, J. M., El-Seoud, S. A., & El-Sofany, H. (2006). E-Learning model based on semantic web technology. *International Journal of Computing & Information Sciences, 4*(2), 63–71.

He, F., & Le, J. (2007). Hierarchical Petri nets model for the design of e-learning systems. In K. Hui, Z. Pan, R. C. Chung, C. C. L. Wang, X. Jin, S. Göbel, & E. C.-L. Li (Eds.), *Proceedings of the 2nd International Conference on Technologies for e-Learning and Digital Entertainment* (LNCS 4469, pp. 283-292).

Jensen, K. (1991). Coloured Petri nets: A high level language for system design and analysis. In G. Rozenberg (Ed.), *Advances in Petri Nets* (LNCS 483, pp. 342-416).

Learning Disabilities Association of Canada. (2002). *Official definition of learning disabilities.* Retrieved from http://www.ldac-taac. ca/

Murata, T. (1989). Petri nets: Properties, analysis and applications. *Proceedings of the IEEE, 77*(4), 541–580. doi:10.1109/5.24143

Park, S., & Kim, Y. (2008). Applying Petri nets to model customised learning and cooperative learning with competency. *International Journal of Computer Science and Network Security, 8*(2).

Peterson, J. L. (1981). *Petri net theory modelling of systems.* Upper Saddle River, NJ: Prentice Hall.

Petri, C. A. (1962). *Kommunikation mit automaton.* Unpublished doctoral dissertation, Institut fur instrumentelle Mathematik Schriffen, Bonn, Germany.

Petty, N. M. W. (2005). *Using student perceptions to evaluate the effectiveness of education for high school students with vision impairment.* Christchurch, New Zealand: University of Canturbury.

Risse, T., & Vatterrott, H. R. (2004). (in press). *The learning objects structure Petri net.* Retrieved from http://www.eurodl.org/materials/contrib/2004/Risse_Vatterrott.html

Tatnall, A., & Dakich [*Informing parents with the Victorian Education Ultranet.* Novi Sad, Serbia: Informing Science and IT Education.]. *E (Norwalk, Conn.)*.

Valette, R. (1979). Analysis of Petri nets by stepwise refinement. *Journal of Computer and System Sciences, 18*, 35–46. doi:10.1016/0022-0000(79)90050-3

This work was previously published in the International Journal of Actor-Network Theory and Technological Innovation, Volume 3, Issue 4, edited by Arthur Tatnall, pp. 11-21, copyright 2011 by IGI Publishing (an imprint of IGI Global).

Chapter 7

Deconstructing Professionalism:
An Actor–Network Critique of Professional Standards for Teachers in the UK Lifelong Learning Sector

Jonathan Tummons
Teesside University, UK

ABSTRACT

The problematisation of the professional standards for teachers in the UK lifelong learning sector tends to focus on the discourses that the standards embody: discourses that are posited as being based on a restricted or technicist model of professionalism, that fail sufficiently to recognise the lived experiences of teachers within the sector both in terms of professional knowledge and competences, and professional development. This paper takes a different approach, drawing on a branch of material semiotics – actor-network theory – in order to shift the locus of problematisation away from what the standards might mean, to how the standards are physically assembled or instantiated. The paper concludes by suggesting that a first point of problematisation rests not in the discourses that the standards embody, but in the inherent fragilities of any material artefact that has the intention of carrying meaning across spatial, institutional or temporal boundaries.

INTRODUCTION

In 2006, Lifelong Learning UK (LLUK), a quasi-autonomous government-funded body, published a set of professional standards that were intended to provide a framework for the 'professionalisation' of teachers in further, adult, and community education in the UK, a broad and disparate area of provision that is usually referred to as the lifelong learning sector. These LLUK standards themselves replaced an earlier set of standards which had been introduced seven years before by the Further Education National Training Organisation (FEnto). The earlier FEnto standards had been criticised for not adequately meeting the needs of trainee teachers and for failing to reflect the developmental nature of initial teacher education (ITE): they were seen as prescriptive, imposing too heavy a regulatory burden on the

DOI: 10.4018/978-1-4666-2166-4.ch007

ITE curriculum and focusing on what might be termed the desirable attributes of qualified and experienced, rather than trainee, teachers (Elliot, 2000; Lucas, 2004). Similarly, the LLUK standards have been criticised for positing a restricted, technicist discourse of professional knowledge within the learning and skills sector, akin to a competency-based approach to learning (Finlay et al., 2007; Gleeson & James, 2007; Lucas, 2007).

This paper takes a different approach. Rather than problematising the LLUK standards through an exploration of the discourses relating to teaching, to teacher knowledge or to the pedagogy of initial teacher education that they might – or might not – promulgate, I wish to focus on what at first might seem more mundane or even prosaic matters, but which are, I shall argue, fundamental to an understanding of how a body of professional standards might do their 'work'. I am interested in analysing the LLUK standards not from the point of view of embodying a particular set of discourses or of encouraging – or discouraging – the critical use of particular bodies of professional or technical knowledge, but rather as a reification of a series of conversations, ideas and concepts into a material form: a textual artefact that exists either on paper or on screen, that can in turn generate intertextual hierarchies through being quoted and cited (by students in their essays, in textbooks for trainee teachers or in ITE curriculum documentation, for example). What I mean to stress here is that before academics critique the standards, before university programme leaders embed them within their initial teacher education curricula, before the authors of teacher education textbooks list them at the beginning of a book chapter or before trainee teachers cite them in their assignments, all of these people actually have to get hold of a copy of the standards – in full or in part – and read them.

Thus, it is the processes of firstly reifying the standards into a material form and then distributing or transmitting that reified form across social, geographic or institutional boundaries that I wish to problematise here. I shall begin by providing some brief details regarding the empirical data on which some of my argument rests. After this, I shall provide a brief description of the main characteristics of an actor-network theory approach. I shall then briefly comment on the nature of professional or occupational standards more generally, before going on to provide an ANT-informed account of the LLUK standards.

Empirical Data: An Explanatory Note

This paper rests on both theoretical and empirical strands. The empirical data used here is drawn from a larger data set collected during the period 2006 to 2009 as part of a PhD funded by the Economic and Social Research Council, exploring assessment practices on one programme of initial teacher education for the lifelong learning sector at an English university. Interview data was collected through a series of semi-structured interviews with both tutors and students on the PGCE/CertEd course. The narratives produced were analysed both as a form of retrospective meaning making, and also as a form of presentation of the narrator's (that is to say, the interviewee's) point of view (Chase, 2005; Kvale, 2007). Other data was collected through documentary analysis of a range of sources including course handbooks, module specifications, internal moderation reports and external examiners' reports (Rapley, 2007; Tight, 2003). All data has been rendered anonymous through the use of pseudonyms and the disguise of other signifiers such as locations, module titles and the exact names of management groups or committees (Christians, 2005). Data coding and analysis was carried out using Atlas-Ti (Lewins & Silver, 2007).

A THEORETICAL FRAMEWORK: ACTOR-NETWORK THEORY (ANT)

Conceptualising and then investigating the LLUK framework as a textual artefact requires rather different conceptual or theoretical perspectives in comparison to, for example, an investigation of the framework from the point of view of the professional discourses that they might inhabit. If I am going to argue – and I am – that prior to analysing the framework from the point of view of professional discourse or conceptualisation of knowledge it is necessary first to consider how the framework actually 'gets out there', then I need to draw on a coherent theoretical framework that will allow me to explore how such textual artefacts move, how they are distributed and received, and how effectively they manage to transmit their meaning and thus accomplish the actions that they have set out to make happen. An appropriate framework with which to consider these issues is provided by actor-network theory (ANT) (Barton & Hamilton, 2005; Clarke, 2002; Czarniawska & Hernes, 2005; Fenwick & Edwards, 2010; Latour, 2005; Law, 1994, 2004; Nespor, 1994; Tummons, 2009, 2010a).

Perhaps appropriately, bearing in mind its antecedents in post-structuralism, ANT defies a simple definition.

It has been described in several ways: as a component or characteristic of ethnography that is concerned with "the processes of ordering that generate effects such as technologies (Law, 1994, p. 18); as a "way of talking… [that] allows us to look at identity and practice as functions of ongoing interactions with distant elements (animate and inanimate) of networks that have been mobilized along intersecting trajectories" (Nespor, 1994, pp. 12-13); and as a "sociology of the social and … [a] sociology of associations" (Latour, 2005, p. 9). ANT literature allows three key themes to be teased out in such a way that my working definition of ANT can be established. Firstly, ANT is a sociology of association (Latour, 2005), or of ramifying relations (Law, 2004). It is a way of exploring how social projects are accomplished, in ways that can be traced, across networks of associations or links. Such networks can consist of concentrations of all sorts of stuff: stories, people,

paperwork, computer simulations, routines, texts and voices. ANT is not concerned with what such stories or routines might mean, however: rather, the focus of an ANT account is on what such stuff – people as well as objects – might do once they have been linked or associated into a network (Fenwick & Edwards, 2010; Fox, 2000).

This emphasis, on doing rather than meaning, leads to the second key theme: ANT provides ways of thinking about how networks or associations both carry influence and influence each other, and foregrounds the ways in which people are made to do things across networks of geography or time or across institutional boundaries. "How to make someone do something" is a central concern (Latour, 2005, p. 59). In order for a social project to be accomplished, the network (of people and things) needs to be brought together. A network can be established through persuasion, inducement, coercion, or any combination of these. It is important to note that ANT is not concerned to explain or justify such networks, but simply to account for how they might expand or retract, so that the project that they wish to carry through can be successfully accomplished. A network can break down at any point or link. Consequently, the social project can be slowed down, misdirected or even lost, whether the broken link is an object (for example, a text-based document that has been lost or misinterpreted), or a person (for example, someone who has decided for whatever reason not to act in the way that the network requires). Both people and objects can make (or fail to make) other people do something; that is to say, both people and objects are granted agency within ANT.

ANT's insistence on analysing people and things in the same way introduces the third key theme: the principle of symmetry, which states: "humans are not treated differently from non-humans… Humans are not assumed to have a privileged a priori status in the world but to be part of it" (Fenwick & Edwards, 2010, p. 3). In an ANT analysis, therefore, it makes no difference whether the network constituents being explored are people or things. Both human and non-human elements can come together and be held together in order to ensure the performance of the social project in question. Indeed, it may be the case that both human and non-human elements are always present. This is not because such a mixture of people and objects makes a network seem to be more sustainable. Rather, this is a reflection of the fact that to attempt to bifurcate people and things when considering how the social is enacted creates a false dichotomy: it is simply the case that the one cannot be without the other (Latour, 2005).

ANT has predominantly been used as a theoretical and investigative framework in science and technology studies and the study of socio-materialism, but it is increasingly being used within education as well (Fenwick & Edwards, 2010; Tummons, 2011): important ANT studies in education include Nespor's (1994) exploration of curriculum within a US university, Edwards' (2003) ANT account of neoliberal discourses of lifelong learning, Hamilton's (2009) analysis of the use of individual learning plans in adult basic skills education and, of particular relevance to this paper, Fenwick's (2010) exploration of the policy processes associated with educational standards.

PROFESSIONAL OR OCCUPATIONAL STANDARDS: TOWARDS A COMMON DEFINITION

Occupational or professional standards perform two main functions. Firstly, they inform the public about the claims to competence of the profession; secondly, they inform the development of relevant professional qualifications, including the ways in which such qualifications are delivered, mentored and assessed (Eraut, 1994; Taylor, 1997). Both the current LLUK standards and the FEnto standards that preceded them share these characteristics. That said, there has been and continues to be a rigorous debate about the ways in which these two sets of standards have satisfactorily

embodied a model of professionalism that positions practitioners, rather than policy makers and employers, at the centre of the process – in direct opposition to those models of professionalisation that position autonomous professionals at the heart of the processes by which an occupation seeks to advance its status (Eraut, 1994; Lucas, 2004). Notwithstanding the disputed model of professionalism that the LLUK standards embody, a more fundamental concern can be identified in the assumption that "it is possible to capture in written statements – codified knowledge – the richness and complexities involved in the process of teaching" – an assumption that may not stand up to scrutiny (Nasta, 2007, p. 3).

THE LLUK STANDARDS: AN ANT ANALYSIS

What might a network of actors, mobilised in order to accomplish the work of the LLUK professional standards, look like or consist of? Certainly, it would – must – need to consist of both things (for example: the standards themselves, in print or pdf format; textbooks written for trainee teachers; curriculum handbooks for appropriate ITE courses) and people (for example: teacher educators; trainee teachers; authors). And, if this is indeed an actor-network, then we need to account for the nature of the interrelationships between all of these. More accurately, we need to account for the ways in which the people, the human actors within the network and the objects, the non-human actors, move and work within and around each other, making each other do things in particular ways. Nor is there any particular place where this account 'should' begin. Actor-networks are (politically) flat, not hierarchical: it requires the mobilisation and cooperation of all of the components of the network for a social project to be accomplished: as such, our account can begin anywhere, and travel in any direction within and across the network.

VIGNETTE ONE: PEOPLE – TUTORS, TRAINEES, AND THE STANDARDS

Let me provide an example, informed by the empirical data that I referred to above, specifically, to the data that I collected from teacher-training students. Over the course of two academic years (the time it normally takes to complete the course which is delivered on a part-time basis), amongst other kinds of data collection I followed thirteen students (a purposive sample, but a statistically insignificant number compared to the overall number of students on the course, which is over 1,500 (Crang & Cook, 2007), interviewing them at different points during these two academic years, observing a small number of the classes that they attended and also carrying out content analysis on the assignments that they completed. These students were variously taught by five teacher educators, whom I also followed, through both interviews and observations, over the two years. Between them, the students completed 143 assignments (students complete eleven assignments in total during their time on the course) of various kinds: essays, portfolios, teaching observations and such like, all of which are typical of professional courses such as those that trainee teachers follow (Brown, 1999; Klenowski et al., 2006; Taylor, 1997; Tummons, 2010b).

So, enfolded within all of these different kinds of assessment practice, where were the traces of the LLUK standards made visible? Only in the work of one of the students was any explicit reference to the LLUK standards made. This student had not actually read the LLUK standards in their original published form, however: rather, they had used references within a teacher-training textbook to quote them, a textbook that does not contain references to all of the standards, but just to a selection of them. All of the students demonstrated what might be termed at best a technicist understanding of the standards: an awareness of the practices that teachers in the lifelong learning sector were required to do, although without inhabiting any

of the discourses of the 'professionalisation' of the sector that the standards were designed to espouse. But the other students had not read them and when reading textbooks, tended to gloss over references to or lists of the standards as they appeared in the text, concentrating instead on the 'substantive' content of the books. Only one of the tutors made explicit use of any reference to the standards in their feedback practice, encouraging students to draw on the standards when writing their reflections (although only a few of their students actually did so). The other four tutors did not use the LLUK standards as part of their teaching repertoire. The one exception to this is found in the final module that students are required to complete on the course, which places 'teacher professionalism' and the LLUK standards within the module content, although the assessment for the module is predominantly concerned with reflective practice and quality assurance.

What I want to highlight here is that within the curricular practices of this teacher-training course, the LLUK standards inhabit what might be termed a relative material invisibility. The LLUK standards are 'there', receiving the occasional mention, straightforward to look up and make explicit reference to should a tutor or student choose/wish to do so, but the status or condition that they occupy is transient and mutable. They are capable of being foregrounded or of being left behind, of being quoted or being ignored, of being discussed or of being forgotten. However, it is important to remember that the LLUK standards never completely 'go away': they are always present, even if they are only whirring away in the background in a manner akin to the operating system on my laptop that supports the graphical user interface that I work with.

Working out what Works

It would be uncontroversial to state that different people would read the LLUK standards in different ways, and consequently take different meanings from them: texts do not have a single intrinsic meaning; rather, the meanings that we as readers take from and ascribe to them are diffracted through our own prior experiences, ways of knowing and positionalities (Barton et al., 2000; Gee, 1996). Academic authors who have written critiques of the LLUK framework will 'read' them rather differently to a teacher training student who is preparing their final assignment and wants to cite one or more of the standards in their reflections on practice. But any conversation about how people might read them and how they might make or take meaning from them is predicated on the fact of the standards having actually been accessed in some sort of physical form. That is to say, before we can begin to think about how people respond to the standards, we have to make certain assumptions about how those same people actually get to the standards in the first place. Have they read them in full after downloading a pdf to their laptop? Have they picked up a hard copy at a conference? Have they had the standards introduced to them or placed in front of them by somebody?

Assembling the Professional Standards

It seems obvious, nonsensical even, to state that if the LLUK standards are going to be distributed across the lifelong learning sector, they need first to be reified into a physical form (Wenger, 1998). Before we can read the standards and then do something with them (quote them in the textbooks that we write, draw on them to shape our teacher training curricula; refer to them in our essays) we have to have them presented to us in a reified form. Reifications such as these are commonplace in the social world, and are used to capture and make concrete all sorts of more-or-less complicated concepts. As well as professional frameworks (which are numerous), other easily recognisable reifications include government statutes, textbooks, even railway timetables. Reifications do not necessarily need to

be made out of physical stuff, although they may necessarily involve and even create physical stuff: a conference is a reification and so is a meeting. But if it is going to travel across institutional, geographic or spatial boundaries, then a reification needs to be made of physical stuff. And the boundaries that the standards have to travel across are impressive. The standards are designed to be 'read' (whatever that might imply) by college lecturers, teacher-trainers, curriculum designers, endorsement officers and students, inter alia. The readership is vast and diffuse, spread across institutions (universities, colleges of further education, adult education centres). Only a physical reified form is capable of making this journey: if the standards relied solely on voices when travelling, such a journey would be unfeasible (Latour, 2005; Law, 1994). The standards have to be assembled into a material form.

Within ANT such a document or artefact, a physical list of standards, is referred to as an immutable mobile. It is immutable because it is seen as fixed and stable, self-contained and self-evident (Fenwick, 2010). All of the 'behind the scenes' work that went into creating this list of standards in the first place – the meetings, the seminars, the consultations, the discussions (Nasta, 2007) – disappear from view. And it is mobile because it can travel. It can be 'sent out' by government departments, quasi-autonomous non-governmental organisations and/or other professional bodies. But immutable mobiles also need people. Or, to put it another way, once the standards have been collected together in a concrete form, they rely on people to circulate them, to talk about them and to champion their use. It is in the interplay between people and things that an actor-network becomes established. Networks such as these can be highly effective. The interweaving into a network of people and artefacts can allow messages, ideas and practices to travel across significant geographical, temporal or institutional boundaries. But such networks are tentative constructs at best, prone to breaking down if links are put under stress or insufficiently nurtured (Latour, 2005). Texts do travel well, and they can be highly resilient: but they can also be lost or misinterpreted; people can travel but they can only reach so far, and once out of sight, you cannot be sure that they will do what you have told them (Law, 1994). Or, to put it another way: we cannot be sure how people will respond to the standards, whether people will indeed tell other people about them in the ways that they are supposed to, whether they will pay lip service to them or simply abandon them.

VIGNETTE TWO: THINGS – THE TEACHER TRAINING CURRICULUM AND THE STANDARDS

Let me provide a second example that foregrounds the role of other things – other stuff – in establishing an actor-network for the LLUK standards (based on content analysis of previously collected documentary data, as discussed above). In the first example, I highlighted how the two 'main' groups of people involved in teacher-training – the teacher-educators and the trainees – did, or did not, talk or write about the standards, and I made reference to the fact that there was just one module or unit on the course where such a discussion might be foregrounded. In this sense, the accomplishment or establishment of the actor-network can be seen as coming under strain simply because an insufficient number of the people that the network needs are becoming enrolled in the social project at work. I have also established that things as well as people make up an actor-network. And some of the things that are involved have already been referred to in the first example in addition to the actual standards themselves: teacher-training textbooks; teacher training curricula; feedback sheets. These, and perhaps other, textual artefacts – or, more properly, other immutable mobiles – are all enmeshed within the actor-network. That is to say, they are all, in different ways, enrolled

in the social project of ordering the LLUK standards, of getting the standards 'out there'. But these objects are in themselves the products of other ordering, of other network effects. The ways in which the curriculum documents for a teacher training programme, a teacher-training textbook or a feedback sheet firstly come to be as they are and secondly align themselves – to some extent – with the LLUK standards, are far from straightforward.

Take the writing of a textbook. Many of the textbooks that are to be found on the reading lists for teacher training programmes within the lifelong learning sector make reference to the LLUK standards. By this I mean that it is a common feature of such books to list some or all of the standards, sometimes quoting them directly and sometimes supplying references, as the book proceeds. For example, a chapter, or a whole book, about assessment would refer to the standards from Domain E: Assessment for Learning. Sometimes the standards are put at the start of the chapter, sometimes at the end. Within such textbooks, the readers – the trainee teachers – might be encouraged to reflect on the standards, to think about how they apply to their own professional practice. Many students – and tutors – encounter the standards in this way, rather than downloading the full pdf from the LLUK website. But what are the standards 'doing' within textbooks such as these?

Many of the textbooks that students on these courses use are now published in third, fourth or fifth editions, and have been in print for a decade or more. That is, they have been in print since before the LLUK standards were published. Six years ago, a textbook would have been citing the earlier FEnto standards. Six years before that, there were no professional standards for the authors to cut and paste. What is noteworthy, if you read and then compare different textbook editions from this period of time, is that the content of the different editions remains relatively unchanged: certainly, the imposition over the last decade or so of two – quite different – sets of professional standards does not seem to have impacted on the content of books, apart from the fact that as such books are updated, the relevant standards are 'plugged in', in a manner akin to the ways in which I have to install new plug-ins for my web browser before I can access some forms of online content.

CONCLUSION: WHAT ARE THE STANDARDS DOING?

Up to this point, I have presented two vignettes within which I have provided deliberately small-scale accounts of just two of the kinds of actions or practices that the LLUK standards are enfolded within. In the first vignette, I explored the extent to which students and tutors do or do not make reference to the LLUK standards within the assessment processes of a teacher training course; in the second, I considered the ways in which the authors of teacher-training textbooks cite from the standards. Focusing on such relatively tiny episodes may seem at first look to be rather trivial or prosaic – irrelevant even. And yet it is within tiny episodes such as these that an actor-network might be established or collapse, and thus why the ANT researcher is characterised not by their subscriptions to overarching theories or schema, but by their myopia that only allows them to see small things, close-up (Latour, 2005).

Small stories such as these are important because they allow us to see how stuff such as the LLUK standards sometimes gets used. During episodes such as these, the standards are not being disputed, contradicted or challenged: there is no discourse to challenge managerialism, employer-led professionalisation or competence-based models of professional knowledge here. What there is, indeed all that there is, is a text-based artefact, a thing made up of some physical stuff, that we all agree is called 'the LLUK standards' or, to give it it's full title, 'new overarching professional standards for teachers, tutors and trainers in the lifelong learning sector'. It might be a pdf file or a hard copy, lying on a desk or in a box file, stored on an usb memory stick or on an email attachment: these are the ways in which the standards get sent out and about. And then what happens to them? They get cited from; they get ignored or left on a shelf; or they get saved to a folder that gets lost sight of on an already crowded hard drive. The important point to hold on to here is that once the standards get sent 'out there', on very many occasions the journey that they take does not last very long and certainly does not result in the kind of end use for the standards that its initial sponsors - the people who wrote and promulgate them – envisaged (Brandt & Clinton, 2002). They are employed in manners that are more or less closely aligned to the intentions that lie behind them.

Some kinds of action or response are in close alignment. When university teacher-training programme leaders write or revise their curricula so that they 'map onto' the required professional standards, the work of the standards is being accomplished: the central tenets of their discourse of professionalism are in some ways being circulated and established. References to the standards within textbooks also helps establish the network, although here the accomplishment of the standards might be seen as being somewhat inadvertent, even accidental: several of the authors of such textbooks that I have spoken to have admitted to 'tacking on' the standards after the book or the chapter in question has been written. But at other times, people who 'could' and 'should' be being enrolled within the network are clearly not being sufficiently engaged, or interested, in order to get them to do so. This is why so many teacher educators, as well as trainee teachers, simply allow the standards to pass them by. They do not challenge or critique them; nor do they read and reflect on them: they simply ignore them.

In this paper I have drawn on just two very small exchanges or interactions that involve and envelop the LLUK standards. There are lots of others. And the role of the ANT researcher is to slowly, painstakingly map out all of these tiny episodes and events, finding out who does actually read the standards and who does not, and what they do with them afterwards. Only then will it become possible to start to account for the power that such standards, within and through an actor-network, actually embody. And this is important because the ways in which the standards can be said to be informing a discourse of professionalisation need to take account of the fact that many of the people who actually work in the lifelong learning sector do not read or even pay much meaningful attention to them.

REFERENCES

Barton, D., & Hamilton, M. (2005). Literacy, reification and the dynamics of social interaction. In Barton, D., & Tusting, K. (Eds.), *Beyond communities of practice: Language, power and social context*. Cambridge, UK: Cambridge University Press. doi:10.1017/CBO9780511610554.003

Barton, D., Hamilton, M., & Ivanic, R. (Eds.). (2000). *Situated literacies: Reading and writing in context*. London, UK: Routledge.

Brandt, T., & Clinton, K. (2002). Limits of the local: Expanding perspectives on literacy as a social practice. *Journal of Literacy Research*, *34*(3), 337–356. doi:10.1207/s15548430jlr3403_4

Brown, S. (1999a). Assessing practice. In Brown, S., & Glasner, A. (Eds.), *Assessment matters in higher education: Choosing and using diverse approaches*. Buckingham, UK: Open University Press.

Chase, S. E. (2005). Narrative inquiry: Multiple lenses, approaches, voices. In Denzin, N., & Lincoln, Y. (Eds.), *The Sage handbook of qualitative research* (3rd ed.). London, UK: Sage.

Christians, C. (2005). Ethics and politics in qualitative research. In Denzin, N., & Lincoln, Y. (Eds.), *The Sage handbook of qualitative research* (3rd ed.). London, UK: Sage.

Clarke, J. (2002). A new kind of symmetry: Actor-network theories and the new literacy studies. *Studies in the Education of Adults*, *34*(2), 107–122.

Crang, M., & Cook, I. (2007). *Doing ethnographies*. London, UK: Sage.

Czarniawska, B., & Hernes, T. (Eds.). (2005). *Actor-network theory and organising*. Malmö, Sweden: Liber and Copenhagen Business School Press.

Edwards, R. (2003). Ordering subjects: Actor networks and intellectual technologies in lifelong learning. *Studies in the Education of Adults*, *35*(1), 54–67.

Elliott, G. (2000). Accrediting lecturers using competence-based approaches: A cautionary tale. In Gray, D., & Griffin, C. (Eds.), *Post-compulsory education and the new millennium*. London, UK: Jessica Kingsley.

Eraut, M. (1994). *Developing professional knowledge and competence*. London, UK: Routledge.

Fenwick, T. (2010). (un)Doing standards in education with actor-network theory. *Journal of Education Policy*, *25*(2), 117–133. doi:10.1080/02680930903314277

Fenwick, T., & Edwards, R. (2010). *Actor-network theory in education*. London, UK: Routledge.

Finlay, I., Spours, K., Steer, R., Coffield, F., Gregson, M., & Hodgson, A. (2007). The heart of what we do: Policies on teaching, learning and assessment in the learning and skills sector. *Journal of Vocational Education and Training*, *59*(2), 137–153. doi:10.1080/13636820701342442

Fox, S. (2000). Communities of practice, Foucault and actor-network theory. *Journal of Management Studies*, *37*(6), 853–867. doi:10.1111/1467-6486.00207

Gee, J. (1996). *Social linguistics and literacies: Ideology in discourses* (2nd ed.). London, UK: Routledge.

Gleeson, D., & James, D. (2007). The paradox of professionalism in English Further Education: A TLC project perspective. *Educational Review, 59*(4), 451–467. doi:10.1080/00131910701619340

Hamilton, M. (2009). Putting words in their mouths: The alignment of identities with system goals through the use of individual learning plans. *British Educational Research Journal, 35*(2), 221–242. doi:10.1080/01411920802042739

Klenowski, V., Askew, S., & Carnell, E. (2006). Porfolios for learning, assessment and professional education in higher education. *Assessment & Evaluation in Higher Education, 31*(3), 267–286. doi:10.1080/02602930500352816

Kvale, S. (2007). *Doing interviews*. London, UK: Sage.

Latour, B. (2005). *Reassembling the social: An introduction to actor-network theory*. Oxford, UK: Oxford University Press.

Law, J. (1994). *Organising modernity*. Oxford, UK: Blackwell.

Law, J. (2004). *After method: Mess in social science research*. London, UK: Routledge.

Lewins, A., & Silver, C. (2007). *Using software in qualitative research: A step-by-step guide*. London, UK: Sage.

Lucas, N. (2004). The 'FENTO Fandango': National standards, compulsory teaching qualifications and the growing regulation of FE college teachers. *Journal of Further and Higher Education, 28*(1), 35–51. doi:10.1080/0309877032000161805

Lucas, N. (2007). Rethinking initial teacher education for further education teachers: From a standards-led to a knowledge-based approach. *Teaching Education, 18*(2), 93–106. doi:10.1080/10476210701325077

Nasta, T. (2007). Translating national standards into practice for the initial training of further education (FE) teachers in England. *Research in Post-Compulsory Education, 12*(1), 1–17. doi:10.1080/13596740601155223

Nespor, J. (1994). *Knowledge in motion: Space, time and curriculum in undergraduate physics and management*. London, UK: Routledge.

Rapley, T. (2007). *Doing conversation, discourse and document analysis*. London, UK: Sage.

Taylor, I. (1997). *Developing learning in professional education*. Buckingham, UK: Open University Press.

Tight, M. (2003). *Researching higher education*. Maidenhead, UK: Open University Press.

Tummons, J. (2009). Higher education in further education in England: An actor-network ethnography. *International Journal of Actor-Network Theory and Technological Innovation, 1*(3), 55–69. doi:10.4018/jantti.2009070104

Tummons, J. (2010a). Institutional ethnography and actor-network theory: A framework for researching the assessment of trainee teachers. *Ethnography and Education, 5*(3), 345–357. doi:10.1080/17457823.2010.511444

Tummons, J. (2010b). The assessment of lesson plans in teacher education: A case study in assessment validity and reliability. *Assessment & Evaluation in Higher Education, 35*(7), 847–857. doi:10.1080/02602930903125256

This work was previously published in the International Journal of Actor-Network Theory and Technological Innovation, Volume 3, Issue 4, edited by Arthur Tatnall, pp. 22-31, copyright 2011 by IGI Publishing (an imprint of IGI Global).

Chapter 8
Knowledge Conversion Processes in Thai Public Organisations Seen as an Innovation:
The Re-Analysis of a TAM Study Using Innovation Translation

Puripat Charnkit
Victoria University, Australia

Arthur Tatnall
Victoria University, Australia

ABSTRACT

This article uses data collected for a study undertaken in the mid-2000s using the Technology Acceptance Model (TAM) to investigate knowledge conversion processes in a Thai Government Ministry. The authors re-analyse this study making use of the power of actor-network theory. The original TAM study, based on technological innovation, investigated the relationship between technology support and management of the knowledge conversion process in a government ministry in Thailand to increase knowledge sharing. The original study found that a number of external variables impacted on the knowledge conversion process, including personal details, training, tools of persuasion, national background and culture, management and policies, employee behaviour, management, and policies and computing support. This paper briefly outlines the findings of the original study and discusses how an ANT study would have approached this material. An analysis is then made of how an Innovation Translation approach differs fundamentally from one using the Technology Acceptance Model.

DOI: 10.4018/978-1-4666-2166-4.ch008

INTRODUCTION: THAI PUBLIC ORGANISATIONS

In 2003 in Thailand a Royal Decree on Principles and Procedures for Good Public Governance (B.E.2546, section 11) set the way for the development of a knowledge-based agency:

In order to enable the administration of the government agency to be in compliance with the public administration for the efficient result of the mission of the State, the government agency shall have the duty to develop knowledge base within its agency regularly so as to make itself as the knowledge base agency. In this regards, the government agency shall analyse all received information in order to produce analytical knowledge which is necessary to its practical use in its public administration correctly, rapidly and suitably for any circumstance. The government agency shall also promote and develop knowledge and capability of, and create vision and alter attitude of, its public servants so as to be efficient and co-learning personnel. (THAILAWS, 2003) (Translation)

The Government then promoted knowledge management (KM) as part of its development strategy (2003-2004) (OPDC, 2004), prompting the public sector in Thailand to transform itself into a learning organization and a knowledge-based agency. The main objective of this strategy was to modify processes and working procedures so as to raise the competency and working standards of Thai Government service units to an international level by using good governance practices. The objective of good governance is ensuring the Government's mission of efficiency. It also involves leveraging cost benefits by reducing redundant operational processes and offering end-to-end solutions. Thailand lags, however, in terms of KM execution compared with other developed countries as the processes for knowledge management are still currently being researched. The principal unit of the government sector in

Thailand responsible for identifying and evaluating the benefits of ICT and KM is the Ministry of Commerce (MOC). This Ministry has authority and responsibilities regarding trade in goods and services, intellectual property rights and other duties as assigned by laws. The MOC was the first government unit to initiate and execute this KM project and have since established an independent group to work exclusively on KM, called the 'KM Group', whose role is to analyse KM and communicate to other units in the organisation the importance of KM along with its benefits and uses. This unit works closely with the ICT unit of the Ministry of Commerce to develop efficient KM strategies that are in line with the Government's service development plan and the Government's goals (Charnkit, 2011).

KNOWLEDGE AND KNOWLEDGE MANAGEMENT

In a dynamic and complex global market, success in business necessitates co-operation among various players. Such co-operation can help businesses grow and sustain themselves (Charnkit, 2011). Relationships in a business network become more flexible if they are associated with trust and based on mutual benefits (Lipnack & Stamps, 2000). There are many factors that offer businesses a competitive edge the most critical being knowledge-sharing within the business organisation. Knowledge is an important asset of any global business and Amin and Thrift (1994) suggest that a characteristic factor of an extending and deepening global economy is the increasing importance assigned to knowledge. It can be argued that knowledge is the economic resource in a new economy (Carlsson, 2003). Knowledge is critical to every business and knowledge management is one domain that organisations are increasingly focusing on as the success of business organisations is dependent on creating knowledge and enhancing the ability to learn (Birchall & Tovstiga, 1999). In the organisational network, knowledge-sharing is one strategy that can help companies gain competitive advantage. Some literature reports that organisations often try to enter into collaborative partnerships to buy knowledge and extend their company's capabilities or build intellectual capital (Jane, 2005). Knowledge however, can be managed within an organisation or business network by using several tools including some form of knowledge management process and the implementation of Information and Communication Technology (ICT). Davenport and Prusak (1998) regard knowledge as:

A fluid mix of framed experience, values, contextual information, expert insight and grounded intuition that provides an environment and framework for evaluating and incorporating new experiences and information. It originates and is applied in the minds of knowers. In organizations, it often becomes embedded not only in documents or repositories but also in organizational routines, processes, practices, and norms.

Wikipedia (2011) defines Knowledge Management as comprising "a range of strategies and practices used in an organization to identify, create, represent, distribute, and enable adoption of insights and experiences. Such insights and experiences comprise knowledge, either embodied in individuals or embedded in organizational processes or practice". KM can be seen as an innovation with the potential to affect the whole of an organisation's business, especially its processes and information systems (De Grooijer, 2000).

Tacit and Explicit Knowledge

Polanyi (1958) was the first researcher to making a clear distinction between tacit and explicit knowledge. He suggested that explicit knowledge should refer to knowledge that can be expressed in words or numbers. Such knowledge can be shared formally and systematically in forms including:

data, specifications, manuals, drawings, audio and video tapes, computer programs and patents (Fernandez et al., 2004). For example the basic principles for stock market analysis contained in a book or manual are considered explicit knowledge, and this knowledge can be used by investors while making decisions about buying or selling stocks. Explicit knowledge can be transmitted through various formats including: data forms, handbooks, reports, letters and scientific formulae. This knowledge can be stored and processed in databases so it can be used by anyone in an organisation (Civi, 2000).

Tacit knowledge, however, cannot be formally exchanged and is difficult to communicate or share with others (Nonaka, 1994). "A person knows more than he can express in words. For example, a painter cannot describe in detail how he goes about drafting a new picture" (Krogh et al., 1998). While explicit knowledge is material knowledge, Tacit knowledge is systematic knowledge (Hamel, 1991). Civi (2000) has argued that tacit knowledge can be divided into two dimensions: one dealing with technical skills, and another with a cognitive dimension that refers to beliefs, values, ideals and mental models (Civi, 2000). Fernandez et al. (2004) supported the idea that tacit knowledge includes insights, intuitions and hunches which are difficult to express, formalise and share. It is more likely to be personal and based on individual experiences and activities. For example it is through years of observing a particular industry that stock market analysts gain knowledge that helps them make recommendations to investors regarding short-term and long-term prospects of stocks of companies within that industry.

KNOWLEDGE MANAGEMENT AND KNOWLEDGE CONVERSION

Nonaka and Takeuchi (1995) explain that knowledge is created by humans and will increase social interaction via a correlation between tacit knowledge and explicit knowledge. They also expound a conversion model, known as the Knowledge Creation Process, in which it is possible to change the nature of knowledge by using tools like concepts, metaphors and hypotheses. They term this conversion model Externalization and suggest that it can frequently be seen in human activity. For example people write reports after participating in workshops. When they distribute and copy the report, they are actually converting tacit knowledge to explicit knowledge (Civi, 2000). Nonaka and Takeuchi (1995) use the distinction of knowledge from Polanyi's concept of tacit and explicit knowledge to explain the interaction between these two knowledge forms by creating a 'knowledge creation spiral' to illustrate the relationship between the epistemological and ontological dimension of knowledge creation. The objective of this model is to show the new concept in term of creating knowledge.

Nonaka (1994) proposes that tacit knowledge can be transformed into explicit knowledge through communication. His work focuses on the process of knowledge creation during the new product development phase in an organisation. He also states that organisations can use the benefits of this knowledge and amplify their new knowledge base if they convert tacit knowledge to explicit knowledge. Nonaka and Takeuchi (1995) have outlined four models of knowledge creation (Figure 1), or as they call it: Knowledge Conversion (KC) and suggest that knowledge can be converted by:

- **Socialisation:** From individual tacit knowledge to group tacit knowledge.
- **Externalisation:** From tacit knowledge to explicit knowledge.
- **Combination:** From separate explicit knowledge to systemic explicit knowledge.
- **Internalisation:** From explicit knowledge to tacit knowledge. This mode is generated by learning and by doing (Krogh et al., 1998).

These processes are often denoted in abbreviated form as SECI. Knowledge conversion (KC) is thus a critical interaction where human knowledge is created and expanded through social interaction between tacit knowledge and explicit forms of knowledge. The study reported in this paper focuses on conversion of knowledge between its tacit and explicit forms (Charnkit, 2011).

THE TECHNOLOGY ACCEPTANCE MODEL (TAM)

The Technology Acceptance Model (TAM) was developed by Davis (1989) from the Theory of Reasoned Action (Ajzen & Fishbein 1980). The Technology Acceptance Model was designed to

Figure 1. The four modes of knowledge conversion (adapted from Nonaka & Takeuchi, 1995)

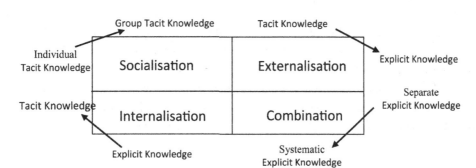

evaluate "… the effect of system characteristics on user acceptance of computer-based information systems" (Davis, 1986, p. 7). TAM is a theoretical model that assumes that a user of technology is generally quite rational and uses information in a systematic manner to decide whether to use, or not to use this technology. "Computer systems cannot improve organizational performance if they aren't used. Unfortunately, resistance to end-user systems by managers and professionals is a widespread problem. To better predict, explain and increase user acceptance, we need to better understand why people accept or reject computers" (Davis et al., 1989, p. 982). This stance is quite different to that adopted by actor-network theory.

The TAM model used the Theory of Reasoned Action as a theoretical basis for specifying the causal linkages between two key concepts: Perceived Usefulness (PU) and Perceived Ease Of Use (PEOU) that it suggests affect to users' attitudes, intentions and actual computer usage behaviour (Kripanont, 2007; Kripanont & Tatnall, 2011).

Perceived Usefulness (PU)

Davis (1989) and Davis et al. (1989) suggest that perceived usefulness can be defined as the degree to which a person believes that using a particular system or technology would enhance their job performance. PU is seen as a direct determinant of usage behavior and suggests that a person will use a particular technology if they believe that that it would be useful.

Perceived Ease of Use (PEOU)

Davis (1989) and Davis et al. (1989) define perceived ease of use as the degree to which a person believes that using a system would be free of effort. Perceived ease of use is thus considered to be a direct determinant of usage behaviour because it is expected that someone would use the technology if they believe that the technology is easy to use.

In TAM, behavioural intention is seen as jointly determined by attitude and perceived usefulness, while attitude is determined by perceived usefulness and perceived ease of use. The goal of TAM is to provide an explanation of the determinants of computer acceptance that is in general capable of explaining user behaviour across a broad range of end-user computing technologies and user populations, while at the same time being both parsimonious and theoretically justified. As it incorporates findings accumulated from much IS research TAM is seen by many as well-suited to modelling computer acceptance (Davis, 1989).

Much research using TAM investigates 'external variables' that may affect a potential user's views on the perceived usefulness or perceived ease of use of the technology in question. Such factors may include: age, attitude towards technology and Knowledge Management, human factors such as abilities and skills, organisational culture and background, management support, understanding of the technology and its applications, government (or leaders) policies, and behaviour and collaborations between managers and employees.

RESEARCH METHODOLOGY

Davis' (1986) conceptual framework proposed that a user's motivational factors are related to actual technology usage and hence act as a bridge between technology design and actual technology usage (Al-Hajri & Tatnall, 2011), meaning that information obtained from the prediction of actual usage at the early stage will guide ICT designers and implementers to enhance the chance of implementing ICT successfully or even avoid the risk of failure. Davis (1986) assumes that stimulus variables, such as system features and capabilities, trigger user motivation to use the technology and in turn users respond by actually using the technology.

The conceptual framework of the original research made use of TAM to explain the adoption and increased effectiveness of the knowledge conversion process in Thailand (Figure 2). The following research questions were investigated:

1. Which external variables impact technology acceptance in Thai public organisations by improving or reducing the knowledge conversion processes?
2. Which technologies have been used with knowledge conversion processes in Thai public organisations?
3. Does the sharing of knowledge in Thai public organisations increase after improvements in the knowledge conversion process?
4. Does TAM help explain the knowledge conversion process in Thai public organisations?

The location for the data collection was the Thai Ministry of Commerce (MOC). At the MOC several departments are involved in knowledge management practices, but only to play an important role in designing technology strategies and planning development:

- The ICT Department which looks after technology and communication channels,
- The Human Resource Development Department (HRD) which offers course training and development of human resources.

Members of both departments participate in knowledge management activities within the MOC and meet to consult about technology that will support people in the organisation and create knowledge management plans. Two groups involved in knowledge conversion activities (SECI) within the MOC were the ICT Team and the KM Team.

Ten members of each department participated in the research. Data was collected using a semi-structured interview method to gain an in-depth understanding of subject perspectives. Respondents were able to supply details and as

Figure 2. Conceptual framework of enhancement of Thai public knowledge conversion

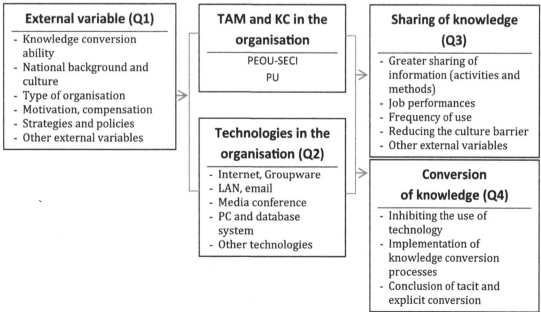

many facts and opinions as they wanted. For anonymity interviewees are listed as Person A, B, C etc. These people included senior technical officers, computer technical officers, the technical manager, human resource and development officers, senior human resource and development officers and the HR manager.

FINDINGS FROM THE RESEARCH

Which External Variables Have an Impact on Technology Acceptance in Thai Public Organisations by Improving or Reducing the Knowledge Conversion Process?

After data review and immersion in the data by the researcher the results were integrated, analysed, and categorised by referring to the issue of technology usage and knowledge management. To answer the research question, the research needed to find out the external variables that had an impact on technology acceptance by investigating knowledge-sharing activities and information technology usage. The results can be illustrated using two dimensions:

- An ICT dimension consisting of ICT usage, the technologies most used by MOC Officers and external variables that impact on technology acceptance, and
- A KM dimension consisting of KM tools, frequency of use, problems of knowledge management, status of KM, key obstruc-

tions in implementation, status of KM and its limitation and barriers.

ICT usage in the MOC involves the technology and communication systems necessary to convert knowledge, share knowledge, communicate with people in the organisation, make decisions, solve any problems, and collect data and knowledge. Eight technologies were used in the Ministry of Commerce: MOC website, MSN MESSENGER, phone, video conference, e-mail, fax, network including Internet and intranet and e-service. The technologies that are most used in order to communicate with others are MSN MESSENGER, phone and email, however the influence of these ICT tools spans opportunities and events. Table 1 shows the relationship between technology, opportunities and events.

From the interviews it is clear that most Officers use MSN MESSENGER as a common communication tool which they use mainly to transfer knowledge between each other. Some view of MSN MESSENGER follow:

Participant D: *Normally, classified information will be transferred through official e-mail system in the organisation. MSN MESSENGER will be used only when that information is unclassified. To interact with chiefs or bosses, who mostly do not apply for an MSN MESSENGER id, we usually send the information by using e-mail, phone call, or seeing them by ourselves.*

Participant B: *MSN MESSENGER can only be used in an already-in contact group, mean-*

Table 1. ICT and frequency of usage

Influence of ICT	MSN MESSENGER	Phone	Email
Opportunities and events	Individual Group Normal events Communication in ICT team Send message to receivers when they are not available.	Urgent events Communicate with other departments	Send important file or document Distribute/share knowledge and information

ing; to use MSN MESSENGER, you need to have the other person's MSN Messenger account or e-mail address. For those who do not use MSN MESSENGER (do not apply for one account), you will not be able to reach them.

The Knowledge Management dimension involves itself with the presentation of data which is related to KM implementation in the MOC. The investigation showed that two tools were used by the KM team to implement a knowledge-sharing process in the organisation: community of practice (COP) and storytelling.

Participant E: Storytelling is the technique I use the most to share my knowledge with my co-workers, since this technique offers unlimited time and topics for one conversation. We can use this technique easily by telling our co-workers what we will be talking about. If the topic is interesting and useful for our work, we will use the tape recorder to record the conversations, and convert them into documents and, finally, distribute them to other co-workers.

Participant H: COP is a pattern that provides the ability to place duty towards an organisation's leader. The leader can lead the team members to join the activities he organizes and jot the information he receives by observing usage of those information again in annual performance measurement.

Which Technologies Have Been Used with the Knowledge Conversion Processes (SECI) in Thai Public Organisations?

When asked about SECI process in the organisation, while most had heard about this when they were training few could identify what technologies could apply to it. The Head of the KM Team,

however indicated that a form of SECI is really used in the organisation but consisting only of the socialisation and externalisation process (Table 3).

Does the Sharing of Knowledge in Thai Public Organisations Increase after Improvements in the Knowledge Conversion Process?

Although it was not possible in this pilot study to come up with a definitive answer to this question, tentative results suggest that it does increase (Table 2). This study cannot say that the sharing of knowledge in Thai public organisations has increased rapidly or decreased dramatically. As the results show, further recommendations through an analysis of the qualitative data on problems that occurred in the sample group could be expected to show that the level of sharing of knowledge and behaviour of use of technology to support knowledge management in the organisation might increase after the organisation has concerned itself will all issues and considered positive ways to improve their strategic management in the future.

Data from the interviews suggested that the Ministry of Commerce was attempting to adapt its existing technologies and communication methods to help implement KM and that although still at the beginning level, the organisation does attempt to use new technology with their KM strategy. The competences of employees were such that they only understood the basic concept of knowledge management and learnt new knowledge by using the provided activities within their

Table 2. Frequency of use and KM practices and activities in organisation

KM Tools and Activities	Frequency
KM Days	1 per year
KM Topic	1 Topic per department
COP	7 Topics per year
Storytelling	1 Topic per department

organisation. Internet technology, for example, is used as a media centre to distribute and share knowledge with staff. It also includes an e-learning system that is used as a tool to share knowledge with the staff.

Does TAM Help Explain the Knowledge Conversion Process in Thai Public Organisations?

TAM focuses on the usability of ICT by studying perceptions and values and is used for determining the relationship between human needs and other technological factors. TAM offers a basis to determine people's technology perceptions with the aid of two factors: comfort and ease of use, and user benefit. Both of these, however, can be influenced by other factors such as age, gender, and culture. This study found that in some respects TAM did indeed help to explain issues of knowledge conversion and whether it might be adopted. In other respects, however, it was of less use. Many saw ICT in KM as potentially useful in the work, but other people were not interested in the technology because they thought it a waste of their time to attend technology training classes and that it may not be related to their current job. Perhaps a more important factor, however, was how KM related to Thai culture. There are some factors such as ease of use (PEOU) and usefulness

(PU) in TAM that probably mean that the MOC will not be able to influence technology usage among its officers as they lack inspiration for use when Head Office or their supervisor does not support them and does not reinforce usage because of policies, motivation and practices.

AN ANT ANALYSIS OF THIS STUDY

Analysis of this study was initially performed using the Technology Acceptance Model to investigate the uptake of Knowledge Management in a Thai Government ministry. The study's socio-technical nature, however, suggests that a re-interpretation using Innovation Translation from actor-network theory might be useful. While it is not possible to completely re-interpret an existing qualitative study using actor-network theory as the questions that would be asked in the interviews would not be quite the same, there is still some value in re-investigating the actors and interactions that may have been present. Whereas TAM is based on the assumption that a user of technology is generally quite rational and uses information in a systematic manner to decide whether to use, or not to use this technology, Innovation Translation sees this quite differently. Innovation Translation argues that just because a technology has been built and made available does not mean that it can automatically

Table 3. The relationship between ICT in the organisation and SECI process

SECI Process	Technique	Technologies
Socialisation (Tacit to Tacit)	COP Story telling Meeting Direct communication (face to face)	Phone MSN Messenger VDO conference Network (internet and intranet)
Externalisation (Tacit to Explicit)	Training (E-learning) Manual and document	Website, web board (Q&A) MSN MESSENGER E-mail
Combination (Explicit to Explicit)	Undiscovered	Website, web board(Q&A) Share point on public server email
Internalisation (Explicit to Tacit)	Training	Website, web board (Q&A) E-learning on website

be assumed that organisations or individuals will want to adopt or to use it, and even if an organisation does adopt a new innovation, it may not use it in the way that its originator intended. It also cannot be assumed that its employees will want to use it, and even if they have no choice and are made to use it, that they will get the most out of it.

The model of Innovation Translation as proposed in actor-network theory proceeds from a quite different set of assumptions to those used in TAM. Translation can be considered to involve all the strategies through which an actor identifies other actors and arranges them in relation to each other (Callon et al., 1983). It is "... the means by which one entity gives a role to others" (Singleton & Michael 1993, p. 229). Latour (1996) speaks of how 'chains of translation' can transform a global problem, such as the transportation needs of a city like Paris into a local problem like continuous transportation. Latour (1996) contends that the innovation itself has no inertia, and moves only if it interests one group of actors or another. Its movement cannot be caused by an initial impetus as there is none. It is instead a consequence of energy given to it by everyone in the chain. The adoption of an innovation comes as a consequence of the actions of everyone in the chain of actors who has anything to do with it, and each of these actors then shapes the innovation to suit themselves. Innovation Translation has the advantage of being able to easily explain examples of partial adoption, and of situations where what is actually adopted differs somewhat from what was proposed. The Technology Acceptance Model uses some of the ideas originally postulated in the well-known Theory of Innovation Diffusion (Rogers et al., 1980; Rogers, 1995, 2003). In comparing the Diffusion and Translation models, Latour (1986) contends that in a Diffusion model an innovation is "endowed with its own form of inertia and propelled from a central source" (Tatnall, 2009). This enables it to move through space and time without the need for further explanation

and makes it unstoppable except by the most reactionary interest groups. Once the innovation has been pointed out to people then it should just be a matter of time before everyone, except the most immovable, recognise its advantages (McMaster et al., 1997). With the Translation model, on the other hand, the initial idea hardly counts and the innovation is not endowed with autonomous power or propelled by a brilliant inventor (Latour 1996).

The important thing to note here is that each potential adopter 'translates' the innovation into a form suitable for what they consider will meet the needs. Callon (1986) suggests that the process of translation can be considered to have four aspects or 'moments'.

- **Problematisation, or 'how to become indispensable':** In this stage, a group of one or more key actors attempts to define the nature of the problem and the roles of other actors so that these key actors are seen as having the answer, and being indispensable to the solution of the problem (McMaster et al., 1997). This is done in order to convince everyone that they have the answer and that they should all follow.

- **Interessement, or 'how allies are locked in place':** A series of processes which attempt to impose the identities and roles defined in the problematisation on the other actors.

- **Enrolment or 'how to define and coordinate the roles':** Will follow through a process of coercion, seduction, or consent (Grint & Woolgar, 1997), leading to the establishment of a solid, stable network of alliances. After enrolment the innovation has now been adopted.

- **Mobilisation or 'are the spokespersons representative?':** Occurs as the proposed solution gains wider acceptance (McMaster et al., 1997) and an even larger network of absent entities is created (Grint

& Woolgar, 1997) through some actors acting as spokespersons for others to promote adoption of the innovation (Tatnall, 2009).

Whereas TAM tries to identify the perceived usefulness, ease of use and intention to adopt by the potential adopter, ANT instead works to identify actors and their associations and interactions with other actors. The whole research approach and the interview questions used in an ANT study would have been different and it is, of course, not possible to ask new questions in this case. It is, nevertheless possible to give an indication of how the results would be interpreted and to suggest other questions that could be asked if it were possible to conduct some more interviews. In an ANT analysis we begin by identifying the actors. Law (1987) describes an actor as any human or non-human entity that is able to make its presence individually felt by other actors. The human actors in this case can be seen to include: the Ministry of Commerce, KM Team, ICT Team, KM Team Head, senior technical officers, computer technical officers, the technical manager, human resource and development officers, senior human resource and development officers and the HR manager. Non-human actors include: Thai Government policy, Ministry of Commerce policy, information technologies, communication technologies, MOC website, MSN MESSENGER, phone, video conference, e-mail, fax, network including Internet and intranet and e-service, SECI techniques, communities of practice and storytelling.

The original study, and this re-analysis, was a study in innovation – in investigating whether a particular technology was accepted and how this occurred. When framed by Innovation Translation the approach involves looking at how each of the actors relates to the four moments of translation: problematisation, interessement, enrolment and mobilisation through these interactions and associations. But what it is rather more difficult to now do in a re-interpretation of the original study is to fully investigate interactions and associations

between these actors. Some likely interactions between the main actors in this study are shown in Figure 3.

If it was possible to now conduct additional interviews, other actors, interactions and associations would probably emerge. The innovation that we are considering is Knowledge Conversion (KC) in the Ministry of Commerce. We are looking at how the actors might have seen its translation and adoption. We will now consider each of these major actors and their interactions and associations in terms of these moments of translation and speculate on how this may have occurred. As it is not now possible to go back and directly question the actors, of necessity this must be quite speculative.

1. **The Government of Thailand:** The Government's problematisation of Knowledge Conversion (KC) for the Ministry of Commerce (MOC) probably related to what it saw as the benefits to increased government efficiency by adoption of knowledge management. Its interessement probably just involved a directive to this Ministry which then had no choice but to be enrolled. Whether the MOC was fully mobilised, however, is quite another matter.

2. **The Ministry of Commerce:** Having accepted the need to engage in a process of knowledge management as this was required by the Government, the MOC now had the task of convincing its own officers of the value of KM and KC. Its problematisation in this would most likely have been to stress the value of KC to the work of the Ministry and how, when implemented, it would make everyone's job easier and better. To convince its officers (interessement) of the value of making use of SECI techniques it could have done things like offering training and professional development activities or possibly some form of disincentive for not getting involved. It appears from the inter-

Figure 3. Major interactions in the MOC knowledge conversion process

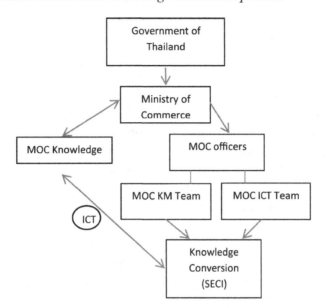

view data that most of the MOC officers were now enrolled, but it could be seen from the interviews that some were mobilised and keen on getting others involved, while others had enrolled reluctantly. As participant E remarked: "Making a trust, this is a very hard practice. People have to show significantly an own effort in job task for example, "if people do not wish to do KM activities, I will work and do not care them to show other people as a KM model and KM worker" This will be firstly shown but it has to depend on what people wish to do or do not wish to do..."

3. **MOC Officers:** The problematisation of Knowledge Management for the Ministry of Commerce Officers may well have depended whether they were in the KM Team or the ICT Team. Members of the KM team would probably have considered that KC was something that they should be involved in and so problematised it in this way, but they may have translated the ideas somewhat in the process. Member of the ICT Team, on the other hand, may have been more interested

in finding another use for ICT. They may have problematised KC as something that could be best implemented through the use of the technologies that they managed. Most members of these teams probably did not need much convincing that enrolment was worthwhile. There is little evidence from the interviews, however, that many were sufficiently mobilised to work on convincing others.

Something else about the MOC Officers that could be investigated further is Thai culture. In Thai culture, differences of opinion are not usually openly expressed during meetings (Charnkit, 2011). Normally, a Thai public Officer always respects those in higher positions such as the director of their department. Following the executive's policies is the principle in Thai society and when a policy has been launched by the executives, it is natural that all employees must follow. In the interviews, Participant I said:

Our organisation culture can be explained as a 'terrified to express an opinion' culture and it also included 'rarely sharing their knowledge' culture. Using a tool like Storytelling will help this organisation fix those problems.

This principle has remained in Thai culture and in Thai organisations: conflicts with those in authority never occur in Thai organisations (Charnkit, 2011). How would TAM handle this? Here is an interaction that lies beneath the surface and has little effect on PU or PEOU. It is, nevertheless, an interaction that would be important to investigate further in a study framed by ANT.

4.   **MOC Knowledge:** This non-human actor, if it had a voice, would probably have seen a big advantage in the value of knowledge conversion as it would potentially make knowledge more accessible. With a large amount of both tacit and explicit knowledge in the Ministry it could have problematised the value of converting this into appropriate forms and its interactions would have worked towards this end.

5.   **ICT:** The interactions also of this non-human actor would probably have been to welcome another important use for itself.

CONCLUSION

To a researcher used to an approach like that of Actor-Network Theory, the criteria used by the Technology Acceptance Model to determine the likelihood of adoption: Perceived Usefulness and Perceived Ease of Use, seem rather self-evident and do not offer much in the way of explanatory power – aren't they a bit obvious? What else do they offer? TAM makes use of a fairly mechanistic approach to checking whether various factors are likely to have increased a potential adopter's perceived usefulness of the innovation and whether they have increased their perception that it is easy to use. ANT makes no such prior assumptions and looks instead to find interactions and associations

between all the actors. It makes no assumptions on what these might be. It also looks seriously at the contributions of other entities like Government policy, SECI techniques and the necessary technology itself. Instead of looking only at a potential user's perceptions of the technology, Innovation Translation allows the possibility that this user might not want to use it in the way originally suggested: that they might want to 'translate' it into another form before adoption.

This re-interpretation of a TAM study of the use of knowledge conversion in the Ministry of Commerce in Thailand made use of actor-network theory and Innovation Translation in place of the original framework using the Technology Acceptance Model. Of course, if an ANT approach is to be used in any research project then ideally it would be used from the beginning of the study so that the data collection and interviews then reflected the sort of questions required to approach the problem from an ANT perspective. In this case it would have been good to find out what officers of the MOC thought about the Government's push to introduce knowledge management, whether they were convinced of the value of this or not. It would have been good to find out what senior management at the MOC thought about KM and whether they saw value in adopting it. There are many other questions that it would be good to ask if this were possible. This article has shown, nevertheless, that it is quite possible to do some re-conceptualisation and re-analysis of the data of a study originally framed by another innovation model and to make good use of an Innovation Translation approach.

REFERENCES

Ajzen, I., & Fishbein, M. (1980). *Understanding attitudes and predicting social behavior*. London, UK: Prentice Hall.

Al-Hajri, S., & Tatnall, A. (2011). A socio-technical study of the adoption of internet technology in banking, re-interpreted as an innovation using innovation translation. *International Journal of Actor-Network Theory and Technological Innovation, 3*(3).

Amin, A., & Thrift, N. (1994). *Globalization, institution, and regional development in Europe.* Oxford, UK: Oxford University Press.

Birchall, D. W., & Tovstiga, G. (1999). The strategic potential of a firm's knowledge portfolio. *Journal of General Management, 25,* 1–16.

Callon, M. (1986). The sociology of an actor-network: The case of the electric vehicle. In Callon, M., Law, J., & Rip, A. (Eds.), *Mapping the dynamics of science and technology* (pp. 19–34). London, UK: Macmillan.

Callon, M., Courtial, J. P., Turner, W. A., & Bauin, S. (1983). From translations to problematic networks: An introduction to co-word analysis. *Social Sciences Information. Information Sur les Sciences Sociales, 22*(2), 191–235. doi:10.1177/053901883022002003

Carlsson, S. A. (2003). Knowledge managing and knowledge management systems in inter-organizational networks. *Knowledge and Process Management, 10,* 199–264. doi:10.1002/kpm.179

Charnkit, P. (2011). *Using the technology acceptance model to investigate knowledge conversion in Thai public organisations: Management and information systems.* Melbourne, Australia: Victoria University.

Civi, E. (2000). Knowledge management as a competitive asset: A review. *Marketing Intelligence & Planning, 18,* 166–174. doi:10.1108/02634500010333280

Davenport, T., & Prusak, T. (1998). *Working knowledge: How organizations manage what they know.* Cambridge, MA: Harvard Business School Press.

Davis, F. (1986). *A technology acceptance model for empirically testing new end-user information systems: Theory and results.* Cambridge, MA: MIT Press.

Davis, F. (1989). Perceived usefulness, perceived ease of use, and user acceptance of information technology. *Management Information Systems Quarterly, 13*(3), 318–340. doi:10.2307/249008

Davis, F., Bagozzi, R., & Warshaw, P. (1989). User acceptance of computer technology: A comparison of two theoretical models. *Management Science, 35*(8), 982–1003. doi:10.1287/mnsc.35.8.982

De Grooijer, J. (2000). Designing a knowledge management performance framework. *Journal of Knowledge and Information Management, 4,* 303–310.

Fernandez, I. B., Gonzalez, A., & Sabherwal, R. (2004). *Knowledge management: Challenges, solutions and technologies.* Upper Saddle River, NJ: Pearson/Prentice Hall.

Grint, K., & Woolgar, S. (1997). *The machine at work - Technology, work and organisation.* Cambridge, UK: Polity Press.

Hamel, G. (1991). Competition for competence and interpartner learning within international strategic alliances. *Strategic Management Journal, 1991,* 83–102. doi:10.1002/smj.4250120908

Jane, M. (2005). How to share knowledge between companies. *Knowledge Management Review, 8*(16).

Kripanont, N. (2007). *Examining a technology acceptance model of internet usage by academics within Thai business schools*. Melbourne, Australia: Victoria University.

Kripanont, N., & Tatnall, A. (2011). Modelling the adoption and use of internet technologies in higher education in Thailand. In Tatnall, A. (Ed.), *Actor-network theory and technology innovation: advancements and new concepts* (pp. 95–112). Hershey, PA: IGI Global.

Krogh, G. V., Kleine, D., & Roos, J. (1998). *Knowing in firms: Understanding, managing and measuring knowledge*. London, UK: Sage.

Latour, B. (1986). The powers of association: Power, action and belief. A new sociology of knowledge? *Sociological Review. Mongraph, 32,* 264–280.

Latour, B. (1996). *Aramis or the love of technology*. Cambridge, MA: Harvard University Press.

Law, J. (1987). Technology and heterogeneous engineering: The case of Portuguese expansion. In Bijker, W. E., Hughes, T. P., & Pinch, T. J. (Eds.), *The social construction of technological systems: New directions in the sociology and history of technology* (pp. 111–134). Cambridge, MA: MIT Press.

Lipnack, J., & Stamps, J. (2000). *Virtual teams: People working across boundaries with technology*. New York, NY: John Wiley & Sons.

McMaster, T., Vidgen, R. T., & Wastell, D. G. (1997). Towards an understanding of technology in transition: Two conflicting theories. In *Proceedings of the IRIS20 Conference on Information Systems Research in Scandinavia*, Hanko, Norway.

Nonaka, I. (1994). A dynamic theory of organisational knowledge creation. *Organization Science, 5,* 14–37. doi:10.1287/orsc.5.1.14

Nonaka, I., & Takeuchi, H. (1995). *The knowledge creating company*. New York, NY: Oxford University Press.

OPDC. (2004). *Annual report*. Bangkok, Thailand: Office of the Public Sector Development Commission.

Polanyi, M. (1958). *Personal knowledge: Towards a post-critical philosophy*. London, UK: Routledge & Kegan Paul.

Rogers, E. M. (1995). *Diffusion of innovations*. New York, NY: Free Press.

Rogers, E. M. (2003). *Diffusion of innovations*. New York, NY: Free Press.

Rogers, E. M., Daley, H., & Wu, T. (1980). *The diffusion of personal computers*. Stanford, CA: Stanford University, Institute for Communication Research.

Singleton, V., & Michael, M. (1993). Actor-networks and ambivalence: General practitioners in the UK cervical screening programme. *Social Studies of Science, 23*(2), 227–264. doi:10.1177/030631293023002001

Tatnall, A. (2009). Innovation translation and innovation diffusion: A comparison of two different approaches to theorising technological innovation. *International Journal of Actor-Network Theory and Technological Innovation, 1*(2), 67–74. doi:10.4018/jantti.2009040105

THAILAWS. (2003). *Royal decree on criteria and procedures for good governance: B.E. 2546*. Retrieved from http://www.opdc.go.th/english/main/content_view.php?cat_id=3

Wikipedia. (2011). *Knowledge management*. Retrieved from http://en.wikipedia.org/wiki/Knowledge_management

This work was previously published in the International Journal of Actor-Network Theory and Technological Innovation, Volume 3, Issue 4, edited by Arthur Tatnall, pp. 32-45, copyright 2011 by IGI Publishing (an imprint of IGI Global).

Chapter 9
Applying Hermeneutic Phenomenology to Understand Innovation Adoption

Stasys Lukaitis
RMIT University, Australia

ABSTRACT

In this paper, the author examines phenomenology and hermeneutics as research traditions and proposes a philosophical basis for their use. The author develops an iterative research process model that meets the needs of socio-technical research into technical innovation. This rigorous hybrid methodology is called hermeneutic phenomenology and is shown to be an excellent approach to dealing with the search for understanding.

INTRODUCTION

Socio-technical approaches to understanding innovation adoption at core rely upon finding meaning from data that must be interpreted. In this paper a theoretical discussion will seek to uncover the philosophical issues of the search for meaning using critical hermeneutics within a phenomenological framework. The discussion will suggest a way of framing research so that a level of trust can be associated with research outcomes.

CONSTRUCTIONISM AND INTERPRETIVISM

Crotty defines constructionism as "all knowledge, and therefore all meaningful reality as such, is contingent upon human practices, being constructed in and out of interaction between human beings and their world, and developed and transmitted within an essentially social context" (Crotty, 1998, p. 42).

Motivation for research is often to construct new understandings associated with a phenomenon rather than confirming and testing existing conceptualisations and theories. Research of this nature is appropriately constructionist.

DOI: 10.4018/978-1-4666-2166-4.ch009

The concept of "researcher-as-bricoleur" (Lévi-Strauss, 1966; Denzin & Lincoln, 1994) describes eloquently the process of constructing meaning from disparate heterogeneous collected objects that will "contribute to the definition of a set which has yet to materialize". Thus the construction of meaning will come from the interpretation of the research data which has already been socially constructed.

Understanding and interpretation then become the goals of this constructionist approach to the data suggesting a theoretical perspective of interpretivism. The understanding and interpretation go hand-in-hand as one feeds the other. As understanding develops then one can begin to interpret and examine potential relationships between the components of the data. As one's interpretation of the material develops then so does a better understanding of the problem at hand.

The research question is interested in understanding people's actions in their socio-organisational context. Understanding will involve interpreting reality (interpretations) as it appears to people (constructions) in their workplace.

PHENOMENOLOGY AS A RESEARCH TRADITION

Engagement with the individuals who are closest to the innovation under investigation requires the asking of questions, participation in discussions and most importantly, capturing, ordering and interpreting their views and opinions.

And thus a phenomenological philosophical approach to the interpretive theoretical approach is suggested. "Phenomenology invites us to set aside all previous habits of thought, see through and break down the mental barriers which these habits have set along the horizons of our thinking... to learn to see what stands before our eyes" (Husserl, 1931, p. 43). This suggests we must critique what we find, not to challenge the phenomena themselves, but our interpretations and understandings and to seek reinterpretation as a new meaning or a fuller meaning or even a renewed meaning (Crotty, 1998).

The research question seeks understanding of the innovation being an aspect of the interactions between individuals and groups in an organisational setting. The development of this understanding will flow from discussions and interviews conducted with individuals who are experts in the innovation and problem domain. Understanding is something that develops as more and more information is contributed to a problem domain. The development of understanding is a complex process that deals with acquiring new pieces of knowledge pertinent to the issue under investigation, examining these pieces, reconciling them against the newly developing understanding and adjusting one's broader view, or horizon, to maintain consistency between the individual fragments of knowledge and the developing horizon.

The lived experiences and opinions of senior executive practitioners people are difficult to probe with surveys and questionnaires as experiences and opinions can often yield surprising and unexpected outcomes that might lead the research and discussions into hitherto unexpected areas (Walsham, 2006). It is the rich and sometimes unexpected data that we search for – lived experiences and professional opinions.

Phenomenology describes the situation where the researcher encounters a "phenomenon" and then experiences it, reflects upon it, then forms an interpretation of it (Husserl, 1931). Husserl insists that one should seek reinterpretation and perhaps a renewal of meaning of the phenomenon.

Phenomenology demands of the researcher a clear mind that allows a newer, fuller and a renewed meaning being constructed, the development of a deeper understanding requires an additional philosophical approach that builds meaning from repeated encounters with phenomena (Spiegelberg, 1982).

The potential danger of naively engaging with people in a specialist real world is that there may be a tacit lacework of presuppositions, biases, prejudices and a meaning system already in place that will colour one's understanding of what is said, or worse still – simply be not understood.

To start to overcome this problem it is necessary to accept its existence then to engage with it in a "recursive process of ontological disclosure" (Introna, 2008) effectively peeling back layers of understanding. This is not to suggest that phenomenology with its insistence on naivety is inappropriate, but rather to temper and perhaps regard this naivety as state of mind that identifies and is able to deal with pre-existing knowledge, biases, prejudices and so on in such a manner that they are "set aside" and not allowed to colour what is emerging in front of our eyes (Creswell, 1997).

Spiegelberg (1982, p. 680) described phenomenology as "a determined effort to undo the effect of habitual patterns of thought and to return to the pristine innocence of first seeing".

Much contemporary research tends to follow safe conventional studies and tries to conform to majority sanctioned approaches (Introna & Whittaker, 2004). A worthwhile study should challenge existing orthodoxies and seek understanding with a clear mind (Gregor et al., 2007).

HERMENEUTICS AS A RESEARCH TRADITION

In studying innovation it is important to acknowledge that the investigator already has some knowledge and understanding of the studied domain. This pre-understanding will allow meaningful communications with the study participants. However, with each subsequent encounter with the study participants and with domain artefacts, the investigator's views and understanding of the studied phenomena will necessarily be altered leading to the construction of a larger meaning.

This process of cyclical growth in knowledge and understanding is a key principle of hermeneutics.

The Oxford dictionary defines hermeneutics as "of interpretation", taken from the original Greek hermeneutikos (Turner, 1987). Hermeneutics as a philosophy of enquiry has been well documented with its roots already evident in the late antiquity where "the Greeks, the Jews and the Christians had been reading and re-reading their vital texts, namely the Homeric epics, the Torah, Talmud and Midrashim, and the Holy Bible, respectively. In the process of their textual labour, these people devised their own idiosyncratic sets of rules for doing interpretation" (Demeterio, 2001).

Demeterio (2001) gives a useful definition of hermeneutics as "a theory, methodology and praxis of interpretation that is geared towards the recapturing of meaning of a text, or a text-analogue, that is temporally or culturally distant, or obscured by ideology and false consciousness".

Thus, the understanding that is sought is found within texts and text-analogues – records that have been created by authors (Klein & Myers, 1999). These records might be as prosaic as a report, or as interesting as a series of captured electronic mails (Lee, 1994), or even as a set of transcripts of interviews and case study notes (Applegate et al., 1999; Montealegre & Keil, 2000). In any event, these documents purport to represent or record some sort of reality or truth.

Often in our studies of innovation the research data and text under investigation will be interview and focus group transcripts, derivative documents such as tables and diagrams and extensive margin and field notes collected over the course of the research. In Information Technology there exist many text analogues that are well understood and which are commonly used in research to convey meaning to a typical IT audience. These text analogues form the basic data of analysis.

According to Crotty (1998, p. 91) hermeneutic theory suggests the prospect of gaining an understanding from the texts under investigation that is "deeper or goes further than the original author's own understanding or intention... (skilled) interpreters may end up with an explicit awareness of meanings, and especially assumptions, that the authors themselves would have been unable to articulate".

This is an especially important aspect of hermeneutic theory – that the final emergent understanding can be greater than the individual contributions (Myers, 1994).

This search for understanding is influenced by several factors that rely on some assumptions that may or may not be all present and at work at any given time. Understanding can be viewed as an ongoing interpretive oscillation between several layers or perspectives. This is often referred to as the "hermeneutic circle or cycle", where one examines a small fragment of knowledge and seeks to understand it, then looks at the "whole" (whatever that means to the enquirer), and seeks understanding there as well – the smaller fragment being part of the whole, and the whole being composed of many smaller fragments. Understanding, then, is achieved when there is a consistency between the whole and all its component parts and vice versa. Or, as stated by Myers (1994, p. 191): "This hermeneutic process continues until the apparent absurdities, contradictions and oppositions in the organization no longer appear strange, but make sense".

Gadamer then says that if the new fact causes your growing horizon of understanding to change then you need to go back and review all your previous beliefs and understanding in the light of the new data (Gadamer, 2004). In other words, each of the previous individual fragments of data is re-reconciled back into your new horizon of understanding.

How does one know that understanding has been achieved? The repeated cycling between the parts and the whole will eventually yield consistency that is driven by the sum of knowledge or data in front of the researcher. Should that knowledge be incomplete, the researcher would

actually have no way of knowing that fact. The only really useful test would be to introduce yet more data or facts and test by hermeneutically cycling through again. If the number of resulting cycles are sufficiently small (or even none), then one could say that there is understanding.

But understanding and the processes of its acquisition must be something more than just the end product of a process. Kidder (1997, p. 1196) cites Hans-Georg Gadamer on understanding:

If I am an English language speaker learning German, for example, I will very likely pursue a course of study in which I learn a linguistic apparatus that is neither spoken English nor spoken German. I will learn patterns of verb endings, noun cases, systems of adjective and noun agreement, and such – categories I may never have applied to language before, although I had been speaking language all my life. This apparatus is a third thing, a bridge to understanding a language that is not the same as understanding that language. When the understanding actually occurs, I recognize it because suddenly the apparatus falls away and I simply speak German. So it is with hermeneutic: the interpretive process creates something that is neither my horizon nor the others. This third thing is a necessary medium; but it is just as necessary that this medium fall away. At this point in transcending the apparatus we can say that understanding occurs. There is still, however, the quality of a kind of third horizon here; one has not dissolved into the other culture; one has not erased one's own horizon; but one's horizon has become entwined with another in a unique instance of fusion. (Kidder 1997, p. 1196)

So it can be reasonable to assume then that understanding can be helped by applying an apparatus (or tool) repeatedly over some data until the apparatus or tool becomes superfluous – that is to say, some understanding has been reached – because the apparatus is no longer needed. Using the Gadamerian analogy, successfully engaging in a conversation with a German would validate one's understanding of the newly learnt language – i.e., testing the understanding with new untried data. If the conversation is unsuccessful, by whatever criteria, then the apparatus is reapplied, learning restarted, and then another test of the understanding employed. This is the hermeneutic circle in its simplest form. The act of understanding flows from understanding the whole to understanding all the little bits that make up the whole. Then when confronted by a new "little bit" that purports to be part of the whole under consideration, if understanding has been achieved, then a consistency between the new knowledge and the context of the existing whole will be maintained without any conflict (Myers 1994).

The apparatus that is so critical to achieving/acquiring understanding in Gadamer's case is specially designed to create a bridge between little understanding and the final goal of complete understanding. The apparatus itself is specific to the task at hand. In the use of critical hermeneutics[1] in the interpretation of texts (and text analogues), Harvey and Myers (1995, p. 20) quote Paul Ricoeur:

In critical hermeneutics the interpreter constructs the context as another form of text, which can then, of itself, be critically analysed so that the meaning construction can be understood as an interpretive act. In this way, the hermeneutic interpreter is simply creating another text on a text, and this recursive creation is potentially infinite. Every meaning is constructed, even through the very constructive act of seeking to deconstruct, and the process whereby that textual interpretation occurs must be self critically reflected upon. (Ricoeur, 1974)

Research should create, analyse and seek to understand these additional texts on the original sources of understanding derived from interviews, focus groups and field notes under investigation. Hermeneutic research demands self-reflexivity, an

ongoing conversation about the experience while simultaneously living in the moment, actively constructing interpretations of the experience and questioning how those interpretations came about (Hertz, 1997).

There are already additional issues to consider. There is a substantial cultural difference between an English-speaking Californian (say) and an English-speaking Berliner. What if we are engaging with text rather than a person? What if the text was written 200 hundred years ago about things that were important at the time, but have become obscure in the twenty first century? (Lukaitis & Cybulski, 2004)

This "distance" between the hermeneutist (the enquirer) and the author (and text) under investigation is referred to as "historicality".

Critical hermeneutics[1] does emphasize the fact that social reality is historically constituted. And one of the key differences between a purely interpretative approach and critical hermeneutics is that the researcher does not merely accept the self-understanding of participants, but seeks to critically evaluate the totality of understandings in a given situation.22 The researcher analyses the participants' own understandings historically, and in terms of changing social structures. The Hermeneutic-dialectic perspective, therefore, as an integrative approach, emphasizes both the subjective meanings for individual actors and the social structures which condition and enable such meanings and are constituted by them. (Myers, 1994, p. 189)

This concept of historicality has also been called "contextualization" where Klein and Myers (1999, p. 73) refer to Gadamer's (1976, p. 133) observation: "… the hermeneutic task consists, not in covering up the tension between the text and present, but in consciously bringing it out".

The distance (historicality) of the investigators from the source text can be manifold. It might be combinations of time, language, culture, intention and social milieu. It is the investigator's responsibility to acknowledge that they have a historicality factor to account for and that the research data or text under investigation may well be a puzzle of many dimensions, even if the investigator doesn't realise it yet. In addition to the historicality issues, there are burdens already surrounding the investigator – their prejudices that will colour their own interpretations. These prejudices are actually "pre-judgments", expectations of understanding. Butler (1998, p. 288) extends the notion of prejudice by including a reference to Heidegger's (1976) notion of "tradition" and suggesting that prejudice is actually a combination of lived experiences, tradition and a sort of socialized comfort zone he refers to as "das Man". Butler (1998, p288) acknowledges the powerful influence exerted on individuals:

According to Gadamer (1976), Tradition influences a social actor's attitudes and behaviour through authority, and such authority is transmitted through time and history via cultural mechanisms. Heidegger (1976) argues that it is the quiet authority of das Man (roughly translated as "the they" or "the anyone") which provides reassurance in the face of existential turbulence. The state of being 'situated' or 'tuned' under the sway of das Man, (e.g., as operationalised through public opinion or group or social norms), provides one with familiar and comfortable surroundings; self-reflection precipitated by existential turbulence (a 'breakdown') shatters this tranquillity and brings about an 'unhomeliness' (Unheimlichkeit) of existence. (Butler, 1998, p. 288)

Gadamer suggested that prejudices are a natural attribute of individuals and should be accepted and dealt with appropriately (Gadamer, 2004). An interesting dilemma then arises when one accepts that an investigator must confront and deal with these issues. What then of the co-researchers' and their own prejudices and biases? How will truth and genuine understanding emerge when all the parties to the dialectic are prejudiced? Gadamer's acceptance of peoples' prejudices as "natural" did not strike a sympathetic chord with Wolin (2000, p. 45) although the basis for his vitriol was not the philosophical aspect, but rather the suggestion that aspects of human nature are somehow "natural" and need to be accepted.

Kidder (1997, p. 1194) on the other hand takes up the issue of the investigator's prejudice as being a useful starting point for the enquiry. He quotes from Augustine that one should "identify the clear and obvious meanings first and then use this understanding to make sense of the more obscure and confusing passages" (Augustine 427). Kidder (1997) goes on to state that "what is clear and obvious to one in reading a text is likely to be a function of one's own cultural orientation and one's own prejudices rather than the function of some given accessibility of the text". He goes on to say:

So where does one begin? If one cannot begin with the obvious, are we to somehow begin with the obscure? The answer is that either option is more or less viable, but the crucial thing is that one avoids allowing the starting point to control the enquiry. False assumptions can be excellent roads to genuine understanding, but only if one is open, in the course of interpreting, to the clues that reveal the inadequacy of those assumptions and point the way to needed revisions. Thus hermeneutic properly manifests a circular or cyclic pattern in its unfolding: the progress of the enquiry returns one to the beginning, and the new beginning sets a new course of progress; the interpretation of parts yields a conception of the whole, but that conception brings new meaning to the parts, whose reinterpretation may again require re-conception of the whole, and so on, in a circle that would be merely vicious were it not propelled by concrete and cumulative acts of genuine understanding (Schleiermacher, 1819; Dilthey, 1990). (Kidder, 1997, pp. 1194-1195)

Laverty (2003) reminds us that an integral part of the hermeneutic circle is the entry point or the beginning as mentioned by Kidder above. This entry point is the baggage that the enquirer carries with them, their prejudices and biases and historicality. This baggage is an integral part of the hermeneutic circle. Critical hermeneutics is often called the hermeneutic-dialectic. There is the dictionary definition of "diale'ctic": the art of investigating the truth of opinions, testing of truth by discussion, logical disputation (Turner, 1987). The accepted usage of this term is taken from the original Socratic dialogues. Kidder's (1997) explanation of dialectic is eloquent:

In an ideal Socratic dialogue, no one is in it to win the debate, but everyone is engaged together in the search for the very best arguments in support of whatever opinion is being considered, along with the very best objections that can be set against those arguments. If in the context of a Socratic dialectic, I propose an argument to which no one can respond with a substantial objection, it may fall to me to become the objector (and Socrates is often put into this situation, particularly with his younger interlocutors). If I discover that my objection is more reasonable than my argument then I do a virtuous thing, from the point of view of the dialectic, if I immediately abandon my original opinion and seek a new one. This sort of reasoning process, then, has everything to do with persuasion, but it is not one person persuading another to hold a particular opinion; it is rather a matter of putting persuasion into a larger context of enquiry and discovery, allowing the power of argument to sway oneself along with the others, and in a way that is open and deeply attuned to the reasoning on all sides of an issue. (Kidder, 1997, p. 1197)

A pilot study using the critical hermeneutic philosophy of enquiry has been brought to bear on the selected case study of the Denver International Airport (DIA) Baggage Handling System (Applegate et al., 1999) to develop a better understanding of the event itself through the supporting documents under investigation and also the actual process of a critical hermeneutical enquiry. The case study is commonly used in Information Systems departments to teach issues related to project management, risk assessment, information systems strategy, etc. The case is so well known that numerous prejudices and preconceptions about the DIA project have been firmly established in the Information Systems community. By re-analysing the case using critical hermeneutics, we have been able to reveal the new horizons of understanding in the roots of the DIA project failure (Lukaitis & Cybulski, 2004).

It seems that innovation can be profitably studied through a hermeneutic phenomenological perspective. The phenomenological aspect suggests approaching the data with a clear mind and seeking to renew or even rebuild understanding from behind a veil of habitual thought, while hermeneutics gives us the tools to engage with the data conscious of these thoughts and our prejudices and to repeatedly plough the data whilst building the developing horizon of understanding.

PHENOMENOLOGY AS A RESEARCH METHOD

The methodological approach as defined by van Kaam (1959, 1966) and modified by Moustakas (1994) is appropriate to the innovation research questions. The rigour of this methodology allows the whole process to be transparently viewed and engaged. The steps from capturing the experiences naively, reconstructing the meaning and deriving the essences can be readily followed. The specific process (from van Kaam & Moustakas) outlined in a pure phenomenological study are:

- Epoche
- Listing and Preliminary Grouping
- Reduction and Elimination
- Clustering of Invariant Constituents into Themes
- Imaginative Variation
- Synthesis and Essences

These processes address the steps in a formalistic and fairly rigorous way so that other researchers might tread the same paths. Perhaps more importantly is the fact that the interpretations become obvious from the data and the resulting synthesis and essences are transparent.

Figure 1 illustrates the chosen phenomenological process research model, derived by Moustakas (1994) from the work of van Kaam (1959, 1966). Table 1 details the individual stages of this process.

HERMENEUTIC PHENOMENOLOGY METHOD

The method suggested here adopts the hermeneutic phenomenological approach that combines the rigour of phenomenology with the cyclical enquiry and development of understanding that is the hallmark of the philosophy of enquiry of hermeneutics.

Modern researchers have successfully utilised these techniques in the field of Information Systems and Technology to reveal hidden or suppressed knowledge and understanding (Boland et al., 1994; Rennie, 2000; Olson & Carlisle, 2001; Lukaitis & Cybulski, 2004).

Koch observed that "...Hermeneutics invites participants into an ongoing conversation, but does not provide a set methodology. Understanding occurs through a fusion of horizons, which is a dialectic between the preunderstandings of the research process, the interpretive framework and the sources of information (1995, p. 835)".

This is consistent with hermeneutics being a philosophy of enquiry as opposed to a specific method. Elements of methodology emerge as

"bridges" or an "apparatus" (Gadamer, 2004) are designed to aid in the process of understanding. In particular, the (bridge/apparatus) approach suggested by Ricoeur (1974, 1981) whereby documents and texts are examined and analysed and derivative texts developed from these analysis, and themselves further analysed and further elaborated into additional texts has been found to be a particularly powerful application of this hermeneutic philosophy (Lukaitis & Cybulski, 2004), and is consistent with the development of derivative documents from the phenomenological process model in Figure 1.

The phenomenological process of Epoche emphasises the prejudices and biases as they existed before the encounters with the co-researchers, then followed by a reflection on how these biases and prejudices have been identified, managed, and then become a part of the fusion of horizons of understanding. I acknowledge that the creation of a clear and naive mind is difficult, however, the articulation of my biases will help in the reception of peoples' lived experiences.

The phenomenological process model as suggested by Moustakas from Van Kaam (1959) operates on data from one or more encounters as a whole, creating a composite description of the meanings and essences of the experience of the group as a whole. The proposed chosen methodology includes the hermeneutic feedback loop acknowledging the growing awareness of understanding as time passes and knowledge growing from successive interviews and reflection and engagement with the data. Implicit in this process model is the recognition of Ricoeur's four collection protocols:

- Fixation on meaning;
- Dissociation at some point from the mental intention of the subject (author);
- The necessity to interpret the protocols (text/transcripts25) as a whole, a gestalt of interconnected meanings;

Figure 1. The phenomenological research model

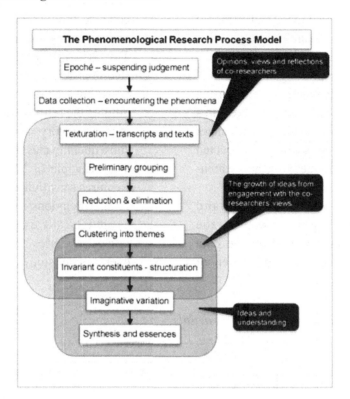

• Their universal range of address, i.e., their potentiality for multiple interpretations. (Titleman, 1979) from Ricoeur.

The suggested research model shown in Figure 2 illustrates the detail of the phenomenological process of the modified van Kaam approach with each successive gathering of data (the rounded rectangles) represented as a discreet hermeneutic cycle. Three such cycles are shown although many more may be performed according to the amount of data collected and the "completeness" of understanding developed. The processes of imaginative variation and synthesis and essences are taken out to show how their outputs are the developing horizons of understanding – the results of smaller pieces of knowledge being constantly reconciled with "the whole". Notice also that this reconciliation allows to completely retrace one's steps back to the first hermeneutic cycle if the developing horizon needs to account for earlier knowledge.

GUIDING PRINCIPLES AND SUCCESS CRITERIA

Klein and Myers' Guiding Principles

Klein and Myers developed a set of guidelines for conducting and evaluating interpretive research in response to Lee et al.'s (1995) call for a discussion on the criteria for judging qualitative and interpretive research (Klein & Myers, 1999).

Their principles are derived primarily from anthropology, hermeneutics and phenomenology and the following outlines their summary of principles:

1. The Fundamental Principle of the Hermeneutic Circle. This principle suggests that all human understanding is achieved by iterating between considering the interdependent meaning of parts and the whole that they form.

2. The Principle of Contextualisation requires critical reflection of the social and historical background of the research setting, so that the intended audience can see how the current situation under investigation emerged.

3. The Principle of Interaction Between the Researchers and the Subjects. This requires critical reflection of how the research materials (or "data") were socially constructed through the interaction between the researchers and the participants.

4. The Principle of Abstraction and Generalisation. Requires relating the idiographic details revealed by the data interpretation through the application of principles one and two to theoretical, general concepts that describe the nature of human understanding and social action.

5. The Principle of Dialogical Reasoning. Requires sensitivity to possible contradictions between the theoretical preconceptions guiding the research design and actual findings ("the story which the data tell") with subsequent cycles of revision.

6. The Principle of Multiple Interpretations. Requires sensitivity to possible differences in interpretations amongst the participants as are typically expressed in multiple narratives of stories of the same sequence of events under study.

Table 1. Phenomenological research process details

Stage	Process	Outcome
Epoché	Declaration and articulation of biases and prejudices. Reflection upon one's position or stance.	A mind free of judgement, receptive to the observed phenomena, capable of fresh and even a naïve view of the world. Receptiveness and criticality of one's own thoughts and interpretations
Texturation – Textural Representation	Capturing the phenomena in text form from interview transcripts, personal observations, sidebar notes and memos. Collection of other pertinent documents.	Raw text in a form suitable for analysis and further manipulation (e.g., word processor format).
Preliminary Grouping	Analysis and grouping of text of text into statements about "something" or an individual aspect of the phenomenon under investigation. Each statement is treated equally (horizonalisation).	A derivative document of individual statements accompanied by a suitable identifier (code) of the nature or aspect of the phenomenon under investigation.
Reduction and Elimination	For each statement test that it contains a moment of the experience and contributes to the understanding; is it possible to extract and label it as a horizon of the experience? Eliminate vague, repetitive or overlapping terms.	A derivative document of statements that are exemplars of the experience described and so labeled. These are the invariant constituents of the experience.
Clustering into Themes	Cluster the invariant constituents of the experience that are related into a thematic label.	This derivative document will hold the core themes of the experience with their component parts.
Invariant Constituents – Textural-Structural Representation	Check the invariant constituents and their accompanying theme against the complete record of the texturation and check that they are explicitly referenced. If they are not they should be deleted.	This derivative document will hold the final invariant constituents, their themes and groupings.
Imaginative Variation	The resulting themes, experiences and component parts are reflected upon. Vary the possible meanings and the possible perspectives of the phenomenon from different vantage points. Explore causality and precedence.	Various outcomes including suggestive diagrams, explanatory statements, reflections on paradoxes and conundrums and dialectical analysis.
Synthesis and Essences	From the results of the imaginative variation develop a composite description of the meanings and essences of the experiences representing the group as a whole.	Essence statement.

7. The Principle of Suspicion. Requires sensitivity to possible "biases" and "systematic distortions" in the narratives collected from participants (Klein & Myers, 1999).

MOUSTAKAS GUIDING PRINCIPLES

Polkinghorne asks "Does the general structural description provide an accurate portrait of the common features and structural connections that are manifest in the examples collected?" (1989, p. 57). The final essence statement attests to this question. Moustakas (1994) then goes on to identify 5 questions that might be usefully asked:

1. Did the interviewer influence the content of the subjects' descriptions in such a way that the descriptions do not truly reflect the subjects' actual experience?

2. Is the transcription accurate, and does it convey the meaning of the oral presentation in the interview?

3. In the analysis of the transcriptions, were there conclusions other than those offered by the researcher that could have been derived? Has the researcher identified these alternatives?

4. Is it possible to go from the general structural description to the transcriptions and to account for the specific contents and

Figure 2. Hermeneutic phenomenological research process model

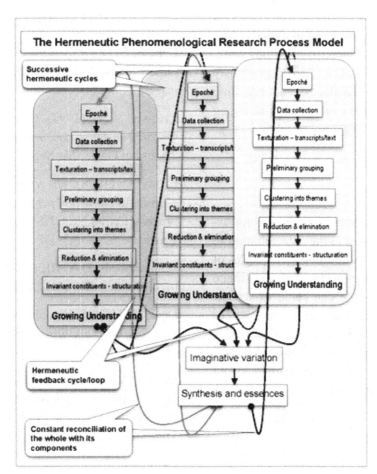

connections in the original examples of the experience?

5. Is the structural description situation specific, or does it hold in general for the experience in other situations? (Moustakas, 1994)

These principles indeed guide the research process and are evident at all the various stages of the process. An additional evaluation measure could be to adopt a process from the school of grounded theory (Fernandez, 2004) that "enfolded" the literature into the findings. In this situation it is a guiding principle that the extant literature will need to be hermeneutically reconciled with the developed findings and horizons of understanding.

It is worth remembering that hermeneutics itself triangulates and constantly evaluates its findings throughout the research process by the reflective fusion of horizons of understanding. Separate evaluations of the research outcomes (as opposed to the processes) is not practised in hermeneutic research in contrast to case study work, as an example. Nevertheless, Caputo cautiously advises that "coming to a place of understanding and meaning is tentative and always changing in the hermeneutic endeavour" (Caputo, 1987).

CONCLUSION

This discussion has centred on the essential issues of finding meaning in the data common to innovation research. By combining the cycles of hermeneutic analysis of text and text analogue with phenomenology we can come to a composite description of the meanings and essences of the experience of the group as a whole. This approach to Innovation research provides a research framework with robust philosophical and methodological underpinnings.

REFERENCES

Applegate, L. M., Montealegre, R., Nelson, H. J., & Knoop, C.-I. (1999). BAE automated systems (A): Denver International Airport baggage-handling system. In Applegate, L. M., McFarlan, F. W., & McKenny, J. L. (Eds.), *Corporate information systems management: Text and cases* (pp. 546–561). New York, NY: McGraw-Hill.

Augustine. (427). *On Christian doctrine.* Indianapolis, IN: Bobbs-Merrill.

Boland, R. J., Tenkasi, R. V., & Te'eni, D. (1994). Designing information technology to support distributed cognition. *Organization Science, 5*(3), 456–475. doi:10.1287/orsc.5.3.456

Butler, T. (1998). Towards a hermeneutic method for interpretive research in information systems. *Journal of Information Technology, 13*(4), 285–300. doi:10.1057/jit.1998.7

Caputo, J. D. (1987). *Radical hermeneutics: Repetition, deconstruction and the hermeneutic project.* Bloomington, IN: Indiana University Press.

Creswell, J. W. (1997). *Qualitative inquiry and research design: Choosing among five traditions.* Thousand Oaks, CA: Sage.

Crotty, M. (1998). *The foundations of social research: Meaning and perspective in the research process.* Crows Nest, NSW, Australia: Allen and Unwin.

Demeterio, F. P. A. III. (2001). Introduction to hermeneutics. *Diwatao, 1*(1), 1–9.

Denzin, N. K., & Lincoln, Y. S. (Eds.). (1994). *Handbook of qualitative research.* Thousand Oaks, CA: Sage.

Dilthey, W. (1990). The rise of hermeneutics. In Ormiston, G. L., & Schrift, A. D. (Eds.), *The hermeneutic tradition: From Ast to Ricoeur.* New York, NY: State University of New York Press.

Fernandez, W. D. (2004). The grounded theory method and case study data in IS research: Issues and design. In Hart, D., & Gregor, S. (Eds.), *Information systems foundations: Constructing and criticising*. Canberra, Australia: ANU E Press.

Gadamer, H.-G. (Ed.). (1976). *The historicity of understanding critical sociology, selected readings*. Harmondsworth, UK: Penguin Books.

Gadamer, H.-G. (2004). *Truth and method*. London, UK: Continuum.

Gregor, S., Bunker, D., Cecez-Kecmanovic, D., Metcalfe, M., & Underwood, J. (2007). Australian eclecticism and theorizing in information systems research. *Scandinavian Journal of Information Systems, 19*(1), 11–38.

Harvey, L. J., & Myers, M. D. (1995). Scholarship and practice. The contribution of ethnographic research methods to bridging the gap. *Information Technology & People, 8*(3), 13–27. doi:10.1108/09593849510098244

Heidegger, M. (1976). *Being and time*. New York, NY: Harper and Row.

Hertz, R. (1997). *Reflexivity and voice*. Thousand Oaks, CA: Sage.

Husserl, E. (1931). *Ideas: General introduction to pure phenomenology*. London, UK: George Allen & Unwin.

Introna, L. D. (2008). Understanding phenomenology: The use of phenomenology in the social study of technology. In Introna, L. D., Ilharco, F., & Faÿ, E. (Eds.), *Phenomenology, organisation and technology* (pp. 43–60). Lisbon, Portugal: Universidade Católica Editora.

Introna, L. D., & Whittaker, L. (2004). Truth, journals, and politics: The case of the MIS Quarterly. In Kaplan, B., Truex, D., Wastell, D., Wood-Harper, A., & DeGross, J. (Eds.), *Information systems research* (*Vol. 143*, pp. 103–120). New York, NY: Springer. doi:10.1007/1-4020-8095-6_7

Kidder, P. (1997). The hermeneutic and dialectic of community in development. *International Journal of Social Economics, 24*(11), 1191–1202. doi:10.1108/03068299710193561

Klein, H. K., & Myers, M. D. (1999). A set of principles for conducting and evaluating interpretive field studies in information systems. *Management Information Systems Quarterly, 23*(1), 67–94. doi:10.2307/249410

Koch, T. (1995). Interpretive approaches in nursing research: The influence of Husserl and Heidegger. *Journal of Advanced Nursing, 21*, 827–836. doi:10.1046/j.1365-2648.1995.21050827.x

Laverty, S. M. (2003). Hermeneutic phenomenology and phenomenology: A comparison of historical and methodological considerations. *International Journal of Qualitative Methods, 2*(3).

Lee, A. S. (1994). Electronic mail as a medium for rich communication: An empirical investigation using hermeneutic interpretation. *Management Information Systems Quarterly*, 143–157. doi:10.2307/249762

Lee, A. S., Baskerville, R. L., Liebenau, J., & Myers, M. D. (1995). Judging qualitative research in information systems. In *Proceedings of the Sixteenth International Conference on Information Systems*, Amsterdam, The Netherlands.

Lévi-Strauss, C. (1966). *The savage mind*. Chicago, IL: University of Chicago Press.

Lukaitis, S. A., & Cybulski, J. (2004). A hermeneutic analysis of the Denver International Airport baggage handling system. In Hart, D., & Gregor, S. (Eds.), *Information systems foundations: Constructing and criticising*. Canberra, Australia: ANU E Press.

Montealegre, R., & Keil, M. (2000). De-escalating information technology projects: Lessons from the Denver International Airport. *Management Information Systems Quarterly, 24*(3), 417–447. doi:10.2307/3250968

Moustakas, C. E. (1994). *Phenomenological research methods*. Thousand Oaks, CA: Sage.

Myers, M. D. (1994). Dialectical hermeneutics: A theoretical framework for the implementation of information systems. *Information Systems Journal*, *5*, 51–70. doi:10.1111/j.1365-2575.1995.tb00089.x

Olson, D. L., & Carlisle, J. (2001). Hermeneutics in information systems. In *Proceedings of the Seventh Americas Conference on Information Systems*.

Polkinghorne, D. E. (1989). Phenomenological research methods. In Valle, R., & Halling, S. (Eds.), *Existential-phenomenological perspectives in psychology* (pp. 41–60). New York, NY: Plenum.

Rennie, D. L. (2000). Grounded theory methodology as methodical hermeneutics. *Theory & Psychology*, *10*(4), 481–502. doi:10.1177/0959354300104003

Ricoeur, P. (1974). *The conflict of interpretations: Essays in hermeneutics*. Evanston, IL: Northwestern University Press.

Ricoeur, P. (1981). *Hermeneutics and the human sciences*. Cambridge, UK: Cambridge University Press.

Schleiermacher, F. D. E. (1819). The hermeneutics: Outline of the 1819 lecture. In Ormiston, G. L., & Schrift, A. D. (Eds.), *The hermeneutic tradition: From Ast to Ricoeur*. New York, NY: State University of New York Press.

Spiegelberg, H. (1982). *The phenomenological movement: A historical introduction*. Boston, MA: Martinus Nijhoff.

Titleman, P. (1979). Some implications of Ricoeur's conception of hermeneutics for phenomenological psychology. In Giorgi, A., Knowles, R., & Smith, D. L. (Eds.), *Duquesne studies in phenomenological psychology* (*Vol. 3*, pp. 182–192). Pittsburgh, PA: Duquesne University Press.

Turner, G. W. (Ed.). (1987). *The Australian concise Oxford dictionary of current English*. Melbourne, Australia: Oxford University Press.

van Kaam, A. (1959). Phenomenal analysis: Exemplified by a study of the experience of "really feeling understood". *Journal of Individual Psychology*, *15*(1), 66–72.

van Kaam, A. (1966). *Existential foundations of psychology*. Pittsburgh, PA: Duquesne University Press.

Walsham, G. (2006). Doing interpretive research. *European Journal of Information Systems*, *15*, 320–330. doi:10.1057/palgrave.ejis.3000589

Wolin, R. (2000). Nazism and the complicities of Hans-Georg Gadamer: Untruth and method. *New Republic (New York, N.Y.)*, *222*(20), 36–46.

ENDNOTES

1. The critical hermeneutics described here is NOT the same as that derived by Jurgen Habermas which is actually an extension of Critical Theory that addresses the hegemony and oppression present in language, an effective extension to Marxist philosophy (Crotty, 1998).

This work was previously published in the International Journal of Actor-Network Theory and Technological Innovation, Volume 3, Issue 4, edited by Arthur Tatnall, pp. 46-59, copyright 2011 by IGI Publishing (an imprint of IGI Global).

Chapter 10
Is a Stock Exchange a Computer Solution?
Explicitness, Algorithms and the Arizona Stock Exchange

Fabian Muniesa
Mines ParisTech, Centre de Sociologie de l'Innovation, France

ABSTRACT

The paper examines, through a case study on the Arizona Stock Exchange, how computerization challenged the definition of the stock exchange in the context of North-American financial markets in the 1990's. It analyses exchange automation in terms of trials of explicitness: the computational formulation of what an exchange is calls for a detailed explication of the (variable, often conflicting and unanticipated) processes and properties of price formation. The paper focuses in particular on the argument of the concentration of liquidity in one single point, which was central to the development of the Arizona Stock Exchange (an electronic call auction). It then asks what kind of revolution is the 'explicitness revolution' in the design of allocation mechanisms.

INTRODUCTION

Expressing markets (or economic institutions in general) in computational terms is an intellectual venture that has often characterized, sometimes quite decisively, the ambitions of economics. But this venture is not only of an intellectual kind. It is also practical, industrial and commercial. Many of the innovations characterizing the organization of markets since the mid-seventies at least are in fact about the introduction of computers at the heart of

market processes, this being particularly visible in the case of financial markets. The Arizona Stock Exchange stands as an interesting example of how the vocabulary of stock exchanges evolved with the introduction of machines. This 'market' (I use inverted comas because its status as such was itself a matter of controversy), although modest and short-lived (launched in the early 1990s and closed in early 2002 due to a lack of volume), was an important player in the history of electronic markets. Its near-paradigmatic character explains that role: spearhead in the struggle for legal recognition of 'alternative trading systems', star in the

DOI: 10.4018/978-1-4666-2166-4.ch010

academic literature on the quality of automated price discovery, and locus of innovation and algorithmic experimentation, the Arizona Stock Exchange enables us to identify salient points of what happens to markets (as objects not only of science but also of engineering) when they are confronted to algorithmic formulation.

This paper posits itself as a contribution to the sociological appraisal of market devices, that is, to the examination of how several kinds of apparatuses do contribute to the formation and deformation of market realities, in resonance with the viewpoints emphasized throughout actor-network theory (Callon & Muniesa, 2005; Callon, Millo, & Muniesa, 2007). The empirical context is the struggle for computer-assisted liquidity enhancement that characterised the transformation of North-American financial markets in the nineteen-eighties and nineteen-nineties. The argument is that computers posed a challenge to the very definition of what an 'exchange' is and also that presenting a market in the terms of a 'computer solution' introduced what I term a 'trial of explicitness': a call for detailed explication of the process and properties of 'price discovery'. The underlying theoretical assumption is that to make something explicit is not about clarifying or implementing something that is already prefigured as a potential reality, but rather about putting that thing to the test of variable, often conflicting and unanticipated forms of actualization – hence the idea of 'trial' (Latour, 1988).

The account which follows draws primarily from archival sources.[1] The next section is a brief presentation of the idea of a trial of explicitness and its intellectual context. In the next section, I examine how electronic trading systems such as the Arizona Stock Exchange challenged existing notions of the stock exchange. Then, I present the connexions between this system and research in economics, and their corresponding investigation on the concrete explication of price equilibrium. I then focus more narrowly on the crucial argument of the concentration of liquidity in one 'single

point' and the electronic call auction. I finally examine the algorithmic advancement of the Arizona Stock Exchange in the face of multiple calls for explicitness. In the concluding discussion, I propose a critical comment on what does it mean to consider markets as computer solutions.

THE PROBLEM OF EXPLICITNESS

The notion of explicitness has two sides. One is the very mundane idea of being called to make a clearer and more detailed statement about something that was initially formulated in rather loose terms or only in terms of general principles. This idea of making something explicit is often linked to the problem of the 'implementation' of something (of an idea, a project, a measure or a rule, for example). The second side of the notion is philosophical – more difficult and complicated. It is linked to the concept of 'explication' ('explicatio' in Latin, perhaps best translated as 'explikation' for instance in German, or 'explicitation' in French).[2] The notion conveys of course something of an idea of unfolding, of deploying, of opening up (opening the fold, the 'pli'), as opposed for instance to an idea of folding, or of complicating. But it is not very clear what this may mean and the philosophical problem of explication is an open one. Of particular interest for instance is the question of how prefigured (how ideated) is the thing that undergoes explication. Is explication about the laborious unveiling (or the working out) of something that is already there, implicit? Or is it a creative, performative, generative, provocative process that adds more reality to reality? And is it about the breath of intelligence tackling an initially chaotic matter and turning it meaningful ('pneuma' over 'plasma')? Or is it rather about a seamless play of folding and unfolding in a world which is constituted only by what happens at its surface?

A possible inclination for the second term of these two sets of questions is visible in a number of philosophical traditions which have been emphasized by Gilles Deleuze (1990). Explication would not be, within this direction, about clarification, about the unveiling of the unnoticed, about the implementation of the prefigured or about the realization of the potential. Explication would rather be about the actualization of the virtual: that is, about expressing something, provoking it in variable, conflicting, unanticipated manners, putting it to the test of becoming an actual configuration, an actual event. Expression (another notion for 'explicatio') would not be, within this direction, about pressing out something latent, but entirely about performing it.[3]

The mundane idea of explicitness rather sides, in my view, with this philosophical alternative. A call for explicitness rarely translates into the unproblematic unfolding of a one single programme, a plan, a code or a detailed set of instructions that may have already been settled in an implicit or latent form. On the contrary, a call for explicitness often translates into the emergence of grey areas, the discovery of new problems and, sometimes, the development of controversies about what is exactly what is to be made explicit and how. Computerization – and information systems at large – is an area in which this feature of explicitness is most visible. Valuation and quantification are too. In a sense, many of the types of practices pertaining to the world of postmodern knowledge in the sense of Lyotard (1984) are characterised by a recurrent exposure to trials of explicitness. From performance indicators to allocation protocols, the crucial step of implementation often translated into the multiplication of issues and interrogations that were not prefigured beforehand, trials of explicitness of the description of what is at stake.[4]

DEFINING AN EXCHANGE

What is an exchange? This question is probably worthy of the most serious and impassioned theoretical debates in the social sciences. Beyond the world of academic research, practitioners grapple

with it as well, in quite pragmatic terms, for instance with regard to legal issues. In the case of North-American stock markets, the question was prominent in the analyses of the Securities and Exchange Commission (SEC) throughout the nineteen-nineties, especially in response to the upsurge of Electronic Communication Networks (ECNs)[5] during that period (Lee, 1998; Domowitz & Lee, 2001). ECNs (Posit, Island or Archipelago among the most well-known) were worrying characters on the stock-market scene in those years, for they could be used in a variety of ways to bypass the official quotation services proposed by the North-American stock exchanges (such as for instance the New York Stock Exchange). ECNs proposed to their clients a more efficient execution of their orders (in terms of the quality of obtained prices) and often at a lower cost (in terms of brokerage and quotation commissions). Although they were registered as brokers or broker-dealers within the SEC and regulated as such, ECNs nevertheless had characteristics similar to those of traditional exchanges, in so far as they served the matching and subsequent execution of buy and sell orders.

The word 'exchange' roughly denotes the place where buyers and sellers come together. But this can be taken in an abstract sense (i.e., a space in which supply and demand schedules intersect) or a concrete one (i.e., the physical site where brokers meet in order to do their business). Controversies in the definition of North-American financial markets in the nineties stemmed in part precisely from the fact that new electronic technologies for the transmission and execution of orders undermined the idea of a stock exchange as a physical place. As the following official opinion attests, the SEC's main concern was the prospect of doing away with physical boundaries defining the exchange:

Thus, we find ourselves attempting to make difficult choices concerning what time and space limitations we will choose to retain, if any, in the absence of any lingering physical or technological necessity, all while being bombarded by continuing automation advances that sometimes make even our most recent market structure and regulatory decisions seem already archaic. (SEC, 1991a, p. 1)

Risks associated with exchange automation were of prime concern in this type of regulatory literature. They were expressed in terms which, like the following, deeply resonate with the vocabulary of computers: "security to prevent unauthorized access and misuse of data", "capacity to support timely operations", and "programs to provide continuous service in the event of system failure" (GAO, 1991, p. 30). This computational parlance may seem natural today, but was quite new to the regulatory appraisal of markets in the 1990s. Documents circulating in the SEC, but also in the US General Accounting Office (GAO) or the International Organization of Securities Commissions (IOSCO) were increasingly populated by this kind of wording.

In addition to generating novel so-called 'operational' risks (Power, 2005), market technologies in general and ECNs in particular triggered a crisis in the very structure of traditional markets. Despite their growing legitimacy based on arguments of liquidity, transparency and efficiency, they were sometimes perceived as tools to bypass instituted stock exchanges, such as the New York Stock Exchange, or more recent market networks that nevertheless still corresponded to historical institutional arrangements, such as the NASDAQ, the communication system of the National Association of Securities Dealers (NASD). In this context, ECNs looked like nothing short of institutional 'monsters'[6] that seriously challenged the definition of an exchange, or rather that made it necessary to clarify exactly what an exchange was and what it was not.

The term 'exchange', used by the SEC, remained ambiguous for quite a time. It was inherited from the Securities and Exchange Act of 1934, the legal underpinning of the regulation of financial activities in the United States:

The term 'exchange' means any organization, association, or group of persons, whether incorporated or unincorporated, which constitutes, maintains, or provides a market place or facilities for bringing together purchasers and sellers of securities or for otherwise performing with respect to securities the functions commonly performed by a stock exchange as that term is generally understood, and includes the market place and the market facilities maintained by such exchange. (US Congress, 1934, Section 3, a.1)

As pointed out by Lee (1998, p. 286), the inclusion of the term 'stock exchange' as part of the definition of 'exchange', or the vague reference to the meaning of the term as it is 'generally understood', made the above definition obscure and potentially difficult for courts to use in granting the status of an exchange to trading services that had applied for it. The introduction, in 1975, of regulation determining the legal definition of ECNs sparked a controversy. These new players were considered to be brokers. But they fulfilled, in practice, functions 'commonly performed by a stock exchange': that is, providing the means 'for bringing together purchasers and sellers of securities' with a view to agreeing on a price and transacting. The SEC, aware of these difficulties, tried to devise appropriate measures and contemplated changes to the very definition of what 'an exchange' is. A radical attempt at making that explicit was the 1997 Concept Release[7] on the theme of stock exchange regulation:

As a result of the technologically-driven developments discussed above, however, the distinctions among market service providers have become blurred, making it more difficult to determine whether any particular entity operates as an exchange, OTC market, broker, or dealer. For example, alternative trading systems incorporate features of both traditional markets and broker-dealers. Like traditional exchanges, alternative trading systems centralize orders and give participants control over the interaction of their orders. Like traditional broker-dealers, alternative trading systems are proprietary and, in some cases, maintain trading desks that facilitate participant trading. Because the activities of alternative trading systems include both traditional exchange and broker-dealer functions, it is often unclear whether such systems should register as exchanges, broker-dealers, or both. Under the existing statutory structure enacted by Congress, however, exchanges and broker-dealers are subject to significantly different obligations and responsibilities.

To date, the Commission has regulated many alternative markets as broker-dealers, rather than as exchanges, in order to foster the development of innovative trading mechanisms within the existing statutory framework. The determination as to whether any particular alternative trading system should be regulated as an exchange or broker-dealer has been decided on a case-by-case basis. This regulatory approach has had two significant, unintended effects: (1) it has subjected alternative trading systems to a regulatory scheme that is not particularly suited to their market activities; and (2) it has impeded effective integration, surveillance, enforcement, and regulation of the U.S. markets as a whole. (SEC, 1997a, pp. 26-27)

The Arizona Stock Exchange, also known as 'AZX', is a fine example of the play of definitions and redefinitions that ECNs prompted at the SEC (Lee, 1998, pp. 279-321). AZX proposed an improvement to the conditions of execution for a number of securities listed on the New York Stock Exchange or on NASDAQ. Despite its name, it was not a proper traditional, geographically-located stock exchange. It was only in 1992, after agreement with the relevant authorities of Arizona (and after moving its central server from New York to Phoenix), that this proprietary trading system (or rather, notwithstanding the controversies, this ECN)[8] adopted this name. Until then and from

its inception in 1990, it was called the Wunsch Auction System, Inc., WASI, after its founder and CEO Steven Wunsch (see Wunsch, 1992, 2000). From then on AZX was considered to be a 'stock exchange' and unofficially recognized as such by the SEC, even though it benefited from a clause exempting it from formal registration as a stock exchange, and also despite differences with a traditional stock exchange, highlighted by Wunsch himself (Wunsch, 1993).[9] In short, AZX was considered to be a stock exchange because it was a market mechanism that determined a trading price based on the matching of supply and demand.

It was thus because the mechanism underlying innovations such as the Arizona Stock Exchange – and not their institutional or corporate form – resembled an exchange, that the very definition of an exchange was to be centred on the structure of the mechanism. The proposal that the SEC seemed to favour in its 1997 Concept Release reflected this: an amendment to the definition of the term 'exchange' and several gradients in the identification of these entities. The SEC thus proposed to rank trading systems on three levels: on the first level, systems with a low volume, with essentially passive call auction mechanisms; on the second level, alternative systems or ECNs that treated large volumes and had active mechanisms of 'price discovery'; and, finally, on the third level, traditional stock exchanges (SEC, 1997a, pp. 48-49). The tendency could even be pushed further, with a clear separation between considerations on the corporate nature of the entity and the regulation of the market structure as such (Lee, 1998, pp. 309-316). In other words, the definition of the market was taken out of its institutional setting (a corporative association, a service provider, etc.), reducing it to its purely mechanistic, algorithmic component (a trading system with a 'price discovery' mechanism). The constraint that electronic trading systems placed on the call for explicitness in the definition of the exchange is evident here. The fact that the algorithmic description of the market can serve as a landmark in the identification of what an exchange is seems to indicate a pragmatic ascendancy of computer vocabulary over that of the market.

LABORATORIES AND REAL MARKETS

The history of electronic exchanges is largely that of an 'explication' of market mechanisms. It is a history shared by both academic research (notably in the fields of experimental economics, game theory and market microstructure) and industrial research (development of market technologies, commercialization of trading solutions). These two types of research do not always communicate easily, even if data, results and people often travel from one environment to the other. They aim at making market mechanisms explicit in quite different ways. The more complex and detailed the description of a mechanism, the closer it actually is to an algorithm, that is, to a functional product that can be implemented and generate economic return, and thus fall within the domain of industrial property and commercial law. On the other hand, the more the description leans towards an outline of the basic principles and resulting quality effects, the more it falls into the arena of academic science, where publication of the explanatory work is valued as such. As some studies on the performativity of economics have shown (e.g., MacKenzie, Muniesa, & Siu, 2007), various modes of research (either 'confined' or 'in the wild') can swap their vocabulary and centres of interest in several respects. The quality of price fixing, although formulated in different styles and from various angles, is a concern that can very well be shared by academic research in experimental economics or in market microstructure, and by the own R&D (research and development) of financial institutions.

The case of the Arizona Stock Exchange is a remarkable example of the encounter between these two types of knowledge. The AZX mechanism was initially set up in New York to enable institutional clients to match their orders by means of a call auction, and the fact that the device ended up migrating to Arizona was by no means irrelevant. The instigator of this move seems to have been Vernon Smith, a reputable pioneer of experimental economics who was based at the time at the University of Arizona (Smith, 1994).[10] In 1988 Smith conducted his first experiments on the economic properties of the call auction (which he called a 'uniform price double auction'). According to his own account, he subsequently learned that Steven Wunsch had been offering institutional clients a similar service since 1990 in New York. Wunsch had based his device on the practice of 'sunshine trading', which consisted in announcing in advance exactly when a large order was going to be sent over to the exchange, with a view to concentrating a maximum of liquidity at that moment. The Arizona Corporation Commission, interested in creating an 'Arizona Stock Exchange' and seeking inspiration, had in the meantime considered Smith's laboratory electronic markets. The properties of call-auction mechanism, as demonstrated in the laboratory, raised some enthusiasm and the decision was taken to inquire about the similar system that Wunsch had developed in Wall Street, i.e., in a 'natural environment':

Eventually Wunsch adopted the new name, AZX, and the new exchange has experienced rapid growth since its move in March 1992. Had it not been for the experiments we would not have come to understand the comparative properties of the uniform price double auction, and would not have been able to recommend it wholeheartedly as a reasonable direction for a new electronic exchange. (Smith, 1994, p. 116)

This is an interesting example of the combination of academic research and the market or, more exactly, of experimental design and institutional design of a market mechanism (see also Guala, 2007). In both cases (that of Smith and that of Wunsch), the characteristics of a market mechanism were subject to explicitness, in one case in the field of economic theory and in the other in that of financial services. The two trials of explicitness, stemming from distinct constraints and following different trajectories, ended up coinciding and sharing their tools.[11]

I talk of the 'explicitness' of the mechanism without however wanting to suggest the existence of an implicit something which would be underlying, potential, 'already there', merely waiting to be confirmed. On the contrary, I consider 'trials of explicitness' as radically inventive work. To be sure, these mechanisms are not imagined *ex-nihilo*, but nor are they already present *a priori*. The process of explication is long and costly, and always results in a 'type' of mechanism, *ad hoc*, limited to a particular circumstance, and localised. But what needs to be explicated in this particular case? Which question does this particular mechanism, this electronic call auction, answer?

CONCENTRATION OF ORDERS IN A SINGLE POINT

The debate on call auctions and sunshine trading is actually about the 'accuracy' of this process that economists often call 'price discovery' – an interesting expression that implicitly fosters an effect of naturalization.[12] Smith (the experimental economist) and Wunsch (the Wall Street entrepreneur) are not the only ones to have tackled the question. It has been the subject of an abundant literature in economics, especially in the tradition of market microstructure. The initial question, as Fischer Black, for example, formulated it in a seminal article, concerns the 'ideal environment' for economic agents to express (and trade at) an optimal price:

It appears that the market for a single stock is most efficient if all orders for the stock come in to a single point, so that all potential buyers can

be exposed to all sell orders, and all potential sellers can be exposed to all buy orders. (Black, 1971, p. 29)

With such a formulation, Black endeavoured to defend his proposal for an automation of quotation, with the case of the New York Stock Exchange on sight. He did so against a background of criticism of the 'fragmentation' of North-American stock markets and the over-powerful role of professionals of quotation, such as the 'specialists' of the New York Stock Exchange. Other proposals for automation stemming from the academic field did also adopt the 'single point' formulation:

The ideal economic environment is one where all interested traders simultaneously submit their complete demand-to-hold curves for each asset, and where an auctioneer finds the single price that clears all crossing orders. (Cohen & Schwartz, 1989, p. 22)

This excerpt is from Robert Schwartz and Kalman Cohen's proposal for an 'electronic call auction' (the call auction can also be referred to as 'batch market', 'uniform-price double auction' or 'single-price auction', sometimes 'fixing' in French). This 1989 proposal, made at a time when electronic markets were on the upsurge, is more elaborate than Black's 1971's one (Domowitz, 1993). It is more explicit, with regard not so much to the economic justifications but rather to the mechanism that is supposed to correspond to those justifications.

Kalman Cohen and Robert Schwartz's system was a discontinuous quotation device: a sequential or discrete auction. Their proposal was addressed quite clearly to the New York Stock Exchange, which functioned as a continuous market. The proposal was motivated, in part, by the stock market crash of 1987. Schwartz and Cohen argued that one of the main causes of the crash was the temporal fragmentation of continuous quotation, which accentuated phenomena of incomplete information and erratic gaming. In general, meeting a counterpart requires orders to converge, not only in space but also in time. According to these authors, the volatility that shook Wall Street in October 19th, 1987 could have been reduced if orders had been gathered together at specific points in time. They explain how a single-price auction, run at regular intervals, increases the probabilities of transactions occurring at a so-called equilibrium price. Because it is time-specific, the call auction ensures a balanced distribution of information and the production of prices which are grounded on realistic assumptions about the state of the market. Prices will thus become steadier. The concentration of orders eliminates fluctuations between the two extremes of the bid-ask spread found in continuous markets since, by definition, there is no bid-ask spread in a call auction market. The market thus tends to be fairer, according to these authors, especially for small investors, since data and reaction time are levelled out, and a single price is fixed. This structure represents the ideal encounter between supply and demand. The authors present (or explicate) it as the best way to concretize the 'single point' idea.

Robert Schwartz and his colleagues have argued for electronic call auctions in many publications (e.g., Economides & Schwartz, 1995; Schwartz, 2001a; Schwartz, Byrne, & Colaninno, 2003). An active member of the New York financial academic scene, professor at the Stern School of Business of New York University and then at the Zicklin School of Business at Baruch College of the City University of New York, Schwartz, perhaps more than anyone else, was responsible for the dissemination of academic research, assessment and scientific promotion of the call auction mechanism. Schwartz has also contributed as editor of a number of publications on the microstructure of financial markets and trading technologies (Bloch & Schwartz, 1979; Amihud, Ho, & Schwartz, 1985; Cohen, Maier, Schwartz, & Whitcomb, 1986; Lucas & Schwartz,

1989; Schwartz, 1995), and as a consultant for a number of stock exchanges and related services, including the Arizona Stock Exchange.

In his introduction to a collective volume devoted entirely to the subject of electronic call auctions (Schwartz, 2001b); Robert Schwartz reviews the argument of the temporal fragmentation of markets. This text was also sent to the SEC, attached to his answer to a Request for Comment on the problem of market fragmentation, put out by the regulatory authority in 2000. In his letter, Schwartz explained the following:

Unfortunately, virtually all of the public debate concerning order flow fragmentation/consolidation has focused on the spatial distribution of orders across multiple markets. However, the time dimension is every bit as important. To achieve trades at reasonable prices, orders must meet. As with any meeting, two dimensions must be specified: place and time. In continuous trading environments (e.g., the New York Stock Exchange and NASDAQ), trades can be made any time two counterpart orders meet or cross during normal trading hours (9:30 a.m. to 4:00 p.m.). Assume one participant submits a buy order at 10:50 a.m., and that a second participant submits a sell order at 10:55. If these orders cannot be brought together, the market is fragmented. How do orders meet in time? In a quote driven market, a market maker solves the time problem by selling to the buyer at 10:50 and buying from the seller at 10:55. In an order driven market, the limit order placed by one participant enables another participant at another moment in time to trade with immediacy by market order. A third alternative is the call auction. The call enables a large number of buyers and sellers to meet because it establishes a predetermined meeting point in time. I suggest that the introduction of electronic call auction trading along with continuous trading would be the most useful innovation that could be made in U.S. equity market structure. (Schwartz, 2000, p. 1)

A continuous market is based, in a sense, on the principle of waiting. Limit orders are put on hold until matching orders arrive into the order book of a particular stock. This is the very principle of the existence of the bid-ask spread: between two transactions, the best selling and buying prices are displayed, pending a transaction opportunity. This is not the case in a call auction market where there is no waiting, for everyone is supposed to arrive on the market (on the electronic order book) at the same time. This idea of 'meeting' in the order book at time *t* was a specific feature of the Arizona Stock Exchange. Steve Wunsch, founder of the AZX, likened the principle to the mechanism of 'sunshine trading' that he had himself experimented with at the derivatives department of Kidder, Peabody & Co. in the eighties. The practice consisted literally in 'making an appointment' in the order book, that is, publicly announcing that a substantial counterpart was going to be posted for a sale or purchase at a specific time. Basically, this amounted to 'calling the market', which was precisely what the call auction was.

The case of the Arizona Stock Exchange thus provided a practical example of the argument for temporal fragmentation of the market that Schwartz promoted. Wunsch also saw the practice of sunshine trading, along with the justification of the 'Wunsch Auction System' that it inspired, from the perspective of the 1987 crash. These attempts to concentrate liquid assets at time *t* could avoid effects of fragmentation of the order book and thus limit phenomena of disorder.

Many economists supported these arguments. In a piece published in the newsletter of the Arizona Stock Exchange (Auction Countdown, the CEO's personal tribune), Steve Wunsch cited Maurice Allais:

The continuous trading market is an aberration from an economic viewpoint and generates a potentially permanent instability favoring fraud and manipulation of the market. [US markets could be improved] by eliminating the continuous market and replacing it everywhere with a single daily trading price for each stock in each market. (Fisher & Tempest, 1989, p. D1; quoted in Wunsch, 1990, p. 1)

Economists' input was not limited to this type of general comment. The AZX electronic call auction also had influential allies among the pioneers of experimental economics. In his endorsement of a 1993 book edited by Daniel Friedman and John Rust on experiments with call action models, Steven Wunsch expressed his debt as follows:

With computer networks loosening the grip of traditional intermediary cartels on market structure, the Friedman-Rust compendium takes on considerable significance. Academic theories tested heretofore only in the laboratory are no longer merely academic; one or more of the models analyzed in this book will undoubtedly serve as the basis for successful real markets in the future. (Friedman & Rust, 1993, back cover)

This book was indeed a milestone in the encounter between the 'computational' side of experimental economics and the study of electronic trading systems in financial markets. As we have seen, Wunsch owes part of the history of his machine's endeavours to one the models analysed in the book: the call auction designed by Vernon Smith and his colleagues in the laboratory (McCabe, Rassenti, & Smith, 1993).

ALGORITHMIC CONFIGURATIONS AND TRIALS OF EXPLICITNESS

Let us revert briefly to 'sunshine trading'. This practice, developed by Wunsch and his colleagues at Kidder, Peabody & Co., consisted in publicly announcing not only that they were available to sell a particular quantity of securities, but also that they were planning to do so (to put them on the market) at midday exactly, for example. In other words, the market is 'called' to an appointment at a specific time (Wunsch, 2000). Many regulators and market-makers saw this practice as controversial, at best, or fraudulent, at worst, for it consisted in bypassing the historically instituted structures for liquidity enhancement. But for the instigators of sunshine trading, it was more than a contrivance for making a good deal on the market. They claimed that if it were generalized this practice could become a generator of transparency, capable of preventing market disorders due to the temporal fragmentation of market access (Wunsch, 1987). Sunshine trading was moreover a subject of research in economics, which concluded that Wunsch's arguments on the stability of prices were relevant (Admati & Pfeiderer, 1991). In 1990 Wunsch developed the Wunsch Auction System, an electronic system in which securities quoted on the New York Stock Exchange and on the NASDAQ could be traded with better conditions of execution, by means of an electronic call auction. As we have seen above, this was the first version of the electronic trading system that would subsequently be called the Arizona Stock Exchange.

The AZX functioned exclusively on the basis of the call auction principle. Periods of reception and accumulation of buy and sell orders followed one another at regular intervals for each of the securities listed on the system. During these periods, brokers had access to the electronic order book for each security. Immediately after the closure of each auction period, the system calculated the execution price according to an algorithm aimed at maximizing the overall exchanged volume, given the state of the order book. The price chosen among all possible transaction prices was the price at which the volume of buy orders levelled off or was closest to the volume of sell orders. Clients who had proposed higher purchase prices, or lower selling prices, than the one determined

by the algorithm, were served at the set auction price, a single price for each security. When it was possible to find a solution at two different prices, the algorithm was limited to picking up the average of the two prices as the execution price.[13]

But there was still the problem of allocation at this price – another trial of explicitness. How matching orders should be served if the volume purchased did not coincide with the volume sold? The solution to this problem evolved through time at AZX. Initially, time priority was secondary compared to price priority. If, at the set equilibrium price, buy and sell volumes were not equivalent, orders were executed first according to a price priority: those sell orders that displayed a lower price (and higher in the case of buy orders) were put through first. After that, time priority was applied to the execution of those orders whose displayed price coincided with the price determined at the call auction. That was initially how time priority was worked out at the Arizona Stock Exchange (Lee, 1998, pp. 318-319).[14]

AZX managers came across a problem of 'scooping' on this configuration, and time priority was a good solution but considered to be limited in this form. Whereas price priority took precedence over time priority, there were situations like the following: if the execution price calculated by the algorithm was $10.5 for a total of 10,000 shares, a buy offer, no matter how modest, entered at the last minute at $10.6 would be given priority over one at $10.5 and put through before it. With strict price priority, the algorithm was supposed to serve shares to this 'scooper' first, and always at $10.5. The solution developed by Wunsch's team in the late nineties was to apply time priority to all executable orders and not only to those that displayed a limit equal to the equilibrium price. From then on, price priority was used only to determine the equilibrium price and not to allocate shares. The measure resulted in a fairly radical restriction on scooping: a last-minute buy order at $10.6 would not get the trade or, rather, could get it only if it is filled for a volume enough to shift the execution price up (but, in that case, it would be served at $10.6).

But solutions engender newer problems, and the question that these market engineers then had to answer, immersed as they were in a context of competition with traditional and alternative trading methods, was how not to cancel out the possibility of 'aggressive' strategies on the AZX – including 'scooping'. The solution devised in response to demands from clients involved the creation of two different types of order book for each security: an 'open book' in which time priority was predominant and orders were publicly displayed (price and volume), and a 'reserve book' in which orders were hidden and executed according to the price priority principle. The equilibrium price was then determined on the open book, which thus took precedence over the reserve book. This mitigated 'scooping' phenomena. But the existence of the reserve book created an environment conducive to aggressive strategy (Wunsh, 1997).[15] In terms of the algorithm's moral tale, this configuration expresses the following: time priority is the privilege of agents who publicly expose themselves (literally, in broad daylight, as the term 'sunshine trading' suggests) in queues. Scooping (ignoring the queue) is however not prohibited; it remains a legitimate action but will be tolerated only 'backstage', and without undermining the rights of those agents who respect the queues.

Time priority was implemented at AZX to solve a crisis in the justification of principles of allocation. The idea was to limit the gains derived from posting an order on the order book at the last second. Yet opportunism as such could not be excluded from the market. Constraints on scooping were thus completed by special treatment of the publicity of orders on the book. It was the concrete experience of expressing trading in algorithmic terms that governed the particular shape and evolution of this market device. The device was set in a specific competitive context: the battle for

liquidity in a fragmented market space dominated by official stock exchanges but also counting on disruptive initiatives in the form of ECNs.

CONCLUSION

What does algorithmic formulation do to its subject matter? Donald Knuth considers the notion of algorithm in the following terms:

The English language has several other words that almost, but not quite, capture the concept that is needed: procedure, recipe, process, routine, method, rigmarole. Like this things an algorithm is a set of rules or directions for getting a specific output from a specific input. The distinguishing feature of an algorithm is that all vagueness must be eliminated; the rules must describe operations that are so simple and so well defined that they can be executed by a machine. Furthermore, an algorithm must always terminate after a finite number of steps. (Knuth, 1996, p. 59)

For a market (or for the idea of a market) to be formulated in algorithmic terms implies in part the possibility (although not the necessity) of being "executed by a machine". This is for sure quite a noticeable characteristic of both the computerization of actual markets and the computerization of market theory (Izquierdo Martín, 1996; Callon & Muniesa, 2005; Mirowski, 2007). For the 'action' of an exchange for instance to be prone to computer language, this has to turn, in fact, into some sort of a 'machine-like action' (Collins, 1990). But Knuth's definition points to one feature that is perhaps more important than the possibility of machine execution: the idea of explicitness. Nothing is to be left to second thoughts, to on-the-spot tinkering or to indeterminacy. Controversies in computational arrangements need to be closed, and, hence, abstract principles or general ideas need to subject to the trial of a concrete, finite configuration. But it is within this process of concretization that problems arise and that conflicts between alternative solutions (which did not exist beforehand) spring.

The history of the Arizona Stock Exchange might seem trivial, especially in view of its lack of economic success. Having failed to generate a critical mass, it declined and eventually closed down in 2002. This market device was nevertheless a paradigmatic case of expressing a market in algorithmic terms. It was at the centre of regulatory discussions on the redefinition of the stock exchange in the face of computerization. It linked advanced academic research to the world of innovation in the financial services industry, and participated in scholarly arguments on the conditions of 'price discovery' in a computer environment. Finally, it put forward specific functionalities as a result of a process of algorithmic explication of the balance of strength that it was supposed to favour.

What computers do to markets is partially a matter of explication – what I call a trial of explicitness. Explication is a fundamental characteristic of any algorithmic configuration. The concrete organization of trading is confronted not only to a definitional quarrel (is this device an exchange or not) but also to a series of problems that have become unavoidable due to the very fact of being put to the algorithmic test (encounter between supply and demand in what place, at what time, in what order, with what priorities, etc.). It is noteworthy that it is precisely a 'computational' view of markets that encourages economists to talk about the 'concretization' of economic equilibrium (e.g., Guesnerie, 2005). But, while it may indeed be reasonable to consider markets as 'computer solutions', it would be also useful to consider these in the very mundane and ordinary sense of that expression – 'computer solutions' actually often consisting in, as we all know, disorderly sequences of additional problems.

REFERENCES

Admati, A. R., & Pfeiderer, P. (1991). Sunshine Trading and Financial Market Equilibrium. *Review of Financial Studies*, *4*(3), 443–481.

Amihud, Y., Ho, T. S. Y., & Schwartz, R. A. (Eds.). (1985). *Market Making and the Changing Structure of the Securities Industry*. Lexington, MA: Lexington Books.

Black, F. (1971). Toward a Fully Automated Stock Exchange. *Financial Analysts Journal*, *27*(4), 28–35, 44. doi:10.2469/faj.v27.n4.28

Bloch, E., & Schwartz, R. A. (Eds.). (1979). *Impending Changes for Securities Markets: What Role for the Exchanges?* Greenwich, CT: JAI Press.

Callon, M., Millo, Y., & Muniesa, F. (Eds.). (2007). *Market Devices*. Oxford, UK: Blackwell.

Callon, M., & Muniesa, F. (2005). Economic Markets as Calculative Collective Devices. *Organization Studies*, *26*(8), 1229–1250. doi:10.1177/0170840605056393

Cohen, K. J., Maier, S. F., Schwartz, R. A., & Whitcomb, D. K. (1986). *The Microstructure of Securities Markets*. Upper Saddle River, NJ: Prentice-Hall.

Cohen, K. J., & Schwartz, R. A. (1989). An Electronic Call Market: Its Design and Desirability. In Lucas, H. C. J., & Schwartz, R. A. (Eds.), *The Challenge of Information Technology for the Securities Markets: Liquidity, Volatility, and Global Trading* (pp. 15–38). Homewood, IL: Dow Jones-Irwin.

Collins, H. M. (1990). *Artificial Experts: Social Knowledge and Intelligent Machines*. Cambridge, MA: The MIT Press.

Deleuze, G. (1990). *The Logic of Sense*. New York: Columbia University Press.

Didier, E. (2007). Do Statistics "Perform" the Economy? In MacKenzie, D., Muniesa, F., & Siu, L. (Eds.), *Do Economists make Markets? On the Performativity of Economics* (pp. 276–310). Princeton, NJ: Princeton University Press.

Didier, E. (2009). *En quoi consiste l'Amérique? Les statistiques, le New Deal et la démocratie.* Paris: La Découverte.

Domowitz, I. (1993). Automating the Continuous Double Auction in Practice: Automated Trade Execution Systems in Financial Markets. In Friedman, J., & Rust, J. (Eds.), *The Double Auction Market: Institutions, Theories, and Evidence* (pp. 27–60). Reading, MA: Addison-Wesley.

Domowitz, I., & Lee, R. (2001). On the Road to Reg ATS: A Critical History of the Regulation of Automated Trading Systems. *International Finance*, *4*(2), 279–302. doi:10.1111/1468-2362.00074

Economides, N., & Schwartz, R. A. (1995). Electronic Call Market Trading. *Journal of Portfolio Management*, *21*(3), 10–18. doi:10.3905/jpm.1995.409518

Fisher, D., & Tempest, R. (1989, October 26). Allais: "Wall Street Has Become a Veritable Casino". *Los Angeles Times*, D1.

Friedman, D., & Rust, J. (Eds.). (1993). *The Double Auction Market: Institutions, Theories, and Evidence.* Reading, MA: Addison-Wesley.

GAO (United States General Accounting Office). (1991). *Global Financial Markets: International Coordination Can Help Address Automation Risks* (Tech. Rep. No. GAO/IMTES-91-62). Washington, DC: General Accounting Office.

Guala, F. (2005). *The Methodology of Experimental Economics.* Cambridge, UK: Cambridge University Press. doi:10.1017/CBO9780511614651

Guala, F. (2007). How to Do Things with Experimental Economics. In MacKenzie, D., Muniesa, F., & Siu, L. (Eds.), *Do Economists make Markets? On the Performativity of Economics* (pp. 128–162). Princeton, NJ: Princeton University Press.

Guesnerie, R. (2005). Réflexions sur la concrétisation de l'équilibre économique. In Bensimon, G. (Ed.), *Histoire des représentations du marché* (pp. 49–63). Paris: Michel Houdiard Editeur.

Hertz, E. (2000). Stock Markets as "Simulacra": Observation that Participates. *Tsantsa*, *5*, 40–50.

Izquierdo Martín, A. J. (1996). Equilibrio económico y racionalidad maquínica: del algoritmo al sujeto en el análisis económico moderno. *Politica y Sociedad*, *21*, 89–111.

Knuth, D. E. (1996). Algorithms. In Knuth, D. E. (Ed.), *Selected Papers on Computer Science* (pp. 59–86). Cambridge, UK: Cambridge University Press.

Latour, B. (1988). *The Pasteurization of France.* Cambridge, MA: Harvard University Press.

Latour, B. (2006). Air. In Jones, C. A. (Ed.), *Sensorium: Embodied Experience, Technology, and Contemporary Art* (pp. 104–107). Cambridge, MA: The MIT Press.

Lee, R. (1998). *What is an Exchange? The Automation, Management, and Regulation of Financial Markets.* Oxford, UK: Oxford University Press.

Lucas, H. C. J., & Schwartz, R. A. (Eds.). (1989). *The Challenge of Information Technology for the Securities Markets: Liquidity, Volatility, and Global Trading.* Homewood, IL: Dow Jones-Irwin.

Lyotard, J.-F. (1984). *The Postmodern Condition: A Report on Knowledge.* Minneapolis, MN: University of Minnesota Press.

MacKenzie, D., Muniesa, F., & Siu, L. (Eds.). (2007). *Do Economists make Markets? On the Performativity of Economics*. Princeton, NJ: Princeton University Press.

McCabe, K., Rassenti, S., & Smith, V. (1993). Designing a Uniform-Price Double Auction: An Experimental Evaluation. In Friedman, D., & Rust, J. (Eds.), *The Double Auction Market: Institutions, Theories, and Evidence* (pp. 307–332). Reading, MA: Addison-Wesley.

Mirowski, P. (2007). Markets Come to Bits: Evolution, Computation and Markomata in Economic Science. *Journal of Economic Behavior & Organization, 63*(2), 209–242. doi:10.1016/j.jebo.2005.03.015

Muniesa, F. (2007). Market Technologies and the Pragmatics of Prices. *Economy and Society, 36*(3), 377–395. doi:10.1080/03085140701428340

Muniesa, F., & Linhardt, D. (2009). *At Stake with Implementation: Trials of Explicitness in the Description of the State* (CSI Working Papers Series 015). Paris: Centre de Sociologie de l'Innovation.

Muniesa, F., & Trébuchet-Breitwiller, A.-S. (2010). Becoming a Measuring Instrument: An Ethnography of Perfume Consumer Testing. *Journal of Cultural Economics, 3*(3), 321–337. doi:10.1080/17530350.2010.506318

Power, M. (2005). The Invention of Operational Risk. *Review of International Political Economy, 12*(4), 577–599. doi:10.1080/09692290500240271

Satterthwaite, M., & Williams, S. (1993). The Bayesian Theory of the *k*-Double Auction. In Friedman, D., & Rust, J. (Eds.), *The Double Auction Market: Institutions, Theories, and Evidence* (pp. 99–124). Reading, MA: Addison-Wesley.

Schwartz, R. A. (Ed.). (1995). *Global Equity Markets: Technological, Competitive and Regulatory Challenges*. Chicago, IL: Irwin.

Schwartz, R. A. (2000). *Re: Release No. 34-42450; File No. SR-NYSE-99-48; Market Fragmentation. Letter to the Securities and Exchange Commission, Response to Request for Comments*. Washington, DC: Securities and Exchange Commission.

Schwartz, R. A. (Ed.). (2001a). *The Electronic Call Auction: Market Mechanism and Trading*. Boston, MA: Kluwer Academic Publishers.

Schwartz, R. A. (2001b). The Call Auction Alternative. In Schwartz, R. A. (Ed.), *The Electronic Call Auction: Market Mechanism and Trading* (pp. 3–25). Boston, MA: Kluwer Academic Publishers.

Schwartz, R. A., Byrne, J. A., & Colaninno, A. (Eds.). (2003). *Call Auction Trading: New Answers to Old Questions*. Boston: Kluwer Academic Publishers.

SEC. (Securities and Exchange Commission, Division of Market Regulation). (1991a). *Automated Securities Trading: A Discussion of Selected Critical Issues. IOSCO Annual Meeting, Washington DC*. Washington, DC: Securities and Exchange Commission.

SEC. (Securities and Exchange Commission, Division of Market Regulation). (1997b). *Re: Arizona Stock Exchange. Response to Request to Division of Market Regulation*. Washington, DC: Securities and Exchange Commission.

SEC (Securities and Exchange Commission). (1991b). *Self-Regulatory Organizations; Wunsch Auction System, Inc.; Order Granting Limited Volume Exemption from Registration as an Exchange under Section 5 of the SEA. Release No. 34-28899, File No. 10-100*. Washington, DC: Securities and Exchange Commission.

SEC (Securities and Exchange Commission). (1997a). *Regulation of Exchange: Concept Release. Release No. 34-38672, File No. S7-16-97*. Washington, DC: Securities and Exchange Commission.

Sloterdijk, P. (2009a). Airquakes. *Environment and Planning. D, Society & Space, 27*(1), 41–57. doi:10.1068/dst1

Sloterdijk, P. (2009b). *Terror From the Air.* Cambridge, MA: The MIT Press.

Smith, V. L. (1994). Economics in the Laboratory. *The Journal of Economic Perspectives, 8*(1), 113–131.

US Congress (United States Congress). (1934). *Securities and Exchange Act of 1934.* Washington, DC: United States Congress.

Wunsch, R. S. (1987, October 20). Market Innovations. *Financial Futures Department Newsletter.* New York: Kidder, Peabody & Co.

Wunsch, R. S. (1990, August 13). Myths of the Continuous Market. *Auction Countdown.* Phoenix, AZ: Arizona Stock Exchange.

Wunsch, R. S. (1992). *Re: Market 2000, the U.S. Equity Market Structure Study, Release No. 34-30920, File No. S7-18-92. Letter to the Securities and Exchange Commission, Response to Concept Release.* Washington, DC: Securities and Exchange Commission.

Wunsch, R. S. (1993). *Statement of Steve Wunsch, President, AZX, Inc, Propietary Trading Systems Hearing. Subcommittee on Telecommunications and Finance of the Committee on Energy and Commerce, U. S. House of Representatives.* Washington, DC: United States House of Representatives.

Wunsch, R. S. (1997, March 24). Calls for Reform. *Auction Countdown.* Phoenix, AZ: Arizona Stock Exchange.

Wunsch, R. S. (2000). *Re: Release No. 34-42450; File No. SR-NYSE-99-48; Market Fragmentation. Letter to the Securities and Exchange Commission, Response to Concept Release.* Washington, DC: Securities and Exchange Commission.

ENDNOTES

1. The research this paper draws from was conducted in 2000 and 2001. I use in particular materials obtained from the library of the Commission des Opérations de Bourse in Paris (which has since become the Autorité des Marchés Financiers) or downloaded from the websites of the Securities and Exchange Commission and the (now defunct) Arizona Stock Exchange. The on-line newsletter Auction Countdown included for instance commentaries from Steven Wunsch, CEO of the Arizona Stock Exchange. Robert Schwartz and Steven Wunsch kindly granted me interviews (in July 2000 in New York) and supplied me with further documents. I thank them for their support. I also thank Liz Libbrecht for her help with an earlier version of this paper and Nikiforos Panourgias for our discussions on the problem of explicitness in relation to markets and computers.

2. Recent developments include for instance Peter Sloterdijk's use of the notion of 'explikation' to refer to the anthropological revolution introduced by gas warfare, air conditioning and comparable technologies in the early twentieth century. These technologies partake of a process of explication of the atmospheric conditions of breathability and human subsistence, and they contribute in so doing to the constitution of a world of continuous extension, provocation and exacerbation of these conditions. See for instance Sloterdijk (2009a; 2009b) and Latour (2006).

3. See also, for instance, Hertz (2000), Didier (2007, 2009) and Muniesa and Trébuchet-Breitwiller (2010) for further explorations of the vocabulary of Gilles Deleuze in the study of economic reality.

4. See Muniesa and Linhardt (2009) for the examination of this idea in regards to the reform of public administration.

5. The very notion of 'Electronic Communication Networks' is unstable throughout the literature: we also find expressions such as 'Electronic Crossing Networks', 'Alternative Trading Systems' or 'Proprietary Trading Systems' to refer to these sorts of services. Today electronic trading is commonplace and the notion mostly stands as a remnant of debates from the nineteen-nineties.

6. Amusingly, Lee (1998, p. 1) proposes the acronym MONSTER for 'Market-Oriented New System for Terrifying Exchanges and Regulators'.

7. Concept Releases are a type of publication often used by the SEC to elicit comments on a question of regulation. They are similar to Green Papers.

8. In 1996, following an amendment to the meaning of the term 'ECN' in certain SEC documents, the AZX asked to no longer be considered as such. The new definition emphasized the fact that ECN 'continuously' listed prices whereas the AZX functioned on the principle of electronic call auction (and therefore with only one price per auction). See SEC (1997b).

9. The main argument for exempting AZX from formal registration with the SEC was the low volume of trading on this exchange. See SEC (1991b).

10. For a presentation of experimental economics in general, and of the work of Vernon Smith in particular, see Guala (2005).

11. This was of course a partly fortuitous occurrence, possibly facilitated by simultaneous attention to the present state of North-American stock markets and to frontier research in economics.

12. Prices are artificial things, immanent to the trading practice, but can also be referred to as external, somewhat transcendent realities. For a semiotics of prices in that line of inquiry, see Muniesa (2007).

13. But see Satterthwaite & Williams (1993) for a theoretical solution.

14. In his book published in 1998, Ruben Lee reported – without going into further details – the recent extension of the time priority examined below.

15. This solution evolved in fact from a reflection in terms of 'stop orders': the possibility for the system to accept hidden, 'dormant' orders that would be triggered only if the order book allowed for them to be matched. But, market engineers discovered, for this solution to be empirically acceptable by market players, the moment of triggering would indefectibly be at the last second, just before the closing of the auction. This amounted to presenting the filing of aggressive orders independently of that of the main order book.

This work was previously published in the International Journal of Actor-Network Theory and Technological Innovation, Volume 3, Issue 1, edited by Arthur Tatnall, pp. 1-15, copyright 2011 by IGI Publishing (an imprint of IGI Global).

Chapter 11
Making Information Systems Material through Blackboxing:
Allies, Translation and Due Process

Jim Underwood
University of Technology, Sydney, Australia

Edin Tabak
Curtin University of Technology, Australia

ABSTRACT

In this paper, a case study of the evolution of an organisational intranet is used to compare the concepts of "materiality" with actor-network theory's black-boxing. The authors argue that information systems need to become material through "due process". Through this paper, questions arise as to what types of material allies are useful in this process, and whether these allies can co-evolve (or "co-materialise") with the system. In this case there seemed to be existing technical actors, but the authors question whether this is always the case.

INTRODUCTION

Sociomaterality can be regarded either as a broad category of research approaches which includes actor-network theory (ANT), or as a particular theoretical view which is in some ways an alternative to ANT - emphasising performance, embodiment and mutual constitution rather than inscription, symmetry and translation. In this paper we argue briefly for the second view, and interpret becoming "material" as reaching the final stage of ANT translation, mobilisation or "black-boxing". We then describe an interpretive case study in which we ask what it is that allows an information system to be successfully black-boxed, using the concept of "due process" in systems development (McMaster, Vidgen, & Wastell, 1998). We then re-analyse the case results to investigate whether successful black-boxing depends on a wise choice of allies, in particular "material" allies. In our case these seemed to be existing technical actors, but we question whether this is always the case.

DOI: 10.4018/978-1-4666-2166-4.ch011

CONSTRUCTING MATERIALITY

'Sociomateriality' has recently become an important stream of discussion in the literature on information systems theory (Orlikowski & Scott, 2008; Dale, 2005). While this recent research claims to recognize the performative entanglement of the social and the material and 'their mutual (albeit different) constitution and the performed or enacted nature of the boundaries between them' (Orlikowski & Scott, 2008, p. 25), there is little explanation of what the social and the material actually are and how they differ. Orlikowski contrasts the sociomaterial approach with that of Actor-Network Theory, saying that sociomateriality concentrates on performance and embodiment rather than networks (ibid), while at the same time quoting with apparent approval Latour's derisive rejection of any division between social and material (p. 40). Hayles distinguishes between 'informatics' (probably meaning information systems), representing the material and 'incorporation', and information, representing the conceptual (mental? social?) and 'inscription'.

By "informatics" (a term appropriated from Donna Haraway, who uses it in a somewhat different sense), I mean the material, technological, economic, and social structures that make the information age possible. Informatics includes the late capitalist mode of flexible accumulation; the hardware and software that have merged telecommunications with computer technology; the patterns of living that emerge from and depend upon access to large data banks and instantaneous transmission of messages; and changing habits of posture, eye focus, hand motions, and neural connections that are reconfiguring the human body in conjunction with information technologies. (Hayles, 1993, p. 149)

This seems a long way from any usual sense of 'material'. It sounds very much like an actor-network, a hybrid of the social and the technical, a hybrid that undermines the meaning of the distinction on which it is built. Perhaps one difference is that ANT's scripts have traditionally been in terms of external ends ('close the door') rather than behavioural means.

A more helpful approach is provided by Law (2004), who begins from the concept of 'material culture' in anthropology. Here the expatriate anthropologist observes tools, living arrangements, sacred objects, rituals - in fact all the outward signs of everyday life - and from this creates a narrative of the culture. The advantage is that the anthropologist does not need to see 'inside the heads' of their subjects; the disadvantage (as I'm sure Hayles would argue) is that the anthropologist may not even notice important objects of the material culture unless the anthropologist has been fully incorporated into that culture. Law then uses this idea to explain Latour's experience at the Salk institute (Latour & Woolgar, 1979). As a non-scientist Latour would have had great trouble understanding what the researchers were looking for, but he could observe how they were looking for (or constructing) it - and this involved desks, whiteboards, computer printouts, draft academic papers, meetings and a variety of laboratory equipment. These were the materiality of the research practice but, especially in the case of the more complex equipment, they were obviously socially constructed, embodying sophisticated biomedical theory.

Whether something is regarded as material by the practitioners depends to some extent on its existence and function being accepted as non-problematical. From an ANT point of view we can say that the material is a network that has mobilised, that has been black-boxed, that no longer needs to be described as a network. Our question in this paper is how the social (in the non-ANT sense) is involved in this black-boxing.

The 'sociology of translation' to materiality was described by (Callon, 1986) in his study of scallop fisheries. Callon sees translation (of exactly what is not made clear in Callon's paper) as a progression through four stages or 'moments' which attempts to co-opt the other actors to the project in question. These moments are problematisation, intéressement, enrolment and mobilisation. This sequence of steps mirrors common co-option strategies, its main novelty being the heterogeneous collection of actors involved. Of course the process can fail at any stage and it may be necessary to backtrack if previous commitments weaken.

Problematisation: Involves constructing the problem. Some question or issue comes up and the sponsor identifies other actors who could be interested in the project. These actors are also constructed, in the sense that they are interpreted by the sponsor, but not yet themselves, in terms of how they need the project. The project needs to be conceived as an obligatory passage point: the actors must learn not only that they have needs which the project will satisfy but also that the project is the only way these needs can be achieved.

Intéressement: For this, the sponsor must make the actors aware of their needs and have them acknowledge that the project may indeed provide the means of meeting those needs. This may mean, among other things, detaching some of the actors from interests in competing projects or perhaps including secondary actors who will help convince an original actor of their interest in the project. All sorts of technical devices, concepts, procedures and personal performances may be used in this process. As well as their own needs and the project, the actors should also be made aware of the other actors who are "supporting" the project.

Enrolment: The actors must now be enrolled into a solid alliance and each start delivering on their part of the deal (which is not yet in writing). In many cases committees will form, documents will be produced, goals set and plans made. Many actors and performances need to be represented, by delegates, diagrams, mathematical models or test specifications. This is all achieved through the usual mixture of consent, negotiation, coercion, seduction, tricks and trials of strength.

Mobilisation: The last stage of translation. The original idea now needs to become commonplace

and material (in the senses of both solid and relevant) for a multitude of as yet absent actors (Callon, 1986, pp215-216). If successful the project loses its identity and becomes part of everyday life. The success or otherwise of the project at this stage is a test of the representations made during the translation process. There was no way of telling, until now, whether these representatives (be they diagrams or elected delegates) had the support of the masses. The proof of the project is in its acceptance.

McMaster, Vidgen, and Wastell (1998) analysed the issue of acceptance in terms of 'due process'. Using Whitley's (1999) model of the formation of collectives according to Habermassian principles, they produced a four step model of due process for translation (Figure 1).

If due process is not followed (for example, steps are left out or fail to complete) then the translation process will fail. The steps could be seen as a relabeling of Callon's steps of translation, drawing attention to what are the important issues at each stage. In our project we interpreted due process as necessary within each of Callon's stages. We did this partly because the overall intranet project that we were studying came into being gradually. A number of other applications were developed over time; some became allies of the intranet, some didn't. By applying the due process model to each of these applications we were better able to understand the (partial) success of the overall intranet project. This hybrid model is shown in Figure 2.

THE CASE STUDY

An empirical study was conducted in an entertainment organisation, which is for the purpose of this paper named "AU Entertainment". The main business of the organisation was distribution and marketing of home entertainment products such as DVD movies and music CDs in Australia and New Zealand. The fundamental unit for budget allocation was a product (movie, game, or music

Figure 1. Due process model (adapted from McMaster, Vidgen, & Wastell, 1998)

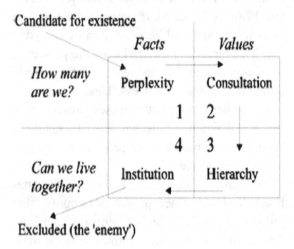

at his previous company, wished to move some marketing activities to the web and to promote collaboration among departments, while the internet content manager looked forward to a portal as a single entry point to the company's currently unconnected web applications. The vision of a single portal was not accepted by top management, so individual applications were developed opportunistically, with the vision of AU intranet in the background. The following discussion describes how some of these applications aligned to aid in the materialisation of the eventual (if somewhat reduced) AU intranet.

Figure 3 summarizes the trajectory of the organisational intranet related to the strength and time. Time is presented as Callon's four moments of translation: problematisation, intéressement, enrolment, and mobilization. The strength of an application was measured by completed stages of the due process stages: perplexity, consultation, hierarchy, and institution. Alliances between applications are indicated by the connecting lines.

In relation to time, the first moment of the intranet development started at the beginning of 2003. This problematisation stage was finalised with a web site that was named 'AU intranet'. The web site was a result of using the organisational web server by the art director and the customer service manager for their daily jobs. When their two web applications had become obligatory passage points for some employees, they made a decision to integrate the applications into a common interface - a web site called 'AU intranet'. However, it was obvious that this was not a fully functional organisational intranet. Only the customer service department and the art department were enrolled to the intranet, while probably the two most important departments in the organisation - sales and marketing - were excluded from the activities on the intranet.

So, it was the main objective during the next stage of intéressement, which lasted the first half of 2004, to align these departments to the intranet. This was done by creating the 'online dealer kit',

album). So, all everyday job activities were organised around a product. Typical procedure of marketing and distribution of a product was as follows. When a new product is released the marketing department creates promotion strategies, the art department creates design for promotions and product packaging, the sales department negotiates sales activities with customers (retailers), and the warehouse distributes the product to customers. The customer service department communicates with the customers, and answers to their queries, while the management looks for new products and plans their release. The project with which we are concerned was the establishment of a corporate intranet, which we call the AU intranet.

At the time the intranet was conceived, the information system of AU Entertainment consisted of local area networks connected via a wide area network to Melbourne corporate offices. The accounting, ordering and financial activities were managed by SAP, and the organisation had two large web sites: a B2B web site and a consumer web site used for marketing. The AU intranet was envisioned by two human actors: the art director, who had experienced a successful intranet

Figure 2. An example of integration of translation and due process model

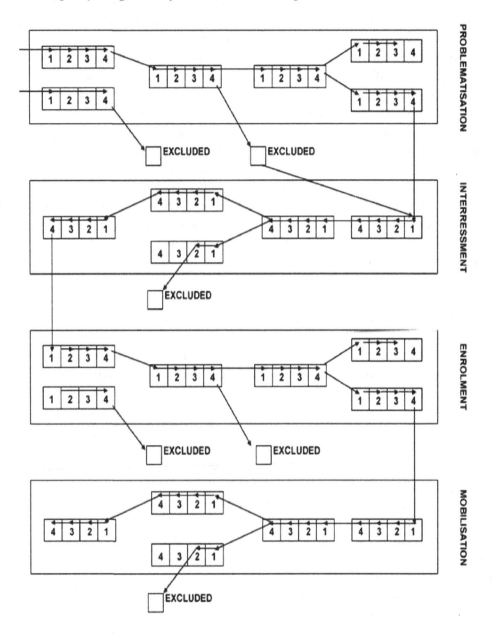

a digital version of the existing hard copy dealer kit, a catalogue used by marketing and sales people in their everyday communication with customers. This application aligned the interests of marketing and sales departments to the intranet. The enrolment stage, which lasted the second half of 2004, was marked by the full enrolment of these departments to the intranet through the creation

of the trade file application. The application was based on an excel file, called trade file, containing major information for each organisational product. When the intranet application of the trade file replaced the excel file, the opportunity was created to link the data to many outputs. The first important output was the business planning application. The success of this application and the trade file application resulted in enrolment of most of the human and organisational actors to the intranet. The mobilization of these actors, during the next stage, made the intranet an institution that became 'just another part of the organisation's normal operation or infrastructure' (Underwood, 2001, p. 197). The mobilization stage produced many new applications, allied to the trade file, and the intranet became a significant part of the organisation's everyday life.

This trajectory indicates that the development of the intranet was dependent on the alignment of interests of human and organisational actors to the main non-human (material) actors - the organisational products. As we saw, a product was the fundamental unit of the allocation of organisational budget, and the main everyday job activities were organised around organisational products. So, a major event in the trajectory was development of the trade file application, which allied the intranet with the main product information. This enabled enrolment and mobilization of the major organisational actors and resulted in development of many new intranet applications. Successful applications were those allied to the main material actor - an organisational product. The strength of an intranet application, indicated in Figure 3, was measured by the due process stages completed. The following paragraphs discuss the due process of several intranet applications.

The customer service application was developed to manage customers' queries to the organisational call centre. The perplexity was brought to the project by the use of the so called 'escalation form', a web form used by call centre operators to send (escalate) customers' queries to an appropriate person. The customer service manager had noticed that call operators write queries on a piece of paper before they fill the web form. He believed this process to be redundant, so he had consultation with a senior customer officer about a need to develop a more useful web form. Based on this analysis, the application was developed in

a process that could be described as rapid application development. This seemed to be a successful method to inscribe information behaviour of the customer service officer to the customer service application. However, the application has never mobilized a critical mass of actors to become an institution. Since the customer service manager and the senior customer officer left the organisation, the application has never been used again.

The dealer kit was a monthly catalogue of products, which would be released three months after the publication of this catalogue. Such a situation has caused perplexity, as last-minute changes were inevitable. The most affected were sales and marketing presentations. Some marketing and sales managers had started to use a combination of the dealer kit and an organisational B2B web site to create presentations in order to address the issue. Sales and marketing managers had a consultation with the web designer, and the inscription of their information needs started, which resulted in creation of an online dealer kit application. It consisted of a number of dynamic pages that could be converted to PDF files, which were then printed as a paper catalogue. As the application resulted in savings of $60,000 per month, it gained very high place in the organisational hierarchy and has become an institution, mobilizing new actors to the intranet.

The main weakness of this application was the additional effort that marketing managers had to perform. They were entering the same data in two places: an excel file called trade file and the intranet. This has created a perplexity and some frustration for marketing people. They had consultation with the web designer and the manager of the sales department to find a way to fill the intranet database from the excel trade file. The excel trade file was always a central point of information. Many participants described it as "the bible" of the organisational information. The importance of the trade tile was the reason to redesign the intranet to place the trade file as

Figure 3. Summary of the trajectory

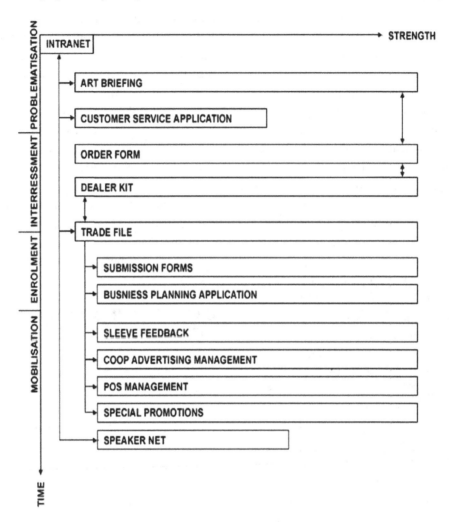

a central application of the intranet. Its highest place in the hierarchy has enabled the trade file to mobilize other actors in the organisation and become an institution itself. Many employees were referring to the intranet as the trade file. Some new applications were initiated because of the success of the trade file.

One of these applications was the business planning application. The perplexity of the situation was caused by the tedious manual job performed by the business planning manager - copying enormous data from the trade file, and performing calculation in the excel file before any

major meeting involving business forecast. After a consultation with the web designer, the business planning manager found that all data used on the trade file could be sufficient for his business planning. A new application gained a high place in the hierarchy of the sales department as soon as it was built, but it became an institution when it became a major information tool in the department, frequently being used by management and the marketing department.

Creation of the trade file and the business planning application made management aware of opportunities to materialize some organisational processes through the intranet. At the time the management of point of sale (POS) items was in significant perplexity. There was a lack of communication of the marketing, sales, and art departments with the organization's warehouse and an external printing company. Items were missing, not coming on time or coming to wrong destinations. Activities of all actors involved in this process were consulted, and inscribed in the new POS application on the intranet. Supported by top management, the application has been placed on a high place in the organisational hierarchy. It changed the communication of all involved in the process. Anyone was now able to track an item at any time on the intranet. The application was regarded as very successful, and it became an institution for the people involved in design and distribution of the POS items.

However, not all applications were so successful, although great efforts have been made to institutionalise them. One of the applications that was not able to mobilize the actors was the 'SpeakerNet' application. The perplexity was brought by the web designer, who was proposing the use of communities of practice to manage organisational knowledge. While there was not any consultation with users (employees), the great support of the management enabled the application to reach a place in the organisational hierarchy. When the application had been completed, it was advertised in the big organisational meeting. The employees were encouraged to the use application and asked to leave the comments on that meeting. The next day, only one employee left a comment, and nobody has ever used the application again. It was obvious that the application was a failure, despite the significant effort of several organisational actors.

Successful applications followed all stages in the due process and they were aligned to important human (the management) and non-human (products) actors. Two unsuccessful applications were allied with important human actors (the management), who tried to place them in high positions

in the organisational hierarchy, but that was not enough to make them institutions that could last longer. When the customer service manager and the senior customer service officer, who secured the place in the hierarchy of the customer service application, left the organisation, there was no actor to keep the application running. If the application was allied with a material actor (product), it could last longer regardless of the main human actors leaving the organisation. If the project of SpeakerNet did not skip the consultation with users, it might be allied with the material actors and avoid being a failure despite the great support from the management. Successful applications did not rely on merely social actors.

MATERIALISING WITH THE AID OF REAL FRIENDS

While imaginary friends might be comforting, they will not provide the useful love that is necessary for a project to be realised (Latour, 1996). Real friends are allies that are material, that have been institutionalised. They might be important human actors within the organisation, 'current trends' in technology, existing IT infrastructure, or even concepts - legal, economic, scientific or ethical (Underwood, 2001); but they are, for the time being, accepted without question or analysis.

Making information systems material through blackboxing is what makes them durable. In this case study, the blackboxing of a new application was a process of aligning it to the most important material actor in the organisation (product information) through opportunistic translation (Tabak, 2010). The existing product data were frequently calculated (opportunistically translated) to create new information. For instance, the intranet database was translated to the business planning application. By moving the process of very complex calculation and editing from the excel file to the web server, this application was blackboxed, so the users were provided with the latest business plan with a click of a button, without being aware of the complex translations.

To be successfully blackboxed, each application had to complete all stages of the due process. The typical trajectory of a successful application development in this study was as follows. First, an opportunity was presented through perplexity; then, consultation with users provided representational requirements for a new system; third, the project needed support from the important human actors to gain its place in the organisational hierarchy; finally, to become an institution, the requirement from the second step needed to be materialized and blackboxing of the system would be completed. In this stage, the system needed to be allied to a material actor to make it durable. In this case study, the most important material actor was a product. In short, the translation process was in great part social. An opportunity was recognised in a perplexity; users' information needs should be consulted; and there was a need for support of important human actors to place the system in the organisational hierarchy, which could mobilize wide acceptance of the system in the organisation. However, in the above narrative, only non-human (material) actors, through blackboxing, could make a system a durable institution.

The discussion in this paper so far is based on the analysis that was done at the time of the original case study research. A reconsideration of the data raises a number of questions, particularly with regard to which actors are considered 'material' and whether projects can help each other to jointly materialise (or co-evolve). We found, for instance, that the human actors were insufficient allies in this case. The particular examples involved strong supporters of projects who held apparently important organisational positions, but who left before the project was fully mobilised; so in this case the individual human actors were less material than had been imagined. In other cases it may

still be worth the risk or even be necessary to ally with key human actors, for example the CEO for large IT projects. An alternative might be to align with an organisational position or department. In a fairly rigid bureaucracy, alliances formally agreed with one incumbent of a position are likely to be honoured (though not perhaps so enthusiastically) by their successors. Another type of social actor is the professional, cultural or interest group, such as sales and marketing and their enrolment with the online dealer kit application. These actors can be regarded as more material since they have a longer history and are more self-producing (McCabe & Underwood, 2008) than either role incumbents or formal organisational groups, which may be subject to organisation restructuring. Unlike Latour (2005), we would argue that these social actors are 'real', although their behaviour in a translation trajectory is contingent, and cannot be predicted by any independent rule of 'the social'.

On the 'other side' we have technical actors such as the trade file and SAP, and (we claim above) the very material 'product'. Orlikowski and Scott (2008) in fact seem to equate technology with 'material' and work with 'social'. From the point of view of Hayles (1993), however, technical actors only became material through being incorporated by the humans, by becoming part of their life. (For further research it might be worth considering this a 'mutual incorporation', with the humans incorporating the system into their work, and the system incorporating their work into its design.) And this incorporation was of course contingent. The materiality of SAP is more enduring (providing its company remains solvent) and its alliances are more one-sided; once an organisation has decided to use SAP it must incorporate the SAP model into its work practices. As for the 'product', with which in our case it was so important for all projects to align, it is in no way a physical thing. In the entertainment industry in particular individual products are ephemeral (and are of course consructed by an extremely complex social system). It is the continuous stream of products and the discourse of product that is important. In our case study this is demonstrated through the centrality of the trade file, and by the fact that most of the information systems rely heavily on product data. In addition, the various departments, with their differing professional cultures, see each other through their work on products. At the global level, the materiality of 'the product' is demonstrated by the dominance of marketing in most organisations. To analyse the trajectory of this particular blackbox might be a fascinating exercise in ANT.

The question of co-evolution also requires further investigation. The online dealer kit and the trade file grew together as allies; later the trade file seemed part of the material environment, but itself became stronger with each new application that used it as an ally. We need to further understand how co-evolving projects inscribe or incorporate each other.

CONCLUSION

We have interrogated the concept of socio-materiality by relating it to the ANT concept of mobilisation or black-boxing. We have confirmed in the case studied that successful mobilisation depended on adherence to due process, and also to the acquisition of "material" allies. We have not, however, established a clear meaning for "material" that might be applicable to a variety of cases. This is not surprising, since ANT does not claim general theories, but it leaves a number of interesting questions for future research, particularly using comparisons across a variety of cases.

REFERENCES

Callon, M. (1986). Some Elements of a Sociology of Translation: Domestication of the Scallops and the Fishermen of Saint Brieuc Bay. In Law, J. (Ed.), *Power, Action and Belief: a new Sociology of Knowledge?* (pp. 196–233). London: Routledge and Kegan Paul.

Dale, K. (2005). Building a Social Materiality: Spatial and Embodied Politics in Organizational Control. *Organization*, *12*(5), 649–678. doi:10.1177/1350508405055940

Hayles, N. K. (1993). The Materiality of Informatics. *Configurations*, *1*(1), 147–170. doi:10.1353/con.1993.0003

Latour, B. (1996). *ARAMIS, or the love of technology*. Cambridge, MA: Harvard UP.

Latour, B. (2005). *Reassembling the Social*. London: Oxford UP.

Latour, B., & Woolgar, S. (1979). *Laboratory Life*. Beverly Hills, CA: Sage.

Law, J. (2004). *After Method*. London: Routledge.

McCabe, B., & Underwood, J. (2008). Enrolling actors in the co-evolution of inter-organisational information systems. In *Proceedings of the 12th Pacific Asia Conference on Information Systems,* Suzhou, China.

McMaster, T., Vidgen, R., & Wastell, D. (1998). Networks of association in due process of IS development. In Larsen, T., Levine, L., & de Gross, J. (Eds.), *Information Systems: current issues and future changes* (pp. 341–357). Helsinki, Finland: IFIP.

Orlikowski, W. J., & Scott, S. V. (2008, February). *The Entangling of Technology and Work in Organizations*.

Tabak, E. (2008). Inscription of information behaviour to communities of practice on an organisational intranet. In *Proceedings of the OZCHI 2008*, Cairns, Australia (pp. 347-350).

Tabak, E. (2010). Opportunistic translation in development and managment of an organisational intranet. In Proceedings of 2010 International Conference on Innovation, Management and Service (ICIMS 2010), SIngapore, 2010 *(pp. 47-52). Liverpool, UK; World Academic Press.*

Underwood, J. (2001). Translation, Betrayal and Ambiguity in IS Development. In K. Liu, R.J. Clark, P.B. Andersen & R. (Eds.), *Organizational Semiotics: Evolving a Science of Information Systems* (pp. 91-108). Boston; Kluwer.

Whitley, E. A. (1999). Habermas and the Non-Humans: Towards a Critical Theory for the New Collective. In *Proceedings of the Critical Management Studies conference*, Manchester, UK (p. 83).

This work was previously published in the International Journal of Actor-Network Theory and Technological Innovation, Volume 3, Issue 1, edited by Arthur Tatnall, pp. 16-26, copyright 2011 by IGI Publishing (an imprint of IGI Global).

Chapter 12
Institutionalisation of the Enterprise Architecture:
The Actor–Network Perspective

Tiko Iyamu
Tshwane University of Technology, South Africa

ABSTRACT

Despite impressive technical advances in tools and methodologies and the organizational insights provided by many years of academic and business research, the underperformance of Information Technology (IT) remains. In the past and even today, organizations experience difficulty in managing technology, changing from system to system, implementing new technology, maintaining compatibility with existing technologies, and changing from one business process to another. These challenges impact significantly on business performance and will continue to do so if not addressed. As a result, many organizations have deployed Enterprise Architecture (EA) in an attempt to address these challenges. However, the design and development of EA has proven to be easier than its institutionalization. The study explored the development and implementation of EA to determine the factors, which influences the institutionalization. Two case studies were conducted and Actor-Network Theory (ANT) was employed in the analysis of the data.

INTRODUCTION

Over the years, there have been efforts to improve information technology (IT) operations, most critically, its relationship with the business and its role in the vision and strategy of the organization (Radeke, 2010). This has led to improvement in the processes and activities in the computing environment of many organizations. According to Kang et al. (2009, p. 3275), using an Enterprise Architecture (EA), enterprises can manage strategies, flexible processes, and supportive resources systematically and can maintain their relations such as: relations between business strategies and execution processes, relations between execution processes and supportive enterprise resources, and so on. Despite these efforts, some organizations still find it difficult to realize the full potential of their IT investments and others are considered woeful. Unfortunately, none of these efforts seem to have solved the problems of how to ensure that

DOI: 10.4018/978-1-4666-2166-4.ch012

the organization's goals are properly met, and that the best value is achieved from investments in new information technology infrastructure (Kilpeläinen, 2007).

EA is a technical mechanism which defines the role of the business, information, technical and application architectures that best enable the business needs of the enterprise, and it provides the migration plan which moves the enterprise from the current to the future architecture. This definition is provided to guide the study. This definition is buttress by many studies such Harmon (2009) who argued that architecture is becoming the prime representation of the enterprise. It is being used more and more as the basis for determining enhancement requirements and rationalizing investments in capability development.

In the last decade, EA has become a popular topic of debate and discussion in recent years, primarily in the IT industry but also elsewhere (Ross et al., 2006). Despite the interest, it is very difficult to find an organization that has successfully designed, developed, implemented and institutionalized the EA concept. In some organizations, EA has been well developed as a blueprint but was never implemented (Armour, et al., 2007), while other organizations experienced challenges during implementation (Iyamu, 2010). In a similar study, Zachman (1987, p. 281) points out that "Many organizations face complex and unwielding challenges in assessing and articulating the components required in the implementation of EA in their organizations". Institutionalization of EA has not been a smooth process. This is attributed to the importance attached to the subject.

In this study, institutionalization is the process where a practice is assimilated into the norm. It is not easily disassociated, dismantled or re-designed. Callon (1991) refers to institutionalization as the degree of irreversibility, which depends on

1. The extent to which it is subsequently impossible to go back to a point where that translation was only one amongst others, and

2. The extent to which it shapes and determines subsequent translations.

The general expectation is that the EA is a promising means of reducing the development cycle time and cost, thus improving quality, and leveraging existing efforts by constructing and applying multi-use and reuse of assets such as patterns, components, and frameworks. The study explored whether, in practice, there is conspiracy which makes EA difficult to be delivered more successfully than one is led to believe by debates and discussions (Yin, 2003).

As such, the problematisation, development and implementation of the EA are critical to the success or failure of its institutionalization. The non-technical factors such as people and policy are critical in the development, implementation and practice of the EA in the organisations. The enrolment of employees in the implementation of the EA primarily dictates its competitive advantage particularly in large organizations. EA is fundamental to processes and activities in the computing environment, this including selection of technologies and modelling of business patterns. Some of the challenges in the deployment of the EA include skill-set. According to Burke (2007), not everyone is an architect. Other challenges include the lack of alignment between IT and Business.

The study adopted a case study, qualitative research method and employed Actor Network Theory (ANT) in the analysis of the data.

RESEARCH APPROACH

Two organizations, a financial institution and a government institution, were selected on the basis that each provides a good example of an organization subject to change, and each provides some evidence of success and failure of institutionalization of EA.

The financial institution is referred to as "Company A" and "Company B" the government institution. There were 450 and 180 employees in the computing environments of Company A and Company B, respectively. A total of 16 and 13 interviews were conducted at company A and company B, respectively. The number of interviewees was reached heuristically. The interviewees were at senior and junior levels from both business and IT departments of the organisations.

The number of interviewees varied, based on the size of the organization. A set of balanced respondent demographics was a key factor in achieving a true reflection of the situations. Targeted respondents were from different units and were at various levels of the structure within the Business and IT departments. They included Business and IT Analysts, IT Architects, IT Managers, IT Project Managers, IT Executives, Business Managers, Network and Systems Administrators.

The interview questions were designed to elicit individual and group involvement and understanding, and how the enterprise architecture was deployed and practiced in the organizations. The case materials were drawn by different means including, semi-structured interviews (Yin, 2003) with some of the key players, documentary sources and *ad hoc* observational and experience-based notes. The primary question was: what are the factors which influence institutionalisation of enterprise architecture in the organisation? There were subsidiary questions to the main question.

This paper focuses on the factors which influence institutionalisation of EA in the computing environment and the entire organisation. In such a context, an interpretive research approach (Walsham, 2006) was appropriate in order to understand influences from the perspective of social context within the organisation.

The study has three lines of investigation. Firstly, the research uses a qualitative approach to investigate the relationship between technical and non-technical factors in the development and implementation of the EA. Secondly, it investigated within the organizational hierarchy, the roles of the different actors in the development and implementation of the EA in the organizations.

This area of investigation was more carefully phrased because of the sensitive nature of the subject. Finally, the study focuses on the non-technical factors. These were to gain better understanding of how certain factors influence the practice of the EA in the organisations.

A qualitative research approach was selected mainly because it allows for clarification from respondents to questions from the researcher, while the researcher, through close interaction with interviewees, can develop a deeper understanding of the situation. Qualitative research, it has been argued, is a very useful method for complex situations (Myers, 1997). This study was considered complex because of its social-technical nature.

The data was analyzed using the interpretive approach. Interpretative rules create signification or meaningful symbolic systems that provide ways for actors to see and interpret events. Agents reflexively apply interpretative schemes and stocks of knowledge. According to Walsham (1993), the interpretive approach looks at 'reality' from a different perspective. Realism was critical in the research as it was a case study, the practice of the subject in the industry. According to Kaplan and Maxwell (1994), in an interpretive research project, there are no predefined dependent and independent variables, but a focus on the complexity of human sense-making as the situation emerges. Using the interpretive approach, the analysis of the data focused on the implementation, from the individual domains perspectives.

Underpinning Theory

Actor-Network Theory (ANT) was identified as suitable theory to underpin the research. This is primarily because it provides an ontological and epistemological basis for the research: both an understanding of the essence of what is investigated in the study, and how to obtain knowledge about the phenomena studied. This means that the data collection, subsequent analysis of the data and interpretation of the results of the analysis were guided by ANT. An actor-network consists of actors linked together through various interests. ANT emphasises the heterogeneous nature of actor-networks which consist of and link together both technical and non-technical elements. According to Adam and Tatnall (2010:5), Actor-network theory (ANT) reacts against the idea that characteristics of humans and social organizations exist which distinguishes actions from the inanimate behaviour of technological and natural objects. A core assumption in ANT is that no actor is different in kind from another. Instead, how size, power or organisation is generated should be studied unprejudiced (Law, 1992).

ANT provides a fresh perspective on the importance of relationships between actors that are both human and non-human. By their very presence, actors work to establish, maintain and revise the construction of organisational networks of aligned interests. The study followed the four moments of translation in the analysis:

1. **Problematisation:** A focal actor analyses a situation, defines the problem and proposes a solution as an obligatory point of passage (OPP) – implying that the problem resolution can only be negotiated through the OPP.
2. **Interessement:** Other actors become interested in the solution proposed. They change their affiliation to a certain group in favour of the new actor.
3. **Enrolment:** The solution is accepted and a new network of aligned interests starts when actors accept the roles defined for them.
4. **Mobilisation:** The new network starts to operate in a target oriented manner to implement the solution proposed, and grows as actors become mobilised to act as 'secondary focal actors'.

The research questions were analyzed at two interconnected levels: macro and micro. The macro-level addresses issues of how EA is developed and implemented in the organizations. At the micro-level, the roles and impacts of non-technical factors were analyzed from the perspective of its institutionalization. The moment of translation of Actor-Network Theory was followed in the analysis. The empirical data from the two studies were combined in the analysis, which is presented in the next section.

ANALYSIS OF EA DEPLOYMENT

The focus of the study was to gain better understanding of the factors which influences institutionalization of the EA in the organizations. The primary aim of the study was on the non-technical issues in the development, implementation and practice of EA in the organisations.

The EA was initiated by the Chief Technology Officer and Chief Information Officer in Company A and Company B, respectively. Architects, IT Managers, Project Managers and Business Managers were the primary actors which were involved in both the development and implementation of the EA in the organisations. The architects were responsible for the development, whilst the IT Managers, Project Managers and Business Managers were tasked with the implementation of the EA. The IT Managers and Business Managers dominated in the areas of technology and business aspects of the architecture, respective. The Projects Managers facilitated the processes for both the IT Managers and Business Managers. Within the rules and regulations and dictated by the policy of the organisations, the managers could allocate tasks, approve and terminate processes. Other stakeholders included business and IT analysts, software programmers, technology infrastructure specialists and network administrators. Each of these stakeholders was tasked with secondary and detailed activities in the implementation of the EA in the organisations. The allocation of tasks was based on technical know-how, stock of knowledge and level of seniority in the organisation. The detailed nature of the tasks makes the stakeholders very important. The majority of the interviewees knew how critical their service and contribution were to the implementation and practice of the

EA in the organisation. One of the interviewees expressed this as follows "sometimes when I am not at work, I get numerous telephone calls from my peers and other people in the department, requiring help and all sorts of support". This type of domineering attitude gave the employees power to influence the outcome of the implementation of the EA in the organisations. This sometime manipulated the administration of processes and activities, as well manifested into politicking.

Certain activities were considered very important in the organisations, and the EA was intended to execute them through its domains. Some of the activities included the selection, deployment and management of technologies; business processes; information flow and management. The study revealed that the EA is typically developed and implemented with the intention of significant benefits at the level of strategic information technology implementation and business engineering. Also, in practice, the organization expected EA to enable rapid change in an enterprise's business processes and activities. The deliverables of EA were primarily carried out through its domains - Enterprise Business Architecture (EBA), Enterprise Information Architecture (EIA), Enterprise Technical Architecture (ETA) and Enterprise Application Architecture (EAA). The intentions were well articulated, to enable competitive advantage.

The two organisations had 6 and 8 critical success factors (CSFs), respectively. Four CSFs were common among the organisations. They included cost reduction; technology infrastructure rationalization; enable and optimize process; and organized application development and deployment. The CSFs were defined in accordance to the organisational vision and requirements of EA and were regarded as key for competitive advantage. The CSFs were the main intended benefits of the EA. These factors were influenced and manipulated by the practitioners, stakeholders and sponsors, either in the development or implementation phases. Primarily, CSFs were used as measurement and justification of the investment on the EA. Due to the importance

associated to the EA in the organisations, the processes and activities in the development and implementation politics was high, sometimes grossly hyped. Politics is not stable or never in a permanent situation. This therefore has an impact of institutionalization of EA in the organization. Organizational politics involves those activities undertaken within organizations to acquire, develop, and use power and other resources to obtain one's preferred outcomes in a situation in which there is uncertainty, lack of clarity or a lack of consensus about choices. Organizational structure is a key component of organizational politics, and power is the focal point of organizational structure. Pichault (1995) opined that the system of power distribution is characterized by a relative stability: it is part of the organizational structure and may not be modified by a simple managerial intervention since it is related to other variables such as the task environment of the operators and the coordination mechanisms.

Each of the domains of the architectures provided a unique view of the enterprise leading to its own capabilities. In both organizations, the EBA was intended to provide the tools, models, techniques, and participants to manage the impact of change on business activities and processes, including their partners. This practice was supported by EIA to enable the management of change on information flow and exchange; the ETA, to enable the management of change on technology infrastructure, and the EAA, to enable development and the portfolio management of software applications.

In the development, implementation and practice of the EA, specialised skills were needed. Not all IT specialists can be architects without the opportunity to learn and practice the tools and techniques required. A lack of skill implies both the inability to perform competently as well as the inability to recognize and deliver the full potential of the EA. Even where the process was understood, there was evidence that the potential and objectives of the EA were not realized, as such, the investment was threatened. It thus appears that the technical know-how and experiences of architects and managers will be important in achieving future success.

When it came to EA, there was a feeble relationship between the IT and Business departments of the organizations. This was as a result of the hierarchical structure of the organisations. Some of the employees protected their domain from control being taken over by the EA team. Consequently, there was not sufficient input from the business during development and implementation of the EA. As a result, there was more concentration and focus on the Technology and Application architectures than Business and Information architectures. This has led to more investment, in terms training and development of both Technology and Application Architects than other domain architects.

The analysis of the empirical data revealed that simply defining the EA exposes gaps in business processes and strategy, information technology and systems strategy, and the relationship between Business and IT departments of the organization. The process obliges employees to confront difficult questions and make hard decisions they had previously managed to avoid, such as redeployment of certain employees who did not have appropriate skill for the position they hold. This was to make easy and possible the institutionalization of EA in the organizations.

In one of the case studies, the organization formulated a policy to guide the deployment of the EA into institutionalization. The policy was to ensure successful design, development, implementation and maintenance of EA, through fundamental principles. These principles were basic philosophies which were intended to guide the process from the problematisation to institutionalization stages. The principles apply to all the domains of the EA. They provided guidelines and rationales for the constant examination and re-evaluation of technology and systems plans. This approach is however not new; it is supported by Youngs et al. (1999). The principles were generally derived from an intensive discussion with senior IT and Business Managements, then validated

in discussions with the highest IT Committees. Non-technical factors such as financial budget, personal or group interests and the capability of the organization influenced the formulation of these principles.

The primary object of the institutionalization of EA was to provide methods, processes, disciplines, and organizational structures to create, manage, organize, and use models for managing the impact of change. The research finds, in both case studies that typically organizations did not take a holistic view, and that the practice of EA was deficient when measured against the organizations' requirements. This has been acknowledged and was attributed to a manifestation of lack of cooperation and understanding between the Business and IT departments of the organizations. In Company A, one of the senior managers expressed his frustration as follows: "I'd lock all architects and senior business management in a room for a week or two, and only allow them out once I was satisfied they understood each other's role. Once the appreciation for each other's contribution is understood, I'd expect a less expedient approach towards "establishing business capability" and in this climate, architecture would have a better chance of being able to contribute to its full potential." The misunderstanding between the Business and IT personnel were both conscious and unconscious acts. The conscious was as a result of lack of understanding, and those who understood did not buy-in into the concept of the EA in the organisation. These acts impacted mobilisation of peers and subordinates, specifically in the implementation and practice of EA in the organisations.

The sequence of the EA development phases - business visioning (extracted from business strategy), defines and refines the respective domains, EBA, EIA, ETA and EAA. This was conveyed in a logical sequence of development, which was based on relationships and dependencies of these phases, rather than a linear sequence of events. Though interrelated, each of the domains had their unique focuses. The scope of the EA was therefore the union of the enterprise, the business engineering and development that was applied to it, and the technical domains that supports it. Thus the scope of the EA was defined through a pragmatic need: the need to design and redesign as well as continuously as was intended, to improve the functioning of the organization.

During the study, it became evident that the EA defines the scope, scale and nature of required changes within an organisation and that it helps to identify the resources that must become involved. There were validation points or checkpoints during the development and implementation of the EA. These were influenced by factors, which result to negative and sometimes positive outcomes. This was the case in both organisations. But it was more visible in Company B, where an architect opined as follows:

I'd change the way we fund technology initiatives. I'd make silo's illegal. I'd teach "community" concepts to the business and attempt to demonstrate the value of synergy. I'd get greater CEO support - he needs to understand that architecture really is a business issue, not a technology thing. I'd financially reward those that pursue properly architected routes and disincentives those that don't. I'd either centralize architecture (ALL the interrelated disciplines) probably physically or at worst establish a capacity to govern all architecture teams as if they were a single unit. And I'd make architecture a mandatory.

Some employees including managers feared that architects could become too powerful if given the necessary support. Others thought that institutionalisation could render them redundant. This behaviour was most from the business units who didn't understand the EA. These actions contributed to the IT been a cost centre and hampered innovation in the organisations.

The study indicates that problems routinely experienced in organisations include a perception of poor value for money from IT investments. It revealed that this was as a result of poor linkage and alignment between the strategic goals and IT investments of the organisations. When the business environment is dynamic; and when unavoidable change is forced upon the organization; an inability to link exploitation of IT investments with changes to strategic business goals leads to greater difficulties.

RESULTS

Some findings have been extracted from the above analysis. These findings are presented and discussed as follows:

This study examined the development, implementation and practice of EA in two organizations. This was done to establish and determine the factors which influence institutionalization of EA in the organization which deploys it. As revealed by the analysis, there are four key elements in the development and implementation of EA. The four elements were considered as the key elements because they were more prevalence, and most importantly, they are interconnected. As illustrated in Figure 1 below, they include adaptation, innovation, uniformity and alignment.

Adaptiveness

The EA requires adaptiveness in order to effectively and efficiently support and enable the business objectives through its domains. It is more beneficial when it is applied uniquely to specific needs of the organization, depending on its business strategies, architectural maturity, priorities, organizational culture, and political environment. Explicitly, infrastructures are to be adaptive to ensure return on investment. Through adaptiveness consolidation and reuse are achieved.

Innovation

The EA engineers innovations through its processes, and activities in the organizations. Each of the various domains (as defined by the organization)

Figure 1. Factors of EA institutionalization

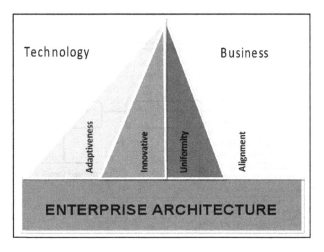

of EA has their various deliverables in relation to innovations. The primary aim of the continuous innovations was to enhance competitive advantage of the organization's businesses, processes and activities. Innovation proactively promotes and supports the initiative of the organization to achieve its critical success factors.

Uniformity

EA provides a uniform process and procedure for selecting technology infrastructure, of documenting the current business, the future business, and the gap between the two. This is important and applies to the autonomous business units of organizations. It begins from project initiation and problematisation to implementation stages.

As the case of the case study, uniformity was instrumental to focusing on skill auditing, development and assessment in alignment to organizational needs.

Alignment

The analysis revealed that EA will not work if there is no understanding between the Business and IT Managements. The lack of cooperation manifests itself to rivalry on many issues including in the methods and selection of technology, Business

process standard, Governance approach and Assessment criteria. This has a serious influence on the practice of EA in the organization.

Only when the above identified key elements are made norm through the EA is it that institutionalization becomes feasible. Unfortunately, other critical factors influence and impact the above key elements of EA in its success or failure. The interrelationships between the key elements and critical factors are illustrated in Figure 2 below. If not well managed, the manifestations of these factors could derail the institutionalization of EA in the organization that deploys it. The factors discussed below.

FACTORS INFLUENCING INSTITUTIONALISATION OF EA

The findings presented above are now interpreted, with focus on how they influence institutionalisation of EA in the organisation. The interpretation was in terms of the concept of, and primarily based on responses from the interviewees, pertinent to the present case analysis and based on the findings above, which includes critical success factors and business requirements. Six factors were found to be most influential in the institutionalization of EA in the organization. The factors include

Figure 2. Factor influencing institutionalization of EA

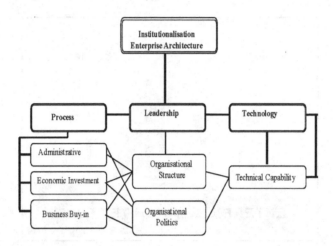

organizational structure, economic investment, administrative, organizational politics, technical capability and buy-in. As depict in Figure 2 below, the factors are grouped in three categories, namely, Process, Leadership and Technology. These categories are reached on the basis of the analysis in which they were relatively prevalence.

The advantage of a general framework shown in Figure 1 is that it enables a greater understanding of how institutionalization of EA is influenced in the organization that deploys it. While the factors could enhance institutionalisation, using this framework, Figure 2 and assist in counteracting them with appropriate measures.

The analyses of the case studies revealed the following as depict in Figure 2, the influencing in the institutionalization of EA in the organizations:

Organisational Structure

The organisational structure plays a critical role in the development, implementation and practice of EA. The EA is problematised through the structure of the organisation. This includes the development and implementation of EA and how the architects and managers carry out their individual and group tasks. Without structure it will be difficult the deploy EA in the organisation. However, structure within the organisation is embedded with roles, responsibilities and power to execute the mandate of the organisation. As such, the organisational structure impacts how alignments between units and department within the organisation are shaped and adapt. How the organisation adapts and aligns its goals manifests and influences the innovation and uniformity across the organisation.

Development, implementation and practice of EA require a deep understanding of technical needs and business vision and requirements. As business processes change, projects are initiated and technology grows, it becomes hard to structure an organization to provide effective feedback loops which run between these constituencies. Although EA is intended to address this very area, if the organization is predisposed to managing them badly in all circumstances, then EA will not be an effective solution.

Employees use the enactment of power to manoeuvre activities and processes within the organizational structure. Power as mandated was exercised to protect individual and group interests rather than the interests of the organization in the practice of EA.

Economic Investment

Funding for the development, implementation and practice of EA in the organisation is critical. What is also important is the roles and responsibilities of the stakeholders, this includes who sponsors and owns the EA in the organisation. This is depended and influenced by the structure of the organisation. For example, in company A, the Chief Architect was in the IT department, which was different from company B, where the head of architecture was situated in the business.

The investment of EA is influenced by where the EA is situated, whether in the business or IT department. The investment on EA determines how it's aligned with the IT and business objectives; shapes its innovation capability; and its uniformity across the organisation.

Supporting EA requires an economic investment, particularly if EA operates as a cost-centre. Many organizations find it difficult to institute appropriate measures to fund their cost-centre because the benefits are only indirectly evident, and rarely are they evident as simple financial benefits. Most architects are not able to articulate, translate and quantify their work into monetary value. This could be attributed to non-immediate realization of their contributions. As a result, its value is hotly contested by the business stakeholders.

Administrative

The administration of the EA is carried out through the organisational structure. This is primarily to ensure manageability, which covers both technical and non-technical factors during the development, implementation and practice of the EA in the organisation. The management focuses on how to gain uniformity across the units of the organisation. Otherwise, processes and activities would be duplicated and exorbitant.

However, the administrative process depend on the participation of employees, particularly, the stakeholders in the deployment of the EA. The administrative process of the EA could be employed to promote adaptiveness, innovation and alignment across the organisation. For example, the administrative provide a channel through which innovation is embarked upon, this includes those who legitimately get involved, and who leads the team.

The nature of EA as process oriented makes it inevitable to align with the administrative process and the structure of the organization. However, it is difficult to catalogue, archive, and retrieve the "as-is" (or silo) architectures across multiple business units within large organizations. Although it is common to scavenge small classes or functions opportunistically from existing programs, architects often find it hard to consolidate suitable architecture outside of their immediate area. This could be achieved through effective and efficient administration of processes and activities. A domain manager (manages specialized architects) who reports to the Chief Architect or Chief Technology Officer is therefore recommended.

Organisational Politics

Employees both in the IT department and in the Business units often view architects with suspicion. This is because they resent the fact that they may no longer be empowered to make key technology and related decisions. They also perceive a threat to their job security and resource control. There is also rivalry between architects and other IT specialists over domination.

These factors manifest themselves to acts of organizational politics, which result in lack of trust and cooperation. The factors have a negative impact on the relationship between the Business and IT departments on one hand and on the other, between the IT specialists and Architects.

Technical Capability

EA efforts often and frequently fail because architects lack the appropriate skills, and the enterprise at large lacks the competencies necessary to deploy EA. Most Architects are appointed on the basis of their seniority in the organization. For instance, architects often lack knowledge of, and experience with, fundamental design patterns in the domain they are assigned to.

As a result many of the Architects lack the abilities, knowledge or skills required to effective deploy EA. This was attributed to lack of awareness to narrowness in vision, leading to very different interpretations and definitions of EA. This leads to incompatible views about the full range of EA processes and phases that are required and deprives the participants of any possibility to achieve best practice, through a failure to take the holistic view of what must be done. This makes it hard for them to understand how to implement the EA frameworks and components effectively.

Business Buy-in

Strategy for communication with the Business is critical. Poor communication with the business leads to a general view that architecture is not important. If EA is not understood, the business always finds difficulty in getting "buy-in" into the concept. As a result of lack of buy-in, EA will always fail to achieve its aims and objectives.

An emphasis on technical architecture increases lack of interest and understanding of EA by the business. Arising from these factors is new pressure on IT departments to improve value for money, but many would argue the IT department has no means to achieve it because of the gulf between it and the business. EA addresses this gap, but if it is not supported or sponsored by the business then it – the EA – will also fail and the problems will remain.

Many organizations face complex and unwieldy challenges in assessing and articulating the changes necessary in their organizations. This includes the factors, which influence the practice of EA across the entire organization. If an organization is to be successful in bridging the context gap between development and implementation of EA, a mechanism must be deployed to articulate the impact of the influencing factors on the enterprise.

The factors revealed above are critical to the success or failure of EA, which influences the institutionalization of EA in the organization. Some of these factors have been speculated, but there was never empirical evidence to substantiate it.

CONCLUSION

The contribution of the study arises from implications for the key stakeholders, sponsors and architects responsible for the deployment of EA in the organization. They need to understand the factors impacting the institutionalization of EA, in which they wholly play parts and more importantly, how to mitigate against the risk posed by these factors.

A further contribution of this study is its aim to be of significance to decision makers, managers and employees of the organization within the computing environment. It is expected that the key contribution will arise from the understanding of the fundamental elements through which EA impacts change. Through this, a better understanding of the contribution of non-technical factors in the deployment of EA will be gained.

Also, academia needs to take cognizance of the dynamics and causes of what, why and how EA could be institutionalized in practice, based on the empirical evidence of the study.

REFERENCES

Adam, T., & Tatnall, A. (2010). Use of ICT to Assist Students with Learning Difficulties: An Actor-Network Analysis. In *Proceedings of the IFIP TC 3 International Conference (KCKS 2010)*, Brisbane, Australia.

Armour, F., Kaisler, S., & Bitner, J. (2007). Enterprise Architecture: Challenges and Implementations. In *Proceedings of the 40th Annual Hawaii International Conference, System Sciences* (pp. 117-217).

Burke, B. (2007). *The Role of Enterprise Architecture in Technology Research*. Gartner Inc.

Callon, M. (1991). Techno-economic networks and irreversibility. In Law, J. (Ed.), *A sociology of monsters. Essays on power, technology and domination* (pp. 132–164). London: Routledge.

Cook, M. A. (1996). *Building enterprise information architectures: reengineering information systems*. Upper Saddle River, NJ: Prentice-Hall, Inc.

Harmon, K. (2009). *The "Systems"*. Nature of Enterprise Architecture.

Iyamu, T. (2010). Theoretical Analysis of the Implementation of Enterprise Architecture. *International Journal of Actor-Network Theory and Technological Innovation, 2*(3), 27–38.

Kang, D., Lee, J., & Kim, K. (2009). Alignment of Business Enterprise Architectures using fact-based ontologies. *Expert Systems with Applications, 37*, 3274–3283. doi:10.1016/j.eswa.2009.09.052

Kaplan, B., & Maxwell, J. A. (1994). Qualitative Research Methods for Evaluating Computer Information Systems. In Anderson, J. G., Aydin, C. E., & Jay, S. J. (Eds.), *Evaluating Health Care Information Systems: Methods and Applications* (pp. 45–68). Thousand Oaks, CA: Sage Publications.

Kilpeläinen, T. (2007). Business Information Driven Approach for EA Development in Practice. In *Proceedings of the 18th Australasian Conference on Information Systems* (pp. 447-457).

Law, J. (1992). Notes on the theory of the actor-network: ordering, strategy, and heterogeneity. *Systems Practice, 5*(4), 379–393. doi:10.1007/BF01059830

Myers, M. D. (1997). Qualitative Research in Information Systems. *Management Information Systems Quarterly, 21*(2), 241–242. doi:10.2307/249422

Pichault, F. (1995). The Management of Politics in Technico-Organisational change. *Organization Studies, 16*(3), 449–476. doi:10.1177/017084069501600304

Radeke, F. (2010). Awaiting Explanation in the Field of Enterprise Architecture Management. In *Proceeding of the 16th Americas Conference on Information Systems*, Lima, Peru.

Ross, J. W., Weill, P., & Robertson, D. (2006). *Enterprise Architecture as a Strategy: Creating Foundation for Business Execution*. Boston: Harvard Business School Press.

Walsham, G. (2006). Doing Interpretive Research. *European Journal of Information Systems, 15*(3), 320–330. doi:10.1057/palgrave.ejis.3000589

Yin, R. K. (2003). *Case Study Research, Design and Methods* (2nd ed.). Thousand Oaks, CA: Sage Publications.

Youngs, R., Redmond-Pyle, D., Spaas, P., & Kahan, E. (1999). *A standard for architecture description* (Vol. 38, No. 1). Enterprise Solutions Structure.

Zachman, J. A. (1987). A framework for information systems architecture. *IBM Systems Journal, 26*(3), 276–292. doi:10.1147/sj.263.0276

This work was previously published in the International Journal of Actor-Network Theory and Technological Innovation, Volume 3, Issue 1, edited by Arthur Tatnall, pp. 27-38, copyright 2011 by IGI Publishing (an imprint of IGI Global).

Chapter 13

Actor-Network-Theory in Medical E-Communication:
The Role of Websites in Creating and Maintaining Healthcare Corporate Online Identity

Magdalena Bielenia-Grajewska
University of Gdansk, Poland

ABSTRACT

In this article, an attempt will be made to discuss how websites create and maintain the online identity of medical care providers. To discuss this issue in greater detail, the author has chosen Actor-Network-Theory since an ANT approach makes it possible to study the role of living and nonliving entities in shaping the online identity of healthcare suppliers and to concentrate on the networks and systems within e-healthcare as well as the flows and interrelations constituting it. The primary aim of this research is to show the communicative aspect of healthcare corporate websites by using the selected notions of ANT methodology and their potential implications for corporate identity creation and maintenance.

INTRODUCTION

Modern reality is shaped by some complicated nets built of various entities and ties (Blommaert, 2010) and it is determined by the dependence on other human beings (Laszlo, 2001). Thus, the modern world is a networked entity (e.g., Castells, 2009; Corallo, 2007; Hardt & Negri, 2004) and its interconnectedness is represented in various domains of life, including the networked

economy (Aurik, Jonk, & Willen, 2003). For example, modern business, with its grids and lattices, can be observed on the organizational level. Since modern companies do not exist in a vacuum, but are rather connected with other entities on an everyday basis, the organization and its relations can be viewed through the prism of networks and ecosystems (Andrew & Sirkin, 2006; Davenport, Leibold, & Voelpel, 2006). The multispectral character of corporations is also reflected in their identities which are constituted of multiple personalities (e.g., Bergen & Braith-

DOI: 10.4018/978-1-4666-2166-4.ch013

waite, 2009), of both individual and social types. Among various factors shaping the networked organizational identity it is technology which is the most important one (e.g., Carr, 2004; Fernandez, 2004; O'Kane, Hargie, & Tourish, 2004). The revolution in communication and technological achievements have changed the way companies function and communicate, with technologically sophisticated codes, wires and pulsations being an important part of modern corporate life (Birkets, 2010). The coexistence of technology with other aspects of corporate reality makes it difficult to establish the demarcation line between the human and the technological world (Bukatman, 2002). Some go even further and state that information technologies are starting to become part of our bodies and function as prosthetic technologies that take over or augment biological functions, turning humans into cyborgs, and thereby altering human nature (Brey & Søraker, 2009, p. 1388). Human and nonhuman entities mutually contribute e.g. to information networks (e.g., Masuda, 1983) such as the ones available on the Internet. Since they are online everywhere and anywhere (Richardson, 2005, p. 272), the same applies to the activities related to healthcare which will be discussed in the coming sections. The Internet determines the patient-doctor relation in a number of ways, being a source of information, a community creator, a communication tool and a new technology facilitator, introducing e.g. telemedicine (McLellan, 2004). Since one of the most popular levels of analyzing health discourse is mass communication (Schulz, 2006), in this research an attempt will be made to show that websites are not only the places of putting information on the services offered by the healthcare company and the instruments of health information and disease prevention for many patients, but they also determine personalities of those interested in health issues. At the same time, e-patients (Akerkar & Bichile, 2004) influence the corporate online identity of healthcare providers.

E-HEALTHCARE

All people, whether in good or bad condition, have to conduct heath-related activities in their adult life (Nielsen-Bohlman & Panzer, 2004). With the increasing role of technology in the twenty first century, the issues connected with well-being and health management also take place online. As has been proved by some studies, those looking for health-related information rely on the Internet since 4.5% of all the Internet searches concern health topics (Morahan-Martin, 2004). Some authors even state that health is the second most often searched topic on the Internet (Roberts and Copeland, 2001). Since national and professional barriers are of secondary importance on the Internet (Roberts & Copeland, 2001) and most people are into "e", and if they are not, they plan to be (Goldstein, 2000, p. 6), the health system is also heavily determined by the web. It is especially popular among Digital Natives (Palfrey & Gasser, 2008), those born after 1980, to rely on online health information and favor e-healthcare, with the latest being defined as goods and services provided by healthcare professionals or organizations to patients/customers/end-users via the Internet or other telecommunication pipelines (Pańkowska, 2004, p. 3).

There are different reasons for the popularity of technology, especially the Internet, in healthcare. First of all, the health system has changed significantly, especially in the industrialized countries. The cost policy makes health providers compete for patients since the latter can choose the doctor or health service they want. Additionally, many medical treatments are not covered by the national health service and they have to be reimbursed by patients themselves. Consequently, those interested in health services look for competitive possibilities and cost-saving offers. The other issues are related to demographic factors, such as aging societies, with older people being the growing group which relies heavily on the national health system. What is more, since individuals are more educated (Sieving, 1999) and a healthy life style is more popular, people are interested in looking for relevant health topics. The constant need for information is also related to the chance of health dangers. In the past infectious diseases drew more public concern, whereas nowadays chronic lifestyle diseases are the most important ones (Zarcadoolas, Pleasant, & Greer, 2006). Moreover, information and communication technologies enable distance healthcare systems, in particular the remote monitoring of patients' state of health, as well as supervising traditional care (Cellary, 2002). Additionally, patients turn to the Internet for medical help since it offers them anonymity, which is important when they are not satisfied with the standard medical treatment (Eysenbach & Diepgen, 1999; Overberg, Toussaint, & Zwetsloot-Schonk, 2006; Winefield, Coventry, & Lambert, 2003) or if they are ashamed of their health problems (McLellan, 2004). In the latter case, online health communication makes it possible to choose between the pseudo identity when a person uses a pseudonym or a number and the untraceable identity when no identifiable name or code is used (Kizza, 2010). What is more, the lack of face-to-face communication gives the possibility to mask an identity or even to use a false identity (Brey & Søraker, 2009; Burnett, Consalvo, & Ess, 2010; Wallace, 2001).

New information technologies and their implications for patient-doctor communication are connected with both advantages and disadvantages (e.g., Berger, 2009). Online health information can reduce the sufferers' anxiety, increase patient knowledge on health issues (Rice, 2001) and offer more autonomy in choosing healthcare providers and treatments (Howell, 2004). As far as the advantages of website communication are concerned, customers can be provided with the information they need very quickly (Neuman, 2007), at a lower cost than available offline sources (Lipsey, Fischer, & Poirier, 2007; Neuman, 2007),

or even, in most cases, free of charge (Kim & Chang, 2007). What is more, it is more convenient to search for medical information online since it is available 24 hours a day, in any place where access to the web is available (Anderson, Rainey, & Eysenbach, 2003). Another advantage is that published materials can be very quickly modified or erased (Cantoni & Tardini, 2010).

As far as potential disadvantages of e-healthcare are concerned, the issues of security, privacy and confidentiality, encompassing legal, social, psychological and technological factors, are very important and should be treated with great care (Shoniregun, Dube, & Mtenzi, 2010). What is more, not all offline materials can be simply placed onto the website (Tourish & Hargie, 2004).

The Internet encompasses different ways of providing and exchanging health information. One of them is the corporate websites of companies offering healthcare services.

HEALTHCARE CORPORATE WEBSITES

As far as the definition is concerned, a corporate website is the Internet site mainly concerned with information about the company. Thus, a healthcare corporate website is a website created by a medical company to provide information on health-related services. Its purpose is to build relations with existing and potential stakeholders by praising such values as goodwill, loyalty and trust (e.g., Kotler et al., 2008; Lipsey, Fischer, & Poirier, 2007). Taking the above-mentioned aspect into account, corporate websites are often perceived as a marketing tool (Foglio, 2007; Palkhivala, Anderson-Lemieux, & Mappin, 2000) since they can be a public calling card, the street-side façade, the cover of the book, the gilded entrance to an otherwise function-first interior design (Potts, 2007, p. 90). Such items as negative comments are very rarely to be found on company websites (Cass, 2007). Thus, such information as a company's history, mission statement, corporate philosophy, products and services, financial information and career possibilities should be provided on the website (Capriotti & Moreno, 2007). Since company websites are said to be among the most important tools in customer-company communication (e.g., Barker & Angelopulo, 2007; Bastian, 2008; Chan, 2004; Sieving, 1999), the creation and maintenance of these Internet sites should be done by different specialists, coming from different departments to cope with different issues publishable on the website (Ace, 2001). It should be also remembered that there is no one communicative procedure adopted throughout the website but there are different strategies to meet different audiences and aims (Garzone, 2009; Roberts & Copeland, 2001; Winefield, Coventry, & Lambert, 2003) and to attract the ones potentially interested in the products or services offered by the company (Galea, 2000; Mishra, 2009). Since medicine is determined by such notions as mythologies, rituals, opinions on life and death, religious beliefs and lay medical opinions (Root Wolpe, 2002), the profile of online users is of primary importance for the creators and administrators of healthcare websites. As far as diversified audience is concerned, there are different factors determining the content of websites. For example, in the case of health websites, the notion of 'national medical culture' should be analyzed which comprises the methods of managing health as well as the group of values and beliefs popular among national medical communities (Last, 1999). At the individual level, websites should take into account the diversified health literacy of its users (Nutbeam, 2000). Health literacy is defined as the degree to which individuals can obtain, process and understand basic health information and services needed to make appropriate health decisions (Elliott & Shneker, 2009, p. 434). People of low health literacy have problems with following doctors' advice, do not take medications as prescribed or do not take care of their health very much (Wilson, 2003). Conse-

quently, people of a low literacy level can misinterpret information on the website which may lead to maltreatments. However, literacy is dynamic and may change according to the circumstances (Zarcadoolas, Pleasant, & Greer, 2006). Since health-literate patients are beneficial for healthcare providers (Rubinelli, Nakamoto, & Schulz, 2009), corporate websites are very important and effective tools for improving health literacy. The other factor determining how the website is used is the stage of advancement (Caiata, Zufferey, & Schulz, 2009). Thus, the stage of illness determines the type and frequency of online searches. The environment related to health issues is the next factor. Health contexts differ from standard settings since they often contain fear or stress factors (Nielsen-Bohlman & Panzer, 2004). Thus, people look for support networks which will help them to offset stress and negative emotions (Wright, 2009). They are also more responsive to the information they need. Being under stress related to the uncertainty of health condition, some may over interpret or understand the web content in the wrong way. What is more, nowadays we can observe the shift from passive to active patients who demand more information (Anderson, Eysenbach, & Rainey, 2003; Schulz, 2006). The relations between patients and doctors have also changed. The paternalistic model has been replaced by a more partnership-related attitude (Kasztelowicz, 2004). Corporate websites should also take into account the so-called patient centeredness (Del Piccolo, Mazzi, Scardoni, Gobbi, & Zimmermann, 2008) which is connected with much more than prescribing and medicine-taking (Bond, 2004, p. 12). Stewart et al. (2006) discuss some components comprising the patient-centered approach: disease and illness experience, understanding the whole person, finding common ground, incorporating prevention and health promotion, enhancing the patient-doctor relationship. Let me discuss the above-mentioned components with regard to the health care websites of corporations. As far as disease and illness experiences are concerned, the dichotomy between these two should be taken into account. A disease is an objective clarification made by physicians to explain to patients the malfunctions of their body. To compare, an illness is a subjective understanding made by the sufferers, including their feelings and thoughts (Stewart et al., 2006). This attitude can be also reflected in the case of health corporate websites. Apart from some questions concerning how long the health problem lasts and what the symptoms are, there can be enquiries dealing with how much it disrupts everyday activities, how the health service provider can enhance patients' quality of life. Thus, apart from eliciting health facts, the website should also adapt an emotional attitude towards patients' doubts. The second issue important for website creators is the holistic approach to e-patients. Thus, not only the particular problem should be dealt with, but also the issue, not necessarily linked to the indisposition. For example, the patient should be provided with information not only on necessary treatments and consultations, but also on the post-healing phase. This is also in line with not separating health prevention and health promotion. The next element, finding a common ground, is the ability to use the communicative strategies which will enable various patients to understand the web content. What is more, the technological devices available on the website should enhance the patient-doctor communication. Thus, chat tools, questionnaires, email contacts and telephone lines reduce the emotional gap between the sufferers and the healers and may compensate for the physical distance present in e-communication.

The web as such can be studied by taking two aspects into account: the navigational aspect and the corporate identity aspect (Meissner, 2005). In this paper I will concentrate on identity issues. Since a website itself can be considered a community of people running and accessing that website (Lorenzo & Cantoni, 2010, p. 228), it can be treated as an instrument of corporate identity creation.

CORPORATE ONLINE IDENTITY OF HEALTHCARE PROVIDERS

Although complex personalities existed in other centuries, it is the network society which has led to the proliferation of different identities (Rüsen & Laass, 2010). The multitude of individualities is also visible in the net. Since identities are geographic in that sense that they are constructed in and through particular spaces (Del Casino, 2009, p. 56), the web is also the place where personalities are created and maintained (Holt, 2004; Monteiro, 2004). Identity is treated as an ontological concept since life can be projected or cast in similar but not identical existential settings (Capurro and Pingel, 2002), with the Internet being one of them. However, the identity created online differs from the one created in printed media since it can be changed very quickly and can neither be predicted nor kept fully under control by writers or by readers (Schäfer, 2010, p. 29). This is also determined by its interactivity and interconnectivity (Harison, Barlow, & Williams, 2007; Rossmann, 2010; Sassen, 2004) since the site handles interactive communication initiated by the customer (Kotler et al, 2008, p. 850). What is more, there is no demarcation line between online and offline corporate identities. The offline identity is important since it is the corporate offline image which makes customers consult the website (Danet & Herring, 2007; Thurlow, Lengel, & Tomic, 2004). In the case of searching for health information, most people look for sites which are owned by well-known and well-respected organizations. Reputation is an important factor in choosing companies and people feel that they would be more likely to trust a site that they have heard of before rather than the one that they have simply found in a search engine (Sillence, Briggs, Harris, & Fishwick, 2007). Consequently, online and offline communications do not exclude each other (Cantoni & Tardini, 2006; Christensen, 2003), but it is rather the process of mediamorphosis (Fidler, 1997), when old media do not disappear with the appearance of new modes of mass communication, but they rather change and adapt to the new environment. In the case of the discussed corporate health websites, offline materials can enhance those interested to consult the webpage for updated and new information. What is more, not only offline and online identities are interrelated, but also corporate and social personalities. Health corporate websites determine a patient's identity. As Schau and Muniz (2002) state, consumers create their identities during computer-mediated communication. Since patients are also consumers of health services, their identity will be also influenced by online interactions. At the same time, the online representation of healthcare providers will be determined by patients since people choose brands or products that reflect or communicate a specific personality (Schau & Gilly, 2003) Health websites can also help restore one's identity, especially if a pessimistic diagnosis makes one question the value of life. Reading the stories of people who are in a similar situation or who have managed to fight the illness helps to build up the disturbed identity (Overberg, Toussaint, & Zwetsloot-Schonk, 2006).

CORPORATE ONLINE IDENTITY OF HEALTHCARE PROVIDERS THROUGH THE ACTOR-NETWORK PERSPECTIVE

The approach taken into account by me is also in line with the perspective adopted by Cantoni and Tardini (2006) who highlight in their research the communicative function of websites, viewing them not only as technological tools but also as communication artifacts. Thus, the structural features such as the name of the company, address, telephone number, privacy policy statement, links to other websites and navigation menu, being rather stable elements of a website (Rains & Donnerstein Karmikel, 2009), will not be given a detailed study. However, it must be remembered

that visual appearance, especially familiar images or logos, influences the choice of websites (Sillence, Briggs, Harris, & Fishwick, 2006).

To study the nuances of the online identity represented by healthcare providers on their websites, one of the popular network theories has been chosen, namely Actor Network Theory.

There are different reasons for the adoption of ANT into the discussion on healthcare websites. The first one is the increasing demand for technology, and consequently, the popularity of technology-related approaches, such as Actor-Network-Theory (Kien, 2009). Secondly, ANT underlines the social creation of technological progress (Meyer, 2005) and, at the same time, helps to analyze how technology determines the change of social systems (Tsohou et al., 2010). In the case of this research, the attempt of this paper is to stress the social shaping of healthcare websites and the technological influence on the web users. The third cause is that ANT relies strongly on semiotics. Analyzing the semiotic character of ANT literally allows us to treat websites as the place where the magnitude of signs appear. For example, logos, colors and layouts can be treated as the signs representing corporate identity. However, by looking at the semiotics more metaphorically and treating a sign as anything which produces meaning (Thwaites, Davis, & Mules, 2002 p. 9), all elements of a website can be studied by taking into account its meaningfulness. Thus, even the website elements which are not signs themselves can be treated as the visual representation of corporate image. As has been already highlighted, it is very difficult to draw the line between the offline and online life. This is also stressed in ANT which underlines the lack of strict and fixed boundaries between different realities, such as social, natural and technical ones (Murdoch, 2005). Thus, people, technology and artifacts simultaneously take part in the mutual production of reality (Lindstrøm, 2010). What is more, neither the technical vision nor the social vision will come into being without the other (Sismondo,

2010, p. 81-82) and neither social nor technical positions are privileged (Adam & Tatnall, 2010, p. 5). In the case of corporate websites, they can be treated as networks built of various social and material elements (Mitev, 2009). Drawing from the terminology of ANT, an actor-network is a set of relationships between human and nonhuman entities drawn together by a particular activity of concern (Moreira, 2010, p. 7). What is more, ANT stresses that not only networks determine entities but also a single entity determines a given network. Any introduction of a new element to a network does not go unnoticed (Geels, 2005). In the case of medical corporate websites, they are determined by living (e.g., administrators, users) and nonliving (e.g. access to the web, technical obstacles) elements whose mutual aim is to provide an online service for patients and stakeholders. In this case, its permanence will depend on the durability of composing bonds, the strength of constituting networks (Tatnall, 2010) and the ability of actors and actants to interpret and translate one's behavior (Warf, 2009). What is more, the discussed lack of boundaries is also present at the individual level, since actants possess simultaneously socio-material qualities (Mainz, 2009). This hybridity, at both the actant and network positions, can be observed also during the discussion on corporate health websites. Depending how corporate websites are treated, at the individual level of actants or at the more collective position of networks, their character is determined, among others, by technological advancement, company characteristics and user-related features. Moreover, since any changes related to one element determine the entire system (Yang, Hu, & Chou, 2010), the failure of one element can lead to the deterioration of the whole website.

Taking its interconnected and networked nature, the website can be viewed as a system. In the organizational context, the concept of a system is applied to whole companies, or any part of the corporation that can function on its own (Burgess, 2004). As far as medical corporate websites are

concerned, they can be classified as information systems, with such elements as computer hardware, software, people, procedures and data, acting together to collect, store, process, transmit and display information (Tatnall et al., 2002). They can be also understood as representations of a technical system, being the collective outcome of the intertwined social, political, economic and cognitive processes and structures (Andersson-Skog, 2009, p. 72). In my previous research (Bielenia-Grajewska, 2009; Bielenia-Grajewska, in print) I wanted to draw attention to the concept of an ecosystem as a method of studying organizations. The same can be applied in the case of healthcare websites. Taking into account the online environment of websites, the concept of an electronic ecosystem (Sacristán, 1999) can be also used. Since an ecosystem is a system formed by the interaction of a community of organizations and their environment (Daft, 2009, p. 176), a website, with all its relations and interactions, constitutes such an example. What is more, networks and ecosystems share many common features, but what makes ecosystems different is that ecosystems are chosen more voluntary, according to the required conditions (Leibold, Probst, & Gibbert, 2005). This feature is also valid in the case of healthcare websites which are selected by patients according to their requirements, by taking into account different factors, such as geographical proximity or specialized services. The ecosystem can be viewed from different perspectives. Taking the micro level into consideration, a website can be treated as a small ecosystem. According to ANT, actors ad networks are more important than the space as such (Pedersen, 2009), thus an ecosystem operating on a smaller scale can be more innovative and effective than a large ecosystem (Andersson, Curley, & Formica, 2010) since, for example, it is more adaptable to new circumstances (Wilkinson, 2006). In the case of the conducted research, a website representing a healthcare unit can be more informative than large national or international health campaigns. However, an ecosystem can be also viewed by using the macro perspective. In this case, healthcare companies and their websites will be a part of a large health ecosystem sharing technological achievements (Iansiti & Levien, 2004). What is more, since environment influences the studied ecosystem and the studied ecosystem influences the environment (Allen & Andriani, 2007), the website will mirror the environment and at the same time, the content of the website will determine the environment. To add, healthcare systems of course compete to attract patients but, at the same time, they are interested in the good condition of the mutual ecosystem (Iansiti & Levien, 2004) they are part of. Thus, the ecosystemic approach, concentrating on relations rather than single entities can be used to discuss patient-doctor communication, with e.g. the notion of a communicative ecosystem (e.g., Martin-Barbero, 2006; Mackin, 1997; Gómez Mompart, 1990) serving as a point of discussion. For example, as Mackin (1997) states, those so far marginalized who feel that they have any decisive power in their communicative ecosystem will have strong ties to the community. In the case of the conducted research, patients who feel that their opinion matters and their demands are met by the website will rely on the service offered by the particular health centre. What is more, ANT, as other postmodern theories, concentrates on flows and processes rather than on individuals and artifacts themselves. This dynamic approach is also popular in the studies on health communication since communicative interactions between doctors and patients, including such elements as values, perceptions and preferences, are given a detailed study (Schulz, 2006).

As far as the notion of identity is concerned, identities undergo the so called constant translation to adapt to the network conditions (Barry, 2006; Munro, 2005, p. 134; Prior, Glasner, & McNally, 2000; Singleton, 1995; Thompson, 2003). To translate means to displace, to act and speak for someone else (Lindqvist, 2010, p. 79), thus the

identity has to be modified in order to adjust to the personalities of others. As has been already mentioned, corporate websites change according to the demands of their users. What is more, this is not a one-way process. At the same time, after being exposed to the online content, the identity of website's users change. Translation itself is a very dynamic process, being the combination of negotiations, intrigues, calculations, acts of persuasion, and violence by which an actor or force acquires the authority to speak or act on behalf of other actors or forces (Luna & Velasco, 2010, p. 314). Thus, it takes time for the healthcare provider and its website to build trust and relationships and have the right to speak on behalf of patients and for patients.

Contrary to other studies, ANT stresses the role of nonhumans in network creation and maintenance (Michael, 1996). ANT does not treat artifacts as worse elements in any network or system, but as equally important actors (e.g., Bauchspies, Croissant, & Restivo, 2006; Tatnall & Davey, 2005). They constitute a crucial part of any network because of their durability since they last far longer than the interactions that fabricated them (Latour, 2010, pp. 56-57). Thus, in the case of this research, even the website, being a nonhuman factor in shaping doctor-patient relation, becomes the core of the study. To digress, it should be stressed that ANT is not the only theory stressing the role of nonhumans in social networks. For example, Magnani's characterization of 'moral mediators' also discusses the role of nonhumans (Adam, 2008). In the case of my research, the Internet can serve the role of a moral mediator since it enhances democracy by providing the access to different sources of information and improving civic engagement (Magnani & Bardone, 2008). However, since the ANT approach treats living and nonliving entities in the same way, such a special human feature as culture is not extensively treated in ANT (Sismondo, 2010). Thus, in this paper I made the attempt to highlight one of the cultural issues, namely the concept of identity, to discuss some selected notions of online medical communication.

CONCLUSION

The aim of this paper was to stress the role of corporate websites in patient-healthcare provider interactions. Since this topic can be discussed in many ways, the concept of identity has been chosen to highlight the most important aspects of corporate medical communication. In order to encompass different notions shaping the online identity of healthcare providers, such as technology and communication as well as individual and social identity, Actor Network Theory, which treats living and nonliving entities with equal respect, has been chosen to stress the role of the Internet, in this case the website, in medical communication.

However, although technology is very important in modern healthcare, it is always the person who is and should be responsible for the final shape of health-related interactions. It should be remembered that people cannot be substituted with technology since technology can never write that easy-to-understand sales pitch for a product, never write that simple-to-follow installation guide for a piece of software, never write that exciting job description that makes someone want to join an organization (McGovern & Norton, 2002, p. 11). What is more, especially in the case of e-healthcare, it should be noticed that Digital Settlers, the older people who rely on more traditional forms of doctor-patient interaction (Palfrey & Gasser, 2008), should be provided with analog forms of communication. Thus, as ANT suggests, both the offline and online side of corporate identity is important for serving patients.

REFERENCES

Ace, C. (2001). *Successful Marketing Communications. A Practical Guide for Planning and Implementation*. Oxford, UK: Butterworth-Heinemann.

Adam, A. (2008). Ethics for things. *Ethics and Information Technology, 10*, 149–154. doi:10.1007/s10676-008-9169-3

Adam, T., & Tatnall, A. (2010). Use of ICT to assist students with Learning Difficulties: an Actor-Network Analysis. In N. Reynolds & M. Turcsányi- Szabo (Eds.), *Proceedings of the Key Competencies in the Knowledge Society: IFIP TC 3 International Conference, KCKS 2010, Held as Part of WCC 2010,* Brisbane, Australia. Berlin: Springer.

Akerkar, S. M., & Bichile, L. S. (2004). Doctor patient relationship: Changing dynamics in the information age. *E-Medicine, 50*(2), 120–122.

Allen, P. E., & Andriani, P. (2007). Diversity, interconnectivity and sustainability. In Bogg, J. R., & Geyer, R. (Eds.), *Complexity, science and society* (pp. 1–32). Abingdon, UK: Radcliffe Publishing Ltd.

Anderson, J. G., Rainey, M. R., & Eysenbach, G. (2003). The Impact of CyberHealthcare on the Physician–Patient Relationship. *Journal of Medical Systems, 27*(1), 67–84. doi:10.1023/A:1021061229743

Andersson, T., Curley, M. G., & Formica, P. (2010). *Knowledge-Driven Entrepreneurship: The Key to Social and Economic Transformation*. New York: Springer.

Andersson-Skog, L. (2009). Revisiting railway history: the case of institutional change and path dependence. In Magnusson, L., & Ottosson, J. (Eds.), *The evolution of path dependence* (pp. 70–80). Cheltenham, UK: Edward Edgar Publishing Ltd.

Andrew, J. P., & Sirkin, H. L. (2006). *Payback: reaping the rewards of innovation.* Boston: Harvard Business School Press.

Aurik, J. C., Jonk, G. J., & Willen, R. E. (2003). *Rebuilding the corporate genome: unlocking the real value of your business.* Hoboken, NJ: John Wiley & Sons.

Barker, R., & Angelopulo, G. (2007). *Integrated Organisational Communication.* Cape Town, South Africa: Juta & Co. (Pty) Ltd.

Barry, A. (2006). Actor-Network-Theory. In Harrington, A., Marshall, B. L., & Müller, H. P. (Eds.), *Encyclopedia of social theory* (pp. 4–5). Abingdon, UK: Routledge.

Bastian, H. (2008). Health literacy and patient information: Developing the methodology for a national evidence-based health website. *Patient Education and Counseling, 73*(3), 551–556. doi:10.1016/j.pec.2008.08.020

Bauchspies, W. K., Croissant, J., & Restivo, S. (2006). *Science, technology, and society: sociological approach.* Oxford, UK: Blackwell Publishing.

Bergen, K. M., & Braithwaite, D. O. (2009). Identity as Constituted in Communication. In W. F. Eadie (Ed.), *21st Century Communication: A Reference Handbook* (pp. 165-176). Thousand Oaks, CA: Sage Publications.

Berger, T. (2009). Meet the e-patient: Chancen und Risiken des Internets für das Verhältnis von Gesundheitsfachleuten und ihren Klienten. In Stetina, B. U., & Kryspin-Exner, I. (Eds.), *Gesundheit und Neue Medien. Psychologische Aspekte der Interaktion mit Informations- und Kommunikationstechnologien* (pp. 73–83). New York: Springer.

Bielenia-Grajewska, M. (2009). Actor-Network Theory in intercultural communication. Translation through the prism of innovation, technology, networks and semiotics. *International Journal of Actor-Network Theory and Technological Innovation, 1*(4), 53–69.

Bielenia-Grajewska, M. (2011). A Potential Application of Actor Network Theory in Organizational Studies. The Company as an Ecosystem and its Power Relations from the ANT Perspective. In Tatnall, A. (Ed.), *Actor-Network Theory and Technology Innovation: Advancements and New Concepts.* Hershey, PA: IGI Global.

Birkerts, S. (2010). Into the Electronic Millenium. In Hanks, C. (Ed.), *Technology and Values: Essential Readings* (pp. 491–499). Malden, MA: Blackwell Publishing.

Blommaert, J. (2010). *The Sociolinguistics of Globalization.* Cambridge, UK: Cambridge University Press.

Bond, Ch. (2004). *Concordance: a partnership in medicine-taking.* London: Pharmaceutical Press.

Brey, P., & Søraker, J. H. (2009). Philosophy of Computing and Information Technology. In Gabbay, D. M., Meijers, A., Thagard, P., & Woods, J. (Eds.), *Philosophy of Technology and Engineering Sciences* (pp. 1341–1408). Amsterdam: North Holland. doi:10.1016/B978-0-444-51667-1.50051-3

Bukatman, S. (2002). *Terminal identity: the virtual subject in postmodern science fiction.* Cheltenham, UK: Duke University Press.

Burgess, M. (2004). *Analytical network and system administration: managing human-computer networks.* New York: John Willey & Sons Ltd. doi:10.1002/047086107X

Burnett, R., Consalvo, M., & Ess, Ch. (2010). *The Handbook of Internet Studies*. Malden, MA: John Willey and Sons Ltd.

Caiata Zufferey, M., & Schulz, P. J. (2009). Self-management of chronic low back pain: An exploration of the impact of a patient-centered website. *Patient Education and Counseling, 77,* 27–32. doi:10.1016/j.pec.2009.01.016

Cantoni, L., & Tardini, S. (2006). *Internet*. Abingdon, UK: Routledge.

Cantoni, L., & Tardini, S. (2010). The Internet and the Web. In Albertazzi, D., & Cobley, P. (Eds.), *Media: An Introduction* (pp. 220–232). Harlow, UK: Pearson Education Limited.

Capriotti, P., & Moreno, A. (2007). Communicating corporate responsibility through corporate websites in Spain. *Corporate Communications, 12,* 221–237. doi:10.1108/13563280710776833

Capurro, R., & Pingel, Ch. (2002). Ethical issues of online communication research. *Ethics and Information Technology, 4,* 189–194. doi:10.1023/A:1021372527024

Carr, N. G. (2004). *Does IT matter? information technology and the corrosion of competitive advantage*. Boston: Harvard Business School Publishing Corporation.

Cass, J. (2007). *Strategies and tools for corporate blogging*. Burlington, MA: Butterworth-Heinemann.

Castells, M. (2009). *Communication power*. Oxford, UK: Oxford University Press.

Cellary, W. (2002). Healthcare. In W. Cellary (Ed.), *Poland and the global information society: logging on* (pp. 97-98). Poznań: Grupa Wydawnicza INFOR Sp z o.o.

Chan, T. S. (2004). Web design for international business. In Samii, M., & Karush, G. (Eds.), *International Business and Information Technology* (pp. 83–110). New York: Routledge.

Christensen, N. B. (2003). *Inuit in cyberspace. Embedding Offline Identities Online*. Copenhagen, Denmark: Museum Tusculanum Press, University of Copenhagen.

Corallo, A. (2007). The business ecosystem as a multiple dynamic network. In Corallo, A., Passiante, G., & Prencipe, A. (Eds.), *The digital business ecosystem* (pp. 11–32). Cheltenham, UK: Edward Elgar Publishing.

Daft, R. (2009). *Organization Theory and Design*. Mason, OH: South-Western Cengage Learning.

Danet, B., & Herring, S. C. (2007). *The multilingual Internet: language, culture, and communication online*. Oxford, UK: Oxford University Press.

Davenport, T. H., Leibold, M., & Voelpel, S. (2006). *Strategic management in the innovation economy: strategy approaches and tools for dynamic innovation capabilities*. Erlangen, Germany: Publicis Corporate Publishing and Wiley-VCH Verlag.

Del Casino, V. J. (2009). *Social geography: a critical introduction*. Malden, MA: John Willey and Sons.

Del Piccolo, L., Mazzi, M. A., Scardoni, S., Gobbi, M., & Zimmermann, Ch. (2008). A theory-based proposal to evaluate patient-centred communication in medical consultations: The Verona Patient-centred Communication Evaluation scale (VR-COPE). *Health Education, 108*(5), 355–372. doi:10.1108/09654280810899984

Elliott, J. O., & Shneker, B. F. (2009). A health literacy assessment of the epilepsy.com website. *Seizure,* (18): 434–439. doi:10.1016/j.seizure.2009.04.003

Eysenbach, G., & Diepgen, T. L. (1999). Patients Looking for Information on the Internet and Seeking Teleadvice. *Motivation,* Expectations, and Misconceptions as Expressed in E-mails Sent to Physicians. *Archives of Dermatology,* (135): 151–156. doi:10.1001/archderm.135.2.151

Fernandez, J. (2004). *Corporate communications: a 21st century primer.* New Delhi, India: Response Books.

Fidler, R. F. (1997). *Mediamorphosis: understanding new media.* Thousand Oaks, CA: Pine Forge Press.

Foglio, A. (2007). *Il marketing sanitario. Il marketing per aziende sanitarie, ospedaliere, centri salute, ambulatori e studi medici.* Milan, Italy: FrancoAngeli.

Galea, D. (2000). E-mail and Website Feedback. In Keyes, J. (Ed.), *Internet Management* (pp. 513–522). Boca Raton, FL: CRC Press.

Garzone, G. (2009). Multimodal analysis. In Bargiela-Chiappini, F. (Ed.), *The Handbook of Business Discourse* (pp. 155–165). Edinburgh, UK: Edinburgh University Press.

Geels, F. W. (2005). *Technological transitions and system innovations: a co-evolutionary and socio-technical analysis.* Cheltenham, UK: Edward Edgar Publishing Limited.

Goldstein, D. E. (2000). *E-healthcare: harness the power of internet e-commerce & e-care.* Gaithersburg, MA: Aspen Publishers, Inc.

Hardt, M., & Negri, A. (2004). *Multitude:War and Democracy in the Age of Empire.* New York: Penguin.

Harison, S., Barlow, J., & Williams, G. (2007). The content and interactivity of health support group websites. *Health Education Journal, 66*(4), 371–381. doi:10.1177/0017896907080123

Holt, R. (2004). *Dialogue on the Internet: language, civic identity, and computer-mediated communication.* Westport, CT: Greenwood Publishing Group.

Howell, J. D. (2004). Transforming healthcare. X rays, Computer and the Internet. In Friedman, L. D. (Ed.), *Cultural sutures: medicine and media* (pp. 333–350). London: Duke University Press.

Iansiti, M., & Levien, R. (2004). *The keystone advantage: what the new dynamics of business ecosystems mean.* Boston: Harvard Business School Publishing Corporation.

Kasztelowicz, M. (2004). Medical Information Asymmetry in the Cyberworld of Manuel Castells. In Duplaga, M., Zieliński, K., & Ingram, D. (Eds.), *Transformation of healthcare with information Technologies* (pp. 21–27) Amsterdam: IOS Press.

Kien, G. (2009). *Global Technography: ethnography in the age of mobility.* New York: Peter Lang Publishing.

Kim, D., & Chang, H. (2007). Key functional characteristics in designing and operating health information websites for user satisfaction: An application of the extended technology acceptance model. *International Journal of Medical Informatics, 76,* 790–800. doi:10.1016/j.ijmedinf.2006.09.001

Kizza, J. M. (2010). *Ethical and Social Issues in the Information Age.* London: Springer Verlag.

Kotler, P., Armstrong, G., Wong, V., & Saunders, J. (2008). *Principles of Marketing.* Harlow, UK: Pearson Education Limited.

Last, M. (1999). Understanding Health. In Skelton, T., & Allen, T. (Eds.), *Culture and Global Change* (pp. 72–86). London: Routledge.

Laszlo, E. (2001). *Macroshift: navigating the transformation to a sustainable world.* San Francisco, CA: Berrett-Koechler Publishers.

Latour, B. (2010). A collective of Humans and Nonhumans. In Hanks, C. (Ed.), *Technology and Values: Essential Readings* (pp. 49–59). Malden, MA: Blackwell Publishing.

Leibold, M., Probst, G., & Gibbert, M. (2005). *Strategic management in the knowledge economy: new approaches and business applications.* Erlangen, Germany: Publicis Corporate Publishing and Wiley-VCH Verlag.

Lindqvist, K. (2010). Entrepreneurial success and failures in the arts. In Bill, F., Bjerke, B., & Johansson, A. W. (Eds.), *De)mobilizing the Entrepreneurship Discourse: Exploring Entrepreneurial Thinking and Action* (pp. 75–96). Cheltenham, UK: Edward Edgar Publishing Limited.

Lindstrøm, M. D. (2010). Deep translations. In Simonsen, J., Bærenholdt, J. O., Büscher, M., & Scheuer, J. D. (Eds.), *Design Research: Synergies from Interdisciplinary Perspectives* (pp. 109–122). Abingdon, UK: Routledge.

Lipsey, M. J., Fischer, R. R., & Poirier, K. L. (2007). *Systems for Success: The Complete Guide to Selling, Leasing, Presenting, Negotiating & Serving in Commercial Real Estate.* Gretna, LA: Pelican Publishing Company.

Luna, M., & Velasco, J. L. (2010). Knowledge networks: integration mechanisms and performance assessment. In Viale, R., & Etzkowitz, H. (Eds.), *The Capitalization of Knowledge: A Triple Helix of University-Industry-Government* (pp. 312–334). Cheltenham, UK: Edward Edgar Publishing Limited.

Mackin, J. A. (1997). *Community over chaos: an ecological perspective on communication ethics.* Tuscaloosa, AL: The University of Alabama Press.

Magnani, L., & Bardone, E. (2008). Distributed Morality: Externalizing Ethical Knowledge in Technological Artifacts. *Foundations of Science, 13*(1), 99–108. doi:10.1007/s10699-007-9116-5

Mainz, J. (2009). *Blending Spaces: Actor-Network Interactions of an Internet-Based E-Learning.* Münster, Germany: LT Verlag.

Martin-Barbero, J. (2006). Communication and Culture in the Global Society. A Latin American View. In Gumucio Dagron, A., & Tufte, T. (Eds.), *Communication for social change anthology: historical and contemporary readings* (pp. 649–653). South Orange, NJ: Communication for Social Change Consortium.

Masuda, Y. (1983). *The information society as post-industrial society.* Bethesda, MD: World Future Society.

McGovern, G., & Norton, R. (2002). *Content critical: gaining competitive advantage through high-quality Web content.* Upper Saddle River, NJ: FT Press Prentice Hall.

McLellan, F. (2004). Medicine.com: the Internet and the Patient-Physician Relationship. In Friedman, L. D. (Ed.), *Cultural sutures: medicine and media* (pp. 373–385). London: Duke University Press.

Meissner, C. (2005). *Balancing Cultural and Corporate Identity Aspects in Standardising and-or Localising Websites. A Contingency Approach.* Hamburg, Germany: Diplomica Gmbh.

Meyer, M. S. (2005). *Between Technology And Science: Exploring an Emerging Field: Knowledge Flows And Networking on the Nano-Scale.* Boca Raton, FL: Dissertation.com.

Michael, M. (1996). *Constructing identities: the social, the nonhuman and change.* London: Sage Publication Ltd.

Mishra, P. (2009). *Sales Management. Keys to effective sales.* New Delhi, India: Global India Publications Pvt Ltd.

Mitev, N. (2009). In and out of actor-network theory: a necessary but insufficient journey. *Information Technology & People, 22*(1), 9–25. doi:10.1108/09593840910937463

Monteiro, E. (2004). Actor network theory and cultural aspects of interpretative studies. In Avgerou, Ch., Ciborra, C., & Land, F. (Eds.), *The social study of information and communication technology: innovation, actors and contexts* (pp. 129–139). Oxford: Oxford University Press.

Morahan-Martin, J. M. (2004). How Internet users find, evaluate and use online health information: a cross-cultural review. *Cyberpsychology & Behavior, 7*(5), 497–510.

Moreira, T. (2010). Actor-Network Theory. In Hornig Priest, S. (Ed.), *Encyclopedia of Science and Technology Communication* (pp. 7–9). Thousand Oaks, CA: Sage.

Munro, R. (2005). Actor Network Theory. In Clegg, S., & Haugaard, M. (Eds.), *The SAGE Handbook of Power* (pp. 125–139).

Murdoch, J. (2005). Ecologising sociology. Actor-Network Theory, co-construction and the problem of human exemptionalism. In Inglis, D., Bone, J., & Wilkie, R. (Eds.), *Nature: From nature to natures: contestation and reconstruction* (pp. 282–305). Abingdon, UK: Routledge.

Neuman, J. (2007). *The Complete Internet Marketer. A Practical Guide to Everything you Need to Know about Marketing Online*. With-A-Clue Press.

Nielsen-Bohlman, L., & Panzer, A. M. (2004). *Health literacy: a prescription to end confusion*. Washington, DC: The National Academies Press.

Nutbeam, D. (2000). Health literacy as a public health goal: a challenge for contemporary health education and communication strategies into the 21st century. *Health Promotion International, 15*(3), 259–267. doi:10.1093/heapro/15.3.259

O'Kane, P., Hargie, O., & Tourish, D. (2004). Communication without frontiers: the impact of technology on organizations. In Tourish, D., & Hargie, O. (Eds.), *Key Issues in Organizational Communication* (pp. 74–95). London: Routledge.

O'Kane, P., Hargie, O., & Tourish, D. (2009). Auditing electronic communication. In Tourish, D., & Hargie, O. (Eds.), *Auditing Organizational Communication: A Handbook of Research, Theory and Practice* (pp. 195–223). New York: Routledge.

Overberg, R., Toussaint, P., & Zwetsloot-Schonk, B. (2006). Illness stories on the Internet: Features of websites disclosing breast cancer patients' illness stories in the Dutch language. *Patient Education and Counseling, 61*, 435–442. doi:10.1016/j.pec.2005.05.010

Palfrey, J., & Gasser, U. (2008). *Born Digital. Understanding the first generation of digital natives*. New York: Basic Books.

Palkhivala, K., Anderson-Lemieux, A., & Mappin, Ch. (2000). Serving Many Masters. In Keyes, J. (Ed.), *Internet Management* (pp. 537–546). Boca Raton, FL: CRC Press.

Pańkowska, M. (2004). Value-Driven Management in e-Healthcare. In Duplaga, M., Zieliński, K., & Ingram, D. (Eds.), *Transformation of healthcare with information technologies* (pp. 3–11). Amsterdam: IOS Press.

Pedersen, M. A. (2009). At Home Away from Homes: Navigating the Taiga in Northern Mongolia. In Kirby, P. W. (Ed.), *Boundless worlds: an anthropological approach to movement* (pp. 135–152). New York: Berghahn Books.

Potts, K. (2007). *Web Design and Marketing Solutions for Business Websites*. New York: Springer Verlag.

Prior, L., Glasner, P., & McNally, R. (2000). Genotechnology: Three Challenges to Risk Legitimation. In Adam, B., Beck, U., & Van Loon, J. (Eds.), *The risk society and beyond: critical issues for social theory* (pp. 105–121). London: Sage Publications Ltd.

Rains, S., & Donnerstein Karmikel, C. (2009). Health information-seeking and perceptions of website credibility: examining web-use orientation message characteristics and structural features of websites. *Computers in Human Behavior, 25*(2), 544–553. doi:10.1016/j.chb.2008.11.005

Rice, R. E. (2001). The Internet and health communication: a framework of experiences. In Rice, R. E., & Katz, J. E. (Eds.), *The Internet and health communication: experiences and expectations* (pp. 5–46). Thousand Oaks, CA: Sage.

Richardson, H. (2005). Consuming passions in the 'global knowledge economy. In Howcroft, D., & Trauth, E. M. (Eds.), *Handbook of critical information systems research: theory and application* (pp. 272–292). Cheltenham, UK: Edward Edgar Publishing Limited.

Roberts, J. M., & Copeland, K. L. (2001). Clinical websites are currently dangerous to health. *International Journal of Medical Informatics, 62*, 181–187. doi:10.1016/S1386-5056(01)00162-9

Root Wolpe, P. (2002). Medical culture and CAM Culture: Science and Ritual in the Academic Medical Center. In Callahan, D. (Ed.), *The role of complementary and alternative medicine: accommodating pluralism* (pp. 163–171). Washington, DC: Georgetown University Press.

Rossmann, C. (2010). Gesundheitskommunikation im Internet. Erscheinungsformen, Potenziale, Grenzen. In Schweiger, W., & Beck, K. (Eds.), *Handbuch Online-Kommunikation* (pp. 338–363). Wiesbaden, Germany: VS Verlag. doi:10.1007/978-3-531-92437-3_14

Rubinelli, S., Nakamoto, K., & Schulz, P. (2009). Health literacy beyond knowledge and behaviour. *International Journal of Public Health, 54*, 307–311. doi:10.1007/s00038-009-0052-8

Rüsen, J., & Laass, H. (2010). *Humanism in Intercultural Perspective: Experiences and Expectations*. Berlin: transcript Verlag.

Sacristán, A. (1999). Art, Autopistes i cintes de video. In Franquet, R., & Larrègola, G. (Eds.), *Comunicar en la era Digital* (pp. 115–118). Barcelona, Spain: Societat Catalana de Comunicació.

Sassen, S. (2004). Towards a sociology of information technology. In Avgerou, Ch., Ciborra, C., & Land, F. (Eds.), *The social study of information and communication technology: innovation, actors and contexts* (pp. 77–102). Oxford, UK: Oxford University Press.

Schäfer, J. (2010). Reassembling the literary. In J. Schäfer & P. Gendolla (Eds.), *Beyond the Screen: Transformations of Literary Structures, Interfaces and Genre* (pp. 25-70). Berlin: transcript Verlag.

Schau, H. J., & Gilly, M. C. (2003). We Are What We Post? Self-Presentation in Personal Web Space. *The Journal of Consumer Research*, 385–404. doi:10.1086/378616

Schau, H. J., & Muniz, A. M. Jr. (2002). Brand communities and personal identities: negotiations in cyberspace. In Broniarczyk, S. M., & Nakamoto, K. (Eds.), *Advances in Consumer Research* (pp. 344–349). Valdosta, GA: Association for Consumer Research.

Schulz, P. J. (2006). Maximizing health outcomes through optimal communication. *Studies in Communication Sciences, 6*(2), 215–232.

Shoniregun, Ch. A., Dube, K., & Mtenzi, F. (2010). *Electronic Healthcare Information Security*. Berlin: Springer.

Sieving, P. C. (1999). Factors Driving the Increase in Medical Information on the Web - One American Perspective. *Journal of Medical Internet Research, 1*(1), e3. doi:10.2196/jmir.1.1.e3

Sillence, E., Briggs, P., Harris, P., & Fishwick, L. (2007). Health Websites that people can trust – the case of hypertension. *Interacting with Computers, 19*, 32–42. doi:10.1016/j.intcom.2006.07.009

Singleton, V. (1995). Networking Constructions of Gender and Constructing Gender Networks: Considering Definitions of Woman in the British Cervical Screening Programme. In Grint, K., & Gill, R. (Eds.), *The gender-technology relation: contemporary theory and research* (pp. 146–173). London: Taylor & Francis Ltd.

Sismondo, S. (2010). *An Introduction to Science and Technology Studies*. Chichester, UK: John Wiley & Sons.

Stewart, M., Brown, J. B., Wayne Weston, W., McWhinney, I. R., McWilliam, C. L., & Freeman, T. R. (2006). *Patient-centered medicine: transforming the clinical method*. Abingdon, UK: Radcliffe Medical Press.

Tatnall, A. (2010). Using actor-network theory to understand the process of information systems curriculum innovation. *Education and Information Technologies, 15*, 239–254. doi:10.1007/s10639-010-9137-5

Tatnall, A., & Davey, B. (2005). An Actor Network Approach to Informing Clients through portals. In Cohen, E. B. (Ed.), *Issues in informing science and information technology* (pp. 771–780). Santa Rosa, CA: Informing Science Press.

Tatnall, A., Davey, B., Burgess, S., Davison, A., & Wenn, A. (2002). *Management information systems—concepts, issues, tools and applications*. Melbourne, Australia: Data Publishing.

Thompson, G. (2003). *Between hierarchies and markets: the logic and limits of network forms of organization*. New York: Oxford University Press.

Thurlow, C., Lengel, L. B., & Tomic, A. (2004). *Computer mediated communication: social interaction and the Internet*. London: Sage Publications Ltd.

Thwaites, T., Davis, L., & Mules, W. (2002). *Introducing Cultural and Media Studies. A Semiotic Approach*. Basingstoke, UK: Palgrave Macmillan.

Tourish, D., & Hargie, O. (2004). *Key issues in organizational communication*. Abingdon, UK: Routlegde.

Tsohou, A., Karyda, M., Kokolakis, S., & Kiountouzis, E. (2010). Analyzing Information Security Awareness through Networks of Association. In Katsikas, S., Lopez, J., & Soriano, M. (Eds.), *Trust, Privacy and Security in Digital Business* (pp. 227–237). Berlin: Springer. doi:10.1007/978-3-642-15152-1_20

Wallace, P. (2001). *The Psychology of the Internet*. Cambridge, UK: Cambridge University Press.

Warf, B. (2009). Teleology, Contingency, and Networks. In Meusburger, P., Funke, J., & Wunder, E. (Eds.), *Milieus of Creativity: An Interdisciplinary Approach to Spatiality of Creativity* (pp. 255–268). Berlin: Springer.

Wilkinson, J. (2006). Network theories and political economy: from attrition to convergence? In Marsden, T., & Murdoch, J. (Eds.), *Between the local and the global: confronting complexity in the contemporary agri-food sector* (pp. 11–38). Oxford, UK: JAI Press.

Wilson, J. F. (2003). The Crucial Link between Literacy and Health. *Annals of Internal Medicine, 139*, 875–878.

Winefield, H. R., Coventry, B. J., & Lambert, V. (2003). Setting up a health education website: practical advice for health professionals. *Patient Education and Counseling, 53*, 175–182. doi:10.1016/S0738-3991(03)00149-6

Wright, K. B. (2009). Increasing Computer-Mediated Social Support. In Parker, J. C., & Thorson, E. (Eds.), *Health communication in the new media landscape* (pp. 243–266). New York: Springer.

Yang, W. H., Hu, J. S., & Chou, Y. Y. (2010). Analysis of Network Type Exchange in the Health Care System: A Stakeholder Approach. *Journal of Medical Systems*.

Zarcadoolas, Ch., Pleasant, A. F., & Greer, D. S. (2006). *Advancing health literacy: a framework for understanding and action*. San Francisco: Jossey-Bass.

Chapter 14

Opening the Black Box of Leadership in the Successful Development of Local E-Government Initiative in a Developing Country

Johanes Eka Priyatma
Sanata Dharma University, Indonesia

Zainal Abidin Mohamed
Universiti Putra, Malaysia

ABSTRACT

Leadership has been identified as one of the critical factors in the successful development of e-government projects especially so in developing countries. Unfortunately, empirical studies linking the outcome of e-government projects and the role of leadership are very limited. Moreover, these studies did not comprehensively discuss the role of leadership in implementing e-government projects involving social, political, and technological transformation. Using the four moments of Actor Network Theory (ANT) translation framework, this paper presents detailed actions taken by leaders in the development of a local e-government project. The paper argues that ANT translation provides an appropriate framework to trace and monitor how leadership has been practiced effectively in an e-government project in a developing country.

INTRODUCTION

Implementation and development of e-government projects have never been an easy task. In many developed countries, e-government failed to meet the initial promise to promote better public participation and improve administrative efficiency (Bolgherini, 2007). But in developing countries, e-government development faced more fundamental problems that include the lack of appropriate technological infrastructure, limited financial and human resources, and the incompatibility to their political, social and cultural

DOI: 10.4018/978-1-4666-2166-4.ch014

environments (Nguyen & Schauder, 2007; Imran & Gregor; 2007). These might explain why 85% of e-government initiative in developing countries failed (Heeks, 2003). Ciborra (2005) argues that e-government thus might not yet be suitable for developing countries and Fife and Hosman (2007) even suggested instead to spend money for "bread" rather than for "broad-band."

However, there are some reports of successful e-government initiatives in developing countries. Gudea (2007) reported a successful cooperative approach and innovative strategy to develop home grown internet in Romania. In Ecuador, Karanasios (2007) gave evidence how small tourism enterprise successfully copes with digital divide. In Asia, two studies were documented. In India, Misra (2007) described how a self-reliance approach contributed to successful e-government implementation, while in Indonesia the success of e-government project at municipal level was reported by Furuholt and Wahid (2008).

Because of the differences in technological readiness and other factors, the implementation and development of e-government in developing countries need to adapt the strategies and approaches that have been applied in developed countries, or even develop totally new ones (Chen et al., 2006). Some researchers (Stanforth, 2006; Akhter et al., 2007; Imran & Gregor, 2007) proposed that focus should be given more to the social and political factors surrounding the e-government projects (rather than the technological factors) as these are not only dominant but are also quite diverse. Amongst these, leadership seems to be very important and crucial as reported in several occasions. Accenture (2001) reported that leadership was the more important factor (such as political will, commitment, and accountability) than others. Studies supporting such stand were also reported by Ebrahim and Irani (2005), as they found that strong government leadership to support the organizational and procedural changes during the development of e-government was needed. Torres et al. (2005) and Kim et al. (2009)

also found that strong leadership was considered as the most outstanding drivers to e-government success. Imran and Gregor (2007) further observed that leaders' vision and their willingness to initiate changes within the government sector as significant strategies to succeed in implementing an e-government project.

Although it has been convinced that leadership does play important roles in e-government development but the number of empirical studies are rather limited (Prybutok et al., 2008). Moreover, the few that could be traced focused only on outlining some important features of an effective leadership that are related to the vision, commitment assurance or political will. They failed to describe how such features were exercised in government work setting that was much influenced by political negotiation and constrained by rules and regulations. Such has been the environment that the more static notion of leadership such as characteristics and traits are probably simpler compared to exploring the process of enacting, organizing, explaining, and managing collective actions (Pye, 2005). Therefore, the research question should be on how to explore and analyze the various leadership practices that result in the success of the e-government projects in a developing country. Answering this question will offer some valuable insights and guide for leaders involved in such projects that has to deal with many political, technical and social challenges.

Exploring and analyzing such practices require the use of an established research framework and this paper opted for the use of the Actor Network Theory (ANT). ANT was chosen mainly for its capability to capture the complexity of the interaction between the socio-cultural components as well as the involvement and the need to align the technical and political factors. Consequently, the paper also aims to expose that ANT is a useful framework to explore leadership in action in e-government projects. The focus will be on ANT's four moments of translation for it provides detailed and step-by-step framework to trace the various actions related to leadership. The exploration and analysis has been done on one successful e-government project in Indonesia (a case study approach).

LITERATURE REVIEW

The literature review focusing on e-government, leadership and ANT aims to identify the knowledge gap in the field of leadership role and e-government development. It is also presented to support the argument that ANT is able to provide an appropriate theoretical framework to study this knowledge.

E-Government Development

Under normal circumstances, information and communication technology (ICT) has been recognized as the main trigger and driver for e-government initiatives in delivering services to citizen. But this is no longer true since such recognition is quite myopic as it also plays significant roles in the process of transformation. Alternatively, e-government projects can also be looked from the process perspective which allows analysis up to the deliveries or the end outcomes (Grant & Chau, 2005). Understanding these processes will help recognize the key players involved and the consequences of power redistribution amongst them (Jonas, 2000). Moreover, conceptualizing e-government projects from the process perspective will also reveal many radical prerequisite changes before a certain service can be delivered. These changes include formulating new business processes, adjusting information flows, managing changed policies, mastering new kinds of data recording, and implementing new system security measures. These intense and diverse transformational activities will then require the appropriate application of various leadership styles and characteristics (Dawes, 2002).

Despite its complexity and difficulties, many have embarked on e-government initiatives.

Central as well as local governments all over the world are moving toward e-government (Jansen, 2005). Though the motive varies (Helbig et al., 2009), most e-government initiatives are directed to provide better quality services to citizens. Unfortunately, the failure rate of such initiative is also quite high as partial and total failures reach 85% (Heeks, 2003). Special attention should then be directed to development of e-government in developing countries so as to prevent the waste of their already limited resources.

Generally, the most common strategy proposed was to focus on assuring that bureaucratic reform happens rather than employing sophisticated technologies. Since such reform is difficult then it should be carried out by incorporating significant variables that are within the social and political context (Ndou, 2004). In other words, developing e-government initiatives should consider countries' respective characteristics and conditions (Chen et al., 2006). For example, "self-reliance" had been identified to be an effective strategy in many successful e-government developments in India (Misra, 2007). Another proposed strategy was the stakeholder participation since understanding between the roles of government agencies and its citizen created a more profound impact than technology (Akhter et al., 2007; Anthopoulos et al., 2007). However, stakeholders might have different motives and even conflicting interest (De', 2005; Priyatma & Han, 2008). Using this understanding, Stanforth (2006) argued that any e-government initiative should recognize its nature as an information system in which its outcome will be the result of contested interest of several actors linked together in a complex network.

The Role of Leadership

Executing any of the strategies mentioned earlier needs managers with strong leadership traits since they have to change or move the present condition to a different new situation. This assertion was supported by many research findings that leadership did matter in the e-government development cycle. Leadership is necessary before, during and after e-government project implementation (Ndou, 2004). For example, the clearly articulated vision of the Singaporean government (early part of project) had inspired mindset changes and enabled government agencies to understand the move toward e-government in the country (Ke & Wei, 2004). In addition, managerial innovativeness and managerial orientation (more so during the project) were the most compelling determinants of e-government adoption as reported in several municipalities (Moon & Norris, 2005). In contrast, when analyzing the source of failures of e-government initiatives, inadequate and lack of leadership was the main constraint as reported by Gautam (2006), Gauld (2007), and Wong et al. (2007).

Despite its vital role, only few empirical studies had been conducted to investigate the role of leadership in the development of e-government (Prybutok et al., 2008). In these studies, leadership was always discussed as an important and crucial factor for e-government development but there had no thorough description of how to practice it. Leadership as a form of social influence process was rarely discussed (Pye, 2005). Consequently, most articles on leadership links to e-government development only identified some characteristics attributed to an effective or a strong leadership. Nevertheless, understanding the role of leadership in e-government by exploring the process of enacting, organizing, explaining, and managing collective activities would contribute empirically to the data-base for e-government development. However, exploring the leadership content in e-government development needs an appropriate approach and framework that fit the condition where power and political alignment might be very influential.

Morrel and Hartley (2006) argued that the four main theories of leadership namely traits, contingency, situational and constitutive approaches, were not suitable to understand the role of political leadership. They proposed the use of the "figurational sociology" approach to develop a model for political leadership because "figuration" refers to a network of interdependent actors and they themselves provided a useful framework to rationally talk about the complex domains that characterize the different arenas of politics. Meanwhile Drath et al. (2008) proposed a new ontology on leadership which was totally different from the common tripod ontology of leaders, followers, and shared goals. Instead, they proposed a DAC ontology in which the essential entities were three leadership outcomes:

1. **Direction:** Widespread agreement in a collective basis on overall goals, aims, and mission;

2. **Alignment:** The organization and coordination of knowledge and work collectively; and

3. **Commitment:** The willingness of members of a collective group to subsume their own interests and benefit within the group's interest and benefit.

In addition to the above mentioned DAC model, there is also the ANT model which has been used in power negotiations and also situations involving many parties. Amongst the many characteristics that ANT possesses are its four moments of translation that perhaps can analyse the leadership role from a different perspective. While DAC's model focuses on the outcomes, ANT looks at leadership from the process perspective. Other considerations (Callon, 1986) favouring ANT are:

1. ANT analysis focuses on tracing actor's action to form and stabilize a network of relationship involving human and non-human entities (Callon, 1986; Law, 1992). This kind of analysis can be used to understand the role of leadership in any innovation activity such as an e-government development.

2. Compared to DAC's ontology, the four moments of ANT translation provide more a detailed and comprehensive framework

to open up the notion of leadership that most researchers have taken for granted or normally treated as a black-box.

3. ANT has a rich vocabulary to especially deal with socio-technical reality and power redistribution that always become the main theme for e-government development and its leadership role. It is especially important as Scholl (2007) has identified that since 2002 e-government research has broadened its perspective beyond the role of information systems in order to incorporate the "complex socio-technical work reality" in public administration.

So far, the ANT model has been used to study how power negotiation amongst actors influences an innovation project trajectory (Law & Callon, 1992; Heeks & Stanforth, 2007). ANT then became a well known theory to understand information system development for it always involved interest alignment. However, there were only few studies using ANT methodology on e-government development itself since the latter is a relatively new discipline. Amongst these were:

1. Madon et al. (2004) employed ANT's four moments of translation concept to trace the development of taxation system in India.

2. Heeks and Stanforth (2007) used ANT's concept of global/local framework to understand the development of e-government by Indian Ministry of Finance.

3. Ochara (2010) used ANT to trace inscription process in the development of e-government in Kenya and found that global actors' interest were stronger inscribed than the local actors' interest.

They concluded that ANT helped analyze the ways in which actors formed alliances and enrolled other actors to strengthen such alliances surrounding a technology innovation.

If ANT has been proven to be a useful framework to recognize the process of forming actor's

alliance and mobilizing them in an innovation project, then ANT also seems to be a suitable framework to trace how leaders practice or lead an e-government initiative. Since leading is very close to the notion "of movement, of progress, of transition from one place to another, literally and metaphorically" (Pye, 2005, p. 35), then it is also close to ANT's translation (Callon, 1986, Law, 1992). ANT's four moments of translation seem more comprehensive and although they have never been used as a model for understanding leadership in general and e-government leadership in particular, it is argued that their application here will contribute to the knowledge of leadership's role in e-government projects from the process perspective as well as provide useful lessons for practitioners.

Briefly, some specific and unique characteristics of ANT that justify its use as an analytical framework are:

1. ANT perceives social reality as a complex network of relationship that always involves human and non-human entities (Law, 1992).

2. It holds radical assumption that neither human nor non-human should be given a privilege in determining the stability of certain social reality (Callon, 1986).

3. It rejects essentialism and instead embraces "relational" point of view by stating that both human and non-human entities are just an effect or outcome of a network (Law, 1992; Doolin & Lowe, 2002).

4. ANT refers all entities (human or non-human) involved in this complex network of heterogeneous element as "actors" or "actor-network" (Latour, 1992).

5. It labels a stable actor-network as a black box so its analysis may focus only on its inputs and outputs (Law, 1992). Since a black box is an actor-network then its stability is also influenced by all material involved. Consequently, a relatively stable network is one embodied in and performed by a range of durable materials. One strategy to impose

a stable network is then to employ some durable materials. However, this argument is not that simple because for ANT durability is also an effect and they are not automatically given by the nature of materials. That is why "the more automatic and the blacker the box is, the more it has to be accompanied by people" (Latour 1987, p. 137). The black box could be opened up and analyzed as an actor-network by tracing all its relevant actors and their relationship (May & Powel, 2008 p. 143).

In opening up a "black box" of reality, ANT uses the notion of translation (Callon, 1986) to make sense why certain social reality finally becomes stable/unstable over time. Translation can be described as a process in which actor(s) mobilizes resources or another actor-network to form allies that result in a stabilized actor-network. For example, in developing functional e-government systems there must be actor(s) who mobilizes the needed resources (money, ICT, programmer, stipulations, et cetera) in such a way that these resources become an alliance working together and influence each other to result in a working e-government. Therefore, translation explores the ways that the networks of relations are composed, maintained, and made more durable over time. The translation process involves four moments (phases), namely:

1. **Problematization:** In this moment one or more key actors define the nature of the problem and the roles of other actors to fit the proposed solution. The solution is offered in such a way that all actors that participated will be subjected to some centralised control mechanism labelled as an "obligatory passage point (OPP)."

2. **Interessement:** Here all actors identified in the first phase are given specific roles and identities and the strategies that need to be acted upon which will attract them. This

attraction is implemented through some interessement strategies that will lead them to the next phase.

3. **Enrolment:** The success of the interessement strategies will result in the enrolment of actors to participate in establishing a stable network of alliance. However, the stability of this alliance depends on the negotiation process to define their roles in the network.

4. **Mobilization:** Once the proposed solution gains wider acceptance, then an even larger network of absent entities are created through some actors acting as spokespersons for others.

There are many criticisms of ANT from different perspective such as in neglecting the influence of broader social structure to the local situation (McLean & Hassard, 2004), its suitability for interpretive stance (Cordella & Shaikh, 2006), its contribution to the critical theory of organization (Whittle & Spicer, 2008). However, there are only two relevant critics related to this research namely the problem of inclusion/exclusion of actors and its symmetrical treatment to human and non-human. The first critic relates to the decision of who to include and who to exclude in ANT analysis. Law (1992) argues that an investigator surely cannot follow actors everywhere and consequently he/she should in practice employ certain ordering, sorting, or selection. Meanwhile Miller (1996) suggests that investigative work should be directed at contextualizing the specific event as a way of cutting the endless network.

The second critic has been the subject of controversy for it is morally problematic to make no distinction between human action and the behaviour of things (Collins & Yearley, 1992; Knights & Murray, 1994). Actor–network scholars have argued that they accept the divisions and distinctions, but only when they are understood as effects (Law, 1992) and they refuse to consider the distinctions a priori (Latour, 1996). Law (1992) also argues that Sociology is not Ethics and the concern of ANT is not on ethical issue. For ANT, equal treatment between people and objects is an analytical stance, not an ethical position.

METHODOLOGY AND DATA GATHERING

Data were gathered from a one stop service project located at Badan Pelayanan Terpadu /BPT (Bureau of Integrated Services) of Sragen regency Central Java Indonesia. The project (from now referred as Sragen One Stop Service (SOSS)) was selected since it was recognized as being the most successful regional e-government development in Indonesia by central government and many private institutions. Since it is located in relatively remote regency and has limited resources, the success of SOSS has been attributed to its leadership approach (Furuholt & Wahid, 2008). Therefore, SOSS is a suitable case for this study.

Data gathered include factual (numerical), textual, audio, and visual event. They were collected by observing at the project site, inspecting archival documents, and recording semi structured interviews for two months. The interviews were conducted in local language and included 19 human actors who were involved in the development of SOSS. This included nine management staffs of SOSS (the head, secretary, all six sub-section heads, and two staffs from personnel administration sub-section and customer service respectively), four heads of offices (Electronic Data Processing, Health, Industry and Commerce, Civil Registration), a computer programmer coordinator from Electronic Data Processing Office, two citizens applying license, a guest doing comparative study, and the leader of Sragen regency referred to commonly as "Bupati." All interview sessions lasted from 30 to 90 minutes. Recorded interviews and the narration of video presentation were transcribed fully before they were analyzed. Since SOSS was perceived as a complex socio-technical reality, topical themes (Rychards, 2005

p. 92) which were used to extract information from transcribed interviews were developed based on the four moments of ANT translation and information system elements. Table 1 provides sample of themes and its extracted texts.

Since following the actor(s) is the basic guideline of an ANT analysis (Callon, 1986; Latour, 2005) then what will be described in the analysis section is mainly tracing the decisions and actions taken by the Bupati of Sragen starting from the conceptualization to the implementation of SOSS. In tracing Bupati's works, some other connected human and non-human actors will also be followed. Following Law (1992) in handling inclusion/exclusion of actors, only those that have significant contribution to the design and implementation of SOSS will be included. Meanwhile, the description of each moment of translation will be linked to its suitable context as a way of interpreting the event appropriately as proposed by Miller (1996).

DATA ANALYSIS I: CASE DESCRIPTION OF SRAGEN ONE STOP SERVICES (SOSS)

Sragen Regency located at the eastern part of Central Java Province is one of the 330 regencies in Indonesia, covers an area of 941.55 km^2 and has 22 kecamatan (sub-districts), 208 kelurahan (smaller areas within each sub-district). Its population has remained quite stable over the last two years with 855,244 inhabitants and a density of 908 per square km. About 412,206 people (48% of total) are employed, with 51% of them in the agricultural sector, 19% in services, and 13% in hotel, trade and restaurants. The agricultural sector contributes 34.46% to the total RGDP (Regional Gross Domestic Product) with a value of IDR 835,005.58 million (US$ 83,500.6 thousand). Meanwhile, per capita income is only IDR 929,230.79 or about US$ 100.

Table 1. Sample of themes and its extracted text

Theme	Extracted Texts	Source
Problematization	All of these are the idea of the Bupati. Actually the authority to issue license is himself but then he delegated to the respected office. However, consequently public who apply license should go to many offices with uncertain processes. These conditions created high cost. When the Bupati retracted these authorities, the head of offices might lose their financial opportunities as you said. It is what we want to reform.	Section Head of Customer Services
Interessement	We got financial incentive and it is in line with ministry regulation that staff working at one stop service unit may be given additional salary and its amount depend on each regency capability.	Sub-section Head of Certificates Issuance
Enrolment	The expansion of one stop service unit from only as a unit in 2003 and finally became a bureau of integrated services in 2006 was a result of the commitment from our top executive and legislative leaders. Thus its success came from both executive and legislative as well as from all participating heads of offices who delegated their authority in issuing license to our unit. All of these are meant to provide easy, quick, transparent, and not complicated services.	Sub-section Head of Certificates Issuance
Mobilization	We are their servants. We are public servants and we try to provide good services. If this situation is changed then public will be disappointed. So we really expect that there will be no action to destroy all of these. We should not think that this is part of our rival, because in reality it could happen.	Head of BPT
Performance	Luckily, the customer satisfaction evaluation done every six month showed the increasing performance. From the last two evaluations, it reached 83,995% in December 2007 and 84,005% in June 2008.	Sub-section Head of Information, Documentation and Customer Services

Using the strategic planning process approach, the local administration of Sragen has developed a set of guidelines for its development. These include the formulation of its vision, mission, strategy and development priorities that can be easily accessed from www.sragen.go.id. For the year 2006 – 2011, Sragen's vision is to be a smart regency and its mission is to have its citizens achieve excellence, be productive and prosperous. This mission is being realized through the implementation of a set of strategies and one of them is creating an innovative entrepreneurial administration providing excellent public services.

As a former business man, the Bupati of Sragen was fully aware of how complicated and difficult it is to deal with government bureaucratic procedures. After being inaugurated as Bupati in 2001, he decided to do a major reform to his administration. One of his objectives was to establish a simple yet effective and efficient process of issuance of various licenses for the general public and investors. He believes that enforcing simple investment procedure would trigger more business activities that in turn would increase local government revenue. Although in 2000 Sragen already had the so-called Integrated Services Unit or One-Roof services unit (Unit Pelayanan Terpadu/UPT) but its performance was considered as unsatisfactory. The main drawback of this unit was its inability to provide transparent and simple procedures.

On June 16th, 2002 the Bupati of Sragen established an ad-hoc team comprising of nine respected government officers to study the matter. The team came up with a proposal to modify the existing "one-roof" to a "one-door" service. The previous one-roof service unit had no authority to issue any licenses but the new one-door service unit does. As the consequence for the formation of the one-door service unit, former offices which used to issue licenses had to delegate this authority to this new service unit. The delegation was not simple since it brought some consequences to the staff working in the respective offices, ranging from the change of administrative procedures to the lost of authority and some financial benefits. The Bupati resolved this problematic situation by reminding all heads of offices that in principle the ultimate authority of issuing license was the Bupati. It was then his prerogative to retract that authority and delegate it to another office. Bupati finally endorsed Bylaw No. 17 / 2002 which transferred the authority for issuing licenses where the issuance of licenses to the one-door service unit of SOSS.

The new UPT then gradually became popular because of its effective and efficient services. At the beginning, it handled only 15 licenses but now it issues 59 licenses and 10 certificates (non-license such as birth certificate and citizen identity card). In line with its increasing volume of services, with Regional Government Regulation (RGR) No. 15/2003 the status of this unit was upgraded to that of an office and it began to be called KPT/Kantor Pelayanan Terpadu (One-Door Service Unit) and then later with RGR No. 6/2006 it was made into a bureau (and called BPT/Badan Pelayan Terpadu).

Some indicators could be attributed to verify the success of SOSS. From the citizen's point of view, the simple, transparent, and accountable services had satisfied them. Based on two recent service satisfaction survey involving 150 respondents conducted twice a year, the customer satisfaction index scored 83.995% and 84.005% respectively. From some government and non-government organizations' point of view, SOSS was also considered a good model of a quality public service provider. From the economic point of view, SOSS managed to directly and indirectly increase revenue for the local government. In 2002 Sragen's revenue was only IDR 22.6 billion but in 2005 it rose to IDR 72.8 billion. Within 3 years, it increased by 300%. One small and medium enterprise (SME) owner testified that the SOSS personnel had helped him obtain financing for his business said:

I managed to get a loan from a bank immediately because all the required documents were timely provided by the SOSS personnel and it saved a lot of my time. For me, SOSS is really helpful.

DATA ANALYSIS II: USING THE FOUR MOMENTS OF ANT ANALYSIS ON LEADERSHIP INVOLVEMENT

Each of the four moments of ANT translation will be used consecutively to review and analyze the various activities that the Bupati of Sragen has done but looking only from the leadership perspective which is the focus of this paper.

The central problem faced by SOSS was to serve the public better by providing simple, transparent, accountable, and one-stop license services. In addition to the endorsement by the Indonesian central government since 1998, the establishment of SOSS was also motivated by the Bupati's concern to reform local government public services. He fully believed that introducing a company-like work culture to the government service sector was possible and ICT should be used intensively as a main driver for such an initiative. This was due to his vast experience in the private sector and his full commitment to develop SOSS to support the prosperity of his regency.

Bupati was much perceived by most of his staffs as a genuine but decisive, creative, innovative, confident, ICT-literate, and powerful leader. This is portrayed in the city billboard welcoming commuters to Sragen. His emergence from a laptop screen while holding a stack of rice crops is a "rich text" that reflects his concern and his stance toward the use of ICT. He was also described as an unselfish passionate leader, who is concerned with his country's development problems. He wanted to make Sragen better and supports the overall development of the country. His popular motto was "what Sragen does should colour Indonesia."

By ensuring that SOSS issues business-related licenses efficiently, the Bupati hoped to attract more investors and this eventually would increase the local government's revenue. This increase was an important agenda of every regency leader since the stipulation of the Autonomy Act No.32/2004. This Act delegates local government administrations to manage some public affairs, ranging from regency development, general health services, primary and secondary education, civil administration to local investment administration.

Problematization Moment

The most crucial part in ensuring SOSS's success was to get support from heads of various offices that were authorised to issue licenses. It was common that not only the senior staff from these offices but even some lower-level staffs abused this "power" and make it difficult to issue license for their own benefit. The other problem was to run the one-door service efficiently just like a private entity. To manage this situation Bupati conducted many meetings to promote, explain and solicit support involving related heads of offices, some important personnel from his office and other local legislative bodies. He then problematized the establishment of SOSS by defining the roles of all involved actors. The description of the roles and relationship of some important actors (human and otherwise) involved are as follows:

The Heads of Participating Offices

There were 10 different offices directly involved in the issuance of business licenses. At first, the heads of these offices were not willing to delegate their authority to SOSS personnel. But the Bupati reminded them that in principal he had the sole authority to issue the licenses but had delegated and empowered to the various offices for logistical reasons and smoother operations. He autocratically decided to retract the authority given and pass it on to his own SOSS personnel. However, he clarified that each office still had the authority to monitor the operation of every related activities. In addition, they still participated in the decision making process and fees collected would be posted as revenue for the respective office which formerly had the authority. This "win-win" problematization proposed by the Bupati resulted in no significant

resistance from various offices so that the head of Industry, Commerce and Cooperation Office who should delegate his authority to SOSS gave his commitment by saying:

As part of regency administration which is determined to improve its public service through the establishment of SOSS unit, we have no objection. Moreover, in fact the Bupati is the one who hold the authority to issue licenses. If now the Bupati wants to retract this authority and pass it on to SOSS unit then it is not a problem for us.

SOSS Staffs

As of May 2009, SOSS had 31 staffs managing 59 various licenses and 10 certificates. The educational qualification of these staffs varied: six had master degree, seventeen with bachelors, four with vocational degree, and four with high school qualification. [At the initial establishment in 2002, the number of SOSS staffs was only 21]. All of them had good performance records and worked at different offices before they were selectively recruited. All SOSS staffs got additional enumerations above their monthly salary as incentive. The incentive made them have a take-home pay higher than other employees holding similar posts in the government services.

Technology Infrastructure

SOSS had an appropriate ICT infrastructure. Every staff in SOSS was provided with a computer set that was connected to the local computer network and the internet. The local computer network was part of a larger network connecting almost all important local government offices and village offices across the regency. Although the ICT infrastructure and its related information systems were regarded as the most important non-human technological actors, there were also other important actors such as the air-condition, the CCTV system, and the TV sets.

The technology infrastructure seemed to cooperate well since Bupati regarded it as an important actor for his government innovation initiative. He perceived that ICT played important roles not only as a facilitator but also as a controller. His vision of Sragen as "Being a Smart Regency" reflected how strongly he believed to the important role of technology in general and ICT in particular to support the regency development.

Stipulations

These are conditions, provisions or terms that are created to be placed on to SOSS's shoulders for serious considerations. Historically, the notion of improving public services quality came from Indonesian President Instruction No. 1/1995. It was then operationally stipulated by the Ministry of State Apparatus Empowerment' Decree No. 81/1998. However, the notion of one-stop service was first articulated by the Ministry of Home Affairs through Decree No. 25/1998. In the context of Central Java Province Government, the Governor issued Decree No. 28/1999 on the guidelines for the establishment of integrated public service units for local governments.

Based on Bupati's Decree No. 17/2002, Sragen reformed the existing one-stop service to the one-door service approach. Meanwhile, there was also Presidential Instruction No. 3/2003 which instructs the implementation of e-government across all government agencies. Since then Bupati and local government of Sragen had issued many stipulations as SOSS underwent dynamic development in term of its organizational structure, its services, and its relation to other offices. The Central Government finally appreciated what had been practiced in SOSS and even Ministry of Home Affairs issued Decree No. 24/2006 on the guidelines of the formation of one-door integrated public services. This stipulation significantly adopted some best practices from SOSS. Unfortunately, the Central Government then issued Decree No. 41/2007 on

the new guidelines on the establishment of local government offices and departments structure, and based on this decree, the one-stop service was just an optional unit with a one-roof approach and had no direct authority to issue license. Therefore, this stipulation was not in line with Ministry of Home Affairs' Decree No. 24/2006. Sragen local government and with some others then urged the Ministry of Home Affairs to respond to this contradicting regulation. The Ministry of Home Affairs responded by issuing Decree No. 20/2008 that facilitated the establishment of a one-stop service either in the form of an office or even a bureau. Though this last stipulation resolved the conflicting regulation but the outlined structure of one-stop service office or bureau was less powerful than to the one Sragen had. This condition brought a sort of disappointment to some staffs at SOSS since it might lower their echelon rank and that would decrease their salaries.

KPDE (Kantor Pengolahan Data Elektronik/Electronic Data Processing Office)

KPDE was responsible for managing ICT infrastructure across Sragen regency as well as developing e-government systems to support local administration. Most of the license processing systems were jointly developed by these two offices. However, the permanent role of KPDE toward SOSS was to maintain the ICT infrastructure and also to assure the data and systems integrity among various e-government systems in Sragen. *Kantaya*, (short for "Kantor Maya / Virtual Office"), which was developed and maintained by KPDE, was the most frequently used systems to support SOSS. It enabled departments and village offices to easily share data in which the Bupati could remotely monitor. KPDE also plays vital role in assisting Sragen regency's vision to be a "smart government" which is linked with the intensive use of ICT to support its development programs. The performance of SOSS had significant impact on KPDE since it would reflect the success of KPDE in developing e-government in Sragen. Therefore, KPDE positively supported SOSS and was an important actor.

Citizens of Sragen

Although many citizens of Sragen wanted to serve the public more, but interestingly, none was ever directly involved in the development process. Their only direct participation was involved in a survey to evaluate SOSS performance twice a year. Although SOSS had provided many communication channels such as email, SMS (Short Messaging System), and hot-lines facilities to enable individuals to articulate their concerns, so far their participation and feedbacks were very limited.

Visitors to SOSS

Although at the design stage visitors did not play any significant role to the actor-network developed by the Bupati, eventually, especially after SOSS received a lot of recognition, they had an important role in shaping its continuous development. What made them important was not because of their numbers (more than 1000 for the last three years) but their intention to do a comparative study and this also created unique interessement. Having many visitors to recognize their performance brought a valuable psychological effect to most SOSS staffs as they felt supported, successful, and knowledgeable when being praised. A customer service staff member even commented:

We should treat all our visitors well because if even one visitor got wrong impression of us then he could easily spread around bad news that would ruin our reputation.

After identifying all actors involved, Bupati made himself an indispensable member and de-

fined the obligatory passage point (OPP) as "how to provide simple, transparent, and be accountable services for processing various licenses for the citizens of Sragen." The Bupati was aware that either positive or negative interest of those actors to this OPP determined the success of this initiative. Figure 1 presents these network of interest toward OPP from all involved actors.

The problematization process showed how bureaucratic reform introduced by Bupati was an essential component of this e-government initiative. It also showed that the reform had to deal with legal, procedural, organizational, managerial, as well as mental and cultural issues. Although the reform was only about providing license at regency level but it was not an easy one as similarly reported by many researchers (Grant & Chau, 2005; Stanforth, 2006; Yildiz, 2007). This reform was actually harder to manage within the Javanese culture context where most people do not want any conflict with others since their valued scenario is to live in harmony (Kartodirjo, 1984 p. 185). However, the Bupati seemed to be able to manage this reform successfully. Though many interviewees acknowledged that the reform was successful mainly because of the Bupati's decisive stance and a "win-win" power sharing with heads of offices but the contextual understanding suggests that it was also because of the way staffs perceived the Bupati's role as their leader. From the Javanese culture perspective, a public leader is always perceived as "God chosen" and is never merely part of a human democratic system (Ali, 1986 p. 203). Consequently, a good leader should be not only strong, powerful, decisive, but also the same time kind-hearted since he/she is to represent God in governing people and nature at the same time. To some extent, the Bupati's authoritarian style of leadership, was not only accepted by his staffs but was also supported. This situation, where the citizens understand the role and importance of their leader, originates from an agricultural society. Although only 51% of the people in Sragen work in the agricultural sector,

Figure 1. Problematization network of SOSS

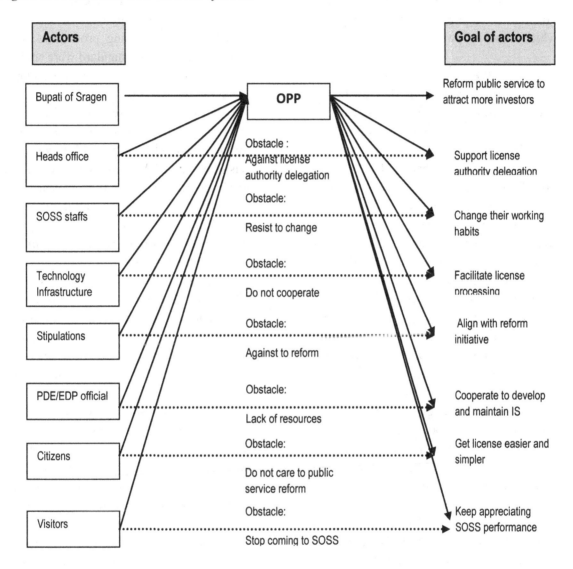

the rest still also live in a very close relationship with this culture.

Interessement Moment

The Bupati attempted to influence and stabilize all the actors he defined in the problematization process by introducing several interessement strategies. These strategies extended and materialized the hypothesis he made concerning the success of SOSS which included:

- License inquiry should be simple, fast, and transparent,
- Involved offices should support by returning their authority to the Bupati,
- SOSS staffs can be transformed to become professional workers,
- ICT systems and private sector practices can be fully adopted,
- Excellent license services would attract more investors.

Under these hypotheses, the Bupati implemented three new important interessement strategies which are as follows:

1. **Granting SOSS unit an authority to issue licenses after retracting that authority from various offices:** The Bupati reminded each office that conceptually he was the one who held the authority to issue licenses. Therefore, the Bupati had the legal right to transfer it to SOSS. Nevertheless, fees collected from license processing, before they were transferred to Local Finance Office, would be posted to the account of the respective office that formerly issued the licenses and each related office would be represented in the technical team to review license application and to recommend its approval.

2. **Facilitating SOSS to adopt corporate work culture and management equipped with new reward system:** All SOSS staffs (new and old) should participate in a series of compulsory training programs to change their mind-set from being served to providing service, to improve their skills in serving public, and to master ICT. To get real experience on how to serve public excellently, these staffs participated in a week internship training program at Gianyar Regency in Bali. Every week SOSS staffs would also join an in-house training program given by internal speakers and motivators with different specializations. As part of the efforts to change their work culture, SOSS staffs wore new office attire, different from that of other government employees. They wore a long-sleeved shirt and a neck-tie in order to look like professional workers in a private company. They also received a supplement to their previous monthly salary as incentive to maintain their performance and to prevent corruption practices.

   To maintain its good performance, SOSS had a good management and control systems.

First, in 2005 it adopted the ISO managerial standards. Although only 16 (out of 62) licenses processing procedures were certified by ISO, the standard were applied to all other licenses processing procedures. Second, the Bupati, heads of office, and monitoring team could easily monitor SOSS performance using many channels such as through the weekly and monthly reports, site visits, or via CCTV. Third, SOSS conducted performance evaluation twice a year using 14 performance variables and involving at least 150 respondents.

3. **Providing incentives to members of the business community who wants to initiate operation in Sragen:** Since the main objective of SOSS was not merely to provide excellent services for license processing and issuance, but also to increase business investment, the Bupati also provided some incentives to business community to complement the quality services offered by SOSS. He provided free business licenses for those who were new. He also had set up a business complex at Kalijambe, located about 30 km from Sragen with its appropriate land size and infrastructure. He even reminded people in Sragen to stop asking companies to provide any community facility since his administration should be the one responsible for such a request. As a result, the number of business-related license application increased significantly and resulted in fee growth of 300% in 2004.

The Bupati elegantly managed to transfer licenses-issuing authority from several offices to SOSS because of his awareness and knowledge on how power and authority can be conceptually distributed and exercised within the local government systems. Uniquely, although the authority to issue non-license (certificates) was not transferable to SOSS because of some stipulations and restriction from the central government, in practice this authority was digitally transferable. It happened whenever SOSS issued new certificates which were signed digitally not by the SOSS head but by the head of the Civil Registry Office. This solution could be considered quite creative as it innovatively used ICT in this authority reconfiguration. In this case, ICT played an important interessement device. However, this should not be considered as merely an ICT innovation but it reflected more on how the Bupati exercised his leadership effectively in his relationship with office heads. From the interessement moment point of view, ICT was used effectively to make this relationship a reality. In other words, the Bupati was able not only to exercise his formal power that arose from his positions of authority (Silva, 2007) as the top leader in Sragen but he also successfully implemented some devices of interessement to create favourable balance of power (Callon, 1986) amongst his actors.

Enrolment Moment

Generally, all implemented interessement devices resulted in enrolment from respective actors. However to elaborate further, all actors that participated in the enrolments will be represented when coming up with each interessement strategy or policy. The interessement strategy to grant SOSS an authority to issue license finally resulted in enrolment from all involved offices but the heads of offices negotiated some issues (as deliberated earlier). The authority transfer should not result in a reduction of their income.

Most staffs at SOSS seemed happily enrolled to the implementation of corporate work culture introduced by the Bupati. Perhaps the initial incentive provided for them was an important factor to their enrolment but later most staffs no longer considered it as their main drive. By then they were not only fully committed to serving

citizens like the way private sector did but also had internalized their style of service deep down in their heart under the notion of "ikhlas" or sincerity. This "ikhlas" value has been strong and embedded character of the Javanese way of life (Kartodirjo, 1984 p. 188) and since all staffs of SOSS are Javanese, the need for quality public service could be easily enrolled into them. Not only did this success in enrolment made them serve the public excellently but it also made them proud. One of the many similar comments recorded when they were asked about their feeling of their new work culture. Below is one such comment from a staff handling licenses related to health services.

...I am proud that I can serve public better especially now when we are recognized locally and nationally. For us, it is invaluable. There is a sort of satisfaction if the way I serve public is nationally adopted as the best practice. Such is beyond our expectation since initially we just wanted to make an innovation but now it is recognized nationally and even it has been referred to by Home Affairs Minister's Decree No 26/2006.

Their deep-rooted work culture at SOSS contributed significantly to the successful alliance from other actors such as from ICT infrastructure and system, the ISO-based license processing, and some regulations. Indeed, the information systems they were using were basically simple but their positive attitude toward this system then made them easily accept its limitation, such as failed connection, viruses, and frequent system modifications. Although the adopted ISO management system adopted had created some administrative burden, they found it very useful since it made them have the full control of license processing. In addition, despite the Central Government's introduction of regulation No. 41/2007 which does not adequately appreciate the SOSS organizational structure, they perceived it as a challenge and not merely as a threat.

Mobilization Moment

Throughout the project cycle, only few individuals were directly involved and became the spokesperson to represent other individuals who chose to be silent (Callon, 1986). Some of these representations will be reviewed to understand the role of legitimate spokespersons.

During the designing stage of SOSS, the Bupati represented the citizen of Sragen in general and business community in particular who demanded excellent licenses-processing service. The Bupati was a legitimate spokesperson of Sragen's citizen since people had voted him as their top leader. Though there was no process to appoint him as representative of the business community, his long experience as a manager in a private company made him a legitimate spokesperson for them. After being inaugurated as Bupati, he was officially also a legitimate spokesperson of central and provincial government, which had a concern to improve the quality of public services.

The Bupati represented the citizens to negotiate with some offices represented by their respective heads. Of course, every head office was a legitimate spokesperson for all the staffs working in his/her respective office. The Bupati negotiated with the head of offices to provide better license-processing service by asking them to select their qualified staff to work at SOSS. The selected staffs from each office would then be a legitimate representative of the various offices respectively. For the subsequent stage of the development, the SOSS head then became a legitimate spokesperson for all his staffs to negotiate with other representatives.

In promoting his idea to establish SOSS, the Bupati stressed that ICT would be intensively used. In many occasions the Bupati unintentionally became a legitimate spokesperson of voiceless ICT too, especially when he himself frequently used ICT to present his ideas. On one occasion he even removed the out-dated over-head projector from his meeting room to condition all his staffs to

used laptop and LCD projectors. The Bupati also acted as a legitimate and powerful spokesperson of ICT when he strongly encouraged KPDE to come up with a computer-based system which enabled him to digitally monitor the performance of all offices at any time.

The Bupati was a legitimate spokesman for the heterogeneous population where he mobilizes local legislative members to approve the expansion of SOSS from a unit in 2002 into an office in 2003 and finally into a bureau in 2006. This expansion has enabled SOSS to manage more licenses and have more personnel to consolidate the organizational structure with higher echelon staffs. To negotiate with local assembly members, the Bupati represented the citizens of Sragen, who demanded quality licenses-processing; the staffs of SOSS, who were willing to work professionally; the provincial and central governments, which encouraged local government to reform public service; the office heads who supported license authority transfer; ICT; and also KPDE, which supported the SOSS operation.

The above description shows how Bupati became an effective leader and was listened to because he had been "the head" of many groups of actors. He was able to combine the demand of the citizens, ICT, KPDE, SOSS staffs, rules and regulation, assembly members, and office heads. These chains of mediated relationship that finally resulted in an ultimate spokesperson could be referred as a progressive mobilization (Callon, 1986) of actors who formed alliance to successfully deliver excellent licenses-processing procedures. All these actors were first disbanded and then reassembled at a certain place at a particular time at the SOSS office (opened from Monday to Saturday, and from 7.30 am to 02.30 pm).

CONCLUSION

The use of ANT methodology has helped to monitor how a leader stabilizes the whole actor-network of members of local e-government initiative by identifying all involved whether human or otherwise. Their dynamic participation to the network has been noted and much influenced by their enrolment to some interessement strategies directed to achieve common goal defined in the obligatory passage point. It has also helped to understand how effective leadership may take advantage of mobilization process in which a legitimate spokesperson plays important role in stabilizing actor-network. The Bupati became an effective leader when managed to formulate and implement some strong and contextual interessement strategies that accommodated various issues: economic (an additional pay), managerial (the ISO standard), technical (the ICT infrastructure and its system), legal (local and central regulations), as well as spiritual (the notion of "ikhlas") and ideal ("colouring" Indonesia). An effective leadership in e-government development is then closely related to its capability to manage problematization process and to introduce strong and contextual interessement strategies.

Among the four moments of translation, the problematization process is the most crucial one. An effective leader should be careful in proposing e-government's problematization in general and it's obligatory passage point in particular since they will become referrences and affect the selection of effective interessement strategies. Putting a bureaucratic reform as the central issue of e-government problematization seems more appropriate and effective than considering it as an issue of technological innovation. Consequently, translating bureaucratic requires strong leadership because it intensively involves how power negotiation will be managed in certain political and social contexts.

Although ANT has been criticized many times as providing a Machiavellian ontology in understanding power (Whittle & Spicer, 2008), which is considered no longer appropriate for it fails to pay adequate attention to the notion of emanci-

pation and participation, Silva (2007) however argues that a Machiavellian view of power is key for making sense of legitimate and illegitimate power. Since power is always an essential part in understanding leadership in government setting then the Machiavellian ontology of ANT become an appropriate framework to understand leadership. It is especially so to understand how leadership is exercised in the design and implementation of an e-government in which the social relationship is much influenced by patron-client type coming from an agriculture society such as in Sragen regency.

REFERENCES

Accenture. (2001). *eGovernment leadership: Rhetoric vs reality — Closing the gap.* Retrieved from http://www.accenture.com/Global/Research_and_Insights/By_Industry/Government_and_Public_Service/GovernmentsRhetoric.htm

Akther, M. S., Onishi, T., & Kidokoro, T. (2007). E-government in a developing country: Citizen-centric approach for success. *International Journal on Electronic Governance, 1*(1).

Ali, F. (1986). *Refleksi Paham "Kekuasaan Jawa" dalam Indonesia Modern.* Jakarta, Indonesia: P.T. Gramedia.

Anthopoulos, L. G., Siozos, P., & Tsoukalas, I. A. (2007). Applying participatory design and collaboration in digital public services for discovering and re-designing e-government services. *Government Information Quarterly, 24,* 353–376. doi:10.1016/j.giq.2006.07.018

Bolgherini, S. (2007). The technology trap and the role of political and cultural variables: A critical analysis of the e-government policies. *Review of Policy Research, 24*(3), 259–275. doi:10.1111/j.1541-1338.2007.00280.x

Callon, M. (1986). Some elements of sociology of translation: Domestication of the scallops and the fishermen of St Brieuc Bay. In Law, J. (Ed.), *Power, action and belief: A new sociology of knowledge?* (pp. 196–223). London, UK: Routledge.

Chen, Y. N., Chen, H. M., Huang, W., & Ching, R. K. H. (2006). E-government strategies in developed and developing countries: An implementation framework and case study. *Journal of Global Information Management, 14*(1), 23–46. doi:10.4018/jgim.2006010102

Ciborra, C. (2005). Interpreting e-government and development: Efficiency, transparency or governance at a distance? *Information Technology & People, 18*(3), 260–279. doi:10.1108/09593840510615879

Collins, H., & Yearley, S. (1992). Epistemological chicken. In Pickering, A. (Ed.), *Science, practice and culture*. Chicago, IL: University of Chicago Press.

Cordella, A., & Shaikh, M. (2006). *From epistemology to ontology: Challenging the constructed "truth" of ANT*. Retrieved from http://is2.lse.ac.uk/WP/PDF/wp143.pdf

Dawes, S. S. (2002). *The future of e-government*. Retrieved from http://www.ctg.albany.edu/publications/reports/future_of_egov/future_of_egov.pdf

De'. R. (2005). E-government systems in developing countries: Stakeholders and conflict. In M. A. Wimmer, R. Traunmüller, Å. Grönlund, & K. V. Andersen (Eds.), *Proceedings of the 4th International Conference on Electronic Government* (LNCS 3591, pp. 26-37).

Doolin, B., & Lowe, A. (2002). To reveal is to critique: Actor–network theory and critical information systems research. *Journal of Information Technology, 17*, 69–78. doi:10.1080/02683960210145986

Drath, W. H., McCauley, C. D., Palus, C. J., Velsor, E. V., O'Connor, P. M. G., & McGuire, J. B. (2008). Direction, alignment, commitment: Toward a more integrative ontology of leadership. *The Leadership Quarterly, 19*, 635–653. doi:10.1016/j.leaqua.2008.09.003

Ebrahim, Z., & Irani, Z. (2005). E-government adoption: Architecture and barriers. *Business Process Management Journal, 11*(5), 589–611. doi:10.1108/14637150510619902

Fife, E., & Hosman, L. (2007). Public private partnerships and the prospects for sustainable ICT projects in the developing world. *Journal of Business Systems, Governance and Ethics, 2*(3).

Furuholt, B., & Wahid, F. (2008). E-government challenges and the role of political leadership in Indonesia: The case of Sragen. In *Proceedings of the 41st Hawaii International Conference on System Sciences*.

Gauld, R. (2007). Public sector information system project failures: Lessons from a New Zealand hospital organization. *Government Information Quarterly, 24*, 102–114. doi:10.1016/j.giq.2006.02.010

Gautam, V. (2006). E-governance 'paradigms' revisited: Constraints and possibilities. In Sahu, G. P. (Ed.), *Delivering e-government*. New Delhi, India: Global Institute of Flexible Systems Management.

Grant, G., & Chau, D. (2005). Developing a generic framework for e-government. *Journal of Global Information Management, 13*(1), 1–30. doi:10.4018/jgim.2005010101

Gudea, S. (2007). Internet access on the cheap: The power of the co-op. *Journal of Business Systems, Governance and Ethics, 2*(3).

Heeks, R. (2003). *Most e-government-for-development project fail: How can risks be reduced?* Manchester, UK: Institute for Development Policy and Management.

Heeks, R., & Stanforth, C. (2007). Understanding e-government project trajectories from an actor-network perspective. *European Journal of Information Systems, 16*(2), 165–177. doi:10.1057/palgrave.ejis.3000676

Helbig, N. C., Gil-García, J. R., & Ferro, E. (2009). Understanding the complexity in electronic government: Implications from the digital divide literature. *Government Information Quarterly, 26*, 89–97. doi:10.1016/j.giq.2008.05.004

Imran, A., & Gregor, S. (2007). A comparative analysis of strategies for e-government in developing countries. *Journal of Business Systems, Governance and Ethics, 2*(3).

Jansen, A. (2005). Assessing e-government progress– why and what. In *Proceedings of the Norsk Konferanse for Organisasjoners Bruk Av IT.*

Jonas, D. K. (2000). Building state information highways: Lessons for public and private sector leaders. *Government Information Quarterly, 17*(1), 43–67. doi:10.1016/S0740-624X(99)00026-X

Karanasios, S. (2007). Ecuador, the digital divide and small tourism enterprises. *Journal of Business Systems, Governance and Ethics, 2*(3).

Kartodirjo, S. (1984). *Modern Indonesia & transformation.* Yogyakarta, Indonesia: Gadjah Mada University Press.

Ke, W., & Wei, K. K. (2004). Successful e-government in Singapore. *Communications of the ACM, 47*(6), 95–99. doi:10.1145/990680.990687

Kim, S., Kim, H. J., & Lee, H. (2009). An institutional analysis of an e-government system for anti-corruption: The case of OPEN. *Government Information Quarterly, 26*, 42–50. doi:10.1016/j.giq.2008.09.002

Knights, D., & Murray, F. (1994). *Managers divided: Organisation politics and information technology management.* Chichester, UK: John Wiley & Sons.

Latour, B. (1987). *Science in action.* Cambridge, MA: Harvard University Press.

Latour, B. (1992). Where are the missing masses? Sociology of a few mundane artefacts. In Bijker, W., & Law, J. (Eds.), *Shaping technology, building society: Studies in socio-technical change.* Cambridge, MA: MIT Press.

Latour, B. (1996). The trouble with actor-network theory. *Soziale Welt, 47*(4), 369–381.

Latour, B. (2005). *Reassembling the social: An introduction to actor-network-theory.* New York, NY: Oxford University Press.

Law, J. (1992). Notes on the theory of the actor-network: Ordering, strategy, and heterogeneity. *Systems Practice, 5*(4). doi:10.1007/BF01059830

Law, J., & Callon, M. (1992). The life and death of an aircraft: A network analysis of technical change. In Bijker, W. E., & Law, J. (Eds.), *Shaping technology, building society: Studies in socio-technical change.* Cambridge, MA: MIT Press.

Madon, S., Sahay, S., & Sahay, J. (2004). Implementing property tax reforms in Bangalore: An actor-network perspective. *Information and Organization, 14*, 269–295. doi:10.1016/j.infoandorg.2004.07.002

May, T., & Powel, J. L. (2008). *Situating social theory* (2nd ed.). New York, NY: McGraw-Hill.

McLean, C., & Hassard, J. (2004). Symmetrical absence/symmetrical absurdity: Critical notes on the production of actor-network accounts. *Journal of Management Studies, 41*(3). doi:10.1111/j.1467-6486.2004.00442.x

Miller, P. (1996). The multiplying machine. *Accounting, Organizations and Society, 22*(3-4), 355–364. doi:10.1016/S0361-3682(96)00030-X

Misra, D. C. (2007, December 10-13). Sixty years of development of e-governance in India (1947-2007): Are there lessons for developing countries? In *Proceedings of the International Conference on Theory and Practice of Electronic Government*, Macao, China.

Moon, M. J., & Norris, D. F. (2005). Does managerial orientation matter? The adoption of reinventing government and e-government at the municipal level. *Information Systems Journal, 15*, 43–60. doi:10.1111/j.1365-2575.2005.00185.x

Morrell, K., & Hartley, J. (2006). A model of political leadership. *Human Relations, 59*(4), 483–504. doi:10.1177/0018726706065371

Ndou, V. (2004). E-government for developing countries: Opportunities and challenges. *Electronic Journal on Information Systems in Developing Countries, 18*(1), 1–24.

Nguyen, T. T., & Schauder, D. (2007). Grounding e-government in Vietnam: From antecedents to responsive government services. *Journal of Business Systems, Governance and Ethics, 2*(3).

Ochara, N. M. (2010). Assessing irreversibility of an e-government project in Kenya: Implication for governance. *Government Information Quarterly, 27*(1), 89–97. doi:10.1016/j.giq.2009.04.005

Priyatma, J. E., & Han, C. K. (2008). ANT and e-government research in developing countries: A case in BIMP-EAGA. In Rahman, A. A., Ali, N. A., & Han, C. K. (Eds.), *Management research issues* (pp. 187–222). Malaysia: UPM Press.

Prybutok, V. R., Zhang, R., & Ryan, S. D. (2008). Evaluating leadership, IT quality, and net benefits in an e-government environment. *Information & Management, 45*, 143–152. doi:10.1016/j.im.2007.12.004

Pye, A. (2005). *Leadership and organizing: Sensemaking in action*. London, UK: Sage.

Rychards, L. (2005). *Handling qualitative data: A practical guide*. London, UK: Sage.

Scholl, H. J. (2007). Central research questions in e-government, or which trajectory should the study domain take? *Transforming Government: People. Process and Policy, 1*(1), 67–88.

Silva, L. (2007). Epistemological and theoretical challenges for studying power and politics in information systems. *Information Systems Journal, 17*, 165–183. doi:10.1111/j.1365-2575.2007.00232.x

Stanforth, C. (2006). Using actor-network theory to analyze e-government implementation in developing countries. *Massachusetts Institute of Technology. Information Technologies and International Development, 3*(3), 35–60. doi:10.1162/itid.2007.3.3.35

Torres, L., Pina, V., & Royo, S. (2005). E-government and the transformation of public administrations in EU countries Beyond NPM or just a second wave of reforms? *Online Information Review, 29*(5), 531–553. doi:10.1108/14684520510628918

Whittle, A., & Spicer, A. (2008). Is actor network theory critique? *Organization Studies, 29*(4), 611–629. doi:10.1177/0170840607082223

Wong, K., Fearon, C., & Philip, G. (2007). Understanding e-government and e-governance: Stakeholders, partnerships and CSR. *International Journal of Quality & Reliability Management, 24*(9), 927–943. doi:10.1108/02656710710826199

Yildiz, M. (2007). E-government research: Reviewing the literature, limitations, and ways forward. *Government Information Quarterly, 24*, 646–665. doi:10.1016/j.giq.2007.01.002

This work was previously published in the International Journal of Actor-Network Theory and Technological Innovation, Volume 3, Issue 3, edited by Arthur Tatnall, pp. 1-20, copyright 2011 by IGI Publishing (an imprint of IGI Global).

Chapter 15

Mediated Action and Network of Actors:
From Ladders, Stairs and Lifts to Escalators (and Travelators)

Antonio Díaz Andrade
Auckland University of Technology, New Zealand & Universidad ESAN, Peru

Samuel Ekundayo
Auckland University of Technology, New Zealand

ABSTRACT

Both actor-network theory and activity theory call attention to the coexistence of people and technology. Although both theories provide analytical tools to understand the nature of the reciprocal action-shaping of humans and nonhumans, each puts emphasis on different conceptual elements of human activity. In this paper, the authors examine both activity theory and actor-network theory and present their similarities and differences, limitations, and complementarities. Using the theoretical lenses of both theories, the authors trace the evolution of an ordinary artifact to illustrate how researchers on the sociology of technology and innovations can benefit from these parallel theoretical approaches.

INTRODUCTION

The coexistence of humans and nonhumans characterises our lives. We are immersed in a world made of both social and technical artifacts (Callon, 1986; Latour, 1986). The social world cannot subsist without technical artifacts as much as the latter only exists because of the former (Miettinen, 1999). These parallel assertions come from two

realms concerned with the study of the interplay between subjects and objects: actor-network theory and activity theory.

In this paper, we analyse these two – at the same time, similar yet contrasting – approaches. On the one hand, the focus of actor-network theory is on the dynamic and simultaneous interaction of both the social and the technical assuming symmetry between human and nonhuman actors (Callon, 1986; Latour, 1986, 1999a, 1999b, 2005). On the other hand, the dialectic nature of cultural-

DOI: 10.4018/978-1-4666-2166-4.ch015

historical activity theory postulates that human activity is always a materially and socially mediated object-oriented practice, whereby the object of activity is constantly modified and the object itself modifies the activity system (Engström, 1987, 1999; Vygotsky, 1979).

Both perspectives provide analytical tools to understand the nature of the reciprocal action-shaping of humans and nonhumans. Using the theoretical lenses of both actor-network theory and activity theory, in this study we examine an ordinary artifact – a device designed to make possible people going and transporting things up and down – and trace its evolution. We trust this analysis illustrates and makes apparent the merits, limitations and complementarities of these two theoretical perspectives for the study of innovations.

This paper is organised in the following manner. In the next two sections, we introduce actor-network theory and activity theory along with their inherent concepts of translation and tool mediation, respectively. Then, we examine the life of an ordinary artifact from the lenses of these two theoretical approaches. Following a discussion on how each of these perspectives examines innovations, we conclude highlighting the merits, limitations and complementarities of actor-network theory and activity theory.

ACTOR-NETWORK THEORY

Actor-network theory rejects the underlying unalterable view of objects and subjects purported by essentialism, which only recognises their fundamental characteristics and ultimate functionalities. Actor-network theory challenges the generalised assumption that humans and technology constitute a stable and predictable system (Latour, 1987). The origins of actor-network go back to symbolic interactionism, which assumes that the meaning humans ascribe to things determines how the former act on the latter. Furthermore, symbolic

interactionism also recognises that the ascribed meaning is not immutable but emerges from social interaction and is continuously modified through interpretation. In this sense, actor-network theory recognises a continuous negotiation process between people, technology and their context (Hanseth, Aanestad, & Berg, 2004).

Actor-network theory is fundamentally the study of the association between humans and non-humans (Callon, 1986; Latour, 1986). It assumes symmetry between the social and the technical, both equally powerful on influencing each other. Moreover, Latour (1999b, 2005) calls attention to the artificial nature of the entity society, which cannot exist by itself. In actor-network theory vocabulary, collective seems to be a better suited word to describe the association of both humans and nonhumans. Actor-network theory stresses the combined nature of the intertwined dyad formed by people and things – both material and immaterial. Latour (1999b) vigorously claims, "we live in a hybrid world made up at once of gods, people, stars, electrons, nuclear plants, and markets" (p. 16). The elements of this hybrid world only exist in the representational space: "no reality without representation" (Latour, 1999b, p. 304).

Latour (2005) illustrates the symmetric characteristics of the network using the case of the traffic system. There is no difference between the car driver who slows down prompted by a road sign and the car driver who slows down because of a speed hump. The first driver's motivation may be altruism, while the second one simply may not want to damage her car suspension. Regardless of the driver's motivation, the absent road designers – who put up the signs and built the speed humps – conditions the driver behaviour. This example shows the association of cars, roads, traffic signs, drivers and road designers forming a network of actors. Thus, not only the drivers and the road designers but also the traffic signs and the speed humps have agency properties since they all have the capacity to act and influence the actions of others. It should be noted here that agency does not involve intentionality. While speed humps or road signs can transform a state of affairs by modifying the driver behaviour, they have no intrinsic sense of purpose. It is the absent road designer intentions that hide behind them. Only human actors are empowered with intentionality.

Translation and Mediation

Actor-network theory is also known as the sociology of translation (Callon, 1986). Translation and mediation are two inextricably linked terms in the conceptually-rich vocabulary of actor-network theory. Translation refers "to the work through which actors modify, displace, and translate their various and contradictory interests" to modify the state of affairs (Latour, 1999b, p. 311). For the translation to occur – that is, the transformation of the state of affairs – it is necessary the coexistence of actors. Mediation represents the linkage among actors, where both the social and the technical worlds fuse together and exchange properties to form one world (Latour, 1999b). In other words, mediation is the invisible link that makes possible the translation. The aim of actor-network theory is to understand the association among actors: "there is no society, no social realm, and no social ties, but there exist translations between mediators that may generate traceable associations" (Latour, 2005, p. 108, emphasis in the original).

The notion of mediation is particularly relevant to the discussion on innovations we present in this paper. When a collective actor is formed, mediation reveals the goal of the translation. That is, the transformation from each actor's goal to a composite goal due to the interference between the actors. For instance, an individual may walk from point A to point B following a certain, rather flexible, route. However, when the same individual – the first actor – decides to drive a car – the second actor – for transporting herself from A to B, it is neither an individual nor a car anymore but a car-driver dyad. The interaction between these two actors transforms the car from

a static wheeled object parked somewhere into a moving vehicle as well as the pedestrian into a driver. The car-driver association can only move through designated roads – something that the pedestrian is not allowed to do – without going through parks and footpaths – something that the pedestrian is allowed to do. Understanding the functioning of this new collective actor requires abandoning the subject-object dichotomy (Latour, 1999a). In this sense, the alliance of actors may change the original function of each of them taken separately creating a composite goal.

Moreover, it is possible for the associated entities to produce an entirely new goal. For instance, planning a trip using an online booking system to search for flights to and accommodation in a specific location may give a result that differs from the original planned tour depending on the dates, airlines and prices suggested – we emphasise the word suggested – by the virtual travel agency. The designers and managers of this travel agency are the invisible actors. By folding their meaning into nonhuman actors, they express their intentions through a visible artifact – i.e., a computer screen. The designers and managers are the human actors that entrust their intentions into nonhuman actors – the virtual travel agency in this case. The interaction between the virtual travel agency – with its embedded logic – and the traveller – with her particular expectations – prompts a process of successive translations. This example makes apparent the intrinsically provisional and dynamic nature of associations (Latour, 2005).

This analysis demonstrates that networks are unstable. They are permanently collapsing and expanding in space and time (Latour, 1999b). Mediation, the process of establishing the association, transits from dispersed actors – which are far from being a network – to a fully developed collective where the nonhuman actors become invisible to the human actors. For instance, before a watch became a watch, the materials that it was made of were collected from different locations and its components were produced at different times until they were assembled together to form one actor – i.e., the watch. Then, a second actor – i.e., the user – comes to establish the collective. The watch user largely ignores the fact that a watch needs a battery to operate until it stops working. It is at this point that the user realises that there were technical elements inside her watch that made it work. The watch is no longer a "black box" (Latour, 1999b) but an artifact that partially discloses its secrets and makes the network collapse – until it is repaired and becomes a black box again within the network. Therefore, mediation is not only an expression of the translation but also, and most importantly, makes evident the symmetric relationship between human and nonhuman actors in the network.

ACTIVITY THEORY

Activity theory aims at understanding the interaction of human beings and the social entities they compose in their natural everyday setting. Achieving this understanding requires going through an analysis of the genesis, structure and process of human activities (Kaptelinin & Nardi, 2006). The theoretical underpinning of activity theory is rooted in the classical German philosophy of Kant and Hegel, which emphasises both the historical development of ideas as well as the active and constructive role of humans (Jonassen & Rohrer-Murphy, 1999; Lektorsky, 2009). That is, activity theory perceives day-to-day actions of human life as a result of the existence of the human mind as a special component of interaction with the environment.

The development of activity theory came from the work of Soviet scholars – mainly, Sergei Rubinshtein (1935), Alexei Leont'ev (1978), and Lev Vygotsky (1979) – who contributed immensely to set its foundations. As a whole, activity theory's combined origin encompasses Marxist philosophy, Vygotsky's (1979) cultural-historical psychology

as well as Leont'ev's (1978) hierarchical structure of human activity (Blin & Munro, 2007). Because of its non-English language origin, activity theory has encountered a major challenge through the several attempts to translate and formulate its concepts and principles into English language (Bedny & Karwowski, 2004). Nowadays, activity theory has transcended its own origins and become a truly international theoretical approach applicable in multiple disciplines (Engström, 1999).

Activity theory was introduced to overcome the Cartesian opposition between the subject and the object, between the inner world of consciousness and the outer world of stimuli (Lektorsky, 2009). Activity theory postulates that activities can only be properly understood by analysing their historical-cultural development within a specific context. In this sense, activity theory conceptualises the interaction between human beings and their social environment as a system of social relations – that is, an activity system. Activities do not exist without social relations. This is because human activity is enmeshed in a network of social relations working together. Since human activity is the result of historical development, activities are constantly undergoing change and reformation (Quek & Shah, 2004).

An activity system is an object-oriented, artifact-mediated and socially-constructed system, where cognition, behaviour and motivation are integrated and organised by a mechanism of self-regulation towards achieving a deliberate goal (Bedny & Karwowski, 2004). Activities are complex, collective and motivated by the need to transform a material or abstract object into desired outcomes (Blin & Munro, 2007) – e.g., turning grapes into wine, solving a mathematical problem, etc. Thus, different forms of activity within an activity system can be conceptualised as a development process (Bedny & Karwowski, 2004).

Leont'ev (1978) puts forward that an activity system can be represented as a hierarchical structure organised into three levels: activity, actions and operations. Activity, which is driven by a complex, social motive, is at the top level in this hierarchical structure. The motive is the object, which stimulates or motivates the subject to carry out a set of activities. In the long run, the set of activities carried out by the subject is ultimately aimed at attaining the object (Kaptelinin & Nardi, 2006).

Actions represent the second level in the hierarchy of activities. An activity may be composed of a sequence of steps, each of which is not immediately related to the motive even though the sequence as a whole may eventually result in attaining the object (Kaptelinin & Nardi, 2006). This sequence of steps is termed actions. The objects at which they are directed at are referred to as goals. Goals are conscious mental representations of human activity in conjunction with a motive (Blin & Munro, 2007).

The second-level actions can be decomposed into lower-level units; these units of activity are referred to as operations, which represent the third level. Operations are routine processes oriented towards the conditions under which the subject of an activity is trying to attain a goal. Over the course of constantly carrying out an activity, a conscious action may transform into a routine operation. Gradually, these actions may become more and more automatic (Kaptelinin & Nardi, 2006). For instance, after a series of sessions of driving a car with a manual gear system, a driver becomes acquainted to the car and drives without having to consciously think about where, when or how to change the gear. The operation gradually becomes a routine and thus normalised over the course of time.

In summary, the uppermost level of collective activity is driven by an object-related motive. The middle level of individual – or group – action is driven by a specific goal. Finally, the bottom level of collective activity is driven by the conditions and tools of action at hand (Engeström & Meittinen, 1999).

By assuming that the human mind emerges and exists as a special component of interactions with the environment, activity theory highlights the importance of context and consciousness (Jonassen & Rohrer-Murphy, 1999). Consciousness unifies attention, intention, memory, reasoning and speech of humans. Humans are granted with intentionality since they orient and plan their activities. In other words, purposeful actions are realised through conscious intentions. These human intentions are directed at objects of activity. The objects of activity affect the nature of the activity, which in turn affects the object. In this way, a mutual and dynamic relationship is generated. This mutual and dynamic relation is at the core of activity theory, concluding that activities are socially and contextually bound and can only be described in the context of the community in which it operates.

Tool Mediation

Building on Vygotsky's (1979) ideas of collectivity, Engeström (1999) offers a new paradigm of activity theory that models the social and contextual significance of activities. This new paradigm of activity theory criticises the classical representation of activity systems as limited in explicating the societal and collaborative nature of actions within the system. Engeström (1999) makes a vigorous call, "more than ever before, there is a need for an approach that can dialectically link the individual and the social structure" (p. 19).

The new model expands the original conceptualisation of an activity system. It now includes community, division of labour, rules, subjects, objects and tools as its constitutive elements (Figure 1). It conceptualises an activity as a collective and multi-voiced endeavour, taking into consideration multiple points of view, traditions, interests and interactions between participants.

The main components of the new model are the objective of the activity, defined as the goals, motives or intentions of the participants of the activity. The human interactions present in the carrying out of the activities are mediated with

Figure 1. A complex model of an activity system (adapted from Engström, 1999)

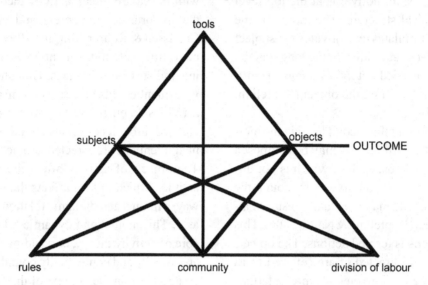

each other as well as objects of the environment through the use of tools, rules and division of labour. The components and the interaction existing between these elements are collectively referred to as the activity system. Mediation represents the nature of relationships existing within and between participants of an activity in a given community (Mwanza & Engström, 2005).

In the uppermost triangle we recognise three elements: subjects, objects and tools. The subjects are the individual or group of actors engaging in conscious actions or chains of operations related to or embedded in the goals of the system (Bedny & Karwowski, 2004; Jonassen & Rohrer-Murphy, 1999). The objects represent the target of the activity within the system. In other words, the objects are the physical or mental products that are sought after – the intention that motivates the activity (Jonassen & Rohrer-Murphy, 1999). Tools are the mediating artifacts that help to achieve the outcomes of the activity; tools alter the activity and are, in turn, altered by the activity. These tools include physical ones such as computers or photocopying papers and mental tools such as mathematical models or heuristics (Jonassen & Rohrer-Murphy, 1999). Physical tools are used to handle or manipulate objects, whilst mental tools

are used to influence behaviour in one way or the other (Mwanza, 2001).

Rules are explicit and implicit regulations, norms and conventions that inherently guide or constrain actions and interactions within the activity system (Jonassen & Rohrer-Murphy, 1999; Mwanza, 2001). Community entails the individual or group of individuals who share the object with the subject (Bedny & Karwowski, 2004). In other words, community represents the social and cultural context of the environment embedding the activity system (Mwanza, 2001). Division of labour stands for the allocation of responsibilities and variations in job roles of the subjects as they carry out the activity in the community (Mwanza, 2001). It describes how tasks are divided horizontally between community members as well as referring to any vertical division of power and status (Bedny & Karwowski, 2004). Finally, the outcome is the desired result of the activity of a system (Bedny & Karwowski, 2004).

Engström's (1999) model makes apparent a set of mutual relationships between the constituents of the activity system. As seen in Figure 1, activities are not isolated units but nodes in crossing hierarchies and networks which are in turn influenced by other activities (Scanlon & Issroff, 2005).

Benson, Lawler & Whitworth (2008) stress that both the subjects of the activity system (internal) and the wider community (external) mediate their activities through tools, rules and roles. Thus, tools mediate the relationship between subjects and objects, while rules mediate the relationship between subjects and the wider community and division of labour mediates the relationship between objects and the wider community.

The new model – recognised for its seemingly encompassing concepts – has been widely accepted among activity theory researchers worldwide. Jonassen and Rohrer-Murphy's (1999) contention that an activity system cannot be understood or analysed independently of the context in which it occurs fully embodies Engström's (1999) ideas. That is, analysing human activity should not only involve the kinds of activities that people engage in but also who is engaging in the activity (subjects), what their goals and intentions are (objects), what products result from the activity (outcomes), the rules and norms that define the activity and the larger community in which the activity is taking place (Jonassen & Rohrer-Murphy, 1999).

Activity theory holds that human beings seldom interact with the world directly. Several artifacts have been developed over time by humans to regulate and mediate their interactions both with the world and among individuals. The use of artifacts symbolises the hallmark of living the life of a human being (Kaptelinin & Nardi, 2006). The significance of artifacts is that they carry with them successful adaptations of an earlier time, either in the life of the individuals who made them or in the lives of those from earlier generations (Cole, 1999). This view conceptualises artifacts as fundamental mediators of purposeful human actions that relate human beings to the present world as well as their culture and history (Kaptelinin & Nardi, 2006).

Artifacts that mediate activities of human beings are referred to as physical artifacts. They also could be simply referred to as tools or instruments. Physical artifacts are easy to recognise as

their effect on the everyday life of humans cannot be overlooked (Kaptelinin & Nardi, 2006) – for instance, the use of simple artifacts like books that we read, phones that we use, road signs on our motorway, cutleries for dinning and so on. These artifacts are inextricably involved with the activities we are engaged in on a daily basis.

Wartofsky's (1979) proposes three levels of artifacts and describes the way each of them influences human activities. Some artifacts are directly involved in human work to mediate the relationship between the subject and object of activity; these are the first hand tools that we use (e.g., bowls, computers, telecommunication networks, etc.) and become the primary artifacts. The second level of artifacts is the combination of both the primary artifacts and models of actions used to preserve and transmit skills in the production and use of primary artifacts; they are referred to as secondary artifacts. The third level is called tertiary artifacts because they contain elements of the imaginative mind that provides conceivable change in the existing practices of human life. According to Cole (1999), "These imaginative artifacts can come to colour the way we see the actual world, acting as tools for changing current praxis" (p. 91).

The emphasis on the mediation of these tools in the interaction between the human mind and an objective is at the core of activity theory. This is because activity theory recognises the role the human mind plays in the cultural-historical development of the human life. For development to occur – that is, the change from an existing practice to a new order – the activity is first of all conceived in the human mind. Imaginative artifacts are put to use to redefine and develop new concepts. This can be further explained using the concepts of internationalisation and externalisation (Engström, 1999). For every phase of development, the mind goes through a reflective analysis of an existing cultural practice, which represents a process of internalisation. However, this reflective analytic exercise alone is not enough. The produced mental structure has to be designed and implemented in the exterior for another level of development to take place; usually in the form of new practice. This is the externalisation process.

We present now in Table 1 a summary portraying actor-network theory vis-à-vis activity theory across the conceptual dimensions described above.

THE LIFE OF AN ORDINARY ARTIFACT FOR GOING UP AND DOWN

In order to illustrate how both actor-network theory and activity theory are well suited to study technological innovations and their evolution, let us follow the trajectory of an ordinary artifact, one that most of us – if not all – use on a daily basis: something that makes possible to go up and, once there, to go down too. Instead of naming it a ladder or a lift, we prefer to refer to it as just an artifact that allows us to going up and down. In this way, we can trace its evolution and the name changes reflecting this evolutionary process. From an actor-network theory perspective, our analysis of the evolution of this artifact will show the dynamic and provisional characteristics of the network of actors. From an activity theory perspective, our analysis will reveal how the goal-directedness of this artifact mediates our actions.

The Actor-Network Theory Perspective

It is hard to establish accurately when the first ladder was made. We can only speculate that the first ladder was used to facilitate the way up when our ancestors were gathering fruits from high trees. They had the need to go to places above the ground surface. Someone – maybe more than one person – creatively devised that an easiest and less dangerous way to go up was by using an artifact composed by two relatively long uprights connected by several rungs in such a way that formed steps that made possible to ascend. Since that moment, a collective actor was formed: the human-ladder dyad. These two elements became an entangled unit.

While this early device to go up had the advantage to be portable or easy to make if it was disposed, perhaps our forebears needed something more stable when they stopped their nomad lifestyle and thought it was a better idea to establish human settlements. By then, living in caves was not the best option; it is when the first dwellings appeared. Thus, someone came up with the idea of building a series of fixed stairs to make possible the ascension from the ground level to the roof or even to a higher story in the dwelling. Perhaps the first reference to a staircase is found in the Book of Genesis: "Go to, let us build us a city and a

Table 1. Actor-network theory and activity theory

	Actor-network theory	Activity theory
Origins	Symbolic interactionism	Dialectical materialism
Unit of analysis	An entangled unit of both humans and nonhumans	A collective activity system, where the subject, tools and objects are immersed in a social assembly
Enacting agency	Both humans and nonhumans	Subjects in their interaction with the environment
Historical understanding	Given by the interaction of humans and nonhumans	Through an expansive cycle of combined internalisation and externalisation
Mediation	Symmetric associations between humans and nonhumans	Tools shape and are in turned shaped by human experiences
Socio-cultural interaction	It recognises the continuous negotiation between humans, nonhumans and their context	No activity system exists of its own accord; other systems contribute to it, directly or indirectly

tower, whose top may reach unto heaven; and let us make us a name, lest we be scattered abroad upon the face of the whole earth" (11:4). The fact that humans used tools to control their environment – cf. Arendt's (1958) notion of "homo faber" – and at the same time the modified environment made humans to modify their tools, represents the chains of translation, by which actors modify, displace and translate their interests (Latour, 1999b). In this case, people designed staircases to reach higher levels in a building in the same way as the availability of staircases allowed people to construct higher buildings.

If the construction techniques allowed people to erect ever-taller buildings, whose higher stories could be reached by means of staircases, the question was when to stop towering. The answer may be given by the effort of going upstairs – how many stories the average person could climb up without becoming a victim of fatigue. In 1853, Elisha Otis designed a safety mechanism for a hoisting platform that made possible and safe riding people and things inside a box moving upwards and downwards by a set of pulleys. This set the origin of the lift, as we know it nowadays. During the reconstruction of Chicago after the devastating fire that destroyed a large area of the city in 1871, architects thought designing and constructing tall buildings. In order to make this plan feasible – and the ascent a less strenuous effort for the building dwellers – lifts were installed in the new buildings marking the rapid expansion of this technology. This expansion signalled the unfolding of the negotiation process between humans and nonhumans to establish the association.

From the times when there were machinists operating lifts, these have evolved into up to a point that they became a "black-box" (Latour, 1999b) – most users unconsciously get in and out of lifts. Nowadays, lifts are part of an everyday sociotechnical network. Some lifts now have available some amenities like background music and videos to make the journey more enjoyable. In addition, some lifts even have audio commands

so human actors can just walk in and out the lift just by following the instructions given by the nonhuman actor through a recorded voice. The precursor of this anthropomorphic device was a humble ringing bell indicating the passengers they have arrived to their destination.

From moving people and things up and down in a vertical way (i.e., perpendicular to the surface level), then the escalator came up making possible to move the crowd up and down at an angle. Most importantly from an actor-network theory perspective is that escalators direct the human actors to specific areas – e.g., displays, terraces, etc. People travelling on escalators have no control at all on the final destination; it has been pre-defined by design. Once again, this feature demonstrates the agency properties of the nonhuman actors.

Now we can enjoy the comfort of travelators. It seems that the evolution of the technology that once made possible moving people upwards and downwards was adjusted to spare people the need to walk over relatively long horizontal distances. We are not going to elaborate further on this artifact, but it is worth noting that travelator creates new associations of humans and nonhumans as ladders, staircases, lifts and escalators did in the past.

The Activity Theory Perspective

From an activity theory perspective, the analysis of a tool for going up relates to the historical development of the human mind. Over the course of their individual development, human beings learn and appropriate concepts already existing in their cultures (Kaptelinin & Nardi, 2006). In other words, though some concepts may have not always been there, they come to be as a result of the positive and negative experiences of people who contributed to the development of culture. As the environment changes, human experience help to shape or modify the tools they use in order to adapt to the changing environment and their consequent needs.

The role of humans, their mind and experiences, is summed up in the term agency in activity theory as the ability to act in the sense of producing effects: "In activity theory, any activity is an activity of a subject. Not any entity is a subject. Subjects live in the world; they have needs that can be met only by being and acting in the world" (Kaptelinin & Nardi, 2006, p. 33). Therefore, the interaction between subjects and objects is not regarded as a symmetrical relationship; rather it is initiated and carried out by the subject to fulfil its needs. This reflects the support of activity theory for the consciousness and intentional trait unique to humans only within an activity system. That is, the ultimate cause for human activity is needs. The need for humans – i.e., the subjects – to go up – i.e., the object(ive) – led to the creation as well as continuous modification and appropriation of tools in this regard.

Human needs are the precursors to their objectives. The objective then defines their activities and the activities define their tools. For instance, the need to go to places above the surface, maybe with the objective in mind to pluck fruits off trees, places a demand for a tool that can take humans above the surface. Human – that is, the subject – therefore need a mediating tool to achieve their objective – in this case, going to places above the surface to pluck fruits. This led to the creation of the ladder. In other words, the major object to which the ladder was applied has to do with heights. Some objects would require a long ladder while some would require short ones. Day after day, humans survive based on their ability to meet their needs using the tools available to them. This is the summary of human existence since inception. The continuous pursuit of meeting human needs relates to the principle of object-orientedness, which presupposes that all humans are directed toward their objects. A way of comprehending this concept of objects is to think of them as objectives. The objective can be seen as the prospective outcomes that motivate and direct activities. The objective of moving humans to through heights led to the development of tools for going up.

The notion of tool mediation allows the analysis of a tool for going up through the lenses of activity theory. Tools mediate humans' relationship with the world. Tools influence human behaviour as well as their mental functioning. It is also germane to know that tools are created and transformed during the development of activity and carry with them the historical evidence of their development; just like the development of a ladder and its evolution to stairs, lifts and escalators. Perhaps after several years of using ladders, it got to a time when they could no longer address the advancing needs of humans. This led to a move from the first concept of ladders to the creation of stairs. Although the goal remains the same, to go up, now we are using a more advanced object due to the development of the human mind as well as the increase of their needs. Human beings then started to build staircases to reach higher levels in a building. After some time, humans discovered that the use of staircases for very distant heights required much energy. Consequently, the need to move to distant heights without stress led to the creation of lifts. Then, humans realised that the lift could only accommodate a certain number of people at a time. There came the need to modify the tool for a more advanced object – moving a crowd on a continuous basis to a distant height. This fresh need led to the creation of escalators. It is important to highlight that these developments emerged as a reflection of the human experience of interacting with the same object: the need to go up (and down).

This account emphasises the mediation of tools in the interaction between the human mind and a particular objective. It also helps to explain the developmental process of both internalisation and externalisation.

DISCUSSION

Both actor-network theory and activity theory have demonstrated their merits in the analysis of the interplay between people and technology as well as how innovations emerge and evolve. The emphasis of actor-network theory on empirical enquiry makes possible observing the process of constructing (or not) the collective between humans and nonhumans around the innovation (Law, 1994). It reveals the ability of one actor to generate interest and enrol other actors in forming the innovation network (Akrich, Callon, & Latour, 2002). Similarly, activity theory rejects the dichotomy subject-object and highlights the dynamic and mutually shaping relationship between people and technology in the creation of innovations. This approach affords visibility of the various participants in the expansive cycle of internalisation and externalisation (Engström, 1999) that guide the evolutionary process of innovations.

Although we have recognised the merits of actor-network theory and activity theory, we feel compelled to discuss the criticisms these two approaches have received. Granting agency properties – that is, the status of active actors – to nonhumans rather than conceptualising them as merely passive artifacts signals the major difference between actor-network theory and activity theory. Some authors claim that bringing the non-social – i.e., the technical – into the sociological fold is seemingly actor-network theory's most controversial feature and perhaps common limitation (Lee & Brown, 1994). Actor-network theory recognises that the association of humans and nonhumans becomes a network of actors as long as all human and nonhuman actors remain faithful to the network. Actor-network theorists regard this characteristic an advantage since it makes visible to the researcher the process of constructing (or not) the network. In contrast, activity theorists see this feature of actor-network theory as a drawback since it somewhat fails to recognise the power of human beings to constitute a network. As Vygotsky (1979) argues, human actors have high order cognitive capabilities and intentional action that are lacking in artifacts. In the same way actor-network theory has been criticised for granting agency characteristics to

nonhumans, activity theory has also been criticised for its bias towards tools. The bias is based on the implicit essentialist assumption and the social abstraction of tools as a means to an end, which may not be the case sometimes. Activity theory tends to neglect issues of power relations that stem from the social embedded nature of technology. That is, technology not only shapes contexts and environments of an activity system; contexts also in turn shape technology.

The aforementioned discussion allows us to see the complementarities between these two theoretical strands. We have already explained the major difference between activity theory and actor-network theory. Unlike the latter, the former grants agency properties to subjects – i.e., human actors – only. Miettinen (1999) points out that one of the shortcomings of assuming symmetry between human and nonhuman actors is that it obscures the intentionality inscribed in technological tools. However, Latour (2005) makes the distinction between agency and intentionality and recognises that while both human and nonhuman actors are granted with agency properties, only human actors possess intentionality – interested readers may refer to Díaz Andrade's (2010) work for a discussion on the difference between agency and intentionality of nonhuman actors. In this regard, we believe that the assumption of conscious goal-directedness of the subject in activity theory allows a deeper understanding of human cognitive capabilities (Mlitwa, 2007), which complements actor-network theory's assumption of symmetry in the study of technological innovation.

CONCLUSION

It is a truism that the day-to-day existence of human beings is made possible through the use of both social and technical artifacts. These artifacts define our survival in a socially constructed world. Both actor-network theory and activity theory back up this claim in a very comparable yet contrasting approach.

We have, in this paper, analysed the concepts of these two theories. Both theories are frameworks for analysing the interaction of humans with their environment. On the one hand, actor-network theory claims a symmetrical relationship between humans and nonhumans, subjects and objects, people and artifacts, the social and the technical. On the other hand, activity theory purports the significance of consciousness and intentionality in humans in an activity system; thus granting agency to human subjects only.

In the analysis of the life and evolution of an innovation, a tool for going up and down, we have examined the conceptual propositions of both theories. From the perspective of actor-network theory, we have described the evolution of the artifact as a typically network of actors forming an entangled unit. The network defines both the translation and mediation mechanism espoused by the tenets of actor-network theory. We have stressed that the evolution of the innovation – from ordinary ladders through stairs and lifts to escalators – describes the way humans and nonhumans constitute an association of actors that is under continuous modification. From the perspective of activity theory, we have emphasised the significance of the recognition of a human need first – in our example, the need to go up and down. This need helps to define the object of an activity, which consequently reveals the indispensability of a tool. It is the need – and its unspoken object-orientedness nature – that puts the human mind to work, recognising the agency role of humans to develop and transform their environment. The evolution of the artifact, from an ordinary ladder to an escalator, describes, through the lens of activity theory, a cultural-historical development. That is, as human needs grow, there is a constant call to advance on the innovation. Thus, innovations shape and are in turn are shaped by human experiences over time.

We have also discussed the merits, limitations and complementarities of both theoretical perspectives. We stressed that both theories are similar in that they help to explain the interaction that takes place between human and nonhuman actors in the actor-network theory vocabulary or between subjects and objects in the activity theory vocabulary. However, they differ in that, actor network theory grants agency to both humans and nonhumans, while activity theory posits that only humans are worthy of the agency ascription. While actor-network theory has been criticised for its dogged claims of a symmetric relationship between human and nonhumans and activity theory has been criticised for its heavy bias towards tools as a means to an end, we recognise that researchers on the sociology of technology can benefit from the complementarities these two theoretical approaches afford.

REFERENCES

Akrich, M., Callon, M., & Latour, B. (2002). The key to success in innovation Part I: The art of interessement. *International Journal of Innovation Management, 6*(2), 187–206. doi:10.1142/S1363919602000550

Arendt, H. (1958). *The human condition*. Chicago, IL: University of Chicago Press.

Bedny, G. Z., & Karwowski, W. (2004). Activity theory as a basis for the study of work. *Ergonomics, 47*(2), 134–153. doi:10.1080/00140130310001617921

Benson, A., Lawler, C., & Whitworth, A. (2008). Rules, roles and tools: Activity theory and the comparative study of e-learning. *British Journal of Educational Technology, 39*(3), 456–467. doi:10.1111/j.1467-8535.2008.00838.x

Blin, F., & Munro, M. (2007). Why hasn't technology disrupted academic teaching practices? Understanding resistance to change through the lens of activity theory. *Computers & Education, 50*(2), 475–490. doi:10.1016/j.compedu.2007.09.017

Callon, M. (1986). Some elements of a sociology of translation: Domestication of the scallops and the fisherman. In Law, J. (Ed.), *Power, action and belief* (pp. 196–233). London, UK: Routledge & Kegan Paul.

Cole, M. (1999). Cultural psychology: Some general principles and a concrete example. In Engström, Y., Miettinen, R., & Punamäki, R.-L. (Eds.), *Perspectives on activity theory* (pp. 87–106). Cambridge, MA: Cambridge University Press.

Díaz Andrade, A. (2010). From intermediary to mediator and vice versa: On agency and intentionality of a mundane sociotechnical system. *International Journal of Actor-Network Theory and Technological Innovation, 2*(4), 21–29. doi:10.4018/jantti.2010100103

Engeström, Y., & Meittinen, R. (1999). Activity theory: A well-kept secret. In Engström, Y., Miettinen, R., & Punamäki, R.-L. (Eds.), *Perspectives on activity theory* (pp. 1–18). Cambridge, UK: Cambridge University Press.

Engström, Y. (1987). *Learning by expanding.* Helsinki, Finland: Orienta Konsultit.

Engström, Y. (1999). Activity theory and individual and social transformation. In Engström, Y., Miettinen, R., & Punamäki, R.-L. (Eds.), *Perspectives on activity theory* (pp. 19–38). Cambridge, UK: Cambridge University Press.

Hanseth, O., Aanestad, M., & Berg, M. (2004). Guest editors' introduction: Actor-network theory and information systems. What's so special? *Information Technology & People, 17*(2), 116–123. doi:10.1108/09593840410542466

Jonassen, D. H., & Rohrer-Murphy, L. (1999). Activity theory as a framework for designing constructivist learning environments. *Educational Technology Research and Development, 47*(1), 61–79. doi:10.1007/BF02299477

Kaptelinin, V., & Nardi, B. (2006). *Acting with technology.* Cambridge, MA: MIT Press.

Latour, B. (1986). The power of association. In Law, J. (Ed.), *Power, action and belief* (pp. 261–277). London, UK: Routledge & Kegan Paul.

Latour, B. (1987). *Science in action: How to follow scientists and engineers through societies.* Cambridge, MA: Harvard University Press.

Latour, B. (1999a). On recalling ANT. In Law, J., & Hassard, J. (Eds.), *Actor network theory and after* (pp. 15–25). Oxford, UK: Blackwell Publishers.

Latour, B. (1999b). *Pandora's hope: Essays on the reality of science studies.* Cambridge, MA: Harvard University Press.

Latour, B. (2005). *Reassembling the social: An introduction to actor-network-theory.* Oxford, UK: Oxford University Press.

Law, J. (1994). *Organizing modernity.* Oxford, UK: Blackwell.

Lee, N., & Brown, S. (1994). Otherness and the actor network: The undiscovered continent. *The American Behavioral Scientist, 37*(6), 772–790. doi:10.1177/0002764294037006005

Lektorsky, V. A. (2009). Mediation as a means of collective activity. In Sannino, A., Daniels, H., & Gutierrez, K. D. (Eds.), *Learning and expanding with activity theory* (pp. 75–87). New York, NY: Cambridge University Press.

Leont'ev, A. N. (1978). *Activity, consciousness and personality.* Englewood Cliffs, NJ: Prentice Hall.

Miettinen, R. (1999). The riddle of things: Activity theory and actor-network theory as approaches to study innovations. *Mind, Culture, and Activity, 6*(3), 170–195. doi:10.1080/10749039909524725

Mlitwa, N. B. W. (2007). Technology for teaching and learning in higher education contexts: Activity theory and actor network theory analytical perspectives. *International Journal of Education and Development using Information and Communication Technology, 3*(4), 54-70.

Mwanza, D. (2001). Where theory meets practice: A case for an activity theory based methodology to guide computer system design. In *Proceedings of the 8th IFIP TC 13 Conference on Human-Computer Interaction*, Tokyo, Japan

Mwanza, D., & Engström, Y. (2005). Managing content in e-learning environments. *British Journal of Educational Technology*, *36*(3), 453–463. doi:10.1111/j.1467-8535.2005.00479.x

Quek, A., & Shah, H. (2004). A comparative survey of activity-based methods for information systems development. In *Proceedings of the International Conference on Enterprise Information Systems*, Stafford, UK.

Rubinshtein, S. (1935). *Foundation of psychology*. Moscow, Russia: Education Press.

Scanlon, E., & Issroff, K. (2005). Activity theory and higher education: Evaluating learning technologies. *Journal of Computer Assisted Learning*, *21*(6), 430–439. doi:10.1111/j.1365-2729.2005.00153.x

Vygotsky, L. S. (1979). *Mind in society: The development of higher psychological processes*. Cambridge, MA: Harvard University Press.

Wartofsky, M. (1979). *Models: Representation and scientific understanding*. Boston, MA: Reidel Publishing.

This work was previously published in the International Journal of Actor-Network Theory and Technological Innovation, Volume 3, Issue 3, edited by Arthur Tatnall, pp. 21-34, copyright 2011 by IGI Publishing (an imprint of IGI Global).

Chapter 16

A Socio–Technical Study of the Adoption of Internet Technology in Banking, Re-Interpreted as an Innovation Using Innovation Translation

Salim Al-Hajri
Higher College of Technology, Oman

Arthur Tatnall
Victoria University, Australia

ABSTRACT

This article presents a re-interpretation of research done in the mid-2000s on uptake of Internet technologies in the banking industry in Oman, compared with that in Australia. It addresses the question: What are the enablers and the inhibitors of Internet technology adoption in the Omani banking industry compared with those in the Australian banking industry? The research did not attempt a direct comparison of the banking industries in these two very different countries, but rather considered Internet technology adoption in Oman, informed by the more mature Australian experience. The original study considered Internet banking as an innovation and used an approach to theorising this innovation that was based on Diffusion of Innovations and the Technology Acceptance Model (TAM). Given the socio-technical nature of this investigation, however, another approach to adoption of innovations was worth investigating, and this article reports a re-interpretation of the original study using innovation translation from actor-network theory (ANT).

DOI: 10.4018/978-1-4666-2166-4.ch016

INTRODUCTION

In developed countries such as Australia, Internet technologies have been strongly embraced by the banking industry and for many years banks have pursued strategies to encourage their clients to engage in Internet banking. For some time Oman has been committed to economic growth but by the mid-2000s had a banking industry that was yet to embrace Internet technology. The study discussed in this article set out to determine inhibitors and enablers to the adoption of Internet technology in the banking industry in Oman, and to inform this by the more mature Australian experience. The original study used a theoretical framework based on the theory of Diffusion of Innovations and the Technology Acceptance Model (TAM). It was conducted in 2005 as a doctoral thesis at Victoria University (Al-Hajri, 2005) and involved in-depth interviews with a sample of bank managers at strategic, tactical and operational levels in both Oman and Australia.

There are, of course, huge cultural differences between Oman and Australia and a direct comparison of the two was not the intent of this research project. The backgrounds, economics, societies and indeed the very way of life in the two countries are all very different. Australian banks had already adopted Internet technologies whilst Omani banks were just beginning to do so. In developed countries such as Australia, Internet technologies have been embraced by the banking industry for some time and bank clients have been encouraged to engage in Internet banking (Al-Hajri & Tatnall, 2008), but while Oman is a developing country committed to economic growth, in 2005 its banking industry had not adopted Internet technology to any great extent.

THEORETICAL FRAMEWORK

It has been suggested that "… explaining human behavior in all its complexity is a difficult task"

(Ajzen, 1991, p. 179). Further to this we will argue that the main complexity in understanding Internet technology adoption behaviour, or the lack of it, within the context of the banking industry in Oman (a non-adopter) and Australia (an adopter) is that this involves people such as bank managers and customers, and that people behave in very different ways.

Innovation can be defined as: "the alteration of what is established; something newly introduced" (Oxford, 1973) or "introducing new things or methods" (Macquarie Library, 1981). Whereas invention refers to creating and building new artefacts or the discovery of new ideas, innovation involves making use of these artefacts or ideas in commercial or organisational practice. (Maguire, Kazlauskas, & Weir, 1994). Just because a new technology has been made available does not mean that it can be assumed that organisations or individuals will want to adopt or use it, and even if an organisation does adopt a new innovation, it cannot be assumed that its employees will be prepared to use it. In deriving a framework for the original study, four existing research frameworks were considered: The Theory of Reasoned Action (TRA), The Theory of Planned Behavior (TPB), The Technology Acceptance Model (TAM) and Diffusion of Innovations.

The Theory of Reasoned Action (TRA)

Fishbein and Ajzen (1975) originally developed the Theory of Reasoned Action (TRA) in 1975, before later comprehensively refining it with empirical evidence to support its validity and reliability (Ajzen & Fishbein, 1980). Their study focused on three major determinants of an individual's behaviour: Behavioral Intention, Attitude and Subjective Norm. TRA assumes that "… human beings are usually quite rationale and make systematic use of the information available to them" (Ajzen & Fishbein, 1980, p. 5). This assumption is important because it indicates clearly that individuals must utilise available information before arriving at any behavioural decision before engaging (or not engaging) in any specific behavioural decision. For example, the banking industry is a shareholder value maximiser and hence it is expected by shareholders to consider benefits/costs. This means that any behavioural decision must undergo a hierarchical sequence of processes and this view has led many researchers to focus on the relationship between cognition of the individual's behaviour and the development of attitude and intention towards performing the behaviour.

Fishbein and Ajzen illustrated their model using these three major variables in a hierarchical sequence to facilitate understanding, postulating that:

- An individual's behavioural intention is the immediate determinant of behavior,
- Their attitude and subjective norm are mediated through behavioural intention,
- Their behavioural and normative beliefs are mediated through attitude and subjective norm.

In summary, Fishbein and Ajzen (1975) developed their concepts, based on this relationship, to provide explanations about why people do (or do not) perform specific behavioural actions as well as to provide suggestions for developing strategies about changing the specific behaviour (or a course of action) to obtain desirable results (Ajzen & Fishbein, 1980).

The Theory of Planned Behaviour (TPB)

After identifying problems with the Theory of Reasoned Action, Ajzen (1991) came up with his Theory of Planned Behavior (TPB) as a significant modification of TRA. His main criticisms of TRA were that it was designed to predict and explain behaviour, or actions, based on the assumption that the behaviour was under a person's volitional control, but that this was often not the case due to the differences in individuals' abilities and in external forces. His arguments were that:

- Actual performance of some behaviours require the availability of opportunities and resources and that there are some behaviours that are not under a person's volitional control.
- There are non-motivational factors that may influence a person's volitional control over the behaviour and hence may affect the performance of the target behaviour.

These volitional control problems were also noted by Ajzen and Madden (1986) and Sheppard, Hartwick and Warshaw. (1988) and were considered to be limitations of the original TRA model. Ajzen's work was based on the original TRA (Fishbein & Ajzen, 1975; Ajzen & Fishbei,n 1980) and Bandura's (1982) concept of "self-efficacy", which is related to the evaluation of "… how well one can execute courses of action required to deal with prospective situations" (Bandura, 1982, p. 122). It concentrated on the non-motivational personal factors of for example: skills, abilities, knowledge, etc… and non-motivational external factors such as time, opportunities, cooperation of others, and so on, and on their influences on the actual performance of the behaviour. This means that lack of opportunities and resources such as time, skills, knowledge, and cooperation of others may present problems for an individual's volitional control over the behaviour and hence failure to perform the behaviour may result.

To address this concern Ajzen extended TRA by adding another construct called Perceived Behavioural Control, which refers to an individual's perception of the "… presence or absence of requisite resources and opportunities" (Ajzen & Madden, 1986, p. 457) required to perform the specific behaviour.

Technology Acceptance Model (TAM)

The Technology Acceptance Model (TAM) is a theoretical model that was designed to evaluate "… the effect of system characteristics on user acceptance of computer-based information systems" (Davis, 1986, p. 7). In a similar way to TRA, TAM assumes that a user of technology is generally quite rational and uses information in a systematic manner to decide whether to use, or not to use this technology. Major benefits claimed for using TAM are two-fold:

- It can provide IS designers with information about how and where to modify design to enhance IS acceptance.
- It can provide IS implementers with information about how and where to manage IS implementation. The information obtained from TAM could assist in forming a strategy to design and implement a successful IT/IS.

Davis' (1986) conceptual framework proposed that a user's motivational factors are related to actual technology usage and hence act as a bridge between technology design and actual technology usage. This means that information obtained from the prediction of actual usage at the early stage will guide IS designers and implementers to enhance the chance of implementing IT/IS successfully or even avoid the risk of failure. Davis (1986) assumes that stimulus variables, such as system features and capabilities, trigger user motivation to use the technology and in turn users respond by actually using the technology.

Davis identified major determinants of technology adoption suggested b previous research studies that relate to cognition and effectiveness and adapted TRA (Fishbein & Ajzen, 1975; Ajzen & Fishbein, 1980) as a basis for causal links between the following factors to explain technology adoption.

- Perceived Usefulness
- Perceived Ease of Use
- Attitude Toward Using Technology
- Behavioural Intention

Diffusion of Innovations

The theory of Diffusion of Innovations as described by Rogers (1995, 2003) is well known and diffusion is described as: "… the process by which an innovation is communicated through certain channels over time among the members of social systems. It is a special type of communication, in that the messages are concerned with new ideas" (Rogers, 1995, p. 5). Rogers asserts that a technological innovation embodies information,

Figure 1. The Technology Acceptance Model (Davis, 1986)

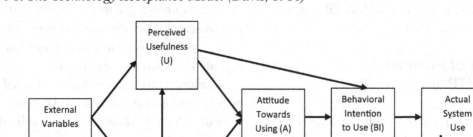

and that this information has the potential to reduce uncertainty. He distinguishes between two kinds of information: software information that is embodied in the technology (or idea) itself, and innovation-evaluation information that relates to an innovation's expected adoption consequences (Rogers, 1995). Diffusion is thus considered to be an information exchange process amongst members of a communicating social network driven by the need to reduce uncertainty. A decision not to adopt an innovation thus relates to the rejection of the available new idea. In the diffusion process, Rogers stresses the importance of communication in an attempt to educate the customer about the innovation concerned, and identifies four main elements that provide an indication of how an innovation is passed to the consumer from first knowledge of this innovation to its final adoption or rejection.

- Characteristics of the innovation itself,
- Relative advantage,
- Compatibility,
- Complexity,
- Trialability,
- Observability,
- Communication channels through which news of the innovation passes,
- The passage of time,
- The social system in which the adoption does, or does not, occur.

DEVELOPING A FRAMEWORK FOR THE ORIGINAL STUDY

The original study involved an exploratory investigation of Internet technology adoption in the Omani banking industry, informed by the situation in the Australia. The various technology adoption models described above suggested that a number of factors might have affected adoption. Relative advantage and ease of use, suggested by Moore and Benbasat (1991), were firstly considered in the analysis. Rogers (1995) originally identified

these two perceptions of technology adoption as relative advantage and complexity. Moore and Benbasat (1991) and Taylor and Todd (1995) explained that these two constructs are similar to those of TAM (Davis, 1986). They highlighted the fact that relative advantage is similar to the perceived usefulness construct and perceived complexity is similar to perceived ease of use due to the similarity in their definitions and in the operation of their measurements. Two additional perceptions, organisational performance and customer/organisational relationship, not previously identified in the ICT literature, were also considered. From an analysis of this literature, and from some preliminary discussions with bank managers, a theoretical framework was devised that suggests that bank managers' perceptions of only four adoption factors might affect any decision to adopt Internet technology here:

- Relative Advantage,
- Organisational Performance,
- Customer/Organisational Relationship,
- Ease of Use.

RESEARCH METHOD

Specifically, the research question was:

What are the enablers and inhibitors of Internet technology adoption in the Omani banking industry compared with those in Australia?

In the original study, twenty-seven interviews were conducted with strategic, tactical and operational managers at each of nine major banks, five in Oman and four in Australia.

Given the exploratory nature of this investigation, data was gathered through semi-structured interviews with these managers, and available internal and public reports were used to facilitate understanding and to explore Internet technology adoption. Interview questions were devised to cover the issues identified from the literature and the research framework. A schedule of semi-structured interviews with these managers was set up to gather field evidence of perceptions of the four adoption factors: Relative Advantage, Organisational Performance, Customer/Organisational Relationship and Ease of Use, as further described below:

Perceived Relative Advantage

This investigated the extent to which a manager perceived that Internet technology would enable their bank to gain relative advantage in the industry.

Perceived Organisational Performance

Here, the extent to which a manager perceived that Internet technology could improve their bank's organisational performance was explored. Clearly, if an organisation expects to improve its performance with Internet technology then the likelihood of their adopting it will be greater.

Perceived Customer/ Organisational Relationship

For this factor the discussion looked at the extent to which a manager perceived that Internet technology would improve their bank's relationship with customers.

Perceived Ease of Use

If a bank officer perceives that Internet technology is easy to use then they will most likely be motivated to adopt this technology.

DATA ANALYSIS

Selective coding can assist the researcher to develop a story that could ultimately establish a theory, and the NVIVO product is useful for this purpose.

NVIVO is a computer software program used for indexing, searching and theorising non-numerical unstructured data (Richards, 2002). Most qualitative software (such as NVIVO) is designed to "… allow the researcher to specify relationships among codes and use these relationships in analysis, and to write memos and link them to text and codes … to allow the researcher to create links between different points in the text (hypertext) … and allow the use of audio and video in place of, or in addition to, text. And there are a variety of approaches to linking categorical and quantitative data (e.g., demographics, test scores, quantitative ratings) to text and for exporting categorical and quantitative data (e.g., word frequencies or coding summaries) to quantitative analysis programs for statistical analysis" (Weitzman. 2000, p. 804). With NVIVO the researcher is required to continuously examine the structure of the core categories and sub-categories to ensure consistent links between these categories (or nodes, which is the term used in NVIVO). In summary, the process involved in the NVIVO analysis is illustrated in Figure 2.

FINDINGS OF THE ORIGINAL TAM/ DIFFUSION STUDY

Although later we will re-analyse this study using an innovation translation approach, it is first necessary to look at the findings of the study using the original TAM/Innovation Diffusion framework.

Perceived Relative Advantage

The study revealed that despite cultural differences there were many similarities in attitudes towards technology adoption as bankers in both countries saw the use of Internet technologies as offering advantages and important enabling factors (Al-Hajri & Tatnall 2008, 2011).

The Omani and Australian banking industries were both found to perceive that Internet technol-

Figure 2. Process involved in the NVIVO analysis

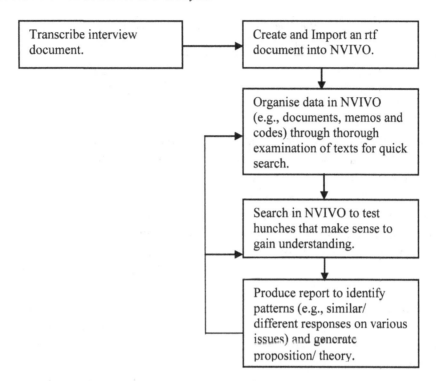

ogy was important and that it could enable the industry to gain relative advantages including the following:

Perceived Organisational Performance

A number of authors (King & Teo, 1996; Dedrick, Gurbaxani, & Kraemer, 2003) have argued from a theoretical perspective that it is possible to increase the rate of Internet technology adoption if a manager perceives that Organisational Performance could be improved. The study showed that in the

Omani banking industry, the majority of managers' responses indicated that this was indeed the case (Al-Hajri & Tatnall, 2010).

Perceived Customer/Organisational Relationship

The role of the customer/organisational relationship in IT adoption has attracted considerable attention in the literature (Sathye, 1999; Athanasso-poulos, 2000; Anderson & Srinivasan, 2003). In this study, participants were asked whether or not they perceived that Internet technology adoption

Table 1. Classification of participants according to country and level of management

Country	Banks	Interviews with Bank Managers			Total
		Strategic	Tactical	Operational	
Oman	5	5 (M1, M4, M7, M10, M13) [1]	5 (M2, M5, M8, M11, M14)	5 (M3, M6, M9, M12, M15)	15
Australia	4	4 (M16, M19, M22, M25)	4 (M17, M20, M23, M26)	4 (M18, M21, M24, M27)	12
Total	9	9	9	9	27

Table 2. Enablers relating to the factor of perceived relative advantage

Major enablers in both Oman and Australia
Convenience of services (- convenience of available service and convenience of location)
Being able to develop innovative ideas
Management of services (- easy to follow up requests/complains)

could improve the relationship with their customers in terms of three focused issues identified in the literature: customer trust, customer commitment and customer satisfaction. Results suggested that the decision to adopt Internet technology is indeed based on what managers perceive about the customer/ organisational relationship in the banking industry.

Perceived Ease of Use

Participants were asked whether they saw Internet technology as easy to use in banks. The literature identified three major issues: easy to navigate, easy to learn and easy to manage (King & Teo, 1996). The findings of this study suggested that the decision to adopt Internet technology was consistent with the literature and that managers' perceptions about Ease of Use were important. Details of the technology were important here, but so were other factors and perhaps these may have been be more important than the technology itself. Bank Managers from both countries saw improvements in productivity of bank employees and customer satisfaction as important enabling factors, but issues of customer trust relating to privacy and Internet security as inhibitors.

Similarities and Differences between the Two Countries

There were, however, some important differences between managers in the two countries. While profitability was regarded as an enabler by Australian banks, which had already installed this technology, it was regarded as an inhibitor by the Omani banks due to the high cost of setting this up. Customer commitment and loyalty was seen as an enabler by Australian banks but as an inhibitor in Oman where bank customers still appreciated the personal attention available in local bank branches (Al-Hajri & Tatnall, 2008). Finally, with their greater experience in using computers and the Internet, Australian banks found the services easy to use, easy to navigate and quite accessible. In Oman, however, where such experience was lacking, issues of Internet navigation were seen as an inhibiting factor to use of the technology (Al-Hajri & Tatnall, 2010).

Initially, this study was analysed using Diffusion of Innovations and TAM, but its socio-technical nature was then also recognised and well understood. Details of the technology were important here, but so were other factors and perhaps these were, in many ways, more important

Table 3. Enablers and inhibitors relating to the factor of perceived organisational performance

	Major enablers	Major inhibitors
Omani banks	Productivity of employees (business efficiency)	Profitability (technology investment cost and the need for economies of scale for Internet technology use)
Australian banks	Profitability (reduction of communication cost	Market environment (customer base expansion)
	Productivity of employees (business efficiency)	

Table 4. Enablers and inhibitors relating to customer/organisational relationship

	Major enablers	Major inhibitors
Omani banks	Customer satisfaction (reduce conflict)	Customer trust (Internet security)
		Customer commitment (customer loyalty)
Australian banks	Customer commitment (customer loyalty)	Customer trust (Internet security)
	Customer satisfaction (reduce conflict)	

to adoptions decisions than the technology itself. Interactions between different bank employees and between bank employees and customers were found to be equally, if not more important than considerations of the technology. Also, issues of dealing with the people involved, and not just the technology, should not be overlooked. This means that another socio-technical approach to adoption of innovations was worth investigating, and so the original study is now re-interpreted using innovation translation from actor-network theory (ANT).

RE-INTERPRETATION AS A STUDY INFORMED BY INNOVATION TRANSLATION

Innovation Translation

Innovation Translation (Latour, 1986, 1996; Law & Callon, 1988), informed by Actor-Network Theory (ANT), makes use of a model of technological innovation which uses the concept of heterogeneity in a world that is full of hybrid entities (Latour, 1993) containing both human and non-human elements. It notes that innovations are often not adopted in their entirety but only after 'translation' into a form that is more appropriate for use by the potential adopter, and uses these notions in an explanation of the adoption, or non-adoption of technology (Tatnall & Davey, 2007). Adoption of an innovation then is a consequence of the actions of everyone in the chain of actors who has anything to do with it. Each actor shapes the innovation to their own ends, and shaping of the innovation is seen as essential for its continued existence. The technological innovation that is actually adopted by different organisations may not be the same – it may be translated into different forms.

Callon et al. (1983) have proposed that translation involves all the strategies that an actor goes through to identify other actors and to arrange them in relation to each other in order to achieve adoption. Latour (1996) speaks of 'chains of translation' and suggests that with the translation model the initial idea hardly counts and the in-

Table 5. Enablers and inhibitors relating to ease of use

	Major enablers	Major inhibitors
Omani banks	Easy to learn (increased automation of process)	Easy to navigate (awareness/knowledge of Internet technology and accessibility of services)
Australian banks	Easy to navigate (user friendly and accessibility of service)	
	Easy to learn (awareness/ knowledge about Internet technology)	
	Easy to manage (customisation of banking services and online tracking of banking/ financial services)	

novation is not endowed with autonomous power, but moves only if it interests one group of actors or another. Callon has theorised four 'moments' in the process of translation: problematisation, interessement, enrolment and mobilisation.

Re-Interpretation of the Original Study vs. Conducting a New Study

It is not possible to completely re-interpret an existing qualitative study using actor-network theory as the questions that would be asked in the interviews would not be exactly the same. Whereas Innovation Diffusion looks particularly at characteristics of the innovation itself and the Technology Acceptance Model tries to identify the perceived usefulness, ease of use and intention to adopt by the potential adopter, Actor-Network Theory instead works to identify actors and their associations and interactions with other actors. The whole research approach and the interview questions used would then reflect this difference. It was, of course, not possible to ask new questions in this case. It is, nevertheless possible to give an indication of how the results would be interpreted and to suggest other questions that could be asked if it were possible to conduct some more interviews. The following analysis will be restricted to a consideration of adoption of Internet technologies in Omani banks.

In an ANT analysis we begin by identifying the actors. In this case they can be seen to include: Bank managers, bank tellers, other bank employees, bank shareholders, banking transactions, customers, the Internet, communications infrastructure, computer systems at the bank, customer's home or business computers, Internet cafés and the mass media. It is often convenient to put elements of the technology into a single group – perhaps called Internet banking technology, and then to consider this as a black box unless we need to investigate or understand details of how it is constituted. Similarly, at times we may also consider the bank, its employees, its technology and its processes as a black box. What it is rather difficult to now do in a re-interpretation of the original study is to fully investigate interactions and associations between these actors.

We should then proceed to identify how these actors relate to each other: to their associations and interactions and to how they arrive at their problematisations, how do they handle interessement and what convinces or entices them to reach enrolment and mobilisation. For any given bank we can quickly identify some important global interactions and associations as involving the following actors:

Some information about important interactions between actors can often identified from what they have to say. One manager (see Table 1 for a

Figure 3. Major interactions in internet banking

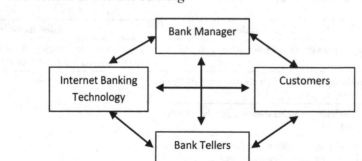

list of the codes for managers interviewed) remarked that:

So it does mean that, you know, there is definitely a perception by customers that we are up 24 hours, every single minute of the day, and in some respects that's extremely hard to meet. (M7)

Two others discussed the problem of encouraging customers to adopt new banking methods:

Not everybody likes changes; many people do not like changes. When people are used to something they wouldn't like to see those changes even within the life style it is not easy to change. It might take a little bit of time but I do not see problem. It will take a little bit of time because we need to train people how to use the Internet. (M3)

While what is happening is that there are many customers who have ideas and they cannot come to the bank because they are far from the bank and they cannot come. The Internet will allow us to know the customers' requirements, their needs for new services, their ideas and then we are going to analyse these ideas and implement them. So I think yes. (M11)

Clearly this indicates a relationship between bank employees and customers that could be investigated further to see how this set of associations is built up. Interview responses from three more Bank Managers point to further actors that should be investigated:

... Internet banking can be operated at different places, I mean, at your home, at your office, in Internet café, you can operate it abroad while travelling and you can still do your Internet banking transactions. In that sense it is convenient. (M1)

While what is happening is that there are many customers who have ideas and they cannot come to the bank because they are far from the bank and they cannot come. The Internet will allow us to

know the customers' requirements, their needs for new services, their ideas and then we are going to analyse these ideas and implement them. (M11)

... we will be able to know better the clientele and their needs, so in that respect that will help a lot and would be beneficial for the Bank. In many cases today we don't have the full picture of our clientele base here. (M10)

Important banking problematisations (reasons by the bank for wanting use of this technology) are also seen in some of the interview responses that can give us an idea of the position taken by some actors in trying to enrol others. These three interview excerpts are examples of this.

As I said before, it costs us less to offer services on the Internet than it does across our branch network and other channels. (M17)

... the cost would not be reduced until the number of customers using the technology increases. Yes, the cost of transaction would be higher at this stage until enough number of customers increase or start using the electronic banking service and even the other benefits which are not relevant to filtering of better information to the customer, it's also coming only when the customer base increase. Adoption by customers is the key here. See any service is dependent upon the number of customers adopting the technology innovation. (M8)

The research that we have suggests that it improves our customer loyalty to our brand. It's a service that if we didn't offer, an Internet banking service to customers that you would see a high volume of our customers going to other banks that did. So it definitely helps in terms of retaining customers that require an Internet banking service, so it definitely improves customer loyalty there. (M24)

We can also see something more of the relationship between bank employees and customers in the following interview quotes:

Going back to what I said before, if we adopt the Internet we would be able know our customers and we would be able to react quickly and we would be able to respond much more quickly too. (M10)

Definitely, it will improve because what happen is that the customer sees his whole banking history in one screen like what are all my deposits, what are all my loans and other things. So to that extent the state of the relationship will improve not in technical terms. For example, conflict could be reduced if the system is correct and other things are maintained. There is no question of conflict here if the customer sees his transaction immediately on performing from wherever he is done his transaction because the history is available. (M5)

In terms of security, I think that's a concern that all customers have, about Internet banking and the safety of their information and their funds. I think it's always at the back of their mind. We offer a security guarantee to try and overcome that issue, but I think it's always something that's present for them. But the convenience of Internet banking probably outweighs the security fears that they do have, and they see the benefits associated with Internet banking, which is why they continue on using the service. I think it's a major issue for any Internet banking service, regardless of the institution, and that's what our research confirms. (M24)

One final example is seen in the relationship between customers, bank employees and the technology in the following:

In Oman it is not that easy yet. You have to have a modem connection and you have to have lot of things to get into the Internet. (M13)

Definitely it is easy. See doing offline transactions you would have to go through the branch whereas through in the Internet most of transactions are done automatically for you online. (M5)

The Internet enhances the customer's commitment to the relationship – no the Internet does not actually, it does not as I said for the reason as I said that you are dealing with totally a machine and customer's loyalty is only built in your beliefs of the Bank as a whole and not necessarily through the services that are performed through the Internet. And customer loyalty comes with you being relaxed with one person or two persons or number of persons who are working for that Bank. And today you know loyalty is not as strong as it used to be previously because the offers people are looking at – different offers given by different Banks. So, you know loyalty does not play a major role nowadays in my opinion. Just like to add to this, people are looking at what more can they get from this Bank than being a loyal that I am committed to this bank, I love the bank and what more can they give me. It's about what am I getting more here than they give to me. (M1)

CONCLUSION

The original TAM/Diffusion-based study suggested that analysis of four perceptions of managers in the banking industry: Relative Advantage, Ease of Use, Organisational Performance and Customer/Organisational Relationship, could shed light on the reasons for adoption (or non-adoption) of Internet technology. As expected, the findings confirmed that Australian managers perceived less inhibitors to the introduction and implementation of Internet technology than did Omani managers, meaning that the Australian banking industry had less challenges to confront than that of Oman.

An important criterion in Innovation Diffusion relates to the characteristics of the innovation itself, but from interviews with the actors is it not hard to see that in many cases this has little relevance to adoption decisions. The criteria used by TAM to determine the likelihood of adoption: Perceived Usefulness and Perceived Ease of Use, seem rather self-evident and do not offer much in the way of explanatory power – aren't they a bit obvious? What else do they offer?

In this article we have re-interpret this study of the uptake of Internet banking in Oman by use of actor-network theory and innovation translation in place of the original framework that was based on Diffusion of Innovations and the Technology Acceptance Model. If an ANT approach is to be used in any research project then ideally it would be used from the beginning of the study so that the data collection and interviews reflected the sort of questions and the approach appropriate to this framework. Nevertheless, this article has shown that it is possible to do some 'after the fact' re-conceptualisation and re-analysis of the data to make use of an innovation translation approach. We argue that in socio-technological studies like this one that actor-network theory and innovation translation have something unique to offer.

REFERENCES

(1973). *The shorter Oxford English dictionary. Oxford, UK.* Oxford: Clarendon Press.

Ajzen, I. (1991). The theory of planned behavior. *Organizational Behavior and Human Decision Processes, 50*(2), 179–211. doi:10.1016/0749-5978(91)90020-T

Ajzen, I., & Fishbein, M. (1980). *Understanding attitudes and predicting social behavior.* Upper Saddle River, NJ: Prentice Hall.

Ajzen, I., & Madden, T. (1986). Prediction of goal-directed behavior: Attitudes, intentions, and perceived behavioral control. *Journal of Experimental Social Psychology, 22*, 453–474. doi:10.1016/0022-1031(86)90045-4

Al-Hajri, S. (2005). *Internet technology adoption in the banking industry business.* Unpublished doctoral dissertation, Victoria University, Melbourne, Australia.

Al-Hajri, S., & Tatnall, A. (2008). Adoption of Internet technology by the banking industry in Oman: A study informed by the Australian experience. *Journal of Electronic Commerce in Organizations, 6*(3), 20–36. doi:10.4018/jeco.2008070102

Al-Hajri, S., & Tatnall, A. (2008). Technological innovation and the adoption of Internet banking in Oman. *Electronic Journal for Virtual Organizations and Networks, 10*, 59–83.

Al-Hajri, S., & Tatnall, A. (2010). Factors relating to the adoption of Internet technology by the Omani banking industry. In Khosrow-Pour, M. (Ed.), *E-Commerce trends for organizational advancement: New applications and methods* (pp. 264–282). Hershey, PA: IGI Global.

Anderson, R., & Srinivasan, S. (2003). E-satisfaction and e-loyalty: A contingency framework. *Psychology and Marketing, 20*(2), 123–138. doi:10.1002/mar.10063

Athanassopoulos, A. (2000). Customer satisfaction cues to support market segmentation and explain switching behavior. *Journal of Business Research, 47*, 191–207. doi:10.1016/S0148-2963(98)00060-5

Bandura, A. (1982). Self-efficacy mechanism in human agency. *The American Psychologist, 37*(2), 122–147. doi:10.1037/0003-066X.37.2.122

Callon, M., Courtial, J. P., Turner, W. A., & Bauin, S. (1983). From translations to problematic networks: An introduction to co-word analysis. *Social Sciences Information. Information Sur les Sciences Sociales, 22*(2), 191–235. doi:10.1177/053901883022002003

Davis, F. (1986). *A technology acceptance model for empirically testing new end-user information systems: Theory and results.* Cambridge, MA: MIT Press.

Dedrick, J., Gurbaxani, V., & Kraemer, K. (2003). Information technology and economic performance: A critical review of the empirical evidence. *ACM Computing Surveys, 35*(1), 1–28. doi:10.1145/641865.641866

Fishbein, M., & Ajzen, I. (1975). *Belief, attitude, intention, and behavior: An introduction to theory and research.* Reading, MA: Addison-Wesley.

King, W., & Teo, T. (1996). Key dimensions of facilitators and inhibitors for the strategic use of information technology. *Journal of Management Information Systems, 12*(4), 35–53.

Latour, B. (1986). The powers of association. In Law, J. (Ed.), *Power, action and belief: A new sociology of knowledge?* (pp. 264–280). London, UK: Routledge & Kegan Paul.

Latour, B. (1993). *We have never been modern.* Cambridge, MA: Harvard University Press.

Latour, B. (1996). *Aramis or the love of technology.* Cambridge, MA: Harvard University Press.

Law, J., & Callon, M. (1988). Engineering and sociology in a military aircraft project: A network analysis of technological change. *Social Problems, 35*(3), 284–297. doi:10.1525/sp.1988.35.3.03a00060

Macquarie Library. (1981). *The Macquarie dictionary.* Sydney, Australia: Macquarie Library.

Maguire, C., Kazlauskas, E. J., & Weir, A. D. (1994). *Information services for innovative organizations.* San Diego, CA: Academic Press.

Moore, G., & Benbasat, I. (1991). Development of an instrument to measure the perception of adopting an information technology innovation. *Information Systems Research, 2*(3), 192–222. doi:10.1287/isre.2.3.192

Richards, L. (2002). Qualitative computing - A methods revolution? *International Journal of Social Research Methodology, 5*(3), 263–276. doi:10.1080/13645570210146302

Rogers, E. M. (1995). *Diffusion of innovations.* New York, NY: Free Press.

Rogers, E. M. (2003). *Diffusion of innovations.* New York, NY: Free Press.

Sathye, M. (1999). Adoption of Internet banking by Australian consumers: An empirical investigation. *International Journal of Bank Marketing, 17*(7), 324–334. doi:10.1108/02652329910305689

Sheppard, B., Hartwick, J., & Warshaw, P. (1988). The theory of reasoned action: A meta-analysis of past research with recommendations for modifications and future research. *The Journal of Consumer Research, 15*(3), 325–343. doi:10.1086/209170

Tatnall, A., & Davey, W. (2007). *Researching the portal. IRMA: Managing worldwide operations and communications with information technology.* Vancouver, BC, Canada: Information Management Resource Association.

Taylor, S., & Todd, P. (1995). Understanding information technology usage: A test of competing models. *Information Systems Research, 6*(2), 144–176. doi:10.1287/isre.6.2.144

Weitzman, E. (2000). Software and qualitative research. In Denzin, N. K., & Lincoln, Y. S. (Eds.), *Handbook of qualitative research.* Thousand Oaks, CA: Sage.

ENDNOTES

[1.] These codes identify individual bank managers and are used later to relate interview material to the response of a given manager.

Chapter 17
Emerging Standardization

Antonio Cordella
London School of Economics and Political Science, UK

ABSTRACT

This paper discusses the dynamics associated with the implementation and deployment of an information infrastructure designed to standardize work practices. The analysis is based on a case study conducted in a pharmaceutical R&D organization. The infrastructure in use, comprising a computerized system and surrounding organizational procedures, seems to support work practices not always as originally planned. The paper discusses the role played by local characteristics, contingencies, and practices in shaping a standardization protocol implemented to standardize work practices. Building on actor-network theory, the paper concludes that the standardization of work practices is the result of the dynamic interplay between technology and its users, rather than the consequence of a planned and well-defined design project.

INTRODUCTION

Information and communication technologies (ICTs) have become one of the most common solutions implemented to standardize work procedures and information flows in private and public organizations. Many authors have discussed how to develop, choose, and implement these technologies in the most effective way. In this context, research on information system development methodologies have proposed and discussed procedures for making the process of developing information systems more efficient and effective. Similarly, managerial studies have focused on researching optimal solutions for analyzing and choosing ICTs to leverage organizations' performances. However, less attention has been given historically to the study of how ICTs enforce and shape work practice standardization. Nevertheless, scholars have recently shown increasing interest in the study of the definition, development and evolution of technological standards and in the role standards play in the deployment of ICTs, designed to define, support and improve organizational practices. Building on actor-network theory, we intend to better explain the complexity of the process which shapes the intertwined effects ICT has on work practice standardization.

DOI: 10.4018/978-1-4666-2166-4.ch017

This paper discusses how an information technology, designed to standardize the process and quality of data collection and analysis in a pharmaceutical company, evolves, changes, and is shaped within the practices of the organization using it so that, rather than standardizing these practices, it changes with them. The paper initially summarizes the debate on the nature and evolution of standards and standardizing technologies and their effects on work flow standardization. It follows a case study conducted at a pharmaceutical company, here referred to as Alpha Company (the names of the organization, its departments, products and applications have all been changed), where an ICT system has been implemented to standardize the work practices involved in collecting data during the drug registration process.

THEORETICAL BACKGROUND

The study of work practice standardization and other means of homogenizing the variety of work behaviours lies at the centre of a vast and multi-disciplinary literature. Historically, the importance of standards and classification protocols as ways of making work procedures and practices uniform has been discussed from different perspectives. Bureaucracies have been described as organizations which rely on rules, norms and routines to reiterate behaviours when similar circumstances occur. Bureaucracies rely on standardized answers, classified and ordered to provide homogeneous paths of responses to similar events whenever they occur (Mintzberg, 1983), to reduce transaction costs and the complexity of an organization's tasks (Ciborra, 1993; Moe, 1984).

The role of norms, rules and resources in a social setting, meanwhile, can be thought of as the set of standards (structure) that affects the process that shapes social order, and therefore organizational practices. Giddens (1984), for example, identifies social structures as being composed of rules and resources that facilitate and/ or constrain interaction in social settings. Rules and resources provide the contextual constraints individuals draw upon when acting and interacting. These rules and resources are the categories through which social orders are constructed and reconstructed recursively. An organization's action is therefore the result of structurational processes that are deeply affected by the norms and rules that constrain the organization's action. Similarly, Avgerou (2000) discusses institutional theory, identifying the nature of institutions as taken-for-granted standardized sequences of activities, which establish and maintain the *modus operandi* of the organization. This path of action can create powerful myths (Avgerou, 2002), which act as the background upon which changes in organizational activities are constrained but also enabled.

These different perspectives show that, at a macro level, the key characteristics of standards and norms are their being the product of social institutions which produce but also reinforce them over time (Douglas, 1986).

Moreover, norms, rules and standards permeate our daily lives as citizens, workers and members of social systems. Our way of coordinating activities, finding places we are looking for, understanding context and other tasks, are mediated by systems of classification which are built on specific norms, rules and standards. These systems of classification are often considered to be in the background of our action, as if they were invisible (Bowker & Star, 1999). However, they are not in the background of the occurring event. They often define the event itself. Think, for example, of the system of classification that defines the admission requirements to a university college. In this case, the system of classification is an important factor in selecting the students who will be accepted to the college and those who will not. The population of the college is hence also defined by the specific system of classification used to filter and rank the submitted applications.

Building on the idea that standards and classification protocols are not neutral in the shaping of organizational practices and actions, we discuss here the role of information systems in standardizing work practices. Within this aim, the paper seeks to provide a better understanding of the micro aspects that define the standardization of work practices that are enforced via the adoption of information systems. The study assesses the effects of technology in the context of its use and then looks at the dynamic that emerges.

A large body of literature has studied both the processes that produce standards and the effects of their adoption on the socioeconomic context in which they are deployed.

These studies can be classified between the extremes of technologically-deterministic and constructivist ontological stances. At one end, technological determinism assumes that technology and its impacts are given and defined; at the other, constructivism tends to assume that technology does not matter because it is always, and inescapably, socially constructed (Lundberg, 2000).

The juxtaposition of these two stances on the relationship between technology and people is the basis for debate on the role of standards and their users in stabilizing and diffusing standards in socioeconomic contexts. Standards can, in fact, be conceived as the result of the process of socio-political negotiation and construction, which is stabilized in technological artefacts (Hanseth & Monteiro, 1996). This view is argued by studies on the social shaping of technology (Bijker, Hughes, & Pinch, 1987; Bijker & Law, 1992; MacKenzie & Wajcman, 1985). On the opposite side, technologically-deterministic stances argue that technology is what fosters organizational change. Here, standards define the nature of technological us use and the direction of the process of change associated with technological implementation (Williams & Edge, 1996). Between these two extremes, a multitude of alternative explanations can be provided. In this paper we choose to take an intermediate position, led by the ontological stances of actor-network theory (ANT). ANT argues that it is the relational process of socio-technical actors that defines the trajectory of their relationships. It is neither technology nor its users in command of this trajectory but the relationship itself; both technology and users are shaped through their relationship (Cordella, 2010).

This choice is justified by the increasing interest that ANT has received in studies on technology and its use (Information technology and People, Special issue: Actor-network theory and information systems, 2004, the establishment of JANTTI) and by the specific focus of the research presented here. We want, in fact, to disentangle the process that defines the relationship between ICT and standardized work practices. We want to shift attention from the actors that define the process, as discussed in socio-constructivist and techno-deterministic studies, to the process that defines their relationships, as suggested by the theoretical formulation of ANT (Cordella, 2010).

STANDARDIZATION IN CONTEXT

Studies of standards and classification protocols have traditionally analyzed either the process that underpins their development or which leads to their stabilization.

Bowker and Star (1999) largely discuss the contextual nature of the process of classifying and hence the socio-technical nature of standards and classification protocols. Their studies specifically emphasize the technical, cultural, social and political elements involved in these processes and their intertwining nature, which they stress is crucial to understanding the nature of a classification protocol. Given this focus, they describe and discuss how standards and classification protocols develop and evolve, and their characteristics in specific contexts. Their studies are based on a detailed analysis of systems set up to categorize diseases, work, races, and other elements and they discuss not only the role of these classification protocols as tools that create groups of homogeneous data, but also the socio-political dimension they play, which provokes advantages or suffering for specific groups, individuals or situations.

The work of Bowker and Star (1999) provides a good example of how classification protocols, standards, and the associated technological systems can be studied as socio-technical networks where physical artefacts and social systems construct and shape the nature of the standard itself (Hughes, 1997).

The complex nature of this socio-technical interplay, however, allows for the use of many different angles, as does the large number of actors that shape the socio-technical network. Hanseth (1996), for example, takes a different analytical approach to that of Bowker and Star (1999), highlighting the role of "the irreversibility of the installed base" as the self-reinforcing mechanism produced by the growth of the technical system. In this case, the focus of the research is on the processes that reinforce the technical characteristics as a consequence of the layering of technical choices over time and of the alignment of technical, institutional and users' choices. This research highlights, once again, the joining of technical and user-related path dependencies as the main factors that shape the socio-technical network. Similarly, Hanseth and Monteiro (1996) discuss the nature of technical standards, looking at how "any given element of an information infrastructure constrains others, that is, how it 'inscribes' a certain pattern of use". Accordingly, standards can be "classified" by the level of their "power of inscription". The stronger the inscription, the more aligned is the socio-technical network and the more effective is the inscribed programme of action. Standards can then be discussed and analyzed by looking at the embodiment of inscription they are made of. Once again, it is the technical actor that is here considered the most appropriate object of study

for understanding the evolutionary path taken by the socio-technical network.

A further insight into the study of the socio-technical nature of classification protocols and standards comes from Timmermans and Berg (1997) that, in studying their nature and configuration, shed light on the diverse nature of standardization outcomes emerging from the interplay in these relational networks. Standardization efforts do not necessary require a central actor. Looking at the evolution of medical protocols, they find that standards procedures emerge as the outcome of the real-time work that occurs in localized processes of negotiation within pre-existing institutional, infrastructural, and material relations. Once again, standards are discussed as the outcome of relational networks defined within time and space contextual variables. Technology can inscribe a path of uses but is de-scribed by the users in the act of using it (Akrich & Latour, 1992; Timmermans & Berg, 1997). The local context and the situatedness of the action that embeds the use of classification protocols and standardization technologies is thus the right place to look, if the aim is to understand the processes that outline the nature of these technologies after considering their socio-technical dimension. Following this idea, Timmermans and Berg (1997) argue that a typical characteristic of classification protocols is their openness because they are "the result of work widely and loosely dispersed through space and time. Neither (their) origin nor (their) development can (thus) be traced back to singularities". According to these authors, a standard and the associated classification protocols are open-ended and closure is never really achieved. The context of the use of a specific protocol of standardization defines, over time and through space, the continuous evolution of the protocol itself.

Using a different focus in the analysis, but reaching similar conclusions, Bowker (2002) highlights the interconnectedness of classification protocols with the legacy of data systems and the technical, cultural, historical, and political reasons underpinning the process that leads to the design of a data collection system. The proposed understanding of the nature of the problem stands on the argument that data collection systems, and hence standards, are the outcome of layering of legacy systems:

what we need to know about data in a database is far more than the measurement standards that were used, and on the other hand, I have argued that atomic elements of a database such as measurement standards, contain complex histories folded (Deleuze, 1996) into them, histories which must be understood if the data is to persist. To summarize, each particular discipline associated with biodiversity has its own incompletely articulated series of objects. These objects each enfold an organisational history and subtend a particular temporality or spatiality. They frequently are incompletely articulated with other objects, temporalities and spatialities – often legacy versions when drawing on non-proximate disciplines. (Bowker, 2002)

All these contributions lead to the view that classification protocols, and in general technologies, are co-defined and emerge through the situatedness of the actions of users, who improvise and invent new programmes of action once the technology is situated and contextualized within routines (Suchman, 1987).

Building on these findings, we argue that the use of a classification protocol as standard to define organizational procedure has to be considered in the specific context and time of action. These are, in fact, the most determinant elements of the nature of the impact of standards on an organization's routines. This conclusion is based on the empirical evidence that emerged from studying the practices and constraints that surrounds the deployment of a classification protocol, implemented to globally standardize data collection and analysis procedures during drug testing at the multinational pharmaceutical company, Alpha.

RESEARCH METHODOLOGY

In this section, we discuss our research design, data collection, and analysis methods. This study employs a case study method. The case study method was chosen because it is well situated to examine the interaction among different contextual variables that define a specific situation, and through it the researcher may use thick description to try to understand the complexity of the phenomenon.

The case study research method uses an empirical investigation to gain detailed knowledge of a contemporary phenomenon within its real-life context, when the borders between phenomenon and context are not clearly evident, and when multiple sources of evidence are used (Yin, 2003). We entered the field with a broad area of study in mind, mainly related to the exploration of how information infrastructures are deployed in large multinational organizations, but with no specific research question. Thus, we hoped to narrow the focus after conducting the initial interviews and observations. Such uncertainty is common before data collection has commenced and case analysis is a useful approach for developing and refining concepts for further study (Benbasat, Goldstein, & Mead, 1987).

Qualitative data collection mechanisms, including in-depth interviews and an analysis of existing documentation, were used to gather evidence about the processes of data standardization. Observations and documentation were used only to confirm the findings of the interviews, which were the main source of data. The case study on which this paper is based was conducted over a period of eight months, during 1999. Interviews were held with study monitors and doctors in Sweden, Germany, Hungary, Spain and Poland. In addition, other personnel involved in the project at the Alpha Corporation were asked questions, and multiple discussions took place with managers at various levels. The interviews were semi-structured, each completed within one to two hours.

When allowed, interviews were tape recorded; when this was not possible, detailed notes were taken by the interviewer. Construct validity was strengthened within the study through the use of multiple sources of evidence, and by having key informants discuss and review the draft case study reports

THE CASE STUDY: BACKGROUND

In late 1997, Alpha Corporation started a project to make data collection uniform in its clinical trials and homogenize the work procedures used to collect data. To achieve this goal, its Clinical R&D department led the implementation of an Internet application named "ODC" and developed new work processes aimed at standardizing the data capture system and process used in the clinical trials. The application was designed to manage and support the remote data capture process used in clinical testing of patients. The aim of the application was to move responsibility for data entry, (i.e. the transcription into specific files of the data collected during the drug testing), from the study managers (the so-called monitors) to the doctors in charge of the study. The purpose of the new system was to improve the homogeneity and quality of the entered data, with the aim of shortening the time needed to correct them and put them in the necessary format (cleaned as per the industry) for the submission of certified documentation to the Food and Drugs Administration (FDA). The quality and homogeneity of the collected data is in fact an important factor in successfully registering a compound with the authorities. If the data are correctly entered and there is no need for extra work and verification before their analysis, the overall registration process is faster and the commercialization phase longer, with obvious benefits for company revenues. Accordingly, the data entry process is a very important aspect of R&D and commercialization activity in the pharmaceutical industry.

THE ODC APPLICATION: HISTORY, CHARACTERISTICS, AND AIMS

ODC was first developed by Alpha as an administrative application to support the management of clinical studies at the corporate level. It was used in the company's headquarters as an Internet Study Administration tool (ISA). During this phase, the application was only accessible to the Clinical Department, where it was used to monitor the various phases of drugs testing and closure. It was not yet developed to homogenize the process of data entry and collection and the associated work practices.

Due to the success of the tool in supporting the Clinical Department, and as a result of the wave of radical change that permeated some of the largest corporations in the industry (Cordella & Simon, 2000), the tool was re-evaluated and subsequently adapted to support the functions needed for the management and standardization of ongoing studies. The application was transformed to satisfy these new requirements and the needs of the new users, the so-called study monitors and the physicians in charge of the drug testing process.

In the new version, the application was developed into two different versions to match the new requirements: one designed to be used by the physicians and the other by the study monitors.

The physicians were to use the application to directly update the corporate central database with the latest data collected from their patients. Their version of the application was a web-based interface, accessed via an internet browser. After a security check, the application led them through the process of entering into the database the data they had collected from the patients. They had only to connect to a specific website, located on the Alpha central server, in order to enter and transfer the locally-collected data to the headquarters. A computer, a modem, and an Internet connection with a provider was given to each physician involved in the project.

Before the introduction of the ODC system, physicians transcribed the patients' data into a paper folder, the Case Report Form (CRF), provided by the Alpha Corporation. When this paper-based system was in place, data registered in the CRF were crossed-checked by the study monitors during their periodic visits to the physician's surgeries, which occurred every one or two months. The data checked during the visits were only entered in the central database once the study was finally finished, at which point the paper CRFs were completed and collected from the physicians' offices. All of the data were entered into the database at the company headquarters by data entry specialists. Only once all these procedures were completed did the data become available for analysis. The overall process was long and time consuming.

With the ODC-based system, the data were inserted directly into the digital CRF, and thus to the central database, by the physicians themselves. The application was designed as an interface to the pre-existing central database of the company, which contained the information collected during the testing phases of all the company's drugs the aim of the ODC platform was to provide the support needed to properly store the data in the database at the precise moment they were collected. The goal was to have all of the data from the drug testing phase cleaned almost on the same day the testing ended. The centrally-stored data could then be used and analyzed to support the preparation of the documentation required by the registration authorities for the commercialization licenses.

The monitors, equipped with a laptop, a modem, and an Internet connection, used different software and different functionalities of the ODC application to those used by the physicians.

The monitors' application was designed to manage the various studies run in the different locations (physicians' centres). Using their ODC application, the monitors could check the data entered by each physician, the number of enrolled patients and the progress of the study, for each patient and each trial site they had to supervise. However, these functionalities did not permit them to verify the consistency between the entered data and the original source. They still had to visit the centres approximately every two weeks to check that the physicians had entered the right data in the system. The monitors had an ad hoc utility in their version of the application that allowed them to remotely control the entered data. However, this function did not prevent physicians from making errors when copying the original medical records into the digital CRF. The correspondence between the collected and entered data could only be guaranteed by matching the original source to the entered records.

The online system and the subsequent methods of data collection and control were conceived as a strategic solution to the data collection process. The development of the application and the maintenance of the ODC system were only considered as technical support and not as being strategically important to the success of the application. Thus, from the outset, the development was outsourced to external consultants.

ODC was in fact implemented to meet the need for standardization and quality across Alpha's global data collection system. The pre-existing IT infrastructure, mainly represented by the central database, was used as the platform for the development of the new system. The central database, once only used at the headquarters to analyze the already collected and cleaned data, was customized to support direct data entry through a web-based interface. These changes in the process required a redefinition of the procedures used to maintain quality control in the data collection process.

In the paper-based data collection methodology, the records were entered into the database once they had already passed the standardization process that ensured a match between the data, the database, and the quality requirements. This standardization process was the result of the interconnected work of physicians, monitors, and corporate data managers. The new methodology, based on the ODC system, changed the standardization process and the role of the agents involved in it. The aim of the project was to ensure the data and data collection process complied with the database structure. The users were strictly guided in the data collection and entering process by the characteristics and structure of the digital CRF. They could not make any ad hoc changes, because the digital interface did not permit local customizations. The requirements of the predefined data collection process were inscribed in the ODC system, as a standard to be followed across multinational environments.

CASE ANALYSIS

The ODC functionality developed to enable the physicians to directly enter data into the database was an HTML interface that "opened" the central database to local data entry by external users. It could be considered as a gateway to the central database. This gateway opened the core corporate database to external users, but also imposed on the users certain rules, characteristics, and structures of data, which they had to follow when they interacted with it. It was not neutral to the definition of the final functionalities of the data collection process.

The web-based interface was customized for the database, which is based on the English language and tailored to recognize only data entered via the English QWERTY-based keyboard. This created problems and errors when users entered data via keyboards based on different standards and/or languages. Local differences were no longer filtered and cleaned as they had previous been by the monitors through ad hoc supervision or by the specialized data entry team when transcribing the data from the paper folders into the database. The process of collecting and entering data, before the ODC system deployment, was divided into steps. Each step represented an opportunity for monitors

and physicians to clean and standardize the data. The data were made to fit the requirements of the database during the process of collecting, cleaning and entering the data. In the new system, it was the web-based interface, customized to accept only data that fit the technological requirements of the central database that filtered and homogenized the entered data.

With the adoption of the ODC system, the role of the monitors in the cleaning process changed. Although the monitor still intermediated in the data entry process to ensure it complied with the ODC system, the main check for errors, mistakes or unusual records, was done on the basis of the information they received from the central system. Once the physician had entered the data into the system, the data were recorded in a temporary folder. When incorrectly-entered data were detected by the system (e.g. out-of-scale measurements), the monitor was informed via a specific functionality in their version of the system. These errors usually referred to predictable data, such as heart rate or blood pressure. If a meaningless unit was entered, the system signalled it. When the physician was informed of the error, by the monitor, he/she was supposed to correct it. This process was supported by a specific function embedded in the software, which allowed the monitor to directly communicate with the physicians using a digital notification tool. However, the monitors usually notified physicians of errors during their regular visits to their surgeries. In order to meet the aim of having final, cleaned data, collected and homogenized at most a few days after the last patient's trial ended, monitors were supposed to re-check the entered data for minor remaining errors.

The ODC system was designed to make the process and procedure of data collection in all locations smoother and homogeneous. Unfortunately, local characteristics, unique to their specific context, were not included or standardized by the ODC system. These specific characteristics, combined with uncontrollable tinkering by the users, affected and made partially vulnerable the attempted standardization by ODC.

In many countries, for specific local, legal or organizational reasons, in combination with the digital CRF of the ODC system, physicians also had to complete a paper CRF during the drug experimentation process. These local requirements had an impact on the output of the overall process of data collection based on the ODC applications. To enter the data into the digital platform could take up to an hour. Due to the important security procedures that had to be followed by the company, the data entry process could not be suspended; each session had to be completed during a single connection. The system automatically interrupted the connection and the data already entered was lost if two minutes of inactivity were detected. These security requirements often did not match the needs of the final users, the physicians. They experienced difficulties; finding an appropriate period of time during their often busy days to complete the data entry in one go. In contrast, the paper folder was always available and could be filled in partially during occasional breaks. The physicians involved in the ODC project that operated in countries or institutions that still required the completion of a paper CRF folder, very often completed the paper option before the digital one. Once they had time, such as in the evening, at weekends, or other non-working times, they transcribed the data registered in the paper folder onto the digital platform. This task was also on occasion delegated to nurses. This un-prescribed behaviour often resulted in a delay between data collection and data availability on the system.

Moreover, the Internet connection was not always and everywhere reliable. When the Internet was not fast enough or where broadband was not yet available, such as in countries with an inefficient IT infrastructure, the paper CRF was still used as a substitute for the digital ODC platform. In these contexts, physician were for-

mally allowed to fill in the paper folder first and complete the digital version later, when the connection was working, or when they had enough time to use the slow web-based application. The overall procedure was thus renegotiated to match the local characteristics and needs. This obviously impacted the overall management of the study and the definition of the monitors' work.

Frequently, for a variety of reasons, including those discussed above, monitors went to trial centres, having checked the digitally-stored data and made related comments and annotations (the so-called proof reading list), only to find that new data and/or patients had been entered. Therefore, the proof reading list, considered the final stage of the data check, did not reflect the real status of the data collected at the study site. This mismatch resulted in a less productive session than hoped for between the monitor and the physician. The monitor had not checked the new data, which was not yet registered in the system, so they could not be reviewed during the meeting with the doctor. This resulted in delays of up to a month in the data registration and cleaning process.

As previously described, to support the data entry and fix the most obvious errors, the system provided an automatic checking procedure. This function worked offline, at night on the central database. The list of errors was then sent to the monitors. Once they received the list, they had to notify the relevant doctors, who then had to correct them. Doctors did not receive any automatic notification by the system if they made errors in data entry. The monitor had two ways of notifying the doctors. One was provided by the system and the other was to use the telephone or inform them in person. The former option consisted of a digital query system, where monitors posed questions to physicians using an ad hoc tool in the system. The latter option was more frequently used and functioned better because the doctors seldom read or answered online queries from the monitors. When the doctor was notified of errors via the online system, they were required to write a report but if the monitor notified them by other means they were relieved of this requirement.

The improvized solutions using direct personal communication rather than the support provided by the electronic platform completely altered the overall effectiveness of the system. The documentation produced during the electronic correction procedure was used to evaluate the efficacy and efficiency of the new, Internet-based system. None of the corrections undertaken via other means was documented, however, and thus the conclusions regarding the success of the system were altered.

LESSON LEARNED: CONTEXTUAL, TECHNOLOGICAL, AND USER CONSTRAINTS

The case provides an interesting insight into the effective role played by information technology in enforcing control and homogenization over organizational activities and work procedures. In this case, information technology is implemented to make the data collection process uniform in different study centres. The technological design and deployment of the system consider the process of data collection as given, and only problematic due to the lack of a standardized procedure across the organization. In the design and deployment of the information system, the users are mainly considered not to affect the output of the new, IT-mediated process. The classic assumption of a dichotomy between technology and people, stemming from the industrial age, still seems to dominate our understanding of the relational interplay between the two. The nature of technology, envisioned as a tool that can process and transform raw material better than humans can, justifies and drives the design and implementation of the ODC application in this organizational context. In the following, we question this dichotic assumption, discussing the roles of both technol-ogy and people in defining the standardization process enacted through the ODC system at the Alpha Corporation. As already discussed, the ODC system appears to constrain and at the same time to be constrained by technological and human features (Orlikowski, 1992; Suchman, 1987). Accordingly, the implications of the system for the data collection process must be re-analyzed in the light of the dynamic interaction that took place between technology and people during the system's implementation and use.

The ODC application was designed and implemented following the perspective that IT is a fundamental tool for enhancing control and co-ordination of organizational activities (Ciborra, 2000). The complex findings that emerge from the analysis of the system implementation show that this vision was too simple to capture the real consequences of the adoption of a new IT system in this organization's multi-layered environment. The new IT-based system and the procedural changes needed to use it, were managed and understood using mental frameworks and "approaches that were effective for the mechanical organization, and assembly-line type of technologies and processes" but that are no longer valid for the adoption of complex IT systems in knowledge-based organizations (Ciborra & Hanseth, 2000). These IT systems are in fact embedded in ramified webs of technologies and social context. They can only be understood if considered in their broad socio-technical context. Only by considering the associated complexity is it possible to understand the technological system, its effects on the organization, and the combined effects of the organization and the system. In a nutshell, the aim of this discussion is to understand the dynamics, drift, domestication, hostility and rejections (Ciborra, 1994, 1999; Dahlbom & Janlert, 1996) that characterize the complexity of the adoption of an IT-based classification protocol and the use of this protocol. In the following, all these unpredictable dynamics are analyzed and considered normal ingredients of the implementation process, rather than pathologies in the deployment of IT systems in organizations.

The complexity of the interplay between the classification protocol and its users is here re-analyzed considering the abovementioned dynamics as lively components that shape and reshape the interplay between technological artefacts and people (Cordella, 2010). Technology and people are here not considered static and stable concepts but are defined and redefined through the interplay that generates dynamic relationships between the two (Callon, 1987; Law, 1992). In the case of the ODC system, all of these dimensions affect the planned, centralized control and coordination strategy. These effects bring about "unplanned constraints" that jeopardize the successful implementation of the new technology. In the design and implementation plan, these events were in fact not even considered possibilities.

One of these constraints is the language used in the data collection system. The American market for pharmaceutical products is very large and has very strict regulations regarding drug registration. Once a drug is registered in the United States, it is very easy to rewrite the application to fulfill the requirements of other countries' drug registration authorities. This is the first reason for customizing the system to the English language. The second is that English is the international language and so it is clearly appropriate that the general process should be standardized based on this language to reduce the costs of data collection and management. The system did not include an English spelling checking function which would have supported users in the data entry process to some extent. However, even if it had been included, such a facility could only correct misspelling errors and not those of translation from the medical folder in the local language to the digital CRF in English. This implies that someone has to check the language and fix the errors. However, the problem of translation requires specialist knowledge, given that it is necessary to translate the anamnesis and illness description. Thus the data have to be carefully cross-checked by the monitors. They have the final responsibility: they amend the language and all others aspects, ranging from doctors' translation errors to unclear data.

The system was changed to satisfy requirements that emerged during its use. Some new problems arose with the greater understanding of the system's requirements. The awareness of customization needs became evident in the implementation phase and more so when the system began to be widely used. Changes introduced when the system was already in use, especially those relating to data checking procedures—new parameters were introduced with the aim of improving the quality of data collection—generated a lot of new problems. Data which complied with the initial protocols failed to comply with the revised one. Corrections had to be made to data that had already been entered and files that had been closed. During the first phase of implementation, the data checking system was based on a pre-defined set of rules and standards. Any errors found were fixed according to these rules. As the system was used, new needs emerged in response to the drug experimentation process and some of the fixed rules had to be changed accordingly. These changes modified the reference set of the system. As a consequence, new errors were found, while others were no longer recognized as errors. Doctors and monitors then had to adapt to the new changes to satisfy the requirements of the newly implemented standards. At the same time, part of the already-collected data had to be re-scanned to guarantee conformity with the newly introduced range of variables. Obviously, this change slowed down the whole procedure and created new and unexpected problems.

To deal with previously entered data, changes were needed in modules of the digital CRF that doctors and monitors had already double-checked and closed. Re-opening and changing these modules required a complex procedure that involved monitors, doctors and the company headquarters. The redefinition of the standards resulted in extra work and complexity for the persons involved in the process, often leading to a longer and more demanding procedure than under the previous paper-based system.

Other emerging problems were related to the use and implementation of the system. To gain access to the system, monitors and doctors had to use an Internet browser. The monitors used the IT-supported systems provided by the local Alpha offices, while the technology for the doctors was provided by the monitor, on the basis of the technological specification provided to them by the Alpha. However, the specifications received by the monitors only covered the necessary hardware configurations. No specific information was given in terms of the software that had to be used. The ODC system was initially based on a specific HTML version that was only fully compliant with specific versions of browsers, such as Internet Explorer 4 and Netscape 4.5 or higher.

Doctors with older versions of the browsers (which was quite common at the time of the study) encountered serious problems in using the system and thus recording and transmitting the collected data. Solving this problem was not as easy as it might seem since the monitors in charge of providing the technology to the doctors were not aware of the problems caused by incorrect versions of browsers. This often resulted in malfunctioning of the system for a long period and, consequently, delays in the registration of the data. The type of browser installed locally also caused problems to the proper functioning of the standardization system. The interface and some simple operations were different when the task was processed via Internet Explorer rather than Netscape. For example, with Internet Explorer, the layout of the page was different and thus the training provided by the monitors had to take these differences into consideration. Moreover, minor "operative" problems were linked with

simple differences between the browsers. For example, in Internet Explorer, the tab key could be used to move the cursor from one entry form to the other, while Netscape did not support this shortcut. The monitors were unaware of these differences, the reasons for them and their implications. The help provided to doctors sometimes resulted in disorienting suggestions. During the implementation and use of the system the monitors had to answer questions related to technical and operative problems, though they were not competent to do so. They had to understand the problem, and find a solution and/or a competent person able to fix it but they did not have sufficient technological knowledge or skill to fulfil this role and thus such problems occupied a large part of their time, leaving less available for their main activity: managing and improving the quality of the data collection process.

A further and unexpected problem emerged when an English version of Internet Explorer was installed on computers running an operating system based on a different language. For example, in Hungary, the installation of the English-based browser was necessary because the required Hungarian version of the browser (see above) was not available. This installation resulted in continuous system crashes because of the conflict between the Hungarian version of the operating system and the English version of the browser. To fix the problem, an English version of the system had to be bought and installed. The solution to the problem seems quite simple, in the end, but the identification and implementation of this solution (the reinstallation of the operating system) was delegated to the monitors.

This incomplete list of effects, problems and "errors" that emerged during implementation could easily be used to blame someone in the organization as incompetent in managing the process. It is obvious that it should have been possible to predict or avoid some of the aforementioned "problems" but it is also true that these problems emerged during and as a consequence of the implementation of the ODC system in the organization. They are easily recognizable ex-post, as consequences of the endogenous changes brought in by the IT-based classification protocol, but some of them were unpredictable ex-ante. IT system development and the following implementation process cannot be considered a straightforward procedure of technology adoption. It requires a broader consideration of the socio-institutional network in which it is embedded (Lanzara, 2009).

The ODC system was designed and implemented by Alpha to standardize and hence increase the central control over its data collection. The aim of the project was to make uniform not only the process of collecting data but also the final, collected data. The system was seen as a machine that would transform the patients' data into homogeneous numbers, comparable regardless of the country, language, or other diverse contexts from which they were gathered, without having any other effect on the organization. No other potential effects were taken into consideration. The IT system was seen as a mechanical system which would help fulfill a specific need in the organization. On the contrary, adopting a new system means re-conceptualizing the nature of the work, the process, and its outcomes (Bloomfield, Coombs, Owen, & Taylor, 1987; Lanzara, 2009). The ODC system was design to increase the uniformity of the process of data collection, using the standard laid down as a tool to translate local differences into a codified, uniform output. The tool was designed to make compatible the differences at the local level. As emerges from the analysis of the case, the effect of the standard on the data collection process was more complex: the ODC system, as with all IT-based systems, cannot simply be considered as a tool for the improvement of organizational performance (Ciborra & Hanseth, 1998), but must be considered in the broad, dynamic context in which it is deployed (Orlikowski, 2000; Star, 1999; Suchman, 1987) and the associated relational dimensions have to be considered, analyzed and discussed (Ciborra, 2000; Cordella & Simon, 2000).

AN ANT PERSPECTIVE: EMERGING STANDARDIZATION

The standardization brought about by the ODC system, which was designed to achieve univocal work practices in the process of data collection, was highly affected by the local dynamics that emerged in, and shaped the use of, the system. To consider these dynamics, we need to look at the standardization process through the relationships involved since it is these relationships that continually shape and reshape the process (Brown & Duguit, 2000; Timmermans & Berg, 1997). As a consequence, the analysis of the standardization protocol (the ODC system) cannot exclude the socio-technical context within which it is deployed. This means considering in more detail the reciprocal interaction between technology and people in the specific context that influences and is influenced by both of them (Law, 1992, 1999). The use of a protocol not only crystallizes and thus shapes the local data into a common framework which makes them manageable at a global level; it also affects and reshapes the associated work practices through the outcome of the process of standardization. Accordingly, the ODC system and work practices of the doctors, monitors and others involved are defined by the struggles faced on many different fronts, at different times, by many different network builders. A process of standardization based on structured work practices and technological standardization means an open-ended network where closure is never really achieved (Timmermans & Berg, 1997). The standardization process has to be considered the dynamic result of continuous interaction between work practices and technical artefacts. It does not have a completely predictable trajectory. It cannot be crystallized except in contingent and specific spatial and temporal references. The standardization process emerges from these complex dynamics (Monteiro & Hanseth, 1995) and is co-constructed within its relational context (Monteiro, Ellingsen, & Munkvold, 2007).

Moreover, the standardization that takes place at the local level is not necessarily uniform as emerges in the case study. Local characteristics, contingencies and practices craft the use of the protocol (Bowker, 2002) so that it is impossible to conceive the overall output as the homogeneous sum of the local activities. The classification protocol produces effects on the local context of data collection but the local data collection process defines how the classification protocol is used and thus, eventually, the associated output. This means that the protocol of standardization, like other global IT systems, is obviously framing part of the process, but is also continually redefined through its implementation and use at the local level (Cordella & Simon, 2000; Ole Hanseth & Braa, 1998).

As already discussed in the literature, IT artefacts are not simple tools that are defined *per se*, but are defined by and define complex networks of relationships (Akrich & Latour, 1992; Callon, 1991; Law, 1999; Suchman, 1987). Only through considering the dynamics of these relational networks is it possible to understand the dynamics associated with the adoption and use of a standardization process. In this case, the consideration of the relational status of the standardization process gives a different understanding of the overall process of standardization and its output.

In the case of the ODC system, the output of the process of standardization and thus the resulting control over it is discussed as the result of a dynamic interplay determined by the interaction between technology and its users.

The standardization process, and in this case the aimed-for centralized control, is discussed as an emerging process, based on adaptation and continuous change, rather than a static monolith reflecting a predefined design. It also changes as a consequence of the output produced by the same process of standardization. Moreover, it is affected by local contingencies where the technology is tinkered with, to satisfy the specific needs of the local context. It is impossible to reconstruct

the original data from the standardized data. The standardization process is tinkered with locally, but is translating the local into an artificial global framework of reference. The consequence is that the expected global uniformity is affected by the contingent and local practices in using the protocol of standardization. This has to be taken into consideration when implementing standardization processes so as to achieve control and uniformity of data collection. The aimed-for uniformity is the output of a dynamic process, so it cannot be considered as the mere result of the implementation of a technological process; standardization occurs as an emerging interaction. Standardization emerges from the context.

CONCLUSION

This article discusses the process through which a standardization process homogenizes data. Based on a case study, the article discusses the process that transforms data collected in different contexts into uniform data that represents a phenomenon that can be defined globally. The means of standardization is an information technology-based protocol that aims to transform the data collection procedure into a homogeneous process. This process is expected to make the quality and characteristics of the collected data homogeneous in turn. The technology used for this standardization is not uniquely analyzed on the basis of the produced output, but within its organizational context. The output of the process of standardization, and thus the ensuing control over it, is considered to be the result of a dynamic interplay between technology and its users.

The standardization process is thus here conceived as a changing process, based on adaptation and continuous changes, rather than a static monolith that reflects the ex-ante design. It also changes as a consequence of the output produced by the process of standardization. Moreover, it is affected by local contingencies, as a result of which the technology is tinkered with, to satisfy specific local needs.

The output of this process of standardization strongly reflects the adaptation and interplay that takes place between the technology and the needs of its users. The consequence is that the expected global uniformity in the data and the collection process is affected by the local use of the protocol of standardization. This has to be taken into consideration when implementing standardization processes to achieve global uniformity. The aimed-for uniformity is the output of a dynamic process and thus cannot be considered merely the result of the implementation of a predesigned and fixed set of rules and standards. Standardization processes emerge from the context, rather than shaping the context according to predefined categories.

REFERENCES

Akrich, M., & Latour, B. (1992). A summary of a convenient vocabulary for the semiotics of human and non-human assemblies. In Bijker, W. E., & Law, J. (Eds.), *Shaping technology / building society: Studies in sociotechnical change* (pp. 259–264). Cambridge, MA: MIT Press.

Avgerou, C. (2000). IT and organizational change: An institutional perspective. *Information Technology & People, 13*(4), 234–262. doi:10.1108/09593840010359464

Avgerou, C. (2002). The institutional nature of ICT and organisational change. *Information Systems and Global Diversity*, 23-50.

Benbasat, I., Goldstein, D. K., & Mead, M. (1987). The case research strategy in studies of information systems. *Management Information Systems Quarterly, 11*(3), 369–386. doi:10.2307/248684

Bijker, W., Hughes, T., & Pinch, T. J. (Eds.). (1987). *The social construction of technological systems: New directions in the sociology and history of technology*. Cambridge, MA: MIT Press.

Bijker, W., & Law, J. (Eds.). (1992). *Shaping technology/building society: Studies in sociotechnical change*. Cambridge, MA: MIT Press.

Bloomfield, B., Coombs, R., Owen, J., & Taylor, P. (1987). Doctors as managers: Constructing systems and users in the national health service. In Bloomfield, B., Coombs, R., Owen, J., & Taylor, P. (Eds.), *Information technology and organizations*. Oxford, UK: Oxford University Press.

Bowker, G. (2002). *Biodiversity datadiversity, manuscript*. Retrieved from http://weber.ucsd.edu/~gbowker/biodivdatadiv.pdf

Bowker, G., & Star, S. L. (1999). *Sorting things out: Classification and its consequences*. Cambridge, MA: MIT Press.

Brown, J. S., & Duguit, P. (2000). Knowledge and organization: A social-perspective. *Organization Science, 12*(2), 198–213. doi:10.1287/orsc.12.2.198.10116

Callon, M. (1987). Society in the making: The study of technology as a tool for sociological analysis. In Bijker, W. E., Hughes, T. P., & Pinch, T. J. (Eds.), *The social construction of technological systems: New directions in the sociology and history of technology*. Cambridge, MA: MIT Press.

Callon, M. (1991). Techno-economic networks and irreversibility. In Law, J. (Ed.), *A sociology of monsters: Essays on power, technology and domination* (pp. 132–161). London, UK: Routledge.

Ciborra, C. U. (1993). *Teams markets and systems*. Cambridge, UK: Cambridge University Press.

Ciborra, C. U. (1994). From thinking to tinkering. In Ciborra, C. U., & Jelassi, T. (Eds.), *Strategic information systems*. Chichester, UK: John Wiley & Sons.

Ciborra, C. U. (1999). Hospitality and IT. In Ljungberg, F. (Ed.), *Informatics in the next millennium* (pp. 161–176). Lund, Sweden: Studentlitteratur.

Ciborra, C. U. (Ed.). (2000). *From control to drift*. Oxford, UK: Oxford University Press.

Ciborra, C. U., & Hanseth, O. (1998). From tool to Gestell. *Information Technology & People*, *11*(4), 305–327. doi:10.1108/09593849810246129

Ciborra, C. U., & Hanseth, O. (2000). Introduction. In Ciborra, C. U. (Ed.), *From control to drift*. Oxford, UK: Oxford University Press.

Cordella, A. (2010). Information infrastructure: An actor network perspective. *Journal of Actor Network Theory and Technological Innovation*, *2*(1), 27–53. doi:10.4018/jantti.2010071602

Cordella, A., & Simon, K. (2000). Infrastructure deployment: Global intent vs. local adoption. In Ciborra, C. U. (Ed.), *From control to drift*. Oxford, UK: Oxford University Press.

Dahlbom, B., & Janlert, S. (1996). *Computer future*. Unpublished manuscript, Göteborg, Sweden.

Deleuze, G. (1996). *Proust et les signes*. Paris, France: Presses Universitaires de France.

Douglas, M. (1986). *How institutions think*. Syracus, NY: Syracuse University Press.

Giddens, A. (1984). *The constitution of society: Outline of the theory of structuration*. Cambridge, UK: Polity Press.

Hanseth, O. (1996). *Information technology as infrastructure*. Unpublished doctoral dissertation, School of Economics and Commercial Law, Goteborg University, Goteborg, Sweden.

Hanseth, O., & Braa, K. (1998). Technology as traitor: SAP infrastructure in global organizations. In *Proceedings of the Nineteenth Annual International Conference on Information Systems*, Helsinki, Finland.

Hanseth, O., & Monteiro, E. (1996). *Inscribing behaviour in information infrastructure standards*. Accounting, Management and Information Systems.

Hughes, T. (1997). The evolution of large technological systems. In Bijker, W. E., & Law, J. (Eds.), *The social construction of technological systems: New directions in the sociology and history of technology*. Cambridge, MA: MIT Press.

Lanzara, G. (2009). Building digital institutions: ICT and the rise of assemblages in government. In Contini, F., & Lanzara, G. (Eds.), *ICT and innovation in the public sector*. New York, NY: Palgrave Macmillan.

Law, J. (1992). Notes on the theory of the actor network: Ordering, strategy and heterogeneity. *Systems Practice*, *5*(4). doi:10.1007/BF01059830

Law, J. (1999). After ANT: Complexity, naming and topology. In Law, J., & Hassard, J. (Eds.), *Actor network theory and after* (pp. 1–14). Oxford, UK: Blackwell.

Lundberg, N. (2000). *IT in healthcare*. Unpublished doctoral dissertation, School of Economics and Commercial Law, Goteborg University, Goteborg, Sweden.

MacKenzie, D., & Wajcman, J. (Eds.). (1985). *The social shaping of technology: How the refrigerator got its hum*. Milton Keynes, UK: Open University Press.

Mintzberg, H. (1983). *Structure in fives: Designing effective organizations*. Upper Saddle River, NJ: Prentice Hall.

Moe, T. M. (1984). The new economics of organization. *American Journal of Political Science*, *28*(4), 4739–4777. doi:10.2307/2110997

Monteiro, E., Ellingsen, G., & Munkvold, G. (2007). Standardization of work: Co-constructed practice. *The Information Society, 23*(5), 309–326. doi:10.1080/01972240701572723

Monteiro, E., & Hanseth, O. (1995). Standardisation in action: Achieving universalism and localisation in medical protocols. In Orlikowski, W. J., Walsh, J., & De Gross, J. I. (Eds.), *Standardisation in action: Achieving universalism and localisation in medical protocols* (pp. 325–343). London, UK: Chapman & Hall.

Orlikowski, W. J. (1992). The duality of technology: Rethinking the concept of technology in organizations. *Information Systems Research, 3*(3).

Orlikowski, W. J. (2000). Using technology and constituting structures: A practical lens for studying technology in organizations. *Organization Science, 11*(4), 404–428. doi:10.1287/orsc.11.4.404.14600

Star, S. (1999). The ethnography of infrastructure. *The American Behavioral Scientist, 43*(3), 377–391. doi:10.1177/00027649921955326

Suchman, L. (1987). *Plan and situated actions: The problem of human machine communication.* Cambridge, UK: Cambridge University Press.

Timmermans, S., & Berg, M. (1997). Standardization in action: Achieving universalism and localisation through medical protocols. *Social Studies of Science, 27*(1), 111–134.

Williams, R., & Edge, D. (1996). The social shaping of technology. *Research Policy, 25*, 856–899. doi:10.1016/0048-7333(96)00885-2

Yin, R. K. (2003). *Case study research: Design and methods.* Thousand Oaks: Sage.

This work was previously published in the International Journal of Actor-Network Theory and Technological Innovation, Volume 3, Issue 3, edited by Arthur Tatnall, pp. 49-64, copyright 2011 by IGI Publishing (an imprint of IGI Global).

Compilation of References

Accenture. (2001). *eGovernment leadership: Rhetoric vs reality — Closing the gap*. Retrieved from http://www.accenture.com/Global/Research_and_Insights/By_Industry/Government_and_Public_Service/GovernmentsRhetoric.htm

Ace, C. (2001). *Successful Marketing Communications. A Practical Guide for Planning and Implementation*. Oxford, UK: Butterworth-Heinemann.

Adam, T. (1993). *Modelling and implementing protocols using high level Petri Nets*.

Adam, T., & Tatnall, A. (2010). Use of ICT to Assist Students with Learning Difficulties: An Actor-Network Analysis. In *Proceedings of the IFIP TC 3 International Conference (KCKS 2010)*, Brisbane, Australia.

Adam, A. (2008). Ethics for things. *Ethics and Information Technology, 10*, 149–154. doi:10.1007/s10676-008-9169-3

Adam, T., Rigoni, A., & Tatnall, A. (2006). Designing and implementing curriculum for students with special needs: A case study of a thinking curriculum. *Journal of Business Systems. Governance and Ethics, 1*(1), 49–63.

Admati, A. R., & Pfeiderer, P. (1991). Sunshine Trading and Financial Market Equilibrium. *Review of Financial Studies, 4*(3), 443–481.

AEEYSOC National Standards Expert Working Group. (2010). *Draft National Professional Standards for Teachers*. Victoria, Australia: Ministerial Council for Education, Early Childhood Development and Youth Affairs.

Ajzen, I. (1991). The theory of planned behavior. *Organizational Behavior and Human Decision Processes, 50*(2), 179–211. doi:10.1016/0749-5978(91)90020-T

Ajzen, I., & Fishbein, M. (1980). *Understanding attitudes and predicting social behavior*. London, UK: Prentice Hall.

Ajzen, I., & Madden, T. (1986). Prediction of goal-directed behavior: Attitudes, intentions, and perceived behavioral control. *Journal of Experimental Social Psychology, 22*, 453–474. doi:10.1016/0022-1031(86)90045-4

Akerkar, S. M., & Bichile, L. S. (2004). Doctor patient relationship: Changing dynamics in the information age. *E-Medicine, 50*(2), 120–122.

Akrich, M., Callon, M., & Latour, B. (2002). The key to success in innovation Part I: The art of interessement. *International Journal of Innovation Management, 6*(2), 187–206. doi:10.1142/S1363919602000550

Akrich, M., & Latour, B. (1992). A summary of a convenient vocabulary for the semiotics of human and non-human assemblies. In Bijker, W. E., & Law, J. (Eds.), *Shaping technology / building society: Studies in sociotechnical change* (pp. 259–264). Cambridge, MA: MIT Press.

Akther, M. S., Onishi, T., & Kidokoro, T. (2007). E-government in a developing country: Citizen-centric approach for success. *International Journal on Electronic Governance, 1*(1).

Al-Hajri, S. (2005). *Internet technology adoption in the banking industry business*. Unpublished doctoral dissertation, Victoria University, Melbourne, Australia.

Al-Hajri, S., & Tatnall, A. (2008). Adoption of Internet technology by the banking industry in Oman: A study informed by the Australian experience. *Journal of Electronic Commerce in Organizations, 6*(3), 20–36. doi:10.4018/jeco.2008070102

Al-Hajri, S., & Tatnall, A. (2008). Technological innovation and the adoption of Internet banking in Oman. *Electronic Journal for Virtual Organizations and Networks, 10*, 59–83.

Al-Hajri, S., & Tatnall, A. (2010). Factors relating to the adoption of Internet technology by the Omani banking industry. In Khosrow-Pour, M. (Ed.), *E-Commerce trends for organizational advancement: New applications and methods* (pp. 264–282). Hershey, PA: IGI Global.

Al-Hajri, S., & Tatnall, A. (2011). A socio-technical study of the adoption of internet technology in banking, re-interpreted as an innovation using innovation translation. *International Journal of Actor-Network Theory and Technological Innovation, 3*(3).

Ali, F. (1986). *Refleksi Paham "Kekuasaan Jawa" dalam Indonesia Modern*. Jakarta, Indonesia: P.T. Gramedia.

Allen, D. E., & Tanner, K. D. (2003). Approaches to cell biology teaching: Learning in context. *Cell Biology Education, 2*, 73–81. doi:10.1187/cbe.03-04-0019

Allen, P. E., & Andriani, P. (2007). Diversity, interconnectivity and sustainability. In Bogg, J. R., & Geyer, R. (Eds.), *Complexity, science and society* (pp. 1–32). Abingdon, UK: Radcliffe Publishing Ltd.

Amihud, Y., Ho, T. S. Y., & Schwartz, R. A. (Eds.). (1985). *Market Making and the Changing Structure of the Securities Industry*. Lexington, MA: Lexington Books.

Amin, A., & Thrift, N. (1994). *Globalization, institution, and regional development in Europe*. Oxford, UK: Oxford University Press.

Anderson, J. G., Rainey, M. R., & Eysenbach, G. (2003). The Impact of CyberHealthcare on the Physician–Patient Relationship. *Journal of Medical Systems, 27*(1), 67–84. doi:10.1023/A:1021061229743

Anderson, R., & Srinivasan, S. (2003). E-satisfaction and e-loyalty: A contingency framework. *Psychology and Marketing, 20*(2), 123–138. doi:10.1002/mar.10063

Andersson-Skog, L. (2009). Revisiting railway history: the case of institutional change and path dependence. In Magnusson, L., & Ottosson, J. (Eds.), *The evolution of path dependence* (pp. 70–80). Cheltenham, UK: Edward Edgar Publishing Ltd.

Andersson, T., Curley, M. G., & Formica, P. (2010). *Knowledge-Driven Entrepreneurship: The Key to Social and Economic Transformation*. New York: Springer.

Andrew, J. P., & Sirkin, H. L. (2006). *Payback: reaping the rewards of innovation*. Boston: Harvard Business School Press.

Anthopoulos, L. G., Siozos, P., & Tsoukalas, I. A. (2007). Applying participatory design and collaboration in digital public services for discovering and re-designing e-government services. *Government Information Quarterly, 24*, 353–376. doi:10.1016/j.giq.2006.07.018

Applegate, L. M., Montealegre, R., Nelson, H. J., & Knoop, C.-I. (1999). BAE automated systems (A): Denver International Airport baggage-handling system. In Applegate, L. M., McFarlan, F. W., & McKenny, J. L. (Eds.), *Corporate information systems management: Text and cases* (pp. 546–561). New York, NY: McGraw-Hill.

Apple, M. (2000). *Official knowledge: Democratic education in a conservative age* (2nd ed.). New York, NY: Routledge.

Arendt, H. (1958). *The human condition*. Chicago, IL: University of Chicago Press.

Argyis, C. (1980). Some limitations of the case method: Experiences in a management development program. *Academy of Management Review, 5*, 291–299. doi:10.2307/257439

Armour, F., Kaisler, S., & Bitner, J. (2007). Enterprise Architecture: Challenges and Implementations. In *Proceedings of the 40th Annual Hawaii International Conference, System Sciences* (pp. 117-217).

Athanassopoulos, A. (2000). Customer satisfaction cues to support market segmentation and explain switching behavior. *Journal of Business Research, 47*, 191–207. doi:10.1016/S0148-2963(98)00060-5

Augustine. (427). *On Christian doctrine*. Indianapolis, IN: Bobbs-Merrill.

Aurik, J. C., Jonk, G. J., & Willen, R. E. (2003). *Rebuilding the corporate genome: unlocking the real value of your business*. Hoboken, NJ: John Wiley & Sons.

Australian Schools Directory. (2011). *The only guide to all Australian primary and secondary schools.* Retrieved from http://www.australianschoolsdirectory. com.au/

Avgerou, C. (2002). The institutional nature of ICT and organisational change. *Information Systems and Global Diversity*, 23-50.

Avgerou, C. (2000). IT and organizational change: An institutional perspective. *Information Technology & People, 13*(4), 234–262. doi:10.1108/09593840010359464

Baldwin, S. E. (1900). Teaching law by cases. *Harvard Law Review, 14*, 258. doi:10.2307/1322548

Bandura, A. (1982). Self-efficacy mechanism in human agency. *The American Psychologist, 37*(2), 122–147. doi:10.1037/0003-066X.37.2.122

Barad, K. (2003). Posthumanist performativity: Toward an understanding of how matter comes to matter. *Signs, 28*(3), 801–831. doi:10.1086/345321

Barker, R., & Angelopulo, G. (2007). *Integrated Organisational Communication.* Cape Town, South Africa: Juta & Co. (Pty) Ltd.

Barnes, L. B., Christensen, C. R., & Hansen, H. (1994). *Teaching and the case method.* Cambridge, MA: Harvard Business School Press.

Barrows, H. (1985). *How to design a problem-based curriculum for pre-clinical years.* New York, NY: Springer.

Barry, A. (2006). Actor-Network-Theory. In Harrington, A., Marshall, B. L., & Müller, H. P. (Eds.), *Encyclopedia of social theory* (pp. 4–5). Abingdon, UK: Routledge.

Barton, D., & Hamilton, M. (2005). Literacy, reification and the dynamics of social interaction. In Barton, D., & Tusting, K. (Eds.), *Beyond communities of practice: Language, power and social context.* Cambridge, UK: Cambridge University Press. doi:10.1017/CBO9780511610554.003

Barton, D., Hamilton, M., & Ivanic, R. (Eds.). (2000). *Situated literacies: Reading and writing in context.* London, UK: Routledge.

Bastian, H. (2008). Health literacy and patient information: Developing the methodology for a national evidence-based health website. *Patient Education and Counseling, 73*(3), 551–556. doi:10.1016/j.pec.2008.08.020

Bauchspies, W. K., Croissant, J., & Restivo, S. (2006). *Science, technology, and society: sociological approach.* Oxford, UK: Blackwell Publishing.

Bedny, G. Z., & Karwowski, W. (2004). Activity theory as a basis for the study of work. *Ergonomics, 47*(2), 134–153. doi:10.1080/00140130310001617921

Benbasat, I., Goldstein, D. K., & Mead, M. (1987). The case research strategy in studies of information systems. *Management Information Systems Quarterly, 11*(3), 369–386. doi:10.2307/248684

Benson, A., Lawler, C., & Whitworth, A. (2008). Rules, roles and tools: Activity theory and the comparative study of e-learning. *British Journal of Educational Technology, 39*(3), 456–467. doi:10.1111/j.1467-8535.2008.00838.x

Bergen, K. M., & Braithwaite, D. O. (2009). Identity as Constituted in Communication. In W. F. Eadie (Ed.), *21st Century Communication: A Reference Handbook* (pp. 165-176). Thousand Oaks, CA: Sage Publications.

Berger, T. (2009). Meet the e-patient: Chancen und Risiken des Internets für das Verhältnis von Gesundheitsfachleuten und ihren Klienten. In Stetina, B. U., & Kryspin-Exner, I. (Eds.), *Gesundheit und Neue Medien. Psychologische Aspekte der Interaktion mit Informations- und Kommunikationstechnologien* (pp. 73–83). New York: Springer.

Berners-Lee, T., Hendler, J., & Lassila, O. (2001). The Semantic Web. *Scientific American.*

Bielenia-Grajewska, M. (2009). Actor-Network Theory in intercultural communication. Translation through the prism of innovation, technology, networks and semiotics. *International Journal of Actor-Network Theory and Technological Innovation, 1*(4), 53–69.

Bielenia-Grajewska, M. (2011). A Potential Application of Actor Network Theory in Organizational Studies. The Company as an Ecosystem and its Power Relations from the ANT Perspective. In Tatnall, A. (Ed.), *Actor-Network Theory and Technology Innovation: Advancements and New Concepts.* Hershey, PA: IGI Global.

Biesta, G. (2009). Disciplinarity and interdisciplinarity in the academic study of education: Comparing traditions of educational theorising. In *Proceedings of the Annual Conference of the British Educational Research Association* (pp. 1-15).

Biesta, G. (2009). How to use pragmatism pragmatically? Suggestions for the 21st century. In *Proceedings of the Annual Meeting of the American Educational Research Association,* San Diego, CA (pp. 1-10).

Biesta, G. (2010). Pragmatism and the philosophical foundations of mixed methods research. In Teddlie, C., & Tashakkori, A. (Eds.), *Handbook of mixed methods research.* London, UK: Sage.

Biesta, G., & Burbules, N. C. (2003). *Pragmatism and educational research.* London, UK: Rowman & Littlefield.

Bigum, C. (2007, July 3-6). Heads up versus heads in: Approaches to quality in teacher education and computing and communication technologies. In *Proceedings of the Australian Teacher Education Association National Conference*, Wollongong, Australia.

Bigum, C. (2004). Rethinking schools and community: The knowledge producing school. In Marshall, S., Taylor, W., & Yu, X. H. (Eds.), *Using community informatics to transform regions* (pp. 52–66). Hershey, PA: IGI Global. doi:10.4018/9781591401322.ch004

Bijker, W., Hughes, T., & Pinch, T. J. (Eds.). (1987). *The social construction of technological systems: New directions in the sociology and history of technology.* Cambridge, MA: MIT Press.

Bijker, W., & Law, J. (Eds.). (1992). *Shaping technology/building society: Studies in socio-technical change.* Cambridge, MA: MIT Press.

Birchall, D. W., & Tovstiga, G. (1999). The strategic potential of a firm's knowledge portfolio. *Journal of General Management, 25,* 1–16.

Birkerts, S. (2010). Into the Electronic Millenium. In Hanks, C. (Ed.), *Technology and Values: Essential Readings* (pp. 491–499). Malden, MA: Blackwell Publishing.

Black, R. (2007). *Crossing the bridge: Overcoming entrenched disadvantage through student-centred learning.* Retrieved from http://www.eric.ed.gov/ERICWebPortal/search/detailmini.jsp?_nfpb=true&_&ERICExtSearch_SearchValue_0=ED501899&ERICExtSearch_SearchType_0=no&accno=ED501899

Black, F. (1971). Toward a Fully Automated Stock Exchange. *Financial Analysts Journal, 27*(4), 28–35, 44. doi:10.2469/faj.v27.n4.28

Blin, F., & Munro, M. (2007). Why hasn't technology disrupted academic teaching practices? Understanding resistance to change through the lens of activity theory. *Computers & Education, 50*(2), 475–490. doi:10.1016/j.compedu.2007.09.017

Bloch, E., & Schwartz, R. A. (Eds.). (1979). *Impending Changes for Securities Markets: What Role for the Exchanges?*Greenwich, CT: JAI Press.

Blommaert, J. (2010). *The Sociolinguistics of Globalization.* Cambridge, UK: Cambridge University Press.

Bloomfield, B., Coombs, R., Owen, J., & Taylor, P. (1987). Doctors as managers: Constructing systems and users in the national health service. In Bloomfield, B., Coombs, R., Owen, J., & Taylor, P. (Eds.), *Information technology and organizations.* Oxford, UK: Oxford University Press.

Boland, R. J., Tenkasi, R. V., & Te'eni, D. (1994). Designing information technology to support distributed cognition. *Organization Science, 5*(3), 456–475. doi:10.1287/orsc.5.3.456

Bolgherini, S. (2007). The technology trap and the role of political and cultural variables: A critical analysis of the e-government policies. *Review of Policy Research, 24*(3), 259–275. doi:10.1111/j.1541-1338.2007.00280.x

Bond, Ch. (2004). *Concordance: a partnership in medicine-taking.* London: Pharmaceutical Press.

Bowker, G. (2002). *Biodiversity datadiversity, manuscript.* Retrieved from http://weber.ucsd.edu/~gbowker/biodivdatadiv.pdf

Bowker, G., & Star, S. L. (1999). *Sorting things out: Classification and its consequences.* Cambridge, MA: MIT Press.

Brandt, T., & Clinton, K. (2002). Limits of the local: Expanding perspectives on literacy as a social practice. *Journal of Literacy Research, 34*(3), 337–356. doi:10.1207/s15548430jlr3403_4

Brey, P., & Søraker, J. H. (2009). Philosophy of Computing and Information Technology. In Gabbay, D. M., Meijers, A., Thagard, P., & Woods, J. (Eds.), *Philosophy of Technology and Engineering Sciences* (pp. 1341–1408). Amsterdam: North Holland. doi:10.1016/B978-0-444-51667-1.50051-3

Brown, J. S., & Conner, M. (2000). *Linking, lurking, listening and learning.* Retrieved from http://linezine.com/2.1/features/jsbmcl4.htm

Brown, J. S., & Duguit, P. (2000). Knowledge and organization: A social-perspective. *Organization Science, 12*(2), 198–213. doi:10.1287/orsc.12.2.198.10116

Brown, S. (1999). Assessing practice. In Brown, S., & Glasner, A. (Eds.), *Assessment matters in higher education: Choosing and using diverse approaches.* Buckingham, UK: Open University Press.

Bukatman, S. (2002). *Terminal identity: the virtual subject in postmodern science fiction.* Cheltenham, UK: Duke University Press.

Burgess, M. (2004). *Analytical network and system administration: managing human-computer networks.* New York: John Willey & Sons Ltd. doi:10.1002/047086107X

Burke, B. (2007). *The Role of Enterprise Architecture in Technology Research.* Gartner Inc.

Burnett, R., Consalvo, M., & Ess, Ch. (2010). *The Handbook of Internet Studies.* Malden, MA: John Willey and Sons Ltd.

Butler, T. (1998). Towards a hermeneutic method for interpretive research in information systems. *Journal of Information Technology, 13*(4), 285–300. doi:10.1057/jit.1998.7

Caiata Zufferey, M., & Schulz, P. J. (2009). Self-management of chronic low back pain: An exploration of the impact of a patient-centered website. *Patient Education and Counseling, 77*, 27–32. doi:10.1016/j.pec.2009.01.016

Callon, M. (1997). *Actor-network theory: The market test.* Retrieved from http://www.lancs.ac.uk/fass/sociology/papers/callon-market-test.pdf

Callon, M. (1986). Some elements of a sociology of translation: Domestication of the scallops and the fisherman. In Law, J. (Ed.), *Power, action and belief* (pp. 196–233). London, UK: Routledge & Kegan Paul.

Callon, M. (1986). The sociology of an actor-network: The case of the electric vehicle. In Callon, M., Law, J., & Rip, A. (Eds.), *Mapping the dynamics of science and technology* (pp. 19–34). London, UK: Macmillan.

Callon, M. (1987). Society in the making: The study of technology as a tool for sociological analysis. In Bijker, W. E., Hughes, T. P., & Pinch, T. J. (Eds.), *The social construction of technological systems: New directions in the sociology and history of technology.* Cambridge, MA: MIT Press.

Callon, M. (1991). Techno-economic networks and irreversibility. In Law, J. (Ed.), *A sociology of monsters: Essays on power, technology and domination* (pp. 132–161). London, UK: Routledge.

Callon, M., Courtial, J. P., Turner, W. A., & Bauin, S. (1983). From translations to problematic networks: An introduction to co-word analysis. *Social Sciences Information. Information Sur les Sciences Sociales, 22*(2), 191–235. doi:10.1177/053901883022002003

Callon, M., Millo, Y., & Muniesa, F. (Eds.). (2007). *Market Devices.* Oxford, UK: Blackwell.

Callon, M., & Muniesa, F. (2005). Economic Markets as Calculative Collective Devices. *Organization Studies, 26*(8), 1229–1250. doi:10.1177/0170840605056393

Cantoni, L., & Tardini, S. (2006). *Internet.* Abingdon, UK: Routledge.

Cantoni, L., & Tardini, S. (2010). The Internet and the Web. In Albertazzi, D., & Cobley, P. (Eds.), *Media: An Introduction* (pp. 220–232). Harlow, UK: Pearson Education Limited.

Capriotti, P., & Moreno, A. (2007). Communicating corporate responsibility through corporate websites in Spain. *Corporate Communications, 12*, 221–237. doi:10.1108/13563280710776833

Capurro, R., & Pingel, Ch. (2002). Ethical issues of online communication research. *Ethics and Information Technology, 4*, 189–194. doi:10.1023/A:1021372527024

Caputo, J. D. (1987). *Radical hermeneutics: Repetition, deconstruction and the hermeneutic project.* Bloomington, IN: Indiana University Press.

Carlsson, S. A. (2003). Knowledge managing and knowledge management systems in inter-organizational networks. *Knowledge and Process Management, 10*, 199–264. doi:10.1002/kpm.179

Carmichael, P., & Garcia Martinez, A. (2009, September 30). Semantic technologies to support teaching and learning with cases: Challenges and opportunities. In *Proceedings of the 1st International Workshop on Semantic Web Applications for Learning and Teaching Support in Higher Education*, Nice, France.

Carr, N. G. (2004). *Does IT matter? information technology and the corrosion of competitive advantage.* Boston: Harvard Business School Publishing Corporation.

Cass, J. (2007). *Strategies and tools for corporate blogging.* Burlington, MA: Butterworth-Heinemann.

Castells, M. (2009). *Communication power.* Oxford, UK: Oxford University Press.

Cellary, W. (2002). Healthcare. In W. Cellary (Ed.), *Poland and the global information society: logging on* (pp. 97-98). Poznań: Grupa Wydawnicza INFOR Sp z o.o.

Chan, T. S. (2004). Web design for international business. In Samii, M., & Karush, G. (Eds.), *International Business and Information Technology* (pp. 83–110). New York: Routledge.

Chappell, C., Rhodes, C., Solomon, N., Tennant, M., & Yates, L. (2003). *Reconstructing the lifelong learner.* London, UK: Routledge. doi:10.4324/9780203464410

Charnkit, P. (2011). *Using the technology acceptance model to investigate knowledge conversion in Thai public organisations: Management and information systems.* Melbourne, Australia: Victoria University.

Chase, S. E. (2005). Narrative inquiry: Multiple lenses, approaches, voices. In Denzin, N., & Lincoln, Y. (Eds.), *The Sage handbook of qualitative research* (3rd ed.). London, UK: Sage.

Chen, Y. N., Chen, H. M., Huang, W., & Ching, R. K. H. (2006). E-government strategies in developed and developing countries: An implementation framework and case study. *Journal of Global Information Management, 14*(1), 23–46. doi:10.4018/jgim.2006010102

Chi, Y.-L., Tsai, M.-H., & Lee, C.-W. (2005). A Petri-net based validator in reliability of a composite service. In *Proceedings of the IEEE International Conference on e-Technology, e-Commerce and e-Service* (pp. 450-453).

Christensen, N. B. (2003). *Inuit in cyberspace. Embedding Offline Identities Online.* Copenhagen, Denmark: Museum Tusculanum Press, University of Copenhagen.

Christians, C. (2005). Ethics and politics in qualitative research. In Denzin, N., & Lincoln, Y. (Eds.), *The Sage handbook of qualitative research* (3rd ed.). London, UK: Sage.

Ciborra, C. (2005). Interpreting e-government and development: Efficiency, transparency or governance at a distance? *Information Technology & People, 18*(3), 260–279. doi:10.1108/09593840510615879

Ciborra, C. U. (1993). *Teams markets and systems.* Cambridge, UK: Cambridge University Press.

Ciborra, C. U. (1994). From thinking to tinkering. In Ciborra, C. U., & Jelassi, T. (Eds.), *Strategic information systems.* Chichester, UK: John Wiley & Sons.

Ciborra, C. U. (1999). Hospitality and IT. In Ljungberg, F. (Ed.), *Informatics in the next millennium* (pp. 161–176). Lund, Sweden: Studentlitteratur.

Ciborra, C. U. (Ed.). (2000). *From control to drift.* Oxford, UK: Oxford University Press.

Ciborra, C. U., & Hanseth, O. (1998). From tool to Gestell. *Information Technology & People, 11*(4), 305–327. doi:10.1108/09593849810246129

Ciborra, C. U., & Hanseth, O. (2000). Introduction. In Ciborra, C. U. (Ed.), *From control to drift.* Oxford, UK: Oxford University Press.

Civi, E. (2000). Knowledge management as a competitive asset: A review. *Marketing Intelligence & Planning, 18*, 166–174. doi:10.1108/02634500010333280

Clarke, J. (2002). A new kind of symmetry: Actor-network theories and the new literacy studies. *Studies in the Education of Adults, 34*(2), 107–122.

Cohen, K. J., Maier, S. F., Schwartz, R. A., & Whitcomb, D. K. (1986). *The Microstructure of Securities Markets.* Upper Saddle River, NJ: Prentice-Hall.

Cohen, K. J., & Schwartz, R. A. (1989). An Electronic Call Market: Its Design and Desirability. In Lucas, H. C. J., & Schwartz, R. A. (Eds.), *The Challenge of Information Technology for the Securities Markets: Liquidity, Volatility, and Global Trading* (pp. 15–38). Homewood, IL: Dow Jones-Irwin.

Cole, M. (1999). Cultural psychology: Some general principles and a concrete example. In Engström, Y., Miettinen, R., & Punamäki, R.-L. (Eds.), *Perspectives on activity theory* (pp. 87–106). Cambridge, MA: Cambridge University Press.

Collins, H. M. (1990). *Artificial Experts: Social Knowledge and Intelligent Machines.* Cambridge, MA: The MIT Press.

Collins, H., & Yearley, S. (1992). Epistemological chicken. In Pickering, A. (Ed.), *Science, practice and culture.* Chicago, IL: University of Chicago Press.

Cook, M. A. (1996). *Building enterprise information architectures: reengineering information systems.* Upper Saddle River, NJ: Prentice-Hall, Inc.

Corallo, A. (2007). The business ecosystem as a multiple dynamic network. In Corallo, A., Passiante, G., & Prencipe, A. (Eds.), *The digital business ecosystem* (pp. 11–32). Cheltenham, UK: Edward Elgar Publishing.

Cordella, A., & Shaikh, M. (2006). *From epistemology to ontology: Challenging the constructed "truth" of ANT.* Retrieved from http://is2.lse.ac.uk/WP/PDF/wp143.pdf

Cordella, A. (2010). Information infrastructure: An actor network perspective. *Journal of Actor Network Theory and Technological Innovation, 2*(1), 27–53. doi:10.4018/jantti.2010071602

Cordella, A., & Simon, K. (2000). Infrastructure deployment: Global intent vs. local adoption. In Ciborra, C. U. (Ed.), *From control to drift.* Oxford, UK: Oxford University Press.

Crang, M., & Cook, I. (2007). *Doing ethnographies.* London, UK: Sage.

Crary, J. (1992). *Techniques of the observer: On vision and modernity in the 19th century.* Cambridge, MA: MIT Press.

Creswell, J. W. (1997). *Qualitative inquiry and research design: Choosing among five traditions.* Thousand Oaks, CA: Sage.

Crotty, M. (1998). *The foundations of social research: Meaning and perspective in the research process.* Crows Nest, NSW, Australia: Allen and Unwin.

Cuban, L. (2004). *The blackboard and the bottom line.* Cambridge, MA: Harvard University Press.

Czarniawska, B., & Hernes, T. (Eds.). (2005). *Actor-network theory and organising.* Malmö, Sweden: Liber and Copenhagen Business School Press.

Daft, R. (2009). *Organization Theory and Design.* Mason, OH: South-Western Cengage Learning.

Dahlbom, B., & Janlert, S. (1996). *Computer future.* Unpublished manuscript, Göteborg, Sweden.

Dale, K. (2005). Building a Social Materiality: Spatial and Embodied Politics in Organizational Control. *Organization, 12*(5), 649–678. doi:10.1177/1350508405055940

Danet, B., & Herring, S. C. (2007). *The multilingual Internet: language, culture, and communication online.* Oxford, UK: Oxford University Press.

Davenport, T. H., Leibold, M., & Voelpel, S. (2006). *Strategic management in the innovation economy: strategy approaches and tools for dynamic innovation capabilities.* Erlangen, Germany: Publicis Corporate Publishing and Wiley-VCH Verlag.

Davenport, T., & Prusak, T. (1998). *Working knowledge: How organizations manage what they know.* Cambridge, MA: Harvard Business School Press.

Davis, F. (1986). *A technology acceptance model for empirically testing new end-user information systems: Theory and results.* Cambridge, MA: MIT Press.

Davis, F. (1989). Perceived usefulness, perceived ease of use, and user acceptance of information technology. *Management Information Systems Quarterly*, *13*(3), 318–340. doi:10.2307/249008

Davis, F., Bagozzi, R., & Warshaw, P. (1989). User acceptance of computer technology: A comparison of two theoretical models. *Management Science*, *35*(8), 982–1003. doi:10.1287/mnsc.35.8.982

Dawes, S. S. (2002). *The future of e-government*. Retrieved from http://www.ctg.albany.edu/publications/reports/future_of_egov/future_of_egov.pdf

De Grooijer, J. (2000). Designing a knowledge management performance framework. *Journal of Knowledge and Information Management*, *4*, 303–310.

De'. R. (2005). E-government systems in developing countries: Stakeholders and conflict. In M. A. Wimmer, R. Traunmüller, Å. Grönlund, & K. V. Andersen (Eds.), *Proceedings of the 4th International Conference on Electronic Government* (LNCS 3591, pp. 26-37).

Dedrick, J., Gurbaxani, V., & Kraemer, K. (2003). Information technology and economic performance: A critical review of the empirical evidence. *ACM Computing Surveys*, *35*(1), 1–28. doi:10.1145/641865.641866

Del Casino, V. J. (2009). *Social geography: a critical introduction*. Malden, MA: John Willey and Sons.

Del Piccolo, L., Mazzi, M. A., Scardoni, S., Gobbi, M., & Zimmermann, Ch. (2008). A theory-based proposal to evaluate patient-centred communication in medical consultations: The Verona Patient-centred Communication Evaluation scale (VR-COPE). *Health Education*, *108*(5), 355–372. doi:10.1108/09654280810899984

Deleuze, G. (1990). *The Logic of Sense*. New York: Columbia University Press.

Deleuze, G. (1996). *Proust et les signes*. Paris, France: Presses Universitaires de France.

Deleuze, G., & Guttari, F. (1988). *A thousand plateaus: Capitalism and schizophrenia*. London, UK: Athlone.

Demeterio, F. P. A. III. (2001). Introduction to hermeneutics. *Diwatao*, *1*(1), 1–9.

Denton, T. (2007). *Tribes of the mind*. Melbourne, Australia: Arts Grant Application.

Denzin, N. K., & Lincoln, Y. S. (Eds.). (1994). *Handbook of qualitative research*. Thousand Oaks, CA: Sage.

Díaz Andrade, A. (2010). From intermediary to mediator and vice versa: On agency and intentionality of a mundane sociotechnical system. *International Journal of Actor-Network Theory and Technological Innovation*, *2*(4), 21–29. doi:10.4018/jantti.2010100103

Didier, E. (2007). Do Statistics "Perform" the Economy? In MacKenzie, D., Muniesa, F., & Siu, L. (Eds.), *Do Economists make Markets? On the Performativity of Economics* (pp. 276–310). Princeton, NJ: Princeton University Press.

Didier, E. (2009). *En quoi consiste l'Amérique? Les statistiques, le New Deal et la démocratie*. Paris: La Découverte.

Dillenbourg, P., Baker, M., Blaye, A., & O'Malley, C. (1995). The evolution of research on collaborative learning. In Spada, E., & Reiman, P. (Eds.), *Learning in humans and machine: Towards an interdisciplinary learning science* (pp. 189–211). Amsterdam, The Netherlands: Elsevier.

Dilthey, W. (1990). The rise of hermeneutics. In Ormiston, G. L., & Schrift, A. D. (Eds.), *The hermeneutic tradition: From Ast to Ricoeur*. New York, NY: State University of New York Press.

Domowitz, I. (1993). Automating the Continuous Double Auction in Practice: Automated Trade Execution Systems in Financial Markets. In Friedman, J., & Rust, J. (Eds.), *The Double Auction Market: Institutions, Theories, and Evidence* (pp. 27–60). Reading, MA: Addison-Wesley.

Domowitz, I., & Lee, R. (2001). On the Road to Reg ATS: A Critical History of the Regulation of Automated Trading Systems. *International Finance*, *4*(2), 279–302. doi:10.1111/1468-2362.00074

Doolin, B., & Lowe, A. (2002). To reveal is to critique: Actor–network theory and critical information systems research. *Journal of Information Technology*, *17*, 69–78. doi:10.1080/02683960210145986

Douglas, M. (1986). *How institutions think*. Syracus, NY: Syracuse University Press.

Drath, W. H., McCauley, C. D., Palus, C. J., Velsor, E. V., O'Connor, P. M. G., & McGuire, J. B. (2008). Direction, alignment, commitment: Toward a more integrative ontology of leadership. *The Leadership Quarterly, 19*, 635–653. doi:10.1016/j.leaqua.2008.09.003

Dugdale, A. (1999). Materiality: Juggling sameness and difference. In Law, J., & Hassard, J. (Eds.), *Actor network theory and after* (pp. 113–133). Oxford, UK: Blackwell.

Ebrahim, Z., & Irani, Z. (2005). E-government adoption: Architecture and barriers. *Business Process Management Journal, 11*(5), 589–611. doi:10.1108/14637150510619902

Economides, N., & Schwartz, R. A. (1995). Electronic Call Market Trading. *Journal of Portfolio Management, 21*(3), 10–18. doi:10.3905/jpm.1995.409518

Edwards, R. (2009). Materialising theory: Does theory matter? In *Proceedings of the Keynote Symposium ontThe Theory Question in Education*, Manchester, UK.

Edwards, R. (2009). Translating the prescribed into the enacted curriculum in college and school. *Educational Philosophy and Theory*.

Edwards, R. (2003). Ordering subjects: Actor networks and intellectual technologies in lifelong learning. *Studies in the Education of Adults, 35*(1), 54–67.

Elliott, G. (2000). Accrediting lecturers using competence-based approaches: A cautionary tale. In Gray, D., & Griffin, C. (Eds.), *Post-compulsory education and the new millennium*. London, UK: Jessica Kingsley.

Elliott, J. O., & Shneker, B. F. (2009). A health literacy assessment of the epilepsy.com website. *Seizure, (18):* 434–439. doi:10.1016/j.seizure.2009.04.003

Encarta Dictionary. (2010). *Definition: Curriculum.* Retrieved from http://encarta.msn.com/dictionary_1861602023/curriculum.html

Engeström, Y., & Meittinen, R. (1999). Activity theory: A well-kept secret. In Engström, Y., Miettinen, R., & Punamäki, R.-L. (Eds.), *Perspectives on activity theory* (pp. 1–18). Cambridge, UK: Cambridge University Press.

Engström, Y. (1987). *Learning by expanding*. Helsinki, Finland: Orienta Konsultit.

Engström, Y. (1999). Activity theory and individual and social transformation. In Engström, Y., Miettinen, R., & Punamäki, R.-L. (Eds.), *Perspectives on activity theory* (pp. 19–38). Cambridge, UK: Cambridge University Press.

Epstein, S. (1996). *Impure science*. Berkeley, CA: University of California Press.

Eraut, M. (1994). *Developing professional knowledge and competence*. London, UK: Routledge.

Ewenstein, B., & Whyte, J. (2009). Knowledge practices in design: The role of visual representations as 'epistemic objects'. *Organization Studies, 30*(1), 7–30. doi:10.1177/0170840608083014

Eysenbach, G., & Diepgen, T. L. (1999). Patients Looking for Information on the Internet and Seeking Teleadvice. *Motivation,* Expectations, and Misconceptions as Expressed in E-mails Sent to Physicians. *Archives of Dermatology, (135):* 151–156. doi:10.1001/archderm.135.2.151

Fails, E. (1988). Teaching sociological theory: The development of an experimental strategy. *Teaching Sociology, 16*(3), 256–262. doi:10.2307/1317527

Fenwick, T. (2010). *How standards are performed in education: Fluid fissures and suspended certainty*. Paper presented at the EASST Conference: Practicing Science and Technology, Performing the Social.

Fenwick, T. (2010). (un)Doing standards in education with actor-network theory. *Journal of Education Policy, 25*(2), 117–133. doi:10.1080/02680930903314277

Fenwick, T., & Edwards, R. (2010). *Actor-network theory in education*. London, UK: Routledge.

Fernandez, J. (2004). *Corporate communications: a 21st century primer*. New Delhi, India: Response Books.

Fernandez, I. B., Gonzalez, A., & Sabherwal, R. (2004). *Knowledge management: Challenges, solutions and technologies*. Upper Saddle River, NJ: Pearson/Prentice Hall.

Fernandez, W. D. (2004). The grounded theory method and case study data in IS research: Issues and design. In Hart, D., & Gregor, S. (Eds.), *Information systems foundations: Constructing and criticising*. Canberra, Australia: ANU E Press.

Fewick, T., & Edwards, R. (2010). *Actor-network theory in education*. London, UK: Routledge.

Fidler, R. F. (1997). *Mediamorphosis: understanding new media*. Thousand Oaks, CA: Pine Forge Press.

Fife, E., & Hosman, L. (2007). Public private partnerships and the prospects for sustainable ICT projects in the developing world. *Journal of Business Systems, Governance and Ethics, 2*(3).

Finlay, I., Spours, K., Steer, R., Coffield, F., Gregson, M., & Hodgson, A. (2007). The heart of what we do: Policies on teaching, learning and assessment in the learning and skills sector. *Journal of Vocational Education and Training, 59*(2), 137–153. doi:10.1080/13636820701342442

Fishbein, M., & Ajzen, I. (1975). *Belief, attitude, intention, and behavior: An introduction to theory and research*. Reading, MA: Addison-Wesley.

Fisher, D., & Tempest, R. (1989, October 26). Allais: "Wall Street Has Become a Veritable Casino". *Los Angeles Times*, D1.

Foglio, A. (2007). *Il marketing sanitario. Il marketing per aziende sanitarie, ospedaliere, centri salute, ambulatori e studi medici*. Milan, Italy: FrancoAngeli.

Fox, S. (2000). Communities of practice, Foucault and actor-network theory. *Journal of Management Studies, 37*(6), 853–867. doi:10.1111/1467-6486.00207

Frank, A. (1994). *At the will of the body*. New York, NY: Mariner Books.

Friedman, D., & Rust, J. (Eds.). (1993). *The Double Auction Market: Institutions, Theories, and Evidence*. Reading, MA: Addison-Wesley.

Fullan, M. (2001). *The new meaning of educational change* (3rd ed.). New York, NY: Teachers College Press.

Furuholt, B., & Wahid, F. (2008). E-government challenges and the role of political leadership in Indonesia: The case of Sragen. In *Proceedings of the 41st Hawaii International Conference on System Sciences*.

Gadamer, H.-G. (2004). *Truth and method*. London, UK: Continuum.

Gadamer, H.-G. (Ed.). (1976). *The historicity of understanding critical sociology, selected readings*. Harmondsworth, UK: Penguin Books.

Galea, D. (2000). E-mail and Website Feedback. In Keyes, J. (Ed.), *Internet Management* (pp. 513–522). Boca Raton, FL: CRC Press.

GAO (United States General Accounting Office). (1991). *Global Financial Markets: International Coordination Can Help Address Automation Risks* (Tech. Rep. No. GAO/IMTES-91-62). Washington, DC: General Accounting Office.

Garfinkel, H. (1967). *Studies in ethnomethodology*. Upper Saddle River, NJ: Prentice Hall.

Garwin, D. A. (2003). Making the case: Professional education for the world of practice. *Harvard Magazine*.

Garzone, G. (2009). Multimodal analysis. In Bargiela-Chiappini, F. (Ed.), *The Handbook of Business Discourse* (pp. 155–165). Edinburgh, UK: Edinburgh University Press.

Gauld, R. (2007). Public sector information system project failures: Lessons from a New Zealand hospital organization. *Government Information Quarterly, 24*, 102–114. doi:10.1016/j.giq.2006.02.010

Gautam, V. (2006). E-governance 'paradigms' revisited: Constraints and possibilities. In Sahu, G. P. (Ed.), *Delivering e-government*. New Delhi, India: Global Institute of Flexible Systems Management.

Gee, J. (1996). *Social linguistics and literacies: Ideology in discourses* (2nd ed.). London, UK: Routledge.

Geels, F. W. (2005). *Technological transitions and system innovations: a co-evolutionary and socio-technical analysis*. Cheltenham, UK: Edward Edgar Publishing Limited.

Ghaleb, F., Daoud, S., & Hasna, A., ALJa'am, J. M., El-Seoud, S. A., & El-Sofany, H. (2006). E-Learning model based on semantic web technology. *International Journal of Computing & Information Sciences, 4*(2), 63–71.

Giddens, A. (1984). *The constitution of society: Outline of the theory of structuration*. Cambridge, UK: Polity Press.

Gleeson, D., & James, D. (2007). The paradox of professionalism in English Further Education: A TLC project perspective. *Educational Review*, *59*(4), 451–467. doi:10.1080/00131910701619340

Goldstein, D. E. (2000). *E-healthcare: harness the power of internet e-commerce & e-care*. Gaithersburg, MA: Aspen Publishers, Inc.

Gomart, E. (2002). Methadone: Six effects in search for a substance. *Social Studies of Science*, *32*(1), 93–135. doi:10.1177/0306312702032001005

Gough, N. (2004). RhizomANTically becoming-cyborg: Performing posthuman pedagogies. *Educational Philosophy and Theory*, *36*(3), 253–265. doi:10.1111/j.1469-5812.2004.00066.x

Gough, N. (2009). AARE President's Address 2008: No country for young people? Anxieties in Australian society and education. *Australian Educational Researcher*, *36*(2), 1–19.

Grant, G., & Chau, D. (2005). Developing a generic framework for e-government. *Journal of Global Information Management*, *13*(1), 1–30. doi:10.4018/jgim.2005010101

Gregor, S., Bunker, D., Cecez-Kecmanovic, D., Metcalfe, M., & Underwood, J. (2007). Australian eclecticism and theorizing in information systems research. *Scandinavian Journal of Information Systems*, *19*(1), 11–38.

Grint, K., & Woolgar, S. (1997). *The machine at work - Technology, work and organisation*. Cambridge, UK: Polity Press.

Guala, F. (2005). *The Methodology of Experimental Economics*. Cambridge, UK: Cambridge University Press. doi:10.1017/CBO9780511614651

Guala, F. (2007). How to Do Things with Experimental Economics. In MacKenzie, D., Muniesa, F., & Siu, L. (Eds.), *Do Economists make Markets? On the Performativity of Economics* (pp. 128–162). Princeton, NJ: Princeton University Press.

Gudea, S. (2007). Internet access on the cheap: The power of the co-op. *Journal of Business Systems, Governance and Ethics, 2*(3).

Guesnerie, R. (2005). Réflexions sur la concrétisation de l'équilibre économique. In Bensimon, G. (Ed.), *Histoire des représentations du marché* (pp. 49–63). Paris: Michel Houdiard Editeur.

Hall, M. (2000). Clinical sociology in service learning. *Sociological Practice: A Journal of Clinical and Applied Sociology, 2*(1), 33-39.

Hamel, G. (1991). Competition for competence and interpartner learning within international strategic alliances. *Strategic Management Journal*, *1991*, 83–102. doi:10.1002/smj.4250120908

Hamilton, M. (2009). Putting words in their mouths: The alignment of identities with system goals through the use of individual learning plans. *British Educational Research Journal*, *35*(2), 221–242. doi:10.1080/01411920802042739

Hanseth, O. (1996). *Information technology as infrastructure*. Unpublished doctoral dissertation, School of Economics and Commercial Law, Goteborg University, Goteborg, Sweden.

Hanseth, O., & Braa, K. (1998). Technology as traitor: SAP infrastructure in global organizations. In *Proceedings of the Nineteenth Annual International Conference on Information Systems*, Helsinki, Finland.

Hanseth, O., Aanestad, M., & Berg, M. (2004). Guest editors' introduction: Actor-network theory and information systems. What's so special? *Information Technology & People*, *17*(2), 116–123. doi:10.1108/09593840410542466

Hanseth, O., & Monteiro, E. (1996). *Inscribing behaviour in information infrastructure standards*. Accounting, Management and Information Systems.

Haraway, D. (1991). *Simians, cyborgs, and women: The reinvention of nature*. New York, NY: Routledge.

Haraway, D. (1997). *Modest-witness@second-millennium.FemaleMan-meets-OncoMouse: Feminism and technoscience*. New York, NY: Routledge.

Hardt, M., & Negri, A. (2004). *Multitude: War and Democracy in the Age of Empire*. New York: Penguin.

Harison, S., Barlow, J., & Williams, G. (2007). The content and interactivity of health support group websites. *Health Education Journal*, *66*(4), 371–381. doi:10.1177/0017896907080123

Harmon, K. (2009). *The "Systems"*. Nature of Enterprise Architecture.

Harvey, L. J., & Myers, M. D. (1995). Scholarship and practice: The contribution of ethnographic research methods to bridging the gap. *Information Technology & People*, *8*(3), 13–27. doi:10.1108/09593849510098244

Hayles, N. K. (1993). The Materiality of Informatics. *Configurations*, *1*(1), 147–170. doi:10.1353/con.1993.0003

He, F., & Le, J. (2007). Hierarchical Petri nets model for the design of e-learning systems. In K. Hui, Z. Pan, R. C. Chung, C. C. L. Wang, X. Jin, S. Göbel, & E. C.-L. Li (Eds.), *Proceedings of the 2nd International Conference on Technologies for e-Learning and Digital Entertainment* (LNCS 4469, pp. 283-292).

Hecht, G. (2007). A cosmogram for nuclear things. *Isis*, *98*(1), 100–108. doi:10.1086/512834

Heeks, R. (2003). *Most e-government-for-development project fail: How can risks be reduced?* Manchester, UK: Institute for Development Policy and Management.

Heeks, R., & Stanforth, C. (2007). Understanding e-government project trajectories from an actor-network perspective. *European Journal of Information Systems*, *16*(2), 165–177. doi:10.1057/palgrave.ejis.3000676

Heidegger, M. (1976). *Being and time*. New York, NY: Harper and Row.

Helbig, N. C., Gil-García, J. R., & Ferro, E. (2009). Understanding the complexity in electronic government: Implications from the digital divide literature. *Government Information Quarterly*, *26*, 89–97. doi:10.1016/j.giq.2008.05.004

Hertz, E. (2000). Stock Markets as "Simulacra": Observation that Participates. *Tsantsa*, *5*, 40–50.

Hertz, R. (1997). *Reflexivity and voice*. Thousand Oaks, CA: Sage.

Holt, R. (2004). *Dialogue on the Internet: language, civic identity, and computer-mediated communication*. Westport, CT: Greenwood Publishing Group.

Holtzman, M. (2005). Teaching sociological theory through active learning: The irrigation exercise. *Teaching Sociology*, *33*(2), 206–212. doi:10.1177/0092055X0503300207

Howell, J. D. (2004). Transforming healthcare. X rays, Computer and the Internet. In Friedman, L. D. (Ed.), *Cultural sutures: medicine and media* (pp. 333–350). London: Duke University Press.

Hughes, T. (1997). The evolution of large technological systems. In Bijker, W. E., & Law, J. (Eds.), *The social construction of technological systems: New directions in the sociology and history of technology*. Cambridge, MA: MIT Press.

Husserl, E. (1931). *Ideas: General introduction to pure phenomenology*. London, UK: George Allen & Unwin.

Hutchins, E. (1995). *Cognition in the wild*. Cambridge, MA: MIT Press.

Iansiti, M., & Levien, R. (2004). *The keystone advantage: what the new dynamics of business ecosystems mean*. Boston: Harvard Business School Publishing Corporation.

Illeris, K. (2009). *Contemporary theories of learning: Learning theorists in their own words*. London, UK: Routledge.

Imran, A., & Gregor, S. (2007). A comparative analysis of strategies for e-government in developing countries. *Journal of Business Systems, Governance and Ethics*, *2*(3).

Introna, L. D. (2008). Understanding phenomenology: The use of phenomenology in the social study of technology. In Introna, L. D., Ilharco, F., & Faÿ, E. (Eds.), *Phenomenology, organisation and technology* (pp. 43–60). Lisbon, Portugal: Universidade Católica Editora.

Introna, L. D., & Whittaker, L. (2004). Truth, journals, and politics: The case of the MIS Quarterly. In Kaplan, B., Truex, D., Wastell, D., Wood-Harper, A., & DeGross, J. (Eds.), *Information systems research* (*Vol. 143*, pp. 103–120). New York, NY: Springer. doi:10.1007/1-4020-8095-6_7

Iyamu, T. (2010). Theoretical Analysis of the Implementation of Enterprise Architecture. *International Journal of Actor-Network Theory and Technological Innovation*, 2(3), 27–38.

Izquierdo Martín, A. J. (1996). Equilibrio económico y racionalidad maquínica: del algoritmo al sujeto en el análisis económico moderno. *Politica y Sociedad, 21*, 89–111.

Jane, M. (2005). How to share knowledge between companies. *Knowledge Management Review, 8*(16).

Jansen, A. (2005). Assessing e-government progress–why and what. In *Proceedings of the Norsk Konferanse for Organisasjoners Bruk Av IT*.

Jensen, K. (1991). Coloured Petri nets: A high level language for system design and analysis. In G. Rozenberg (Ed.), *Advances in Petri Nets* (LNCS 483, pp. 342-416).

Jensen, C. B. (2005). An experiment in performative history: Electronic patient records as a future-generating device. *Social Studies of Science, 35*(2), 241–267. doi:10.1177/0306312705047737

Jonas, D. K. (2000). Building state information highways: Lessons for public and private sector leaders. *Government Information Quarterly, 17*(1), 43–67. doi:10.1016/S0740-624X(99)00026-X

Jonassen, D. H., & Rohrer-Murphy, L. (1999). Activity theory as a framework for designing constructivist learning environments. *Educational Technology Research and Development, 47*(1), 61–79. doi:10.1007/BF02299477

Kang, D., Lee, J., & Kim, K. (2009). Alignment of Business Enterprise Architectures using fact-based ontologies. *Expert Systems with Applications, 37*, 3274–3283. doi:10.1016/j.eswa.2009.09.052

Kaplan, B., & Maxwell, J. A. (1994). Qualitative Research Methods for Evaluating Computer Information Systems. In Anderson, J. G., Aydin, C. E., & Jay, S. J. (Eds.), *Evaluating Health Care Information Systems: Methods and Applications* (pp. 45–68). Thousand Oaks, CA: Sage Publications.

Kaptelinin, V., & Nardi, B. (2006). *Acting with technology*. Cambridge, MA: MIT Press.

Karanasios, S. (2007). Ecuador, the digital divide and small tourism enterprises. *Journal of Business Systems, Governance and Ethics, 2*(3).

Kartodirjo, S. (1984). *Modern Indonesia & transformation*. Yogyakarta, Indonesia: Gadjah Mada University Press.

Kasztelowicz, M. (2004). Medical Information Asymmetry in the Cyberworld of Manuel Castells. In Duplaga, M., Zieliński, K., & Ingram, D. (Eds.), *Transformation of healthcare with information Technologies* (pp. 21–27). Amsterdam: IOS Press.

Kenway, J., Bigum, C., Fitzclarence, L., Collier, J., & Tregenza, K. (1994). *New education in new times*. Geelong, Australia: Deakin University.

Ke, W., & Wei, K. K. (2004). Successful e-government in Singapore. *Communications of the ACM, 47*(6), 95–99. doi:10.1145/990680.990687

Kidder, P. (1997). The hermeneutic and dialectic of community in development. *International Journal of Social Economics, 24*(11), 1191–1202. doi:10.1108/03068299710193561

Kien, G. (2009). *Global Technography: ethnography in the age of mobility*. New York: Peter Lang Publishing.

Kilpeläinen, T. (2007). Business Information Driven Approach for EA Development in Practice. In *Proceedings of the 18th Australasian Conference on Information Systems* (pp. 447-457).

Kim, D., & Chang, H. (2007). Key functional characteristics in designing and operating health information websites for user satisfaction: An application of the extended technology acceptance model. *International Journal of Medical Informatics, 76*, 790–800. doi:10.1016/j.ijmedinf.2006.09.001

Kim, S., Kim, H. J., & Lee, H. (2009). An institutional analysis of an e-government system for anti-corruption: The case of OPEN. *Government Information Quarterly, 26*, 42–50. doi:10.1016/j.giq.2008.09.002

King, W., & Teo, T. (1996). Key dimensions of facilitators and inhibitors for the strategic use of information technology. *Journal of Management Information Systems, 12*(4), 35–53.

Kizza, J. M. (2010). *Ethical and Social Issues in the Information Age*. London: Springer Verlag.

Klein, H. K., & Myers, M. D. (1999). A set of principles for conducting and evaluating interpretive field studies in information systems. *Management Information Systems Quarterly, 23*(1), 67–94. doi:10.2307/249410

Klenowski, V., Askew, S., & Carnell, E. (2006). Porfolios for learning, assessment and professional education in higher education. *Assessment & Evaluation in Higher Education, 31*(3), 267–286. doi:10.1080/02602930500352816

Knights, D., & Murray, F. (1994). *Managers divided: Organisation politics and information technology management*. Chichester, UK: John Wiley & Sons.

Knorr-Cetina, K. (1999). *Epistemic cultures: How the sciences make knowledge*. Cambridge, MA: Harvard University Press.

Knuth, D. E. (1996). Algorithms. In Knuth, D. E. (Ed.), *Selected Papers on Computer Science* (pp. 59–86). Cambridge, UK: Cambridge University Press.

Koch, T. (1995). Interpretive approaches in nursing research: The influence of Husserl and Heidegger. *Journal of Advanced Nursing, 21*, 827–836. doi:10.1046/j.1365-2648.1995.21050827.x

Kotler, P., Armstrong, G., Wong, V., & Saunders, J. (2008). *Principles of Marketing*. Harlow, UK: Pearson Education Limited.

Kripanont, N. (2007). *Examining a technology acceptance model of internet usage by academics within Thai business schools*. Melbourne, Australia: Victoria University.

Kripanont, N., & Tatnall, A. (2011). Modelling the adoption and use of internet technologies in higher education in Thailand. In Tatnall, A. (Ed.), *Actor-network theory and technology innovation: advancements and new concepts* (pp. 95–112). Hershey, PA: IGI Global.

Krogh, G. V., Kleine, D., & Roos, J. (1998). *Knowing in firms: Understanding, managing and measuring knowledge*. London, UK: Sage.

Kvale, S. (2007). *Doing interviews*. London, UK: Sage.

Lampland, M., & Star, S. L. (Eds.). (2009). *Standards and their stories: How quantifying, classifying, and formalizing practices shape everyday life*. London, UK: Cornell University Press.

Lankshear, C., Peters, M., & Kobel, M. (1996). Critical pedagogy and cyberspace. In Giroux, H., Lankshear, C., McLaren, P., & Peters, M. (Eds.), *Counternarratives: Cultural studies and critical pedagogies in postmodern spaces*. London, UK: Routledge.

Lanzara, G. (2009). Building digital institutions: ICT and the rise of assemblages in government. In Contini, F., & Lanzara, G. (Eds.), *ICT and innovation in the public sector*. New York, NY: Palgrave Macmillan.

Last, M. (1999). Understanding Health. In Skelton, T., & Allen, T. (Eds.), *Culture and Global Change* (pp. 72–86). London: Routledge.

Laszlo, E. (2001). *Macroshift: navigating the transformation to a sustainable world*. San Francisco, CA: Berrett-Koechler Publishers.

Latour, B. (1986). The powers of association. In Law, J. (Ed.), *Power, action and belief: A new sociology of knowledge?* (pp. 264–280). London, UK: Routledge & Kegan Paul.

Latour, B. (1987). *Science in action*. Cambridge, MA: Harvard University Press.

Latour, B. (1987). *Science in action: How to follow scientists and engineers through society*. Milton Keynes, UK: Open University Press.

Latour, B. (1988). *The Pasteurization of France*. Cambridge, MA: Harvard University Press.

Latour, B. (1992). Where are the missing masses? Sociology of a few mundane artefacts. In Bijker, W., & Law, J. (Eds.), *Shaping technology, building society: Studies in socio-technical change*. Cambridge, MA: MIT Press.

Latour, B. (1993). *We have never been modern*. Cambridge, MA: Harvard University Press.

Latour, B. (1994). On technical mediation - philosophy, sociology, genealogy. *Common Knowledge, 3*(2), 29–65.

Latour, B. (1996). *Aramis or the love of technology.* Cambridge, MA: Harvard University Press.

Latour, B. (1996). The trouble with actor-network theory. *Soziale Welt, 47*(4), 369–381.

Latour, B. (1999). On recalling ANT. In Law, J., & Hassard, J. (Eds.), *Actor network theory and after* (pp. 15–25). Oxford, UK: Blackwell Publishers.

Latour, B. (1999). *Pandora's hope: Essays on the reality of science studies.* Cambridge, MA: Harvard University Press.

Latour, B. (2005). *Reassembling the social: An introduction to actor-network-theory.* Oxford, UK: Oxford University Press.

Latour, B. (2006). Air. In Jones, C. A. (Ed.), *Sensorium: Embodied Experience, Technology, and Contemporary Art* (pp. 104–107). Cambridge, MA: The MIT Press.

Latour, B. (2010). A collective of Humans and Nonhumans. In Hanks, C. (Ed.), *Technology and Values: Essential Readings* (pp. 49–59). Malden, MA: Blackwell Publishing.

Latour, B., & Woolgar, S. (1979). *Laboratory life: The social construction of scientific facts.* Thousand Oaks, CA: Sage.

Latour, B., & Woolgar, S. (1986). *Laboratory life.* Princeton, NJ: Princeton University.

Laverty, S. M. (2003). Hermeneutic phenomenology and phenomenology: A comparison of historical and methodological considerations. *International Journal of Qualitative Methods, 2*(3).

Law, J. (1986). *On the methods of long distance control: Vessels, navigation, and the Portuguese route to India.* Retrieved from http://www.lancs.ac.uk/fass/sociology/papers/law-methods-of-long-distance-control.pdf

Law, J. (1997). *Topology and the naming of complexity.* Retrieved from http://www.comp.lancs.ac.uk/sociology/papers/Law-Topology-and-Complexity.pdf

Law, J. (2000). *Networks, relations, cyborgs: On the social study of technology.* Retrieved from http://www.lancs.ac.uk/fass/sociology/papers/law-networks-relations-cyborgs.pdf

Law, J. (2007). *Actor network theory and material semiotics.* Retrieved from http://heterogeneities.net/publications/Law2007ANT andMaterialSemiotics.pdf

Law, J. (2009). *Collateral realities.* Retrieved from http://www.heterogeneities.net/publications/Law2009CollateralRealities.pdf

Law, J., & Lien, M. (2010). *Slippery: Field notes on empirical ontology.* Retrieved from http://www.sai.uio.no/english/research/projects/newcomers/publications/working-papers-web/Slippery%20revised%2013%20WP%20version.pdf

Law, J. (1987). Technology and heterogeneous engineering: The case of Portuguese expansion. In Bijker, W. E., Hughes, T. P., & Pinch, T. J. (Eds.), *The social construction of technological systems: New directions in the sociology and history of technology* (pp. 111–134). Cambridge, MA: MIT Press.

Law, J. (1992). Notes on the theory of the actor network: Ordering, strategy and heterogeneity. *Systems Practice, 5*(4). doi:10.1007/BF01059830

Law, J. (1994). *Organizing modernity.* Oxford, UK: Blackwell.

Law, J. (1999). After ANT: Complexity, naming and topology. In Law, J., & Hassard, J. (Eds.), *Actor network theory and after.* London, UK: Blackwell.

Law, J. (2002). *Aircraft stories: Decentering the object in technoscience.* Durham, NC: Duke University Press.

Law, J. (2004). *After method* (1st ed.). London, UK: Routledge.

Law, J. (2006). Pinboards and books: Juxtaposing, learning and materiality. In Krit, D., & Winegar, L. T. (Eds.), *Education and technology: Critical perspectives, possible futures.* Lanham, MD: Lexington Books.

Law, J. (2006). Traduction/Trahision: Notes on ANT. *Convergencia, 42*, 47–72.

Law, J. (2008). On sociology and STS. *The Sociological Review, 56*(4), 623–649. doi:10.1111/j.1467-954X.2008.00808.x

Law, J. (2009). Seeing like a survey. *Cultural Sociology, 3*(2), 239–256. doi:10.1177/1749975509105533

Law, J. (2009). Actor-network theory and material semiotics. In Turner, B. S. (Ed.), *The new Blackwell companion to social theory* (3rd ed., pp. 141–158). Chichester, UK: John Wiley & Sons. doi:10.1002/9781444304992.ch7

Law, J., & Callon, M. (1988). Engineering and sociology in a military aircraft project: A network analysis of technological change. *Social Problems, 35*(3), 284–297. doi:10.1525/sp.1988.35.3.03a00060

Law, J., & Callon, M. (1992). The life and death of an aircraft: A network analysis of technical change. In Bijker, W. E., & Law, J. (Eds.), *Shaping technology, building society: Studies in socio-technical change*. Cambridge, MA: MIT Press.

Law, J., & Hassard, J. (Eds.). (1999). *Actor network theory and after*. London, UK: Blackwell.

Law, J., & Mol, A. (2008). Globalisation in practice: On the politics of boiling pigswill. *Geoforum, 39*(1), 133–143. doi:10.1016/j.geoforum.2006.08.010

Law, J., & Mol, A. (Eds.). (2002). *Complexities*. Durham, NC: Duke University Press.

Law, J., & Singleton, V. (2000). Performing technology's stories: On social constructivism, performance, and performativity. *Technology and Culture, 41*(4), 765–775.

Law, J., & Singleton, V. (2005). Object lessons. *Organization, 12*(3), 331–355. doi:10.1177/1350508405051270

Learning Disabilities Association of Canada. (2002). *Official definition of learning disabilities.* Retrieved from http://www.ldac-taac. ca/

Lee, A. S., Baskerville, R. L., Liebenau, J., & Myers, M. D. (1995). Judging qualitative research in information systems. In *Proceedings of the Sixteenth International Conference on Information Systems*, Amsterdam, The Netherlands.

Lee, A. S. (1994). Electronic mail as a medium for rich communication: An empirical investigation using hermeneutic interpretation. *Management Information Systems Quarterly*, 143–157. doi:10.2307/249762

Lee, N., & Brown, S. (1994). Otherness and the actor network: The undiscovered continent. *The American Behavioral Scientist, 37*(6), 772–790. doi:10.1177/000 2764294037006005

Lee, R. (1998). *What is an Exchange? The Automation, Management, and Regulation of Financial Markets.* Oxford, UK: Oxford University Press.

Leibold, M., Probst, G., & Gibbert, M. (2005). *Strategic management in the knowledge economy: new approaches and business applications*. Erlangen, Germany: Publicis Corporate Publishing and Wiley-VCH Verlag.

Lektorsky, V. A. (2009). Mediation as a means of collective activity. In Sannino, A., Daniels, H., & Gutierrez, K. D. (Eds.), *Learning and expanding with activity theory* (pp. 75–87). New York, NY: Cambridge University Press.

Leont'ev, A. N. (1978). *Activity, consciousness and personality*. Englewood Cliffs, NJ: Prentice Hall.

Lévi-Strauss, C. (1966). *The savage mind*. Chicago, IL: University of Chicago Press.

Lewins, A., & Silver, C. (2007). *Using software in qualitative research: A step-by-step guide*. London, UK: Sage.

Lien, M., & Law, J. (2010). *Emergent aliens: Performing indigeneity and other ways of doing salmon in Norway.* Retrieved from http://www.sai.uio.no/english/research/projects/newcomers/publications/working-papers-web/Emergent%20aliens%20Ethnos%20revised%20WP%20version.pdf

Lindbergh, R. (2001). *No more words*. New York, NY: Simon & Schuster.

Lindqvist, K. (2010). Entrepreneurial success and failures in the arts. In Bill, F., Bjerke, B., & Johansson, A. W. (Eds.), *De)mobilizing the Entrepreneurship Discourse: Exploring Entrepreneurial Thinking and Action* (pp. 75–96). Cheltenham, UK: Edward Edgar Publishing Limited.

Lindstrøm, M. D. (2010). Deep translations. In Simonsen, J., Bærenholdt, J. O., Büscher, M., & Scheuer, J. D. (Eds.), *Design Research: Synergies from Interdisciplinary Perspectives* (pp. 109–122). Abingdon, UK: Routledge.

Lipnack, J., & Stamps, J. (2000). *Virtual teams: People working across boundaries with technology*. New York, NY: John Wiley & Sons.

Lipsey, M. J., Fischer, R. R., & Poirier, K. L. (2007). *Systems for Success: The Complete Guide to Selling, Leasing, Presenting, Negotiating & Serving in Commercial Real Estate*. Gretna, LA: Pelican Publishing Company.

Li, T. M. (2005). Beyond 'the state' and failed schemes. *American Anthropologist, 107*(3), 383–394. doi:10.1525/aa.2005.107.3.383

Lucas, H. C. J., & Schwartz, R. A. (Eds.). (1989). *The Challenge of Information Technology for the Securities Markets: Liquidity, Volatility, and Global Trading*. Homewood, IL: Dow Jones-Irwin.

Lucas, N. (2004). The 'FENTO Fandango': National standards, compulsory teaching qualifications and the growing regulation of FE college teachers. *Journal of Further and Higher Education, 28*(1), 35–51. doi:10.1080/0309877032000161805

Lucas, N. (2007). Rethinking initial teacher education for further education teachers: From a standards-led to a knowledge-based approach. *Teaching Education, 18*(2), 93–106. doi:10.1080/10476210701325077

Lukaitis, S. A., & Cybulski, J. (2004). A hermeneutic analysis of the Denver International Airport baggage handling system. In Hart, D., & Gregor, S. (Eds.), *Information systems foundations: Constructing and criticising*. Canberra, Australia: ANU E Press.

Luke, A. (2002). Curriculum, ethics, metanarratives: Teaching and learning beyond the nation. *Curriculum Perspectives, 22*(1), 49–55.

Luna, M., & Velasco, J. L. (2010). Knowledge networks: integration mechanisms and performance assessment. In Viale, R., & Etzkowitz, H. (Eds.), *The Capitalization of Knowledge: A Triple Helix of University-Industry-Government* (pp. 312–334). Cheltenham, UK: Edward Edgar Publishing Limited.

Lundberg, N. (2000). *IT in healthcare*. Unpublished doctoral dissertation, School of Economics and Commercial Law, Goteborg University, Goteborg, Sweden.

Lyotard, J.-F. (1984). *The Postmodern Condition: A Report on Knowledge*. Minneapolis, MN: University of Minnesota Press.

MacKenzie, D., Muniesa, F., & Siu, L. (Eds.). (2007). *Do Economists make Markets? On the Performativity of Economics*. Princeton, NJ: Princeton University Press.

MacKenzie, D., & Wajcman, J. (Eds.). (1985). *The social shaping of technology: How the refrigerator got its hum*. Milton Keynes, UK: Open University Press.

Mackin, J. A. (1997). *Community over chaos: an ecological perspective on communication ethics*. Tuscaloosa, AL: The University of Alabama Press.

Macquarie Library. (1981). *The Macquarie dictionary*. Sydney, Australia: Macquarie Library.

Madon, S., Sahay, S., & Sahay, J. (2004). Implementing property tax reforms in Bangalore: An actor-network perspective. *Information and Organization, 14*, 269–295. doi:10.1016/j.infoandorg.2004.07.002

Magnani, L., & Bardone, E. (2008). Distributed Morality: Externalizing Ethical Knowledge in Technological Artifacts. *Foundations of Science, 13*(1), 99–108. doi:10.1007/s10699-007-9116-5

Maguire, C., Kazlauskas, E. J., & Weir, A. D. (1994). *Information services for innovative organizations*. San Diego, CA: Academic Press.

Mainz, J. (2009). *Blending Spaces: Actor-Network Interactions of an Internet-Based E-Learning*. Münster, Germany: LT Verlag.

Markussen, T. (2005). Practising performativity: Transformative moments in research. *European Journal of Women's Studies, 12*(3), 329–344. doi:10.1177/1350506805054273

Martin-Barbero, J. (2006). Communication and Culture in the Global Society. A Latin American View. In Gumucio Dagron, A., & Tufte, T. (Eds.), *Communication for social change anthology: historical and contemporary readings* (pp. 649–653). South Orange, NJ: Communication for Social Change Consortium.

Masuda, Y. (1983). *The information society as post-industrial society*. Bethesda, MD: World Future Society.

May, T., & Powel, J. L. (2008). *Situating social theory* (2nd ed.). New York, NY: McGraw-Hill.

McCabe, B., & Underwood, J. (2008). Enrolling actors in the co-evolution of inter-organisational information systems. In *Proceedings of the 12th Pacific Asia Conference on Information Systems,* Suzhou, China.

McCabe, K., Rassenti, S., & Smith, V. (1993). Designing a Uniform-Price Double Auction: An Experimental Evaluation. In Friedman, D., & Rust, J. (Eds.), *The Double Auction Market: Institutions, Theories, and Evidence* (pp. 307–332). Reading, MA: Addison-Wesley.

McGovern, G., & Norton, R. (2002). *Content critical: gaining competitive advantage through high-quality Web content.* Upper Saddle River, NJ: FT Press Prentice Hall.

McLean, C., & Hassard, J. (2004). Symmetrical absence/symmetrical absurdity: Critical notes on the production of actor-network accounts. *Journal of Management Studies, 41*(3). doi:10.1111/j.1467-6486.2004.00442.x

McLellan, F. (2004). Medicine.com: the Internet and the Patient-Physician Relationship. In Friedman, L. D. (Ed.), *Cultural sutures: medicine and media* (pp. 373–385). London: Duke University Press.

McMaster, T., Vidgen, R. T., & Wastell, D. G. (1997). Towards an understanding of technology in transition: Two conflicting theories. In *Proceedings of the IRIS20 Conference on Information Systems Research in Scandinavia,* Hanko, Norway.

McMaster, T., Vidgen, R., & Wastell, D. (1998). Networks of association in due process of IS development. In Larsen, T., Levine, L., & de Gross, J. (Eds.), *Information Systems: current issues and future changes* (pp. 341–357). Helsinki, Finland: IFIP.

Meissner, C. (2005). *Balancing Cultural and Corporate Identity Aspects in Standardising and-or Localising Websites. A Contingency Approach.* Hamburg, Germany: Diplomica Gmbh.

Meyer, M. S. (2005). *Between Technology And Science: Exploring an Emerging Field: Knowledge Flows And Networking on the Nano-Scale.* Boca Raton, FL: Dissertation.com.

Michael, M. (1996). *Constructing identities: the social, the nonhuman and change.* London: Sage Publication Ltd.

Miettinen, R. (1999). The riddle of things: Activity theory and actor-network theory as approaches to study innovations. *Mind, Culture, and Activity, 6*(3), 170–195. doi:10.1080/10749039909524725

Miller, P. (1996). The multiplying machine. *Accounting, Organizations and Society, 22*(3-4), 355–364. doi:10.1016/S0361-3682(96)00030-X

Mintzberg, H. (1983). *Structure in fives: Designing effective organizations.* Upper Saddle River, NJ: Prentice Hall.

Mirowski, P. (2007). Markets Come to Bits: Evolution, Computation and Markomata in Economic Science. *Journal of Economic Behavior & Organization, 63*(2), 209–242. doi:10.1016/j.jebo.2005.03.015

Mishra, P. (2009). *Sales Management. Keys to effective sales.* New Delhi, India: Global India Publications Pvt Ltd.

Misra, D. C. (2007, December 10-13). Sixty years of development of e-governance in India (1947-2007): Are there lessons for developing countries? In *Proceedings of the International Conference on Theory and Practice of Electronic Government,* Macao, China.

Mitev, N. (2009). In and out of actor-network theory: a necessary but insufficient journey. *Information Technology & People, 22*(1), 9–25. doi:10.1108/09593840910937463

Mlitwa, N. B. W. (2007). Technology for teaching and learning in higher education contexts: Activity theory and actor network theory analytical perspectives. *International Journal of Education and Development using Information and Communication Technology, 3*(4), 54-70.

Moe, T. M. (1984). The new economics of organization. *American Journal of Political Science, 28*(4), 4739–4777. doi:10.2307/2110997

Mol, A. (1999). Ontological politics: A word and some questions. In Law, J., & Hassard, J. (Eds.), *Actor-network theory and after* (pp. 74–89). London, UK: Blackwell.

Mol, A. (2002). *The body multiple: Ontology in medical practice.* Durham, NC: Duke University Press.

Mol, A. (2003). *The body multiple: Ontology in medical practice*. Durham, NC: Duke University Press.

Mol, A., & Law, J. (1994). Regions, networks and fluids: Anaemia and social topology. *Social Studies of Science, 24*, 641–671. doi:10.1177/030631279402400402

Mol, A., & Mesman, J. (1996). Neonatal food and the politics of theory: Some questions of method. *Social Studies of Science, 26*(2), 419–444. doi:10.1177/030631296026002009

Montealegre, R., & Keil, M. (2000). De-escalating information technology projects: Lessons from the Denver International Airport. *Management Information Systems Quarterly, 24*(3), 417–447. doi:10.2307/3250968

Monteiro, E. (2004). Actor network theory and cultural aspects of interpretative studies. In Avgerou, Ch., Ciborra, C., & Land, F. (Eds.), *The social study of information and communication technology: innovation, actors and contexts* (pp. 129–139). Oxford: Oxford University Press.

Monteiro, E., Ellingsen, G., & Munkvold, G. (2007). Standardization of work: Co-constructed practice. *The Information Society, 23*(5), 309–326. doi:10.1080/01972240701572723

Monteiro, E., & Hanseth, O. (1995). Standardisation in action: Achieving universalism and localisation in medical protocols. In Orlikowski, W. J., Walsh, J., & De Gross, J. I. (Eds.), *Standardisation in action: Achieving universalism and localisation in medical protocols* (pp. 325–343). London, UK: Chapman & Hall.

Moon, M. J., & Norris, D. F. (2005). Does managerial orientation matter? The adoption of reinventing government and e-government at the municipal level. *Information Systems Journal, 15*, 43–60. doi:10.1111/j.1365-2575.2005.00185.x

Moore, G., & Benbasat, I. (1991). Development of an instrument to measure the perception of adopting an information technology innovation. *Information Systems Research, 2*(3), 192–222. doi:10.1287/isre.2.3.192

Moore, R., & Young, M. (2001). Knowledge and the curriculum in the sociology of education: Towards a re-conceptualisation. *British Journal of Sociology of Education, 22*(4), 445–461. doi:10.1080/01425690120094421

Morahan-Martin, J. M. (2004). How Internet users find, evaluate and use online health information: a cross-cultural review. *Cyberpsychology & Behavior, 7*(5), 497–510.

Moreira, T. (2010). Actor-Network Theory. In Hornig Priest, S. (Ed.), *Encyclopedia of Science and Technology Communication* (pp. 7–9). Thousand Oaks, CA: Sage.

Morrell, K., & Hartley, J. (2006). A model of political leadership. *Human Relations, 59*(4), 483–504. doi:10.1177/0018726706065371

Moser, I. (2008). Making Alzheimer's disease matter: Enacting, interfering and doing politics of nature. *Geoforum, 39*(1), 98–110. doi:10.1016/j.geoforum.2006.12.007

Moustakas, C. E. (1994). *Phenomenological research methods*. Thousand Oaks, CA: Sage.

Mulcahy, D. (2010). Assembling the 'accomplished' teacher: The performativity and politics of professional teaching standards. *Educational Philosophy and Theory*.

Muniesa, F., & Linhardt, D. (2009). *At Stake with Implementation: Trials of Explicitness in the Description of the State* (CSI Working Papers Series 015). Paris: Centre de Sociologie de l'Innovation.

Muniesa, F. (2007). Market Technologies and the Pragmatics of Prices. *Economy and Society, 36*(3), 377–395. doi:10.1080/03085140701428340

Muniesa, F., & Trébuchet-Breitwiller, A.-S. (2010). Becoming a Measuring Instrument: An Ethnography of Perfume Consumer Testing. *Journal of Cultural Economics, 3*(3), 321–337. doi:10.1080/17530350.2010.506318

Munro, R. (2005). Actor Network Theory. In Clegg, S., & Haugaard, M. (Eds.), *The SAGE Handbook of Power* (pp. 125–139).

Murata, T. (1989). Petri nets: Properties, analysis and applications. *Proceedings of the IEEE, 77*(4), 541–580. doi:10.1109/5.24143

Murdoch, J. (2005). Ecologising sociology. Actor-Network Theory, co-construction and the problem of human exemptionalism. In Inglis, D., Bone, J., & Wilkie, R. (Eds.), *Nature: From nature to natures: contestation and reconstruction* (pp. 282–305). Abingdon, UK: Routledge.

Mwanza, D. (2001). Where theory meets practice: A case for an activity theory based methodology to guide computer system design. In *Proceedings of the 8th IFIP TC 13 Conference on Human-Computer Interaction*, Tokyo, Japan

Mwanza, D., & Engström, Y. (2005). Managing content in e-learning environments. *British Journal of Educational Technology, 36*(3), 453–463. doi:10.1111/j.1467-8535.2005.00479.x

Myers, M. D. (1994). Dialectical hermeneutics: A theoretical framework for the implementation of information systems. *Information Systems Journal, 5*, 51–70. doi:10.1111/j.1365-2575.1995.tb00089.x

Myers, M. D. (1997). Qualitative Research in Information Systems. *Management Information Systems Quarterly, 21*(2), 241–242. doi:10.2307/249422

Nasta, T. (2007). Translating national standards into practice for the initial training of further education (FE) teachers in England. *Research in Post-Compulsory Education, 12*(1), 1–17. doi:10.1080/13596740601155223

Ndou, V. (2004). E-government for developing countries: Opportunities and challenges. *Electronic Journal on Information Systems in Developing Countries, 18*(1), 1–24.

Nespor, J. (1994). *Knowledge in motion: Space, time and curriculum in undergraduate physics and management*. London, UK: Routledge.

Nespor, J. (1997). *Tangled up in school: Politics, space, bodies and signs in the educational process*. Mahwah, NJ: Lawrence Erlbaum.

Nespor, J. (2004). Educational scale-making. *Pedagogy, Culture & Society, 12*(3), 309–326. doi:10.1080/14681360400200205

Neuman, J. (2007). *The Complete Internet Marketer. A Practical Guide to Everything you Need to Know about Marketing Online*. With-A-Clue Press.

Newton, I. (1992). Letter to Robert Hooke. In Maury, J. P., & Paris, I. M. (Eds.), *Newton: Understanding the cosmos (New horizons)*. London, UK: Thames & Hudson.

Nguyen, T. T., & Schauder, D. (2007). Grounding e-government in Vietnam: From antecedents to responsive government services. *Journal of Business Systems, Governance and Ethics, 2*(3).

Nicolini, D., Gherardi, S., & Yanow, D. (Eds.). (2003). *Knowing in organizations: A practice-based approach*. Armonk, NY: M.E. Sharpe.

Nielsen-Bohlman, L., & Panzer, A. M. (2004). *Health literacy: a prescription to end confusion*. Washington, DC: The National Academies Press.

Nonaka, I. (1994). A dynamic theory of organisational knowledge creation. *Organization Science, 5*, 14–37. doi:10.1287/orsc.5.1.14

Nonaka, I., & Takeuchi, H. (1995). *The knowledge creating company*. New York, NY: Oxford University Press.

Nutbeam, D. (2000). Health literacy as a public health goal: a challenge for contemporary health education and communication strategies into the 21st century. *Health Promotion International, 15*(3), 259–267. doi:10.1093/heapro/15.3.259

O'Kane, P., Hargie, O., & Tourish, D. (2004). Communication without frontiers: the impact of technology on organizations. In Tourish, D., & Hargie, O. (Eds.), *Key Issues in Organizational Communication* (pp. 74–95). London: Routledge.

O'Kane, P., Hargie, O., & Tourish, D. (2009). Auditing electronic communication. In Tourish, D., & Hargie, O. (Eds.), *Auditing Organizational Communication: A Handbook of Research, Theory and Practice* (pp. 195–223). New York: Routledge.

Ochara, N. M. (2010). Assessing irreversibility of an e-government project in Kenya: Implication for governance. *Government Information Quarterly, 27*(1), 89–97. doi:10.1016/j.giq.2009.04.005

Olson, D. L., & Carlisle, J. (2001). Hermeneutics in information systems. In *Proceedings of the Seventh Americas Conference on Information Systems*.

OPDC. (2004). *Annual report*. Bangkok, Thailand: Office of the Public Sector Development Commission.

Orlikowski, W. J., & Scott, S. V. (2008, February). *The Entangling of Technology and Work in Organizations.*

Orlikowski, W. J. (1992). The duality of technology: Rethinking the concept of technology in organizations. *Information Systems Research, 3*(3).

Orlikowski, W. J. (2000). Using technology and constituting structures: A practical lens for studying technology in organizations. *Organization Science, 11*(4), 404–428. doi:10.1287/orsc.11.4.404.14600

Ottinger, G. (2010). Buckets of resistance: Standards and the effectiveness of citizen science. *Science, Technology & Human Values, 35*(2), 244–270. doi:10.1177/0162243909337121

Overberg, R., Toussaint, P., & Zwetsloot-Schonk, B. (2006). Illness stories on the Internet: Features of websites disclosing breast cancer patients' illness stories in the Dutch language. *Patient Education and Counseling, 61*, 435–442. doi:10.1016/j.pec.2005.05.010

Palfrey, J., & Gasser, U. (2008). *Born Digital. Understanding the first generation of digital natives.* New York: Basic Books.

Palkhivala, K., Anderson-Lemieux, A., & Mappin, Ch. (2000). Serving Many Masters. In Keyes, J. (Ed.), *Internet Management* (pp. 537–546). Boca Raton, FL: CRC Press.

Pańkowska, M. (2004). Value-Driven Management in e-Healthcare. In Duplaga, M., Zieliński, K., & Ingram, D. (Eds.), *Transformation of healthcare with information technologies* (pp. 3–11). Amsterdam: IOS Press.

Park, S., & Kim, Y. (2008). Applying Petri nets to model customised learning and cooperative learning with competency. *International Journal of Computer Science and Network Security, 8*(2).

Pedersen, D. (2010). Active and collaborative leaning in an undergraduate sociological theory course. *Teaching Sociology, 38*(3), 197–206. doi:10.1177/0092055X10370119

Pedersen, M. A. (2009). At Home Away from Homes: Navigating the Taiga in Northern Mongolia. In Kirby, P. W. (Ed.), *Boundless worlds: an anthropological approach to movement* (pp. 135–152). New York: Berghahn Books.

Perillo, S., & Mulcahy, D. (2009). Performing curriculum change in school and teacher education: A practice-based, actor-network theory perspective. *Curriculum Perspectives, 29*(1), 41–52.

Peterson, J. L. (1981). *Petri net theory modelling of systems.* Upper Saddle River, NJ: Prentice Hall.

Petri, C. A. (1962). *Kommunication mit automaton.* Unpublished doctoral dissertation, Institut fur instrumentelle Mathematik Schriffen, Bonn, Germany.

Petty, N. M. W. (2005). *Using student perceptions to evaluate the effectiveness of education for high school students with vision impairment.* Christchurch, New Zealand: University of Canturbury.

Pichault, F. (1995). The Management of Politics in Technico-Organisational change. *Organization Studies, 16*(3), 449–476. doi:10.1177/017084069501600304

Polanyi, M. (1958). *Personal knowledge: Towards a post-critical philosophy.* London, UK: Routledge & Kegan Paul.

Polkinghorne, D. E. (1989). Phenomenological research methods. In Valle, R., & Halling, S. (Eds.), *Existential-phenomenological perspectives in psychology* (pp. 41–60). New York, NY: Plenum.

Popkewitz, T. (2004). Educational standards: Mapping who we are and are to become. *Journal of the Learning Sciences, 13*(2), 243–256. doi:10.1207/s15327809jls1302_7

Potts, K. (2007). *Web Design and Marketing Solutions for Business Websites.* New York: Springer Verlag.

Power, M. (2005). The Invention of Operational Risk. *Review of International Political Economy, 12*(4), 577–599. doi:10.1080/09692290500240271

Prior, L., Glasner, P., & McNally, R. (2000). Genotechnology: Three Challenges to Risk Legitimation. In Adam, B., Beck, U., & Van Loon, J. (Eds.), *The risk society and beyond: critical issues for social theory* (pp. 105–121). London: Sage Publications Ltd.

Priyatma, J. E., & Han, C. K. (2008). ANT and e-government research in developing countries: A case in BIMP-EAGA. In Rahman, A. A., Ali, N. A., & Han, C. K. (Eds.), *Management research issues* (pp. 187–222). Malaysia: UPM Press.

Prybutok, V. R., Zhang, R., & Ryan, S. D. (2008). Evaluating leadership, IT quality, and net benefits in an e-government environment. *Information & Management, 45*, 143–152. doi:10.1016/j.im.2007.12.004

Pye, A. (2005). *Leadership and organizing: Sense-making in action*. London, UK: Sage.

Quek, A., & Shah, H. (2004). A comparative survey of activity-based methods for information systems development. In *Proceedings of the International Conference on Enterprise Information Systems*, Stafford, UK.

Radeke, F. (2010). Awaiting Explanation in the Field of Enterprise Architecture Management. In *Proceeding of the* 16th *Americas Conference on Information Systems*, Lima, Peru.

Rains, S., & Donnerstein Karmikel, C. (2009). Health information-seeking and perceptions of website credibility: examining web-use orientation message characteristics and structural features of websites. *Computers in Human Behavior, 25*(2), 544–553. doi:10.1016/j.chb.2008.11.005

Rankin, J., & Campbell, M. (2006). *Managing to nurse*. Toronto, ON, Canada: University of Toronto Press.

Rapley, T. (2007). *Doing conversation, discourse and document analysis*. London, UK: Sage.

Rennie, D. L. (2000). Grounded theory methodology as methodical hermeneutics. *Theory & Psychology, 10*(4), 481–502. doi:10.1177/0959354300104003

Rice, R. E. (2001). The Internet and health communication: a framework of experiences. In Rice, R. E., & Katz, J. E. (Eds.), *The Internet and health communication: experiences and expectations* (pp. 5–46). Thousand Oaks, CA: Sage.

Richards, L. (2002). Qualitative computing - A methods revolution? *International Journal of Social Research Methodology, 5*(3), 263–276. doi:10.1080/13645570210146302

Richardson, H. (2005). Consuming passions in the 'global knowledge economy. In Howcroft, D., & Trauth, E. M. (Eds.), *Handbook of critical information systems research: theory and application* (pp. 272–292). Cheltenham, UK: Edward Edgar Publishing Limited.

Ricoeur, P. (1974). *The conflict of interpretations: Essays in hermeneutics*. Evanston, IL: Northwestern University Press.

Ricoeur, P. (1981). *Hermeneutics and the human sciences*. Cambridge, UK: Cambridge University Press.

Risse, T., & Vatterrott, H. R. (2004). (in press). *The learning objects structure Petri net*. Retrieved from http://www.eurodl.org/materials/contrib/2004/Risse_Vatterrott.html

Rizvi, F., & Lingard, B. (2010). *Globalizing education policy*. London, UK: Routledge.

Roberts, J. M., & Copeland, K. L. (2001). Clinical websites are currently dangerous to health. *International Journal of Medical Informatics, 62*, 181–187. doi:10.1016/S1386-5056(01)00162-9

Robinson, K. (2006). *Take a chance...let them dance*. Retrieved from http://www.edutopia.org/magazine/ed-1article.php?id=Art_1651&issue=oct_06#

Rogers, E. M. (2003). *Diffusion of innovations*. New York, NY: Free Press.

Rogers, E. M., Daley, H., & Wu, T. (1980). *The diffusion of personal computers*. Stanford, CA: Stanford University, Institute for Communication Research.

Root Wolpe, P. (2002). Medical culture and CAM Culture: Science and Ritual in the Academic Medical Center. In Callahan, D. (Ed.), *The role of complementary and alternative medicine: accommodating pluralism* (pp. 163–171). Washington, DC: Georgetown University Press.

Ross, J. W., Weill, P., & Robertson, D. (2006). *Enterprise Architecture as a Strategy: Creating Foundation for Business Execution*. Boston: Harvard Business School Press.

Rossmann, C. (2010). Gesundheitskommunikation im Internet. Erscheinungsformen, Potenziale, Grenzen. In Schweiger, W., & Beck, K. (Eds.), *Handbuch Online-Kommunikation* (pp. 338–363). Wiesbaden, Germany: VS Verlag. doi:10.1007/978-3-531-92437-3_14

Rubinelli, S., Nakamoto, K., & Schulz, P. (2009). Health literacy beyond knowledge and behaviour. *International Journal of Public Health, 54*, 307–311. doi:10.1007/s00038-009-0052-8

Rubinshtein, S. (1935). *Foundation of psychology*. Moscow, Russia: Education Press.

Rüsen, J., & Laass, H. (2010). *Humanism in Intercultural Perspective: Experiences and Expectations*. Berlin: transcript Verlag.

Rychards, L. (2005). *Handling qualitative data: A practical guide*. London, UK: Sage.

Sacristán, A. (1999). Art, Autopistes i cintes de video. In Franquet, R., & Larrègola, G. (Eds.), *Comunicar en la era Digital* (pp. 115–118). Barcelona, Spain: Societat Catalana de Comumicació.

Sassen, S. (2004). Towards a sociology of information technology. In Avgerou, Ch., Ciborra, C., & Land, F. (Eds.), *The social study of information and communication technology: innovation, actors and contexts* (pp. 77–102). Oxford, UK: Oxford University Press.

Sathye, M. (1999). Adoption of Internet banking by Australian consumers: An empirical investigation. *International Journal of Bank Marketing*, *17*(7), 324–334. doi:10.1108/02652329910305689

Satterthwaite, M., & Williams, S. (1993). The Bayesian Theory of the *k*-Double Auction. In Friedman, D., & Rust, J. (Eds.), *The Double Auction Market: Institutions, Theories, and Evidence* (pp. 99–124). Reading, MA: Addison-Wesley.

Scanlon, E., & Issroff, K. (2005). Activity theory and higher education: Evaluating learning technologies. *Journal of Computer Assisted Learning*, *21*(6), 430–439. doi:10.1111/j.1365-2729.2005.00153.x

Schäfer, J. (2010). Reassembling the literary. In J. Schäfer & P. Gendolla (Eds.), *Beyond the Screen: Transformations of Literary Structures, Interfaces and Genre* (pp. 25-70). Berlin: transcript Verlag.

Schau, H. J., & Gilly, M. C. (2003). We Are What We Post? Self-Presentation in Personal Web Space. *The Journal of Consumer Research*, 385–404. doi:10.1086/378616

Schau, H. J., & Muniz, A. M. Jr. (2002). Brand communities and personal identities: negotiations in cyberspace. In Broniarczyk, S. M., & Nakamoto, K. (Eds.), *Advances in Consumer Research* (pp. 344–349). Valdosta, GA: Association for Consumer Research.

Schleiermacher, F. D. E. (1819). The hermeneutics: Outline of the 1819 lecture. In Ormiston, G. L., & Schrift, A. D. (Eds.), *The hermeneutic tradition: From Ast to Ricoeur*. New York, NY: State University of New York Press.

Scholl, H. J. (2007). Central research questions in e-government, or which trajectory should the study domain take? *Transforming Government: People. Process and Policy*, *1*(1), 67–88.

Schulz, P. J. (2006). Maximizing health outcomes through optimal communication. *Studies in Communication Sciences*, *6*(2), 215–232.

Schwartz, R. A. (2000). *Re: Release No. 34-42450; File No. SR-NYSE-99-48; Market Fragmentation. Letter to the Securities and Exchange Commission, Response to Request for Comments*. Washington, DC: Securities and Exchange Commission.

Schwartz, R. A. (2001). The Call Auction Alternative. In Schwartz, R. A. (Ed.), *The Electronic Call Auction: Market Mechanism and Trading* (pp. 3–25). Boston, MA: Kluwer Academic Publishers.

Schwartz, R. A. (Ed.). (1995). *Global Equity Markets: Technological, Competitive and Regulatory Challenges*. Chicago, IL: Irwin.

Schwartz, R. A. (Ed.). (2001). *The Electronic Call Auction: Market Mechanism and Trading*. Boston, MA: Kluwer Academic Publishers.

Schwartz, R. A., Byrne, J. A., & Colaninno, A. (Eds.). (2003). *Call Auction Trading: New Answers to Old Questions*. Boston: Kluwer Academic Publishers.

SEC (Securities and Exchange Commission). (1991). *Self-Regulatory Organizations; Wunsch Auction System, Inc.; Order Granting Limited Volume Exemption from Registration as an Exchange under Section 5 of the SEA. Release No. 34-28899, File No. 10-100*. Washington, DC: Securities and Exchange Commission.

SEC (Securities and Exchange Commission). (1997). *Regulation of Exchange: Concept Release. Release No. 34-38672, File No. S7-16-97*. Washington, DC: Securities and Exchange Commission.

SEC. (Securities and Exchange Commission, Division of Market Regulation). (1991). *Automated Securities Trading: A Discussion of Selected Critical Issues. IOSCO Annual Meeting, Washington DC*. Washington, DC: Securities and Exchange Commission.

SEC. (Securities and Exchange Commission, Division of Market Regulation). (1997). *Re: Arizona Stock Exchange. Response to Request to Division of Market Regulation.* Washington, DC: Securities and Exchange Commission.

Senge, P., Cambron-McCabe, N., Lucas, T., Smith, B., Dutton, J., & Kleiner, A. (2000). *Schools that learn: A fifth discipline fieldbook for educators, parents, and everyone who cares about education.* New York, NY: Doubleday/Currency.

Shapin, S., & Schaffer, S. (1985). *Leviathan and the air-pump: Hobbes, Boyle, and the experimental life.* Princeton, NJ: Princeton University Press.

Sheppard, B., Hartwick, J., & Warshaw, P. (1988). The theory of reasoned action: A meta-analysis of past research with recommendations for modifications and future research. *The Journal of Consumer Research, 15*(3), 325–343. doi:10.1086/209170

Shoniregun, Ch. A., Dube, K., & Mtenzi, F. (2010). *Electronic Healthcare Information Security.* Berlin: Springer.

The shorter Oxford English dictionary. (1973). *Oxford, UK.* Oxford: Clarendon Press.

Shulman, L. (2004). *The wisdom of practice: Essays on teaching, learning, and learning to teach.* San Francisco, CA: Jossey-Bass.

Shulman, L. (2007). Practical wisdom in the service of professional practice. *Educational Researcher, 36*(9), 560–563. doi:10.3102/0013189X07313150

Sieving, P. C. (1999). Factors Driving the Increase in Medical Information on the Web - One American Perspective. *Journal of Medical Internet Research, 1*(1), e3. doi:10.2196/jmir.1.1.e3

Sillence, E., Briggs, P., Harris, P., & Fishwick, L. (2007). Health Websites that people can trust – the case of hypertension. *Interacting with Computers, 19*, 32–42. doi:10.1016/j.intcom.2006.07.009

Silva, L. (2007). Epistemological and theoretical challenges for studying power and politics in information systems. *Information Systems Journal, 17*, 165–183. doi:10.1111/j.1365-2575.2007.00232.x

Singleton, V. (1995). Networking Constructions of Gender and Constructing Gender Networks: Considering Definitions of Woman in the British Cervical Screening Programme. In Grint, K., & Gill, R. (Eds.), *The gender-technology relation: contemporary theory and research* (pp. 146–173). London: Taylor & Francis Ltd.

Singleton, V., & Michael, M. (1993). Actor-networks and ambivalence: General practitioners in the UK cervical screening programme. *Social Studies of Science, 23*(2), 227–264. doi:10.1177/030631293023002001

Sismondo, S. (2010). *An Introduction to Science and Technology Studies.* Chichester, UK: John Wiley & Sons.

Sloterdijk, P. (2009). Airquakes. *Environment and Planning. D, Society & Space, 27*(1), 41–57. doi:10.1068/dst1

Sloterdijk, P. (2009). *Terror From the Air.* Cambridge, MA: The MIT Press.

Smith, V. L. (1994). Economics in the Laboratory. *The Journal of Economic Perspectives, 8*(1), 113–131.

Sorensen, E. (2007). STS goes to school: Spatial imaginaries of technology, knowledge and presence. *Critical Social Studies, 2*, 15–27.

Sørensen, E. (2009). *The materiality of learning: Technology, knowledge in educational practice* (1st ed.). Cambridge, UK: Cambridge University Press.

Spiegelberg, H. (1982). *The phenomenological movement: A historical introduction.* Boston, MA: Martinus Nijhoff.

Stanforth, C. (2006). Using actor-network theory to analyze e-government implementation in developing countries. *Massachusetts Institute of Technology. Information Technologies and International Development, 3*(3), 35–60. doi:10.1162/itid.2007.3.3.35

Star, S. (1999). The ethnography of infrastructure. *The American Behavioral Scientist, 43*(3), 377–391. doi:10.1177/00027649921955326

Star, S. L. (2010). This is not a boundary object: Reflections on the origin of a concept. *Science, Technology & Human Values, 35*(5), 601–617. doi:10.1177/0162243910377624

Star, S. L., & Griesemer, J. (1989). Institutional ecology, "translations" and boundary objects: Amateurs and professionals in Berkeley's Museum of Vertebrate Zoology, 1907-39. *Social Studies of Science, 19*, 387–420. doi:10.1177/030631289019003001

Stenhouse, L. S. (1975). *An introduction to curriculum research and development*. London, UK: Heinemann.

Stewart, M., Brown, J. B., Wayne Weston, W., McWhinney, I. R., McWilliam, C. L., & Freeman, T. R. (2006). *Patient-centered medicine: transforming the clinical method*. Abingdon, UK: Radcliffe Medical Press.

Strathern, M. (1991). *Partial connections*. Savage, MD: Rowman & Littlefield.

Sturgis, R. (1983). Conversations with theorists: An innovative approach to teaching social theory. *Teaching Sociology, 10*(2), 275–280. doi:10.2307/1317118

Suchman, L. (1987). *Plan and situated actions: The problem of human machine communication*. Cambridge, UK: Cambridge University Press.

Suchman, L. (2006). *Human-machine reconfigurations: Plans and situated actions*. Cambridge, UK: Cambridge University Press.

Sykes, G., & Plastrik, P. (1993). *Standard setting as educational reform*. Washington, DC: American Association of Colleges for Teachers of Education.

Tabak, E. (2008). Inscription of information behaviour to communities of practice on an organisational intranet. In *Proceedings of the OZCHI 2008*, Cairns, Australia (pp. 347-350).

Tabak, E. (2010). Opportunistic translation in development and managment of an organisational intranet. In Proceedings of 2010 International Conference on Innovation, Management and Service (ICIMS 2010), SIngapore, 2010 *(pp. 47-52). Liverpool, UK; World Academic Press*.

Tatnall, A. (2009). Innovation translation and innovation diffusion: A comparison of two different approaches to theorising technological innovation. *International Journal of Actor-Network Theory and Technological Innovation, 1*(2), 67–74. doi:10.4018/jantti.2009040105

Tatnall, A. (2010). Using actor-network theory to understand the process of information systems curriculum innovation. *Education and Information Technologies, 15*, 239–254. doi:10.1007/s10639-010-9137-5

Tatnall, A., & Dakich [*Informing parents with the Victorian Education Ultranet*. Novi Sad, Serbia: Informing Science and IT Education.]. *E (Norwalk, Conn.)*.

Tatnall, A., & Davey, B. (2005). An Actor Network Approach to Informing Clients through portals. In Cohen, E. B. (Ed.), *Issues in informing science and information technology* (pp. 771–780). Santa Rosa, CA: Informing Science Press.

Tatnall, A., Davey, B., Burgess, S., Davison, A., & Wenn, A. (2002). *Management information systems—concepts, issues, tools and applications*. Melbourne, Australia: Data Publishing.

Tatnall, A., & Davey, W. (2007). *Researching the portal. IRMA: Managing worldwide operations and communications with information technology*. Vancouver, BC, Canada: Information Management Resource Association.

Taylor, I. (1997). *Developing learning in professional education*. Buckingham, UK: Open University Press.

Taylor, S., & Todd, P. (1995). Understanding information technology usage: A test of competing models. *Information Systems Research, 6*(2), 144–176. doi:10.1287/isre.6.2.144

THAILAWS. (2003). *Royal decree on criteria and procedures for good governance: B.E. 2546*. Retrieved from http://www.opdc.go.th/english/main/content_view.php?cat_id=3

Thompson, G. (2003). *Between hierarchies and markets: the logic and limits of network forms of organization*. New York: Oxford University Press.

Thurlow, C., Lengel, L. B., & Tomic, A. (2004). *Computer mediated communication: social interaction and the Internet*. London: Sage Publications Ltd.

Thwaites, T., Davis, L., & Mules, W. (2002). *Introducing Cultural and Media Studies. A Semiotic Approach*. Basingstoke, UK: Palgrave Macmillan.

Tight, M. (2003). *Researching higher education*. Maidenhead, UK: Open University Press.

Timmermans, S., & Berg, M. (1997). Standardization in action: Achieving universalism and localisation through medical protocols. *Social Studies of Science, 27*(1), 111–134.

Timmermans, S., & Berg, M. (2003). *The gold standard: The challenge of evidence-based medicine and standardization in health care*. Philadelphia, PA: Temple University Press.

Timmermans, S., & Epstein, S. (2010). A world of standards but not a standard world: Toward a sociology of standards and standardisation. *Annual Review of Sociology, 36*, 69–89. doi:10.1146/annurev.soc.012809.102629

Titleman, P. (1979). Some implications of Ricoeur's conception of hermeneutics for phenomenological psychology. In Giorgi, A., Knowles, R., & Smith, D. L. (Eds.), *Duquesne studies in phenomenological psychology* (Vol. 3, pp. 182–192). Pittsburgh, PA: Duquesne University Press.

Torres, L., Pina, V., & Royo, S. (2005). E-government and the transformation of public administrations in EU countries Beyond NPM or just a second wave of reforms? *Online Information Review, 29*(5), 531–553. doi:10.1108/14684520510628918

Tourish, D., & Hargie, O. (2004). *Key issues in organizational communication*. Abingdon, UK: Routlegde.

Tsohou, A., Karyda, M., Kokolakis, S., & Kiountouzis, E. (2010). Analyzing Information Security Awareness through Networks of Association. In Katsikas, S., Lopez, J., & Soriano, M. (Eds.), *Trust, Privacy and Security in Digital Business* (pp. 227–237). Berlin: Springer. doi:10.1007/978-3-642-15152-1_20

Tummons, J. (2009). Higher education in further education in England: An actor-network ethnography. *International Journal of Actor-Network Theory and Technological Innovation, 1*(3), 55–69. doi:10.4018/jantti.2009070104

Tummons, J. (2010). Institutional ethnography and actor-network theory: A framework for researching the assessment of trainee teachers. *Ethnography and Education, 5*(3), 345–357. doi:10.1080/17457823.2010.511444

Tummons, J. (2010). The assessment of lesson plans in teacher education: A case study in assessment validity and reliability. *Assessment & Evaluation in Higher Education, 35*(7), 847–857. doi:10.1080/02602930903125256

Turner, G. W. (Ed.). (1987). *The Australian concise Oxford dictionary of current English*. Melbourne, Australia: Oxford University Press.

Underwood, J. (2001). Translation, Betrayal and Ambiguity in IS Development. In K. Liu, R.J. Clark, P.B. Andersen & R. (Eds.), *Organizational Semiotics: Evolving a Science of Information Systems* (pp. 91-108). Boston; Kluwer.

US Congress (United States Congress). (1934). *Securities and Exchange Act of 1934*. Washington, DC: United States Congress.

Valette, R. (1979). Analysis of Petri nets by stepwise refinement. *Journal of Computer and System Sciences, 18*, 35–46. doi:10.1016/0022-0000(79)90050-3

van Kaam, A. (1959). Phenomenal analysis: Exemplified by a study of the experience of "really feeling understood". *Journal of Individual Psychology, 15*(1), 66–72.

van Kaam, A. (1966). *Existential foundations of psychology*. Pittsburgh, PA: Duquesne University Press.

Verran, H., Christie, M., Anbins-King, B., Van Weeren, T., & Yunupingu, W. (2007). Designing digital knowledge management tools with Aboriginal Australians. *Digital Creativity, 18*(3), 129–142. doi:10.1080/14626260701531944

Victorian Curriculum and Assessment Authority. (2005). *Victorian essential learning standards: Principles of teaching and learning unpacked*. Retrieved from http://www.education.vic.gov.au/studentlearning/teachingprinciples/principles/unpacked.htm

Victorian Curriculum and Assessment Authority. (2009). *Victorian curriculum and assessment authority homepage*. Retrieved from http://www.vcaa.vic.edu.au/

Vinson, T. (2007). *Dropping off the edge: The distribution of disadvantage in Australia: A report for the Jesuit Social Services and Catholic Social Services Australia*. Retrieved http://www.australiandisadvantage.org.au/pdf/summary.pdf

Vygotsky, L. S. (1979). *Mind in society: The development of higher psychological processes*. Cambridge, MA: Harvard University Press.

Wallace, P. (2001). *The Psychology of the Internet*. Cambridge, UK: Cambridge University Press.

Walsham, G. (2006). Doing Interpretive Research. *European Journal of Information Systems, 15*(3), 320–330. doi:10.1057/palgrave.ejis.3000589

Walsham, G. (2006). Doing interpretive research. *European Journal of Information Systems, 15*, 320–330. doi:10.1057/palgrave.ejis.3000589

Warf, B. (2009). Teleology, Contingency, and Networks. In Meusburger, P., Funke, J., & Wunder, E. (Eds.), *Milieus of Creativity: An Interdisciplinary Approach to Spatiality of Creativity* (pp. 255–268). Berlin: Springer.

Wartofsky, M. (1979). *Models: Representation and scientific understanding*. Boston, MA: Reidel Publishing.

Watson, A., & Huntington, O. H. (2008). They're *here* - I can *feel* them: The epistemic spaces of indigenous and western Knowledges. *Social & Cultural Geography, 9*(3), 257–281. doi:10.1080/14649360801990488

Weiss, L., McCarthy, C., & Dimitriadis, G. (Eds.). (2006). *Ideology, curriculum, and the new sociology of education: Revisiting the work of Michael Apple*. New York, NY: Routledge.

Weitzman, E. (2000). Software and qualitative research. In Denzin, N. K., & Lincoln, Y. S. (Eds.), *Handbook of qualitative research*. Thousand Oaks, CA: Sage.

Whitley, E. A. (1999). Habermas and the Non-Humans: Towards a Critical Theory for the New Collective. In *Proceedings of the Critical Management Studies conference*, Manchester, UK (p. 83).

Whittle, A., & Spicer, A. (2008). Is actor network theory critique? *Organization Studies, 29*(4), 611–629. doi:10.1177/0170840607082223

Wikipedia. (2011). *Knowledge management*. Retrieved from http://en.wikipedia.org/wiki/Knowledge_management

Wilkinson, J. (2006). Network theories and political economy: from attrition to convergence? In Marsden, T., & Murdoch, J. (Eds.), *Between the local and the global: confronting complexity in the contemporary agri-food sector* (pp. 11–38). Oxford, UK: JAI Press.

Williams, R., & Edge, D. (1996). The social shaping of technology. *Research Policy, 25*, 856–899. doi:10.1016/0048-7333(96)00885-2

Wilson, J. F. (2003). The Crucial Link between Literacy and Health. *Annals of Internal Medicine, 139*, 875–878.

Winefield, H. R., Coventry, B. J., & Lambert, V. (2003). Setting up a health education website: practical advice for health professionals. *Patient Education and Counseling, 53*, 175–182. doi:10.1016/S0738-3991(03)00149-6

Wolin, R. (2000). Nazism and the complicities of Hans-Georg Gadamer: Untruth and method. *New Republic (New York, N.Y.), 222*(20), 36–46.

Wong, K., Fearon, C., & Philip, G. (2007). Understanding e-government and e-governance: Stakeholders, partnerships and CSR. *International Journal of Quality & Reliability Management, 24*(9), 927–943. doi:10.1108/02656710710826199

Wright, K. B. (2009). Increasing Computer-Mediated Social Support. In Parker, J. C., & Thorson, E. (Eds.), *Health communication in the new media landscape* (pp. 243–266). New York: Springer.

Wunsch, R. S. (1987, October 20). Market Innovations. *Financial Futures Department Newsletter*. New York: Kidder, Peabody & Co.

Wunsch, R. S. (1990, August 13). Myths of the Continuous Market. *Auction Countdown*. Phoenix, AZ: Arizona Stock Exchange.

Wunsch, R. S. (1997, March 24). Calls for Reform. *Auction Countdown*. Phoenix, AZ: Arizona Stock Exchange.

Wunsch, R. S. (1992). *Re: Market 2000, the U.S. Equity Market Structure Study, Release No. 34-30920, File No. S7-18-92. Letter to the Securities and Exchange Commission, Response to Concept Release*. Washington, DC: Securities and Exchange Commission.

Wunsch, R. S. (1993). *Statement of Steve Wunsch, President, AZX, Inc, Propietary Trading Systems Hearing. Subcommittee on Telecommunications and Finance of the Committee on Energy and Commerce, U. S. House of Representatives*. Washington, DC: United States House of Representatives.

Wunsch, R. S. (2000). *Re: Release No. 34-42450; File No. SR-NYSE-99-48; Market Fragmentation. Letter to the Securities and Exchange Commission, Response to Concept Release*. Washington, DC: Securities and Exchange Commission.

Yang, W. H., Hu, J. S., & Chou, Y. Y. (2010). Analysis of Network Type Exchange in the Health Care System: A Stakeholder Approach. *Journal of Medical Systems*.

Yildiz, M. (2007). E-government research: Reviewing the literature, limitations, and ways forward. *Government Information Quarterly*, *24*, 646–665. doi:10.1016/j.giq.2007.01.002

Yinger, R. (1987). Learning the language of practice. *Curriculum Inquiry*, *17*, 293–318. doi:10.2307/1179695

Yin, R. K. (2003). *Case Study Research, Design and Methods* (2nd ed.). Thousand Oaks, CA: Sage Publications.

Young, M. (2008). From constructivism to realism in the sociology of the curriculum. *Review of Research in Education*, *32*(1), 1–28. doi:10.3102/0091732X07308969

Youngs, R., Redmond-Pyle, D., Spaas, P., & Kahan, E. (1999). *A standard for architecture description* (Vol. 38, No. 1). Enterprise Solutions Structure.

Zachman, J. A. (1987). A framework for information systems architecture. *IBM Systems Journal*, *26*(3), 276–292. doi:10.1147/sj.263.0276

Zarcadoolas, Ch., Pleasant, A. F., & Greer, D. S. (2006). *Advancing health literacy: a framework for understanding and action*. San Francisco: Jossey-Bass.

About the Contributors

Arthur Tatnall is an Associate Professor in the Graduate School of Business at Victoria University in Melbourne, Australia. In his PhD he used actor-network theory to investigate adoption of Visual Basic in the curriculum of an Australian university. Arthur's research interests include technological innovation, history of technology, project management, information systems curriculum, information technology in educational management and electronic business. Much of his research is based on the use of actor-network theory. Arthur is a Fellow of the Australian Computer Society and active in the International Federation for Information Processing (IFIP) as Chair of IFIP WG9.7 – *History of Computing*, Chair of IFIP WG3.4 – *ICT in Professional and Vocational Education* and a member of IFIP WG3.7 – *Information Technology in Educational Management*. He has published widely in journals, books, book chapters and conference proceedings and recently edited the *Encyclopaedia of Portal Technology and Applications*, and *Web Technologies: Concepts, Methodologies, Tools, and Applications* for IGI Global. Arthur is also Editor-in-Chief of the *International Journal of Actor-Network Theory and Technological Innovation*, Editor-in-Chief of the *Journal of Education and Information Technologies* and Editor of the *Journal of Business Systems, Governance and Ethics*.

* * *

Tas Adam is a Senior Lecturer in the School of Management and Information Systems at Victoria University, Melbourne, Australia. He has recently completed a PhD titled: "Determining an e-learning Model for Students with Learning Disabilities: An Analysis of Web-based Technologies and Curriculum" and has worked extensively in this area.

Salim Al-Hajri is Associate Professor and Head of E-Commerce in the Faculty of Business Studies at the Higher College of Technology in Muscat, Oman. His PhD study is about "Internet technology adoption in the banking industry" in which he investigated the enablers and inhibitors of Internet technology adoption in the Omani banking industry and compared them with those in the Australian banking industry. His research interests include e-commerce, management of information systems and technological innovation. He has participated and presented papers in various conferences locally and internationally. Currently he is working towards publishing more papers.

Antonio Díaz Andrade is a Senior Lecturer in Business Information Systems at Auckland University of Technology (AUT), New Zealand. He won the 2010 Emergent Researcher AUT Faculty of Business and Law Award. Before joining AUT in 2009, Antonio was a Lecturer at The University of Auckland, where he obtained his PhD in Management Science and Information Systems in 2007. His doctoral work, *Interaction between Existing Social Networks and Information and Communication Technology Tools: Evidence from Rural Andes*, was nominated for The University of Auckland Best Doctoral Thesis Award. After having spent 15 years in the Peruvian Air Force, Antonio started his academic career at Universidad ESAN, Peru in 2000. His work has been published in a number of international refereed journals, books and conference proceedings in the information systems field.

Dr Magdalena Bielenia-Grajewska is an Assistant Professor at the University of Gdansk (Institute of English, Department of Translation Studies and Intercultural Communication). She is a linguist (MA in English Studies, University of Gdańsk) and an economist (MA in Economics, Gdańsk University of Technology). Her PhD thesis was of an interdisciplinary character, being devoted to intercultural communication, translation and investment banking. She is a member of the Editorial Board of International Journal of Actor-Network Theory and Technological Innovation (IJANTII) and serves as an ad hoc reviewer in some international journals. Her scientific interests include organizational discourse, intercultural and medical communication, sociolinguistics, technological innovation and diffusion as well as ANT and symbolism in management studies. Her email address is magda.bielenia@gmail.com

Patrick Carmichael is Professor of Educational Research at Liverpool John Moores University and since 2008 has been director of the research project: Ensemble: Semantic Technologies for the Enhancement of Case Based Learning. Carmichael is co-author of 'Researching and Understanding Educational Networks' (Routledge, 2010) and author of 'Networking Research: New Directions in Educational Inquiry' (Continuum, 2011). He has written a wide range of conference papers, articles and book chapters on issues as diverse as international media development, teaching and learning in higher education, the design of educational technologies, continuing professional development of teachers, and technology and disability. He is a member of the Research Committee of the Association for Learning Technologies.

Puripat Charnkit has recently completed his degree of Doctor of Business Administration at Victoria University, Melbourne, Australia. His research topic was: *Using the Technology Acceptance Model to Investigate Knowledge Conversion in Thai Public Organisations*.

Antonio Cordella is Lecturer in Information Systems at the London School of Economics and Political Science. His research interests cover the areas of e-Government actor-network theory, and the Social Studies of Information Systems. He has published numerous journal papers, book chapters, and conference papers on the impact of Information and communication technologies on public and private organisations.

Sue De Vincentis (DipT, BEd, MEd) is a PhD student in the School of Education at Deakin University. Prior to becoming a full time student, she taught primary school at various locations around Melbourne and central London. Her research focuses on school and community knowledge practices; ways to include students as valued participants in educational activities; and how to 'do' school differently. Consequently, she finds actor-network theory very useful for challenging the dominant orderings of educational relations.

Samuel Moyosore Ekundayo is a PhD student of Business Information Systems at Auckland University of Technology (AUT), New Zealand. He completed his BSc. Degree in Engineering Business Management at Coventry University (CU), UK and MSc. degree in Knowledge Management at Nanyang Technological University (NTU), Singapore. He is currently exploring the contribution of ICT to the development of higher education in developing countries for his PhD thesis. Samuel is a growing researcher with publications so far linked with subjects such as Activity Theory, ICT for development, E-learning, Leadership, Knowledge-based economy and Knowledge Management. Samuel is also an award winning inspirational speaker and author with his motivational blog (http://www.dynamiqueprofesseur.com) attracting thousands of visitors monthly from over 135 countries worldwide.

Tiko Iyamu is a Professor of information systems at the Tshwane University of Technology, Pretoria, South Africa. He also serves as a Professor Extraordinaire at the Department of Computer Science, University of the Western Cape, South Africa. Before taken fulltime appointment in academic, he heard several positions in both public and private organisations. He was Chief Architect and Head of Architecture & Governance at the Government and Private institutions, respectively. His research interests include Mobile Computing, Enterprise Architecture, Information Technology Strategy; and focuses on Actor Network Theory (ANT) and Structuration Theory (ST). Iyamu is author of numerous peer-reviewed journal and conference proceeding articles. Tiko serves on journal board and conference proceedings committees.

Stasys Lukaitis is an academic in the RMIT School of Business Information Technology and has been now for many years. He is a Fellow of the Australian Computer Society. Stas' teaching and research interests include business and IT alignment and why projects get into trouble, computer security and networking, virtualisation and cloud environments, and qualitative research. He has consulted to industry in various capacities over the years.

Zainal Abidin Mohamed is currently a professor in management and the former Dean of the Graduate School of Management at University Putra Malaysia (UPM). Holds a Bachelor degree in Agricultural Science (Malaya 74), MBA (Wis 76) and PhD (Edin 88). Active in teaching, advisory and research activities in the areas of strategic management, supply chain, innovations and entrepreneurship. Have held several administrative positions in UPM and at University Utara Malaysia (while on secondment in 1999-2002). Attended the Harvard Executive programme in 1984, International Teachers Programme at INSEAD, 1991 and was attached to SPEA in 1995 at University of Indiana, Bloomington under the Fulbright sponsorship for research in Reengineering during his sabbatical. Also an active trainer/coach in EDP programmes for in-house training, such as MAS, PETRONAS, MAYBANK, TELEKOM, Port Klang Authority, as well as public departments and SMEs. Conducted similar programmes in Zimbabwe and Ethiopia. Have twenty-eight publications in the form of three books, twelve chapters in books and the rest in academic journals. Chief editor of the Asian Journal of Case Research, Fellow of EDI of the World Bank, and President of Case writers' Association of Malaysia since 2003.

Dianne Mulcahy is a Senior Lecturer in the Melbourne Graduate School of Education at the University of Melbourne. Her published work in Education spans the areas of education policy, curriculum studies and educators' professional formation and development. Her current research focuses on teacher professional learning and professional teaching standards. Dianne has a longstanding interest in the materiality of educational practice. Pursuing this interest by way of actor-network theory, recent articles have appeared in *Educational Philosophy and Theory, Educational Management Administration & Leadership, Studies in Continuing Education*, and *Curriculum Perspectives,* and include: 'Thinking management and leadership within colleges and schools somewhat differently: A practice-based, actor-network theory perspective'; and 'Performing curriculum change in school and teacher education: A practice-based, actor-network theory perspective'.

Dr Fabian Muniesa is a senior researcher at the Centre de Sociologie de l'Innovation (CSI) in the Ecole des Mines de Paris (now Mines ParisTech), France. His research contributions are mostly located in the fields of science and technology studies and economic sociology. His work primarily aims at developing a pragmatist, materialist approach to the study of calculation, valuation and organization. His past and current research topics include the automation of financial markets, the practice of economics, the implementation of performance indicators, and the pedagogy of business.

Desiree Nelson completed her B.A. in Sociology at the University of Saskatchewan and is pursuing a Masters in Adult Education at the University of Regina. Her research interest involves alternative forms of learning in the post secondary classroom.

Uma Patel is Programme Director for the MA in Academic practice at City University London, and lead researcher at City University on the nationally funded Semantic Technologies for Enhancement of Case-Based Learning project (ENSEMBLE). She moved into Higher Education as an academic in 2004. Her expertise brings together academic studies and work based experience in education, and technology innovation. She has worked as a school teacher, and in adult education and training. She has worked in software design and maintains her links with the sector through consultancy. Some of her past funded research projects include: '3D Visualization of Knowledge Based Systems', 'Intuitive - Multi Media Interface Design' and 'Eurostat - New Technologies and User Requirements'. Her current research interest is in applied pedagogical / technological innovation in complex interdisciplinary domains, participatory design, and claims around technology and empowerment. Her research is informed by writers who draw on science and technology studies and the social science of knowledge.

Johanes Eka Priyatma has been lecturing in the field of Information Systems at Sanata Dharma University Yogyakarta Indonesia since 1994. Since then he lead the design and implementation of information system to support his university academics and management systems until 2006. He also involved the development of e-government system in Indonesia since 2005. He is currently taking a PhD at Graduate School of Management of University Putra Malaysia in the area of e-government looking particularly on the potential contribution of Actor Network Theory to its development. During his study he has been actively participating in several international conferences and writing some journal articles.

Andrea Quinlan is a PhD Candidate in the Department of Sociology at York University, Canada. Her research explores intersections of law, science, technology, and sexual violence. In her PhD work, she draws on Actor-Network Theory and feminist theory to examine the Sexual Assault Evidence Kit, a tool used to collect forensic evidence in legal cases of sexual assault. She explores the mechanisms through which forensic DNA evidence is constructed and legal knowledge of sexual violence is assembled.

Elizabeth Quinlan was one of the first graduates of the Interdisciplinary Studies Doctoral Program at the University of Saskatchewan, Canada, where she now teaches and researches in the Department of Sociology. Her interests lie in the intersection of sociology of health, work, and gender. In her CIHR-funded post-doctoral fellowship, she investigated how members of multi-disciplinary health care teams exchange, create, and apply their knowledge in the context of their collective clinical decision-making. Her recent interests include using arts-based participatory research methods to co-create improved working conditions and quality of life. Recently, Quinlan was awarded a New Investigator grant from Saskatchewan Health Research Foundation to Award to use participatory theatre with health care aides to address workplace bullying.

Sanna Rimpiläinen (MA, MSc) is a doctoral student at the School of Education, University of Stirling, Scotland. Her PhD is linked to an interdisciplinary research and development project *Ensemble* run between Education and Computer Sciences. The team studies case-based learning in a number of settings in Higher Education with a view of developing semantic web-applications for supporting these activities. She studies, employing an Actor-Network Theory approach and multiple ethnographic methods, how a new piece of semantic technology emerges through the heterogeneous research and development practices engaged in the project in one of the settings. Prior to embarking on the PhD, Sanna worked for the Applied Educational Research Scheme of Scotland (2004-2008) as a Research Officer administering and researching the use of Sakai Virtual Research Environment used by collaborative, educational research teams and other groups. She has an MSc in Applied Educational Research (2008), University of Strathclyde; her first degree (MA) is from the Department of Cultural Studies (2000), University of Turku, Finland.

Edin Tabak is a doctoral candidate in the department of the Internet Studies at the Curtin University of Technology in Perth. Prior to this, he spent 12 years in the web industry working as a web designer and the Internet content manager. He holds Bachelor of Science in Interactive Multimedia Technologies (Edith Cowan University), Bachelor of Science (Honours) in Information Technologies (University of Technology Sydney), Master of Internet Communication (University of Canberra), and the Graduate Certificate in Research Commercialisation (Curtin University of Technology). His research interests include information behaviour, information architecture, research management, and politics of information practices. He is currently completing a PhD thesis, which investigates the impact of nationalism on information sharing in academic communities.

Michael Tscholl is a researcher in learning and education at the University of Cambridge (UK). His studies center on questions in collaborative learning, case-based learning, and technology-enhanced learning. His approach to study learning is informed by cognate disciplines, and he has published in conferences and journals of those fields. He has been involved in the ESRC/EPSRC ENSEMBLE project studying ways to enhance case-based learning with the emerging semantic web technology, approaching questions of technology in learning and education through frameworks informed by Science and Technology Studies (STS) and Actor-Network Theory. He holds BSc, MSc and PhD degrees in Cognitive Psychology and Computer Science.

Jonathan Tummons is a Senior Lecturer in Education in the School of Social Sciences and Law at Teesside University, UK. His published work in Education spans the areas of assessment, theory and methodology, and recent articles have appeared in *Studies in Higher Education, Ethnography and Education* and *Assessment and Evaluation in Higher Education*. He is also the author or co-author of several textbooks for trainee teachers. His most recent books are *Contemporary issues in Lifelong Learning* (co-authored with Vicky Duckworth and published by McGraw Hill) and *Assessing Learning in the Lifelong Learning Sector* (third edition, published by Learning Matters). His current research focuses on Actor-network Theory and Institutional Ethnography (with Mary Hamilton at Lancaster University, UK) and e-assessment (with Clive Hedges at Teesside University, UK).

Jim Underwood is a senior lecturer in Information Systems at the University of Technology, Sydney and has been teaching and researching the social aspects of IS development for over 40 years. He was originally a mathematician and has worked for several IT consulting companies. His research combines ANT and Foucault's theory of discourse to the politics of information systems development, considering particularly the intersection of competing discourses and the role of ambiguity in system success.

Index

A

Abstraction 5, 112, 203
activity theory 193-194, 196-197, 199-206
actor-network theory (ANT) 2, 45, 48, 56-57, 78-80,
    88, 133, 144, 146-147, 207, 215, 223
agent of change 18, 23
Alpha Corporation 225-227, 230
analytical tools 193-194
arcs 68-69, 71-72
area network 136
Arizona Stock Exchange 117-118, 121-122, 124-
    126, 128, 130-131
ArtPlay 36-37
AU Entertainment 135-136
Australia 1, 6, 8, 10, 13, 31-32, 42-44, 67, 71, 88,
    101-103, 114-116, 133, 135, 143, 154, 164,
    171, 207-208, 211, 219-220
Autonomy Act 181

B

banking industry 207-209, 211, 213-214, 218-219
bank managers 207-208, 211, 214, 216-217, 220
Behavioral Intention 208
behavioural decision 209
bipartite graph 69
black box 1, 173, 177-178, 196, 216
blood collection 61
Bupati 179-189
Business Case Method 18
business visioning 149
buy-in 149, 152, 154

C

case-based learning 17-18, 24, 28, 45-46
Case Report Form (CRF) 227
complexities 4, 31, 34-35, 38-39, 43, 57, 62, 64, 81
constructionism 103

consultation website 6, 8
corporate identity 156, 160-161, 164, 168
corporate websites 156, 158-164, 166
critical success factors (CSFs) 148
cultural means 193
curriculum 10, 15, 18, 20-21, 25, 29-33, 35-44, 68,
    70, 76-77, 79, 81, 83-84, 87, 171
    standards 32-33

D

DAC model 176
data communications protocol 70
deployment 72, 144-145, 147-149, 153-154, 221,
    225, 228, 230-231, 236
developing countries 173-175, 190-192
Dialogical Reasoning 112
Diffusion of Innovations 102, 207-208, 210, 214,
    219-220
Digital Settlers 164
domain artefacts 105
due process 133, 135-138, 140-142

E

Ease of Use 92, 96, 98, 100-101, 210-212, 214-216,
    218
e-Banking 207
educational practices 17-18
education policy 1, 10, 12-13, 15, 86
    reform 1, 10, 12
e-government 173-179, 183-184, 189-192
    development 175
    failure 175
e-healthcare 156-158, 164, 167, 169
e-learning 67-68, 70-77, 96, 168, 204, 206
Electronic Communication Networks (ECNs) 119
Electronic Data Processing 179, 183
electronic markets 117, 122-123
electronic trading 117-118, 121, 125-126, 132